Praise for **Killin**

'A vivid, absorbing book wh̶
to live through wars, civi̶
and historic ̶ ̶ ̶
Guardian

'If you want to know what journalism is really like,
read her new book: it's wonderful'
Andrew Marr

'A great reporter is clever, fearless and charming:
easy to like but hard to fool. In war zones, tyrannies and
democracies, Ann Leslie has always asked the right questions,
seen the key details and written them down with a passion,
tension and wit which remind us why journalists
call assignments a "good story"'
Mark Lawson

'What worlds she's seen, what a life she's had – at long last,
the memoirs of the fearless, indomitable Ann Leslie'
Deborah Moggach

'Ann Leslie has set the benchmark for modern journalism:
she is without equal, extraordinarily courageous, tenacious,
endlessly surprising, and of course a peerless writer. Armed
with just her notebook, a handbag, and infinite charm
she has brought the world to life for us in all its variety,
its savagery and the infinite heroism of its people'
Roger Alton, Editor, *Independent*

'Ann Leslie – wise, funny and outrageous.
Whether you agree with her or not, you can always be sure
her views are based on her outstanding journalism,
and couched in her own sparkling style'
Esther Rantzen

Killing My Own Snakes

Ann Leslie has been a star writer for the *Daily Mail* for nearly four decades, and regularly appears as a guest on numerous television and radio programmes (including *Question Time* and *Any Questions*). At the Reuters/Press Gazette launch of the Newspaper Hall of Fame she was named as one of the most influential journalists of the last forty years. In David Randall's *The Great Reporters* (celebrating the 13 best British and American journalists of all time) she is profiled as 'the most versatile reporter ever'.

Her awards over many years include the James Cameron Prize for International Reporting 'for work that combined moral vision and professional integrity', and a Lifetime Achievement Award in 1997 from the Media Society which stated: 'Ann Leslie is only the third person to receive the honour, the two previous winners being Sir Alistair Cooke and Sir David Attenborough. The award is an acknowledgement of Ann Leslie's special ability to give readers personality, style and substance in every article she writes.'

She is married with one daughter and lives in London.

To Lisa,
Welcome back to blighty!
Love Murray n Claire
e Beano,
Meow!!

ANN LESLIE

Killing My Own Snakes

A MEMOIR

PAN BOOKS

First published 2008 by Macmillan

First published in paperback 2009 by Pan Books
an imprint of Pan Macmillan Ltd
Pan Macmillan, 20 New Wharf Road, London N1 9RR
Basingstoke and Oxford
Associated companies throughout the world
www.panmacmillan.com

ISBN 978-0-330-44987-8

Picture Acknowledgements

All photographs by courtesy of the author, except the following:
17 – © Tom Blau   18, 25, 28, 33, 36 – © Associated Newspapers
22, 23 – © BBC   31 – © Reuters   34 – © Granada Television
38 – © Christina Fallara   39 – © BCA Films   40 – © Charles Green

A CIP catalogue record for this book is available from
the British Library.

Typeset by SetSystems Ltd, Saffron Walden, Essex
Printed in the UK by CPI Mackays, Chatham ME5 8TD

Visit **www.panmacmillan.com** to read more about all our books
and to buy them. You will also find features, author interviews and
news of any author events, and you can sign up for e-newsletters
so that you're always first to hear about our new releases.

*To my beloved husband Michael
and daughter Katharine*

Acknowledgements

I want to thank all those who've helped me in a long career, and those who've taken the trouble to confirm, or challenge, my memories when I was writing this book; any errors are, of course, my own.

I also owe thanks to the Macmillan team; to my agent, the incomparable Ed Victor; to Matthew Parris for finally convincing me to write it; and above all to the *Daily Mail* and Paul Dacre for giving me so many extraordinary journalistic opportunities over the years.

Those who've been brave enough to help me in the face of sometimes mortal danger to themselves and their families can't be named, but my gratitude to them is boundless: they are the necessarily anonymous heroes and heroines of my – and any foreign correspondent's – story.

Contents

'You're not at the bloody Savoy!'

'There's a dwarf in Oldham, says he was at school with Cary Grant,' growled the News Editor, an irascible Scot. He stared at me malevolently over the huge handle-bar moustache adorning his blotchy face. On his desk, his special 'moustache cup' which had a shelf-like rim on one side designed to keep the facial foliage dry while he slurped his tea, heavily laced with single malt. 'And, while you're about it, lassie, there's a flock of sheep frozen to death on the moors.'

'Er, do we have an address for the dwarf?' I asked nervously. 'Or, indeed, the frozen sheep?' I added. Tom Campbell's expression darkened further. '*You* find the dwarf! This is called J-O-U-R-N-A-L-I-S-M, lassie. Not what you are used to at Oxford University!' (he did a bizarre version of what he perceived to be my 'lah-di-dah' accent). 'You find the dead sheep by looking for hooves sticking up over the snow. And you know what? You're keeping a good man out of a job!'

Yeah, I knew – not least because he never stopped telling me. I was everything he hated: a woman, young, someone whom he could accuse of being 'a bloody intellectual', someone from the despised South, someone who was upper-middle-class, an Oxford graduate, privately educated, and thus someone who was ipso facto a 'stuck-up snob' – and, above all, someone who'd been hired by the loathed London Head Office in Fleet Street.

The only woman he rated was the fearsome Peggie, who he'd decided was one of 'my boys'; I was informed, possibly inaccurately, that she dressed in a camouflage outfit of brown and green blobs, seemed able to match Campbell's remarkable alcoholic intake, and was given to barking 'Kill! Kill!' And she was only covering the Pennines.

I, on the other hand, had been born and brought up as a

'daughter of the Raj' on the subcontinent, surrounded by servants. And later, walled up among nuns in damp, chilblain-riddled English convents. During my early life in India and Pakistan I had survived a riot (and still have small scars on my back), had experienced a bloody massacre on one of the 'killing trains' after Partition, had narrowly escaped death from a black krait snake, been bitten by a dog with rabies, and acquired all the emotion-dampening, shoulder-shrugging stoicism of a lonely expat child. But none of that equipped me for dealing with Tom Campbell.

And in any case, I'd never wanted to be a journalist. I was just filling in time before I decided what I really wanted to do. Forty-six years later I'm still 'filling in time'.

I certainly never expected to find myself being mortared, fired on by snipers and knifed by a would-be rapist in the Gulf, or interviewing a war criminal who boasted that the best way of punishing your enemies is to scoop their eyes out with a rusty spoon.

Or flirting over coffee with a chortling Gorbachev stranded on a ship in a Maltese storm. Or finding the urbane David Niven turn spiteful when I refused his attentions, or being proposed to by James Mason, or being bossed about by Mrs Thatcher over hairdos and campaign 'potty stops'.

Or being there in Communist East Berlin when the Wall came down, or chatting about make-up and their forthcoming execution with two female murderers on America's Death Row, or having my bad back cured by a voodoo priest in Haiti, or watching Nelson Mandela walk to freedom out of his prison gates in South Africa after twenty-seven years.

Or sharing 'substances' with Salvador Dali, or punching Muhammad Ali in the jaw to make him pay attention, or giving a gossip-hungry George W. Bush the latest on Camilla Parker Bowles.

Or indeed trudging blindly across the Buckingham Palace gravel (my contact lenses having popped out), wearing an absurd floral hat, in order to receive a Damehood from the Queen.

On day one of my arrival in the Manchester office, Tom Campbell informed me, 'You're not at the bloody Savoy today!' I had in fact never been to the Savoy, but I'd made the great mistake of turning up on my first day at work wearing what a woman's magazine had said was suitable for a first job: 'neat, but not gaudy'. I'd bought a cheap copy of a Chanel suit.

But today I had to find a dwarf. So with a sinking heart I drove out on to the snow-covered moors. I didn't bother looking for sheep's hooves sticking up out of the drifts. I knew this brief, foolish, 'time-filling' attempt to be a journalist was at its end. I'd never done any university journalism, was at the time deeply incurious about politics, crime and fashion – newspaper staples then and now – and had only got the newspaper job because a nice man from the *Daily Express*, whom I met in an Oxford pub, offered me it at the then stunningly lucrative wage of £20 a week.

I'd been a swot at school so had won a prestigious scholarship to Oxford and had consequently been listed in *The Times*; I was therefore much in demand on the recruitment 'milk round'. Languid young executives from top companies would take rooms in the Randolph Hotel, ply me with warm white wine and peanuts, and ask, 'Have you ever thought of a career in detergents?' '. . . in marketing?' '. . . in thread?' To which, of course, I could only reply 'No' and 'Er, frankly . . .' But I'd said yes to the journalism offer, and look where it had got me. Looking for a dwarf and some dead sheep.

Oldham at the time struck me as being full of deformed people, of often very restricted stature. Later I learned that because of poor nutrition and the historically grotesque working conditions in the mills, a high degree of congenital deformity did exist in the town. It was deeply shocking to me. I was used to the sight of limbless beggars, glaucous blind eyes and general deformity in India's bazaars but, well, the people there were *brown* . . .

But this was England! This was where the British Master Race dwelt, the site of the Mother of Parliaments, the Land of Hope and Glory of which we'd sing in my mountainous south Indian school, the home of Her Majesty, whose Official Birthday my parents had always celebrated on dusty lawns with sedate cocktails, where the invitation would command 'Decorations Will Be Worn.' Somehow I never expected such deprivation at 'home' (as expats in India would always call England, even if they had lived on the subcontinent for decades).

Eventually I tracked down the dwarf in question and found myself standing in a blizzard outside his home, a back-to-back hovel in one of the mill town's soot-stained streets. I began reciting lines from Anglo-Saxon poetry to myself, to remind me that door-stepping dwarfs was not what I was put on earth for: 'Swa cwæð eardstapa earfeþa gemyndig' ('So spake the wanderer, mindful of hardship').

With furious, cold-triggered tears freezing on my cheeks, I suddenly found the dwarf beside me, asking, 'Lookin' for someone, love?'

'I'm from the *Daily Express*. Were you at school with Cary Grant?'

'Yes, love! But of course he were Archie Leach then, we was livin' in Bristol.'

He invited me in. 'Want a cuppa?' He lifted a huge iron kettle off the dead coal fire. He winked at me: 'The missus isn't here – so we can get away with havin' a cuppa!'

The kettle was full of neat Scotch; after quite a few 'cuppas' the dwarf and I were getting on like a house on fire. Then 'the missus' unexpectedly turned up. Unlike her husband, she was not a person of restricted growth; in fact, she seemd to me in my fairly drunken state as huge, wide and black as a coal lorry whose brakes had failed. And she was fizzing with rage. I fled out into the blizzard.

'Get the story?' asked John Scholes, the avuncular agricultural correspondent who shared a desk with me.

'Well, I don't know. I didn't bother looking for the sheep.'

'Good thing too. We know where sheep have been frozen to death because the farmers ring me. He only asked you to do that so you'd get stuck in a snow drift! Prove that, as a soft Southern lassie, you couldn't do the job! What about the dwarf and Cary Grant?'

'Well, I think he *was* at school with Cary Grant: the dates tally. But . . . .' And I told him the story as it happened.

'Write that. Cut out some of the stuff about the booze. Sounds like a short funny.' Which was what the Night Editor thought too: he printed it.

If I naively thought that getting a few paragraphs into an early regional edition might assuage Campbell's loathing, I was soon disabused. 'Bloody try and be clever with that, lassie!' he snarled next day, slapping down a note about a dispute over a budgie between two male pensioners, one dead, one alive. The alive one alleged that his dead friend had promised him his budgie in his will, and the dead budgie owner's family were allegedly disputing it. 'Get a row goin'!' I was commanded.

Actually, I found I got quite emotionally involved in the budgie dispute. As a child in India I had a whole aviary of budgies which I adored. One day, as every day, I'd gone down to the end of the lush, wildly overgrown garden of our old East India Company mansion, the smell of the Indian Ocean filling my lungs, and found my huge budgie enclosure full of dead birds, their legs sticking up in the air, felled by some virus. I was utterly grief-stricken. So I knew how much budgies matter.

Trouble was, there was no row. The budgie owner's family were quite keen on getting rid of 'that scraggy old thing'. I got the impression they felt the same about the dearly departed himself. But I had indubitably failed. 'If you can't get a row goin' over a budgie dispute, you'll never make a journalist!'

My first scoop (though only in the Manchester edition) enraged Campbell even further. There was a woman in hospital, the victim of some crime. I can't remember the crime, or the woman's name, but I do remember the result of my getting the only interview with the woman in question.

The victim had told the hospital staff that she didn't want to speak to any press. Manchester's finest 'dogs of war' did what 'dogs of war' habitually did then: they dressed up as doctors, complete with stethoscopes; they tried climbing through windows; they alleged they were from 'Maintenance'; they asserted that they were concerned relatives and came laden with vast bouquets. Repulsed at every turn.

I thought I'd try a novel tack: I'd do it by the book. I would make an appointment with the Hospital Secretary, tell him who I was and what questions I'd like the crime victim to answer. He returned from talking to her and smiled: 'Mrs A says you sound like a nice, polite young woman, and certainly she'll talk to you.'

'How did you get this bloody story?' barked Campbell the next day.

'I asked the Hospital Secretary . . .'

'You did *what*?' His moustache bristled with rage. 'That's no way to get a story!'

'But,' I pointed out coolly, 'I did get it. And no one else did.'

One evening over a 'jar' (and they were never singular) with some of Campbell's lads, I stupidly mentioned that we had a tennis court at home: one of the lads handed this weapon to his boss. 'You're not on your bloody tennis court today, lassie!'

He constantly put me on the 'dog-watch' which began at 4.30 p.m. and finished in the small hours. I had to do the 'cop-shop round', which meant going to police stations in Dickensian slums like Moss Side, full of squalor and crime, and asking the desk sergeants, 'Do you have a story for the *Daily Express*?' If they did have a story they wouldn't of course give it to this slip of a girl; they'd phone their Crime Desk chums (some of whom paid them handsomely for 'tips'). I would sit there drinking mugs of tea and tell them how miserable I was, how badly I was being treated, and sometimes a sergeant would take pity on me and say, 'There, love, this might help.' For the price of a few tears, I'd get a 'tip'.

Funnily enough, I quite enjoyed this. The desk sergeants were kind, and the 'tips' introduced me to places and people I never suspected existed in Britain: lice-infested bedrooms, carpet cut-offs soaked in urine, foul-mouthed, semi-literate families who constantly thumped their pale, scabby children. But I couldn't afford to do the cop-shop round. The all-night buses were not all-night in the places I was sent to; I couldn't get home except by taxi.

My apparently plutocratic £20 a week was dwindling by the day. John Scholes then told me that I actually had employment rights: 'You can put the cabs on expenses. Join the Union.' Which I did. The National Union of Journalists has enraged me many times over the decades, but because of those early days when it forced an incandescent Campbell to cough up for my late-night cab fares I still remain loyal.

Every night I'd feed coins into a vomit-scented phone box, ring my boyfriend Michael in London and sob, 'I hate this job, this job hates me, I'm chucking it in!' But I didn't. Campbell and I were locked in a deadly battle – about class, education and above all gender – and I was damned if I was going to lose it to this ghastly, failed, fraudulent old drunk. I fully intended to leave – but on my terms. Modern feminism hadn't really been invented then, but I was innately feminist enough to know that I wouldn't be driven out of a job – even one I hated – merely because of the genital arrangements I was born with.

The huge staffs of the Northern branches of the national papers consisted of hordes of feral tribesmen, heavy-drinking, heavy-fighting warriors (there were 700 hacks based in Manchester alone) who regarded namby-pamby talk about 'journalistic ethics' – even if they had ever heard the phrase – as an unforgivable attack on their manhood. 'Aye, lass, but you should see us in Glasgow!' one visiting Scottish newsman told me. 'We're much worse!' he added with pride.

In those days there seemed to be two stories which particularly enthused the Northern ferals: competitive potholing and competitive leek-growing. Perhaps because neither activity took place in the namby-pamby South.

Luckily I didn't have to 'get a row goin'' among the leek-growers of Northumberland. They did that themselves. The mines in the area were still flourishing and so were their fiercely competitive Leek Clubs; Geordie miners were dourly fanatical about rearing their monster leeks, which they fed with a mixture of manure, dried blood, brown ale and various 'secret ingredients', in the hope of winning a prize, perhaps even a three-piece suite. But mostly of course so that they could triumph over their mates down the pit. (The comedian Rob Brydon, despite being Welsh, hates the leek; it is, he notes mysteriously, 'a very *argumentative* vegetable'. Maybe Rob's been to the World Leek-growing Championship in Ashington.)

For a Southerner, Geordie can be fairly incomprehensible, but I understood enough to be amazed at the amount of fear and loathing that was generated by this harmless member of the allium family. I was told many a conspiratorial tale of 'nobblers' who, at dead of night, would creep into a rival's leek beds and stick a needle or fire an airgun pellet into the other man's plants. 'Aye, duck, I know who the nobblers are,' one competitor informed me darkly. 'Why else do you think I've been sitting up all night for the last fortnight wrapped in blankets to make sure me leeks aren't nobbled this time!'

But surely these massive things can't be any good to eat? 'Eat? Eat? You don't want to *eat* a prize-winning leek!' As the son of one competitive leek-grower put it, 'You would no more eat a prize leek than you would a racehorse that had just won the Derby!' He remembered how one legendary self-made millionaire used to take his beloved leeks to the show wrapped up in white towels on the back seat of his Rolls.

As for the potholers: being solitary underground types, they were hardly on the surface long enough to 'get a row goin'' with their rivals. This did not apply, however, to the newsmen above ground. The Northern editions of the nationals were always 'buying up' potholers who were trying to break records for staying underground in dripping caves. Our proprietor Lord Beaverbrook did not approve of cheque-book journalism but his editors would get round that minor inconvenience by putting the sums down as 'hospitality to contacts'.

I was once detailed to 'babysit' the wife of one such potholer we'd bought up. His wife lived in a bleak stone cottage high in the Pennines, with no phone, no electricity, no lock on the door, an outside lavatory and a dingy, deaf, asthmatic dog. The only 'decoration' was a couple of souvenirs of Blackpool Tower and a Kilner jar containing some stones. 'Oh, what are these?' I asked brightly by way of the sort of small talk I'd learned at Karachi cocktail parties. 'Them's his kidney stones,' she replied glumly.

One evening, there was a violent thumping on the door. 'No, no! Don't answer it! That's *my* job!' I trilled at the wife, who was gloomily consuming Strong Lager out of the bottle. Suddenly the door burst open, and a huge ginger thug, whom I recognized as a member of the *Daily Mirror*'s 'heavy mob', appeared in the doorway – and instantly punched me in the face, giving me a black eye. The by then near-comatose potholer's wife suddenly sprang into furious action, firing lumps of coal at him, forcing a retreat. We celebrated our joint victory with another bottle of Strong Lager.

Of course, it never occurred to me to report the *Mirror* man to the police for GBH, or to try to sue him, or indeed complain to the office. The odd black eye from a professional rival was just an occupational hazard. Whenever I hear media commentators talking about how press behaviour has degenerated since the Good Old Days, I find myself thinking, 'Oh really? You evidently weren't at the *Express* in Manchester at the beginning of the Sixties.'

Every journalist dreaded having to do the 'death-knock' routine, which involved knocking on a front door and breaking the news of the sometimes gruesome death of a relative to their loved ones. Mercifully Campbell stopped sending me on 'death knocks', because I was far too squeamish to nick family photos from the house when the bereaved weren't looking. 'You'll never become a proper reporter if you carry on like this!'

Apart from potholers and leek-growing, the Northern editions went big on 'slip editions'. These were special inserts, consisting of up to six pages, full of advertisements, distributed inside the normal paper at agricultural shows, antiques fairs or – my particular nightmare – the Harrogate Toy Fair. Single-handedly I was obliged to produce endless 'amusing' and/or 'heart-warming' stories about teddy-bear manufacturers or gollywog makers (political correctness hadn't yet dawned), get all the biographical details right, and flatter the lot of them. But, I have to admit, it was great training for a job which, I was convinced, would not last long.

At the Toy Fair I met a woman called Jean Rook for the first time. She was working for the *Yorkshire Post* and swept into the toy-crammed auditorium wearing a huge red cloak and what looked to me like a vast black wig in the shape of a medieval warrior's helmet. I suspected she somehow spelled trouble. And so it proved. The *Yorkshire Post* was a respected newspaper but it was regional, and the *Daily Express* was then a powerful and successful national; she clearly resented that fact. I tried to escape the cloak and the wig. After all, it wasn't my fault that I was on a national, albeit in the provinces, and besides, I wasn't going to hang around long enough in the job ever to be a threat to her.

But La Rook descended on me to give me her views on both my pitiful youth and my equally pitiful experience. I quaked. Unfortunately I quaked again when, nearly twenty years later, she and I were obliged, through an organizational mix-up, to share a bedroom in a grand Leeds hotel. We were both getting awards at a Gala Dinner, complete with fanfares from the State Trumpeters, given by the charity the Variety Club of Great Britain. My award was for 'journalism and broadcasting', hers for 'journalism'. She was evidently thoroughly miffed that someone whom she regarded as one of life's obvious also-rans was not only sharing the same room with her but getting a similar award. She treated me to a repeat performance of her Toy Fair put-downs.

By then she'd become the most famous female columnist in Fleet Street, had dubbed herself journalism's 'First Lady', ensured that she was photographed with every luminary she interviewed, and made my husband Michael – who was always fiendishly jealous on my behalf – sourly declare, 'If Jean Rook is the First Lady of Fleet Street, then I'm the Queen of Siam!' She was the original inspiration for *Private Eye*'s Glenda Slagg, and her last column before she died was a love letter to the great tenor she called 'Fatty Pavarotti'. 'This man', she wrote, 'is a mountain any woman yearns to climb!'

What made me so miserable in Manchester – apart from a sexist, bullying News Editor and a brief encounter with a journalistic diva – was the utter 'foreignness' of the North. I was used, as a child, to spending time in Basra in Iraq (all I remember was its charm and its palm trees), Kabul in Afghanistan (full of rose gardens then), and remote parts of India when my oil executive father was 'on tour', where villagers would swathe me, laughing, with heavily scented flower garlands and stuff my eager mouth with brightly coloured sweetmeats. But I had never felt as foreign as I did in Manchester. I remembered how the Regency dandy Beau Brummell, on being told that his regiment was being posted to the city, resigned his commission: 'Sir, when I purchased my commission it was on condition that I was never posted abroad!'

It had begun well though. Michael – then just my boyfriend – told me that he'd take some time off from the BBC and would drive me there. He had a clapped-out Standard Ten: it had no heating, its indicators were short, spavined arms which would regularly, with a thump, shoot out of the side unbidden, and it had great difficulty cresting the most pimply of hills. He'd have to rev the clattering little beast into a fury, then press the accelerator to the rust-thinned floor in the hope that the Standard would manage to catapult itself over the obstacle. This usually worked in Surrey; the Pennines, alas, struck the Standard as the equivalent of the north face of the Eiger.

But we were young, in love, and giggled a lot. On the way we even checked into Coventry's 'finest hotel', the Leofric, as 'Mr and Mrs', which deceit added no end to the sexual excitement. Michael and a previous girlfriend had been evicted at the dead of night from a Cotswold hostelry when the landlady surmised, correctly, that – despite the fake wedding ring – the two of them were 'living in sin'.

At one of the convents I attended, I'd asked the Reverend Mother whether it was okay for me to be godmother to my best friend's baby. She'd been expelled from the school as a 'fallen woman' when she became pregnant, and although she and her boyfriend later married, Reverend Mother was firm: 'God would not be pleased. She has lived in sin, and by agreeing to be this girl's godmother you are, my child, conniving in sin.' (And I'm afraid I did refuse my friend's request.)

Finally, having 'lived in sin' with giddy enjoyment, Michael and I and the exhausted Standard eventually neared our destination: we were driving down the road from Snake Pass into the outskirts of Manchester.

Spread out below us was a vision of a Gustave Doré hell. Night was falling and blotches of yellow, sulphur-smelling fog hung over a devastated, rubble-strewn cityscape. The old slums were being demolished (to be replaced by new slums) and in places Manchester looked like Hiroshima after the bomb; sticking up above the rubble like rotten teeth were blackened churches, chapels and pubs. Oh God, I thought, what have I done, signing up to this benighted city: why didn't I go for a 'career in thread' after all?

The office had assigned me accommodation: the Land O'Cakes pub in Great Ancoats Street, across the road from a mini-version of the *Express*'s Fleet Street HQ (a vast black-glass 1930s edifice, nick-named the Black Lubianka after the KGB headquarters in Moscow). Ancoats was at the rough, fisticuffs end of Manchester, surrounded by still-functioning factories and mills; the *Daily Mail*, then a fading, failing newspaper, dying of genteel good taste, was ensconced in Deansgate, the 'posh' part of the city.

I was shown into my room by the landlady, Mildred. It stank. I soon realized why. An *Express* heavy-mob photographer had been its previous occupant and he had a simple solution to the frequent complaints from his colleagues about his rancid socks: he'd get some new ones and sling the worst-smelling ones under the bed, where they remained radiating an odour like over-ripe Reblochon. They were still there when I checked in.

Breakfast the next morning was a fry-up consisting of watery fried eggs, baked beans, fatty bacon and white doorsteps of bread. None of the other lodgers addressed a word to me, most of them being too hung over to speak. Even Mildred was rather cool. She liked 'her boys' and I was clearly not one of them.

Night-time was worse. The printers used the Land O'Cakes as their local, and although licensing hours were short and strict in those days, 'exceptions' were made in their case: the landlady would simply call 'time' on non-printers and would then institute a lock-in for the 'inkies'. Often included among those locked in would be a local bobby, who'd blackmail the illegal drinkers by demanding 'contributions' to police charity funds.

On late shifts (and I was constantly put on those) I'd have to bang on the door and persuade boss-eyed and drunken printers, who were eating chip butties and 'playing the spoons' (a Northern pastime of which I'd previously never heard), that yes, I was indeed a resident. I would then fight my way through the bar and the catcalls – 'Show us a leg, love!' – up the back stairs and into my sock-stinking room.

There was another 'graduate trainee journalist' in Manchester called Gerry. He too had just come down from a 'posh' university but he had the inestimable advantage of being born a man. Not just any man, but a tall, blond, athletic specimen who was tremendously good at sport and who, moreover, was said to have done national service in the Paras.

Campbell adored the military and aped the lingo of his heroes. He would, on occasion, inform his minions that he was going to ambush the enemy camp at the Fleet Street HQ and 'fight for my lads!' Whether he ever did was a moot point. As for sport, my fellow trainee was able to take time off to play football because, as Campbell informed him, 'We're a sporting regiment here, laddie!' Mind you, there were possibly libellous rumours that Campbell had never actually served in the war: 'in-growing toenails or something'.

Which might explain why he was so horrible to his bullet-headed, stiff-backed deputy Bob Blake, who'd been a tank driver at Alamein and was eventually awarded an MBE. Blake was middle-class and privately educated, sins for which he paid dearly. However, I loathed Blake almost as much as I loathed his boss. Later I learned that, as a protection mechanism in the army he'd affected a cockney accent because, like me, he'd hitherto been rather 'lah-di-dah'. Unfortunately he'd had to join the ranks rather than become an officer because as a schoolboy he'd been hauled up in front of a magistrate for some minor misdemeanour.

In later years, whenever I got a scoop or won an award, I would say to myself, 'Another one in the eye for Campbell and Blake!' When I received the first of two Lifetime Achievement Awards, I got a self-exculpatory letter from Blake admitting that he knew he'd bullied me and regretted it, but that he too was bullied. 'One day I must tell you of the editors (now dead) who drove us on the desk to extend no help to women reporters.'

The 'lads', unlike me, found Blake's bullying madly amusing. The News Desk secretary Jean kept a verbatim, but secret, note of Blake's remarks to his underlings. 'I have no objection to women on newspapers. I think women on newspapers can be a good thing for us. Just so long as they are on other newspapers.' 'Bottle-washing, that's what you university graduates have got to do here! And I'll certainly see that you get a few dirty bottles to wash! Especially you *women* graduates!'

I resented the way Campbell and Blake did all they could to make my male fellow trainee journalist feel at home in the Northern Lubianka. I'd heard rumours of the existence of a document called the Style Book which apparently told new *Express* journalists how to write news stories. I never saw it because, I learned, the Campbell/Blake combo had told my fellow trainee not to give it to me because 'she might learn something'.

Somehow I did learn something, possibly osmotically. According to the Style Book, one must always put the location of a news story near the end of the piece, otherwise people who didn't live there wouldn't be interested in it. Bizarrely, the word 'leukaemia' was *verboten* – apparently our proprietor Lord Beaverbrook (always referred to as the Old Man) found the word alarming – and one had to use the phrase 'a rare blood disease'. One could also never mention Marlene Dietrich (not that, in Manchester, her name was daily on anyone's lips), presumably because the Old Man had an aversion to her.

Whether or not included in the Style Book, the word 'vivacious' if applied to a woman was not to be recommended, because it was seen as code for 'no better than she should be'. Perhaps, on the same grounds, the word 'pert' was to be avoided: I had innocently described someone as 'a pert blonde'; her father came round to the office wanting to thump me for 'casting aspersions' on his daughter. *Express* 'style' seemed to demand that a celebratory family meal would always consist of 'roast beef and all the trimmings' which would always be 'washed down' with 'bubbly'. The *Express* rules for writing stories seemed to be as rigid as those for writing a sonnet or a haiku, but since I didn't know about them, I couldn't obey them. So I just wrote what I saw.

Ever since then I've felt very unconfident about writing straightforward news stories; I've always, not quite truthfully, breezily declared that 'I don't do News: I wouldn't recognize a news story if it bit me in the ankle!' Though I was never as hopeless as the Edwardian journalist who was sent to cover the launch of a ship and returned to inform his editor, 'I'm afraid there's no story. The ship sank.' But I wasn't far off it.

Phil Finn, one of the Ancoats Street heavy mob, who was a fellow Land O'Cakes lodger and went on to be a star news reporter, said, 'Ann could write like a dream, but she couldn't pen a short par about a man falling off his bike in Ancoats.'

Another young journalist who later also became a source of the Manchester News Desk's ire was Paul Dacre, who'd just graduated from Leeds University: apart from being 'too young, brash and cocky', his crime, I later learned, was that he was from the South, had been to public school and had been hired 'only because his father is a famous Fleet Street journalist'. Dacre soon moved South and eventually became the legendarily successful editor of the *Daily Mail*, whereas the Campbell/Blake duo's beloved overstaffed and drunken Manchester *Express* office eventually shrivelled and died.

But mostly what I learned was how to see off assorted sexist, bullying men – like news editors, cross-eyed gunmen, war criminals, prospective rapists, the whole bloody lot – and Campbell (inadvertently) taught me how to deal with them. So, perversely, I'm almost grateful to him.

I picked up other (then invaluable, but now redundant) skills like the removal of diaphragms from the handsets in public phone-boxes to stop your rivals filing their stories. The sharpest rivals would always carry spare diaphragms in their pockets; newspapers were always tut-tutting about the vandalizing of phone boxes, and I sometimes wondered whether much of the vandalism was perpetrated by us. I also learnt how to remove the distributor heads from rivals' cars; to this day the only part of a car engine I can recognize.

And of course, I learned how to drink. These days journalists spend lunch breaks – if they have them – hunched over their computers 'googling', with a Prêt à Manger sarnie and a fruit smoothie. In my youth as a 'trainee reporter' I was mostly trained in how to spend hours in the pub, drinking the 'ferals' under the table. One evening in Yates's Wine Lodge, which had sawdust on the floor – presumably to mop up booze, blood and vomit – I overheard one of my colleagues saying, 'That young Leslie lass has hollow legs.' I'm appalled to remember that I was actually proud of the fact. It meant I was 'one of the lads'.

Not one of Campbell's lads, of course. He'd take a select group of what he called his 'Young Lions' to Yates's or the Crown and Kettle, a former courthouse, run by Carmen who served her favourite lads a peculiar Portuguese red wine called Periquita which tasted of iron filings; they'd reel back to the office moaning, 'I'm completely Periquita-ed!'

The pub's old court benches were always lined with the local ladies of the night, who were Carmen's chums and who gossiped raucously about the rubbish fellers they'd serviced the night before. But for their profession these jolly ladies could have been members of the Women's Institute out on a spree. They always wore curlers and headscarves, which would only be removed when they set off to 'work' of an evening. Actually, most Northern working-class women then wore headscarves all day; in many Northern city suburbs the Muslim hejab is today's equivalent, though donned, of course, for a rather different reason.

Years later John Edwards, my *Daily Mail* colleague in Fleet Street, wrote a nostalgic piece about the now virtually extinct drinking culture of journalism. He recalled how the great wordsmith Vincent Mulchrone would begin every day by taking a cab from Waterloo Station to the Harrow pub next door to the *Mail*'s office. He'd look up and down the street for cops and 'then, at 9.45 a.m., they opened the door quickly for him and he went into the back bar. Half a bottle of Moët et Chandon was always in an ice bucket on the counter. If it was a really bad day, he would take a Fernet Branca as a chaser.'

John was equally misty-eyed recalling the drinking exploits of World War II veteran foreign correspondent Don Wise, who always went to war in a cravat, and who sent a dispatch from Angola which began: 'The first African I saw killed in war almost fell into my drink.' Then, according to John, Wise called the waiter to 'bring him another glass'.

The old Fleet Street cherished tales about its legendary drinkers. Like, for example, the reporter Mick McDonough who one day reeled into the *Sun* office to be greeted by his editor Larry Lamb with the words: 'Pissed again, McDonough!' To which a slurry McDonough managed to reply: 'So am I, Larry, so am I!'

Edwards also described me. 'Ann Leslie usually bought the last one only for herself since the guys she started off with were half-dead on the floor. Sitting later at her desk, the words were hammered into a beaten-up Adler typewriter while she was singing a song. That's how it was then.' Yes, that's how it was. (Though one slight correction, John: I don't sing.)

The new sobriety in what's still called 'Fleet Street' – although no newspaper dwells there now – is, of course, despised by the old-timers. In the words of René Cutforth, one of the greatest foreign correspondents: 'In the old days we were all drunk, late with our stories, and the stuff was good! Now they're all sober, meet their deadlines, and their copy is crap!'

The old Fleet Street, albeit highly competitive, could be surprisingly protective of its fellow tribesmen. When a friend of mine, a particularly affable columnist, was sent to cover the Polisario guerrilla war in the Western Sahara he received a fairly typical Fleet Street war wound: he imbibed a little too freely on the plane, fell over on arrival in the hotel bathroom, broke his leg, and therefore couldn't go to the front line. His fellow tribesmen wrote and filed his dispatches for him. They didn't even take umbrage – let alone rat on him – when 'his' articles received an honourable mention at the British Press Awards.

Surprising numbers of these legendary drunks survived into old age; Don Wise himself lived until he was eighty. And even René

Cutforth, who ended his career doing TV adverts for Krona margarine, didn't expire until he was seventy-five; the obituary in one paper had the headline 'Krona Man Dead'. I'd always assumed that Tom Campbell would die of cirrhosis but 'he could hold his drink, you know,' one of his erstwhile Young Lions told me. 'He died slipping on some icy steps and cracked his skull. And he was sober at the time.'

· One day the Northern editor emerged from his office and came over to my desk. 'There's something going on called a "Youthquake". I want you to write a column for teenagers – pop music, fashion, that sort of thing.' But, I protested, I know nothing about teenagers – my teenage years had been spent overseas or in semi-foster homes or convents. I was also totally ignorant about fashion and had a tin ear for music. The only music I listened to at home was my father's favourites, the Peruvian soprano Yma Sumac and Sibelius's 'Swan of Tuonela', neither of which I thought would equip me for the new 'Youthquake' scene.

'Well, you're the youngest person here, so get on with it.'

And I did, if only to get out from under Campbell's thumb. The only teenagers I was allowed to write about had to exist south of the Scottish border and north of the Potteries.

So I'd ring various spotty youths in Lancashire skiffle clubs who were, alas, rather more articulate on the washboard than on the phone, until I finally found a bright, funny Liverpool boy called John Lennon in a group called the Beatles; I'd keep ringing up his manager, Brian Epstein, would arrange a chat with John, and then gratefully scribble down his funny, sinus-clogged aperçus on more or less anything.

One day the editor told me: 'Too many of these "Insects", or whatever they call themselves, on your page.'

'Actually, as you know, they're called the Beatles.'

'Don't care what they're called – sounds as if you're in their pay.'

Epstein rang me one day: 'Why don't you come to Liverpool and . . .'

'Sorry, Brian, the editor says I'm not to put the Beatles on my page any more.' Barely eighteen months later the Beatles became the biggest pop group in the world, and Epstein never took my calls again.

By now I had moved out of the Land O'Cakes and rented a lace-curtained semi on the Didsbury Road with a young South African actress with curly red hair whom I'd met in the New Theatre Inn, the actors' pub near the Library Theatre. Her real name was Janet Suzman, but her agent had told her to change it because it 'sounds too foreign'. To which Jan replied, 'But what about Ingrid Bergman's name? That's foreign and it doesn't seem to have harmed her!'

'But Bergman is a *Swedish* name.' Unlike Suzman which was, perhaps, a little too Jewish for the time.

So Janet Manners she became for a short while – a rather limp, who's-for-tennis kind of name – which didn't suit her feisty, exotic, witty personality. As a rep actress she was earning £13 for eight performances a week. Our semi soon became open house for all the actors passing through. David Scase, the Library Theatre's director, who reared a host of future stars – among them Anthony Hopkins, Robert Stephens, Alan Rickman, Martin Jarvis and Patrick Stewart – had a tremendous eye for talent. Especially if the talent was young and pretty. 'Though he never made a pass at either of us,' recalls Jan. 'We were not unsexy but I think we were both quite fierce.'

Jan taught me how to cook what we still agree was her 'legendary Spag Bol': we'd buy tins of cheap mince, fish out all the yellow gristly bits, slosh in bottles of red wine and brandy, boil it all up and pour steaming globs of it over some pasta. 'Our drunken cookery was *divine*, wasn't it? Everyone adored it!' remembers Jan. Our Sunday early-afternoon breakfast speciality was toast and marmalade topped with towering pinnacles of whipped cream full of 'lots and lots of brandy'; we and any visiting thesps would spend most of Sunday reeling about with 'huge brandy-cream moustaches on our upper lips'.

And then disaster struck. For me, anyway. John Barton of the Royal Shakespeare Company had seen Jan on stage at the Library and invited her to audition for *The Wars of the Roses*. Peter Hall was watching and hired her on the spot. On hearing Jan's exciting news I once more trudged to the phone box down the road with a sack of tuppenny pieces and rang Michael in London: 'I'm distraught! Jan's left me and gone to Stratford to become a star! I can't stay on in this horrible city without her!' Janet did indeed become a star and, on her marriage to Trevor Nunn, became for a while one half of the most glamorous theatrical couple of the time.

Her departure made me determined to stick to this miserable attempt to be a journalist for precisely one year. After that I would abandon Manchester and journalism for good. And then, eleven months after my arrival, a deus ex machina, a tall, handsome man with a fenderful of startlingly white teeth (he became known to his many enemies as the Smiling Shark) descended on the Ancoats Lubianka and rescued me.

It was Bob Edwards, the *Express*'s Fleet Street editor. In those days of flourishing regional offices it was the custom of Fleet Street editors, like medieval monarchs, to visit their far-flung vassals to give them encouragement. Or, in Edwards's case, to terrify them. The visit resulted in Campbell and Blake instantly transforming themselves, albeit temporarily, into a couple of Uriah Heeps.

Edwards called me in and informed me that I was being transferred to Fleet Street to write a column. He later told me, 'The main reason for giving you a column was because you were young. Besides, I could never get control over the Features Department, and with one or two exceptions none of them were any good. I thought you might improve things.'

On hearing of my promotion Campbell became apoplectic with disbelief. True, he'd wanted to get rid of me from day one. But he didn't want me to leave *in bloody triumph*. The only words he addressed to me were, 'Mark my words, lassie, the editor has made a big mistake!' I feared that he was right, but I was too excited by my liberation from Ancoats to care.

All I had to do was pack up fast and sublet the semi to one of the Library Theatre thesps: a young, but already bald, Patrick Stewart. Over the intervening decades I'd mutter, every time I was channel-flipping and saw him on *Star Trek*, 'Captain Picard, you *still* owe me rent!'

This was the second time that Bob Edwards had become editor of the *Express*. Lord Beaverbrook's son, the Hon. Max Aitken, who was chairman of the board – but whose only discernible talents were for power-boat racing and bedding women – had fired him without consulting Beaverbrook. He was obliged by his furious father to rehire him a year later.

When Edwards was fired for the first time, many on the staff celebrated with champagne. On the return of the Smiling Shark they knew that a night of the long knives awaited them and they'd probably be sacked.

Once I was installed in the large, windowless Features Room in the *Express* HQ, I could see why; very few in there ever seemed to do any work for the paper. One delicate soul would play his violin behind the filing cabinets when upset, which was often. Another would disappear for days on end and the office would have to field calls from far-flung locations – one of which I took from a Dunfermline police station informing me, 'We've got someone here, says he works for the *Daily Express*, but he's run out of money. He's acting a bit funny, and says he can't get home.'

The paper, high on circulation success, was traditionally extraordinarily forgiving towards the many wayward members of its staff. While I was there, one of its numerous foreign correspondents was sent to cover the civil war in the Congo. Before leaving, he had a few snifters in El Vino's in Fleet Street, but nevertheless managed to make it to the plane. Unfortunately it stopped to refuel in Lagos. And so did he. He got so smashed in the transit lounge that after he'd returned to what he thought was his plane it took off and landed, not as he'd expected, in Leopoldville, but back at Heathrow. Nothing for it, of course, but to return to El Vino's where he was discovered by his Foreign Editor. Was he sacked? No, he was merely demoted to being 'Our Religious Affairs Correspondent'.

One of the feature writers who shared my desk never wrote a word unless it was on his expenses sheet; these were highly creative documents, since he never left the office except to go round the corner to Poppins, the *Express* pub. There was an elderly and demented features secretary with dyed cochineal hair who habitually flung the phone at a particular feature writer whom she disliked. Michael Parkinson, a former *Express* man, then working for Granada Television, would wander in and his old colleagues would always have plenty of time for an affable chat.

The William Hickey social diary was situated near us and, from time to time, we'd hear the odd scream as the Diary Editor and his minions would seize their favourite whipping boy, string him up feet first, and dump him in the wastepaper basket. To get to the Diary sadists' den, people had to walk through Features. I kept noticing a cocky young man in a tight, shiny blue suit sashaying through our office scattering laughter and quips. 'Who's that?' I asked.

'Some Aussie called Nigel Dempster who's been hired to shag duchesses.' He eventually married the daughter of a count, then the daughter of a duke, and became the most famous gossip columnist of the time.

A rather eccentric, dreamy girl called Jane Gaskell was always writing novels in office time and seemed to regard being asked to write something for her employer as a violation of her privacy. Thanks to her bestseller about a window cleaner in the Swinging Sixties, *All Neat in Black Stockings* (later made into a film), the *Oxford English Dictionary* credits her with having invented the word 'plonker'.

There were undoubtedly an awful lot of plonkers on the paper then, one of whom was Denis Pitts, who'd made a name for himself covering Suez and Moscow, but Bob Edwards sacked him anyway. 'He just couldn't be bothered; he was always asleep at his desk. He really irritated me. Whenever I remonstrated with him, he treated me like dirt.' Pitts went on to become a film-maker and novelist, with both of which jobs he evidently could be bothered.

In fact it struck me that Bob was always on the point of sacking people, sometimes without justification, apart from irritation with the person concerned. One such example was Nancy Banks-Smith, who went on to work for the *Guardian* and become one of the most consistently witty and brilliant television critics.

One day I was in his office trying to stick up for her copy (and I wasn't a friend of hers). He snapped at me, 'Why does she have to be so ugly?' I was shocked by the remark because obviously what Nancy looked like had no relevance to her writing. Besides, it made me nervous: I was no beauty myself. Bob too was shocked when I reminded him decades later of what he'd said. 'She wasn't ugly, but she was always very unkempt. And I didn't sack her! She left!'

Clearly I too was somewhat unkempt because one day he ordered me to get three smart new outfits and charge them to expenses. The first of these was from Mary Quant, the high priestess of Sixties fashion, who had declared that, thanks to her frocks, 'Middle age has been abolished!'

Bob, who looked tremendously middle-aged to me, was not entranced. The frock was a short, mustard-yellow, 'flapper' tunic dress with black trimming round the neck and a black sash on the hips. I adored it. Later I told Mary Quant that, alas, I could only wear her dress off-duty as it was clearly too 'advanced' for my editor. My second and third outfits were so middle-aged that he could happily declare, 'You could go and interview the Archbishop of Canterbury in those!'

Although I was terrified of him, Bob was never anything but kind to me. But I hated writing the column because, at twenty-two, I felt I was too young to have anything interesting to say. When I told him I didn't want to write it any more, he was astonished: newspapers weren't the thick, column-littered volumes they are today; to be given a column in those more slim-line newspaper days was a much sought-after honour.

'Funnily enough,' he mused years later, 'I always thought you rather resented me for giving you the column in the first place.' But my column embarrassed me, as had my 'Youthquake' page in the Northern editions; I'd cringe every time I saw huge posters bearing my name and face on the sides of Manchester buses urging the populace to read 'The Ann Leslie Page'. And I cringed even more at the first headline over my new column: 'A Provocative New Name – and she's 22!' Why on earth, I thought, would anyone want to read the twitterings of this wet-behind-the-ears young woman?

Mind you, this 'provocative new name' certainly managed to provoke Lady Beaverbrook. The Old Man, who clearly had not yet made up his mind about the new column, passed on his wife's criticisms to the editor. With the smooth, Jeeves-like manner he employed when dealing with the Old Man, Edwards replied, 'Thank you for letting me see Lady Beaverbrook's comments on Ann Leslie's column. I think these criticisms are extremely sound, and I must bear the burden of them, because I passed the column which comes under my personal direction like all the other columns.' But in fact he never asked me to change a word of anything I wrote, and he never told me at the time that my 'provocative' column had seriously provoked the proprietor's wife.

The Old Man, however, soon took an interest in the column himself. Alarmingly, he started sending me letters from his house on Cap d'Ail on the French Riviera.

One such letter in January 1964 began: 'Dear Ann, I have been reading your column. I admire it very much. It is extremely good and I think you are going to make a great columnist.' There then followed alternating paragraphs of praise and criticism. One of the paragraphs took exception to my sympathetic remarks about Jackie Kennedy: 'Someone should remind her that she is the nation's widow – and that the nation's widow should not dine with Brando in public.'

The Old Man's letters terrified me. How was I to respond? Should I try to stick up for myself? This would have been hard since I was convinced that my stuff was dreadful anyway. Should I try to charm him? But I'd never met him and had no idea what he might find charming.

Mercifully, the leader writer George Malcolm Thomson, who was close to Beaverbrook, gave me some useful advice. 'Just remind him that you are still very young, and that you're determined to learn from his *very valid* criticisms. The most important thing, however, is never to send him your reply in an unused envelope: the Old Man thinks that staff who use new envelopes are being very extravagant with his money.'

I would therefore pick up a new envelope, spill coffee on it, stick a stamp on it and grind it underfoot until it was in a fit state to be sent to His Lordship. Bob Edwards's secretary kept a waste-bin full of used envelopes precisely for this purpose.

Then one day a call came from the Old Man's secretary. He was returning from the South of France and wanted me to come and have lunch with him and Lady Beaverbrook at Cherkley Court, his home in Surrey. Wow! Another one in the eye for Campbell and Blake! The Old Man only invited journalists he admired to Cherkley! I'd arrived!

A fortnight before I was due to meet him, I got a call from Cherkley telling me that the Old Man was very ill, so the lunch was postponed. He died not long afterwards, and I was furious. Yes, he was eighty-five, but couldn't he have hung on a bit longer for me?

My fury at the Old Man's 'premature' death suddenly made me realize, for the first time, that a job which I'd embarked on largely by accident was now perhaps in danger of becoming a lifetime career.

2

Daughter of the Raj

The strange thing about having been born in a foreign city, even if you never return to it, is that something about the place always lingers in the roots of your being; the deeply buried loam which once nourished you is never entirely forgotten. I've never been back to Rawal Pindi, where I was born in 1941, in what was then pre-Partition India and is now Pakistan. But whenever I hear old India hands utter the word 'Pindi', I feel an odd tug at the heart.

My father's work was in 'Pindi'. He'd been to public school, had read Latin and Greek at Oxford, and then – instead of becoming one of the so-called 'Heaven Born', the usually public school-educated British members of the Indian Civil Service – he became a 'box-wallah', a business manager, in the oil industry, as his father before him had been in Imperial China.

His mother (her name was Mary but after she moved to China she was always called Ming) was a formidable woman who wrote a privately printed memoir of her life as the wife of a *taipan* in the Chinese Treaty Port of Tianjin, where my father was born.

After the Opium Wars the British obliged the defeated Chinese to open up their ports to foreigners and to trade. Ming remembered how each foreign 'barbarian' nationality largely kept to themselves: there were French, British, Russian, Austrian, Japanese and German territorial 'Concessions' – the German Concession compound in Tianjin was 'very orderly, with a huge metal statue of their Emperor, Kaiser Wilhelm, in the middle'. Each national Concession controlled its own schools, postal service, licensing, municipal affairs and police. It was when motorcars began to arrive in Tianjin and separate driving licences had to be issued by each nationality that this bureaucratic demarcation between the Concessions became, as Ming declared, 'completely ridiculous' – particularly when the distance between each Concession was often no more than a mile or two.

My grandfather, whose family origins were in Scotland, had been born in Australia and he met my grandmother, a vicar's daughter from Stockton-on-Tees, at Oxford where he was a Rhodes Scholar at Balliol and she was working as a midwife in the city's then foetid slums. She'd been born in 1879 and remembered the joy of hearing of the Relief of Mafeking in South Africa when she was twenty-one. Her Reverend father had been extraordinarily liberal for those days and encouraged his blue-stocking daughter to be as independent as convention then allowed. He even encouraged her to learn to ride a bike, a most unladylike thing to do, and she had to endure jeers and catcalling from 'rough' boys in the street; he then took her on a gruelling four-week cycling trip though the high Alps of France and Switzerland.

Ladies' bikes were not yet common and riding a man's bike with its crossbar was difficult while wearing a long, voluminous skirt. The feminist trailblazer in my grandmother's home town was a Mrs Millinchap, who kept a sweet shop and 'electrified the town by riding down the High Street wearing *bloomers* rather than a skirt'. Ming's brazen insistence on riding a bike, albeit in a skirt, caused not only catcalls but much pursing of the lips among the family's 'respectable' neighbours. Her sister's best friend, a doctor's daughter, was invited round to tea after school and replied, 'No thank you. Mother doesn't want me to be friends with people who behave as your family does.'

During the Suffragette movement Ming was, she said, 'no political feminist' and disapproved of their tactics, if not their cause. But she herself had been something of a proto-feminist. She confessed in her memoir that she had been 'considered rather a freak' for insisting on going to Durham University at the turn of the century to read an 'unfeminine' subject like science. She'd won a scholarship to Cambridge but one of her brothers was somewhat spendthrift while there, which meant that there was not enough money left to support her living away from home.

Even more 'freakishly', after graduating in science (which for some reason she had to study in German), she decided to qualify as a Sanitary Inspector or, as the post was more demotically known, an 'inspector of nuisances'. She'd been outraged by the living and working conditions she encountered through her father's pastoral work in the Northern slums – ten adults and children crammed into one filthy room, its walls riddled with bugs which she'd spear with a hatpin.

Experiencing at close hand what she called 'the full blast of poverty, wickedness, hopelessness and ineffectualness' literally made her weep. The job was of course considered very 'unladylike and unwomanly'. Her parents' social circle was shocked that 'a girl they knew, not yet twenty-two, should go alone into factories, slums and elementary schools, and be seen talking to disreputable-looking persons'. Her boisterous brothers called her 'the Insanitary Spectre'.

It was not a safe profession. Sweatshop owners would try to evade her inspections by hiding their grotesquely exploited employees in a lavatory or storage cupboard; others would attempt to bribe her, and at least one enraged employer tried to throw her downstairs. My iron-willed grandmother soon got these 'monsters' sorted. All of which might have given her early practice for dealing with Chinese bandits and warlords in the future.

Grandfather was a tall, athletic, taciturn man, much given to 'nerves' and what my grandmother would refer to darkly in later years as 'his old North China fever'. During the Great War his three brothers, a cousin and an uncle were all killed, and perhaps his habitual melancholy dated from then. One day my grandmother ordered him to come out of his huge garage-cum-workshop under the walnut tree at home in Buckinghamshire, where he frequently hid if there was company (and that included his grandchildren). She told him he had to advise me about going up to Oxford: all he managed to tell me, bafflingly, was that I must 'steer clear of undergraduates who wear yellow shoes; they're all socialists', before loping silently back to his garage sanctuary.

As a young man heading off to live and work in China after graduation, he needed a wife and he was clearly ready to capitulate once Ming had set her determined sights upon him. Not being particularly pretty, and certainly not behaving like the docile ideal of Victorian womanhood, she married 'late', at thirty-four. Which, she later remarked, was something of a blessing: 'Five children are quite enough; if I'd started earlier I might have ended up with eleven like my mother.' They married on Shameen Island, a whites-only (apart from servants) enclave off the southern Chinese port of Canton, now Guangzhou. Ming brought her wedding cake from England, on a sea voyage that lasted five-and-a-half weeks. It was, apparently, still edible.

When working in Oxford in the Child Welfare Department before her marriage my grandmother had campaigned vociferously for the city to provide public lavatories for women. 'Strange to say such comforts were open to men, but women were too modest to mention the need!' Thanks not least to a leaflet written for her campaign by George Bernard Shaw, Ming's fight to provide loos for Oxford's women was a triumphant success. Except that many women, far from congratulating her, were deeply shocked. 'Even one of my own sisters, visiting me and being shown with pride my latest boast [an underground ladies' loo near Balliol] turned away with disgust and called my work "indecent".'

Very little seemed to seriously alarm Ming; indeed, she seemed to regard the warlord period in China as little more than a confounded nuisance; when one warlord's rabble turned up to burn down her house she somehow managed to see them off as though she were still dealing with recalcitrant sweatshop owners back in Cleveland. Her son Kingsley told me, 'I was very young but I do remember that when they fled, leaving behind one of their swords, Ming let me keep it as a souvenir.'

What did shock and sadden her was the miserable status of women in China. An elderly *amah*, or nanny, whom she employed unwrapped her tiny deformed feet one day because they were suppurating from the heat. My grandmother had little truck with the view that the foot-binding of Chinese women was necessary to satisfy the foot-fetishism of Chinese men. The allegedly erotic justification for this bizarre practice was, in her view, stuff and nonsense: the ever-practical Ming concluded that the deliberate and painful crippling of Chinese girls was most likely performed in order to stop the poor creatures from running away from cruel fathers, cruel husbands and, especially, from cruel and equally crippled mothers-in-law. It ensured total subservience, not something which came easily to Ming.

One day she asked the houseboy to go and buy her a couple of canaries in the market. 'He did so and came back with a gorgeous cage of bamboo and a lovely pair.' When asked the cost, the house-boy told her that the male bird cost twice as much as the female. Ming noted witheringly: 'Obviously the sex differential in birds is similar to that of Chinese human beings.'

Travelling through southern China in 1911, she and a woman friend were being transported on palanquins borne along rutted roads by 'coolies'. She'd noticed, as they travelled, 'little structures that puzzled me, and when we came to a stop, to rest the coolies, Mrs Ivy explained to me that these were "baby towers". Each tiny edifice had a small opening in it, some way up one side . . . and this was the place where any unwanted baby girls could be deposited. The Chinese had little use for girls, and when a woman gave birth to a girl, the baby could be deposited here, unless a convent that took in baby girls happened to be nearby. There was always a large basket at convent doors to receive them, dead or alive.'

When Mao came to power he declared that there was to be absolute equality between men and women in China because, as the old Chinese adage had it, 'women hold up half the sky.' But of course it's not so easy to overturn such deeply ingrained, centuries-old prejudices against girl-children.

In 1993, seventeen years after Mao's death, I wrote about the 'dying rooms' in orphanages, where baby girls, who if allowed to live might have 'held up half the sky', were left uncared for, unloved, unfed, all condemned to death for the mistake of being born female. Not that much had changed since Ming first saw the 'baby towers' at the beginning of the twentieth century.

The Dying Rooms article, occasioned by a controversial TV documentary, was denounced by the Chinese authorities for spreading 'lies' and 'malicious propaganda'. They refused to admit that the practice still existed. The adoption by foreigners of discarded Chinese baby girls was not allowed at the time, although later foreign adoptions were approved, not least because orphanages and local officials could charge the 'round eyes' large sums for expenses and require 'donations'. One orphanage official told me later, 'I was never comfortable with the old policy because I'm a woman, and I'm glad I wasn't just left to die as they were. I always tried to keep them warm and comfortable before the end.'

Three years after I wrote about the 'dying rooms' I met an

American couple, Tim and Pam Baker, having breakfast in a noisy restaurant in Beijing with their daughters, who included a funny and fearless little Chinese girl called Esther, her glossy black hair tied in bunches, who was arguing with her blonde elder sister about who had the right to eat the last piece of French toast.

When the Bakers had found Esther in a state orphanage, she was so weak and listless that she couldn't even sit up, and they feared that she might be mentally retarded; a retarded baby girl is considered even more disposable in traditional Chinese culture. The Communists' draconian one-child policy merely accentuated that tradition.

'We don't know how old Esther is but we think she's about three now; we've invented a birthday for her so she doesn't miss out.' The Bakers, who are committed Christians, live and work in China and, through a charity Tim founded, liaise with Chinese orphanages. Apart from the adopted Esther they have three other daughters. 'We and our girls go to the orphanages, unannounced, two or three times a week, to help feed and bathe and love the children. The staff are very poorly paid and overstretched and most of them do the best they can. So our girls help paint rooms, and get hold of wheelchairs, and play with the children.'

The Bakers told me that their Chinese friends, 'knowing that we already had three daughters of our own (a source of pity!) were astonished that we would actually adopt a *fourth* girl. But gradually, once they've seen how happy our family is, their attitude has changed – so much so that they call our girls "the four golden flowers", after a famous Chinese film of the Fifties called *The Five Golden Flowers*. There's a Chinese saying: "Seeing something once is better than hearing about it 100 times." They see with their own eyes that there's no shame or grief in having a girl-child.'

If the convents which took in girl-children abandoned on door-steps (or in the 'baby towers' that Ming saw) couldn't change centuries-old anti-female prejudice, I'm afraid saintly couples like the Bakers aren't likely to succeed either. But the one-child policy has been carried out so cruelly and so corruptly (those with money can bribe local cadres to 'overlook' an extra child or two) that the peasants deeply resent it.

Peasant revolts (such as the one which brought the Communist

Party to power fifty-nine years earlier) terrify the regime. To head off revolt, the law has been modified: now, if you are a peasant (or a member of an ethnic minority like the Tibetans) and your first child is a daughter, or a son who is handicapped, you are allowed the 'privilege' of a second child. But rural incomes are plummeting: these precious only sons – known as Little Emperors – are part of the 'blind flow' of peasants fleeing to the cities to earn money, so that there are too few left to work the farms and feed the still-growing population.

Women do more than 70 per cent of the work on the land, but thanks to the brutal culling of baby girls there are now too few of them left to do it. Older villagers will still describe girl-children as 'maggots in the rice' and as 'useless as spilled water'; no wonder China's female suicide rate is one of the highest in the world.

When in the 2008 earthquake in Sichuan province shoddily built schools collapsed and killed at least 9,000 pupils, while older buildings nearby survived, the agony of the bereaved parents was immeasurably increased by the fact that they had lost their only child. One mother was heard to scream at a local official, 'You forbade me to have more than one! Now he is lost and I have nothing, nothing!'

I worked in Chengdu, the capital of Sichuan province, and went to a giant warehouse in a slum area where peasant youths were milling around like cattle, waiting to be selected by gang-masters for a day or two's work. They knew they'd be badly paid – if at all – but, as one twenty-year-old told me: 'My village is dying and there are no girls of my age to marry. I have to come to the city.'

This is the hidden China, the poverty-stricken 'real' China which Western businessmen, staying in luxury hotels such as mine, plastered with ads for Cartier watches and Gieves & Hawkes shirts, usually never see. Dazzled by the country's growth statistics, they sip their Rémy Martin with their Chinese counterparts in the glamorous cocktail bars of cities such as Shanghai, Beijing, Guangzhou and even Chengdu, and fantasize about China's much-hyped 'billion-strong consumer market'.

But this is not the China in which the vast majority of its citizens live. They are poor, desperate, oppressed by the twin curses of tradition and a callously corrupt Communist regime, unable to afford the expensive gizmos that the West wants to sell them. Those who can afford these pleasures usually have *guangxi*, connections; they enthusiastically endorse the former strongman Deng Xiaoping's assertion that 'to be rich is no sin' (usually rendered as 'to get rich is glorious'), and their own pampered and protected children are now labelled the *yanei*, the 'Red Princes'.

I have been going to China, on and off, since early 1977. On my first visit I knew that my father was dying of cancer in England. I told him I'd be going to Shanghai where he had lived as a child, and he asked me to take a photograph of his parents' house, if it still existed, on the Avenue Foch. Despite the tumultuous and murderous years of the Cultural Revolution, where family ties were rejected as 'bourgeois' and only Chairman Mao could be revered as your 'father', I felt that reverence for the family was probably still buried deep in the Chinese psyche. And of course it was.

So I took one of my Foreign Ministry minders aside and, whispering, explained the situation to him. He looked panicky (who said the Chinese are inscrutable? They're one of the most 'scrutable' races on earth). Despite being Shanghainese, he insisted that he didn't know any of the 'imperialist pre-Liberation' street names, so he couldn't tell me where the old Avenue Foch was. I suspected that he could, but feared to tell me; after all, three of the Gang of Four (Shanghainese themselves) had been arrested only two months earlier and China was still very tense.

How could this hapless bureaucrat be sure that their cruel and arbitrary ideology wouldn't return? There's a stoic peasant saying which declares that all one can hope for in life is to 'keep alive in the bitter sea'. Would the 'bitter sea' engulf the likes of him again? If he helped me there was the risk that one day, if the political tide turned again, he'd be denounced as an 'imperialist running-dog of capitalism'.

Two years later I was back working in Shanghai again and China had stabilized. And I had the same minder. He looked stricken. 'Is your father still alive? Because I can take you to his old home now.' No, I replied, he died. He then told me, his head bent, that he'd felt deep shame for not helping me fulfil my filial duty to my father and his dying wish. The shame, he said, had preyed on his mind ever since. I told him that I quite understood, that he was not to blame – and that anyway I'd visited and photographed Shameen Island where my grandparents had married and that my dying father had been very grateful. All of which was untrue, but I felt it was psychologically helpful to him, and of course I bore him no grudge. He instantly looked less stricken.

My father had died, full of morphine, his once handsome face now carved by cancer into a collection of sharp, yellow-skinned bones, at home in Abney House. He had inherited the house from his parents; it was not an ancestral pile but it did have a certain sombre grandeur and was the west wing of a large, irregular riverside mansion, added to over the years, the central part being an Elizabethan wharf house.

My grandparents had bought it 1935 because it was big enough to house their five children, and had a lengthy river frontage on to the Thames in Buckinghamshire, with a boat house, large paddock, tennis court, billiard room, long lawns and a collection of ancient trees, including a Cedar of Lebanon said to have been planted from one of the seeds brought to England from the Levant by Linnaeus, the naturalist who imported the species to Europe.

Later, when the nationalist Kuomintang under General Chiang Kai-shek took over parts of China, his formidable wife Soong Mei-ling, whom Ming had known in Shanghai, told her she wanted to reforest that blighted country. Ming then sent her seeds from the Abney cedar but Mei-ling told her that, sadly, they never took. There was, of course, rather a lot going on in China at the time (what with Japanese occupiers, the Chinese Communist army and assorted warlords) so perhaps Abney's cedar seeds thought it was hardly worth trying to grow in that turbulent land.

Ming's married life in China had been buttressed by many a docile 'native' servant. And to her surprise and irritation Abney had no servants' quarters, so she had to build something suitably small and pokey behind the kitchen into which a maid or two could be stuffed (an area which we irreverent grandchildren called 'the back passage'). But English servants were more uppity and demanded rather more creature comforts and autonomy than the Chinese; one maid even had the cheek to inspire a teenage crush in my handsome Uncle Kingsley and was of course sacked on the spot.

World War II caused a mass exodus of domestic servants: young women could now get much more lucrative and companionable work in the armaments factories. In any case, being bossed about by Ming – 'No, dear, that's *not* the way you make butter curls!' – can't have been much fun. There was now no one left to answer the bells on the mahogany board in the kitchen quarters labelled 'Drawing Room', 'Billiard Room', 'Dining Room', 'Bedroom 1', 'Dressing Room', 'Bedroom 2' . . .

Ming had to learn to cook and was hopeless at it: her 'speciality' was rock cakes which had, indeed, the tooth-cracking texture of rock. Abney had been largely furnished by Ming with huge, depressing, heavily inlaid mahogany furniture and elaborate screens which she'd had shipped from China. The drawing room, particularly, resembled the Empress Dowager's quarters in the Forbidden City which, when I first saw them, instantly reminded me of Abney. And reminded me too of the long feud between Ming and my mother, which somewhat resembled the imperial feuds within the Qing dynasty, with Ming playing the role of the Empress Dowager and my mother that of the scheming concubine whose beauty had ensnared the eldest son.

My mother's chief sin was to be an Irish Roman Catholic – which showed that she was not descended from the Protestant Anglo-Irish gentry like Ming's side of the family, which had belonged to the so-called Twelve Tribes of Galway. I knew little about my mother's background because she never wanted to talk about it: perhaps all her life she felt (or was made to feel by my father's family) somewhat 'below the salt'. As one of my uncles put it, 'I think Ming blamed your mother for the fact that, when Norman and Theo were both up at Oxford, Norman was so distracted by Theo that he didn't get a First, and didn't become a sporting Blue, as our father had done.'

All I knew about my maternal grandfather was that he'd been a country doctor who died of morphine addiction; he used the drug to ease the aches and pains he got from riding his horse in all weathers to visit his far-flung rural patients. And I knew little about my maternal grandmother (whom we grandchildren always called Little Granny) except that she was a kind, devout woman for whom my mother built a cottage in the Abney paddock. My mother, to her children's dismay, bullied this gentle soul, perhaps because she blamed her for being a non-'gentry' Irishwoman and a Catholic to boot. Because my mother was officially a Catholic by birth she had to get special permission from a bishop to be allowed a 'mixed marriage' to my father. In those days a mixed marriage didn't mean an interracial wedding (although one Irish friend of mine told me that the parents of a mutual friend, while not approving of their daughter's Nigerian fiancé, sighed, 'At least he's a *Catholic* negro!').

Even attending the Anglican church wedding of a friend was frowned on and special permission needed to be sought. The price my mother paid for being allowed to marry my father was that all the resulting children must be brought up as Catholics. Ecumenism was then very far from becoming religiously fashionable. Catholics were, according to one ancient great-aunt, 'the sperm of the devil', so Theo was obviously not greatly welcomed by my father's devoutly Anglican family.

My mother was considered a beauty and a wit, and she frankly found children a bit of a bore. She had sent me off to a distant boarding school in India when I was barely four; as her best friend Alwyne subsequently told me, 'Theo had many wonderful qualities, but being maternal was not one of them.'

Alwyne and her fellow expat mothers in India had arranged to import an English governess to teach their group of small children. 'We asked Theo to join us but she refused. She told me she couldn't cope with you *and* her new baby and you really had to be sent away to boarding school.' Years later in my turbulent teens, when I tried to tell my mother how lonely, homesick and displaced I'd always felt as a small child, her response was: 'Darling, I'm *so* sorry, but you see, I had phlebitis, so it was dangerous for me to look after you *and* Alison.'

She was of course surrounded by servants and ayahs who would look after me and my baby sister day and night for a pittance. But as I had no idea what 'phlebitis' was – and although my mother could evidently cope with acting up a storm in amateur dramatics and starring in a social life where she was always the most beautiful woman present – I somehow never questioned why she couldn't 'cope' with me.

In many ways my mother had been born before her time and it's unfair of me to be so hard on her. She gave birth to three children because – despite the intelligence which had won her an Oxford scholarship – having children, not a career, was what was then expected of an upper-middle-class wife. She had never had a job, bar a brief spell as a governess teaching English to the daughter of a wealthy family in Greece before the war. She'd had to rely on her beauty, not her brains, for her always precarious self-esteem. When she was at Oxford, the poet John Betjeman had said that my mother, Theodora McDonald, with her milky skin and cloud of red Pre-Raphaelite hair, was the most beautiful woman he'd ever seen. He likened her to Elizabeth Siddall, the nineteen-year-old who posed in a bath for John Everett Millais as the drowned Ophelia. (Siddall, who eventually married Rossetti and later committed suicide, nearly died of pneumonia because the forgetful Millais had let the bath-water go cold.)

Once my mother knew she was a Pre-Raphaelite beauty she lived up to it at university by wearing flowing moss-green robes and posies of violets, and letting her coppery, curly mane stream gorgeously in the breeze. The film director David Lean allegedly fell in love with her (which he did often with many other women); one of Scotland's premier earls apparently wanted to marry her. In the tones of Marlon Brando protesting, 'I could've been a contender,' my mother once sighed to me, 'I could've been a Countess.'

She longed for me to be a 'contender' in the title stakes; one day, before I went to university, she told me that a friend of hers had agreed that her daughter and I would do the Season together, and share a coming-out dance. The friend's eldest daughter had nabbed a marquess when she was a deb. I was horrified at the thought, and mercifully my father, who usually acceded to her demands for the sake of a quiet life, told her 'I'm afraid we can't afford for Ann to become a deb.'

Besides, I was well aware that to grab a marriageable marquess – if you didn't have pots of money and/or an aristocratic bloodline – you had to be a beauty. And that I most certainly was not. Growing up as a pale, bespectacled, pig-tailed child with a brace on my disorderly teeth, I always felt ugly, a belief underlined by the fact that I once overheard my mother sighing to a friend, 'I cannot believe I gave birth to such a plain child.' My younger sister, the blonde, blue-eyed Alison, was much prettier than me and, as is so often the way in families, we found ourselves being labelled by kindly but unthinking relatives. As one of them put it to me one day, in what she believed to be consolatory tones, 'Never mind, Ann, your sister may be the pretty one, but you're the clever one!'

It wasn't until many years later that I realized that I was not nearly as plain as family labelling implied, nor was my sister intellectually dim. But because we were deemed to be so unlike each other, judged on our physical appearance, we were sent to different boarding schools. Alison resented the fact that, because she was deemed to be 'pretty but stupid, I was sent to a very pretty but stupid school full of aristocrats and princesses: Mummy probably hoped I'd marry one of their brothers'. Not surprisingly, she and I didn't become friends until adulthood.

3

'A different ghost'

'All your family seem to have fallen out of the womb with "District Commissioner" written on their foreheads!' a friend once remarked to me. Inaccurate, as I know of only one relative who became a District Commissioner in Africa. But perhaps there's something almost genetic in my family's reluctance to spend their lives in England (even if, as rarely happened, they were born there). They were either sorting out tribal disputes in the Yemen, caring for the poor in Tanzania, struggling with a farm in Kenya, running a mining company in South Africa, or in the case of Great-uncle Ernest being a pillar of the community in Hong Kong before enduring imprisonment in a concentration camp at the hands of the invading Japanese. Or in my case becoming a foreign correspondent. I had never planned to do so but maybe it was, in the Chinese phrase *yuen fen*, something fated to happen.

My parents had a peripatetic existence, moving from one city to another all over India and Pakistan: Bombay, Delhi, Agra, Vizag, Madras, Calcutta, and finally Karachi. Pakistan's then Foreign Minister Zulfiqar Ali Bhutto (father of the assassinated Benazir, whom I knew as a child) fell out with my father in a dispute about nationalizing the Burmah Shell oil company for which my father worked. Our family was expelled and my mother never entirely got over it. When Bhutto, having become Prime Minister, was hanged by the military dictator General Zia ul-Haq in 1979, my mother (being Irish and perhaps genetically incapable of forgiving and forgetting) snorted, 'Serves him right for what he did to our family!' I protested, 'But Mummy, I doubt that what he did to the Leslies figured heavily among General Zia's excuses to have him hanged!' As so often, however, my mother wasn't listening.

After our expulsion from the subcontinent my mother, like my grandmother before her, found herself having to endure a life without cooks, dressmakers, gardeners, chauffeurs and other servants. I once asked my father why we always had so many servants, since they seemed to annoy my mother so much.

It was of course the caste system: a man from one caste could not perform the duties of a man from another caste or sub-caste. It was a kind of ancient trade union, full of baffling demarcations. The ancient Hindu text, the *Law of Manu*, declares that if anybody from the lower orders has the temerity to mention the name of someone of a higher caste he should have a red-hot nail thrust in his mouth, and if he makes the mistake of telling a high-caste Brahmin what to do, he should have hot oil poured into his mouth and ears. While hot nails and boiling oil are obviously no longer mandatory, these ancient demarcations linger on. Which is why multi-tasking was impossible: our sweeper, for example, had to be a Dalit, or 'untouchable', as none of the higher-caste servants would do the job.

And of course we British expats always had to have a Christian cook because Christians, unlike Hindus or Muslims, were happy to cook and eat anything. Cooks apart, my father preferred on the whole to employ Muslim servants rather than Hindus. 'You know where you are with Muslims. Straightforward chaps. Strict Hindus have all these rules about the "impurity" of non-Hindus – "untouchable" incidentally applies to foreigners too, so you never quite know where you are with them.'

My mother constantly suspected the servants of trying to swindle her. She would discuss menus for the week with Cook and dole out the money for him to buy food in the bazaar. When he presented the receipts, she was convinced he was cheating her, which he undoubtedly was, but a servant putting a little top-spin on household bills was considered by wiser employers to be an allowable perk. My mother, however, was not one of the wiser employers. I remember being excruciatingly embarrassed when she began screaming at Cook for charging her for papayas when the garden was full of them. Cook was impassive: 'Garden papayas no good.' The garden papayas were very good, but the gardener was picking them, selling them at a discount to Cook, and trading the rest in the bazaar.

She was constantly sacking Cook and Gardener and complaining to my father for 'always siding with the servants against your own wife!' He hated rows and would discreetly rehire the servants – who'd be squatting on a step in their compound awaiting their regular and inevitable recall – and would try to placate my mother by saying 'Well, darling, the next lot wouldn't be any better, so . . .'

Like most Memsahibs – indeed, like most English people these days who go to live in Spain – my mother never bothered to learn more than a smattering of the local language, so that whenever she overheard the servants talking behind her back she was convinced they were plotting against her. The papaya row took a long time to die down, and I was afraid that one day Cook would be sacked and stay sacked. I loved Cook and I loved his food; every time I had to go away to boarding school he'd cook me my favourite meal: dahl, rice and Queen's Pudding with spun sugar. Cook loved spinning sugar into tall, sticky birds' nests; another source of irritation for my mother. 'He wants to put spun sugar on top of *everything*. It'll be on the kedgeree next.'

As a teenager in Karachi I would be obliged to go to dances given for the children of my parents' friends. I learned how to waltz, quickstep and foxtrot, and how to dance The Gay Gordons, as my father was President of the Caledonian Society.

Under my mother's direction, our *derzhi* (dressmaker) would create huge puffballs of tulle and silk roses and, miserable with the knowledge of forthcoming humiliation when no one would ask me to dance, I would set off for the venue wishing the ground would close up over my head.

Our family driver, a taciturn, expressionless man, somehow sensed my agonies and, if I could no longer face the coming ordeal, would accept my request to drive me round for up to three hours before taking me back home. I would then tell Mummy that I'd had a marvellous time but had left early because I had a headache. And Driver would never betray me.

The only time he did was over the matter of Sohail. Some of the teenagers at these dances were the offspring of local Pakistani big-wigs, like Akbar, the son of the first Pakistani Prime Minister who'd been assassinated in 1951. They were always boys, presumably because their fathers, being Muslim, kept their daughters hidden away at home.

One of these boys was Sohail, a beautiful, liquid-eyed youth for whom I developed a passionate crush, not least because he always asked me to dance. One night, after one such party, he told me his driver hadn't turned up and asked if I could give him a lift home. In the back seat, to my terrified and delirious delight, Sohail began kissing me, swearing he loved me, shoving his long, beautiful, brown fingers down into my sturdy bra and putting his hand up the latest tulle absurdity into which I'd been trussed.

Unfortunately Driver reported these teenage fumblings in the back seat to my father; perhaps he disapproved of a Muslim boy behaving like this with any girl, let alone a *kuffar*, an infidel.

After that, my mother informed me that I was never to see Sohail again and, as is the way with teenagers, I thought that my heart was broken. Months later I nervously asked her if she knew how he was; after all, his father and mine were business acquaintances. 'Sohail? Who? Oh, that Pakistani boy. He committed suicide.'

Why was she so cold? Perhaps it was because Sohail was a Pakistani. Would she have behaved like that if he'd been English? But then, if he'd been English, Driver wouldn't have reported us. I didn't dare ask why Sohail had, according to my often unreliable mother, killed himself. I knew it wouldn't have been because of me, but somehow I felt guilty and knew that I could never reveal to my mother how much I grieved for 'that Pakistani boy'.

The fact is that, although she'd spent most of her adult life among foreigners, she never liked them much. When my architect brother, living in Singapore, brought Nellie, his Chinese-Singaporean fiancée, to stay at Abney, he was given a bedroom and Nellie was told firmly that the house was full, so she was to sleep on a camp bed in a corridor. Later, when my mother needed a live-in help, the agency sent a nice black woman; within two days my mother had evicted her and made no pretence to me that it was on the grounds of anything other than her colour.

Over the years, something curdled inside her – particularly when, as was inevitable, her beauty began to fade. I felt that in some way she'd become rather jealous of me and, oddly, that she disliked the fact that by becoming a foreign correspondent I'd unaccountably actually *chosen* to work with foreigners and, especially, dark-skinned ones, all over the world.

She started treating my globe-trotting career as if I'd undertaken it largely to spite her. Typical was the day when she rang to complain that her central heating had gone on the blink, and could I drive down the M4 to Abney and get it fixed.

'But Mummy, you've got a contract with the company, and the phone numbers are on the boiler, and I can't come, because I've got to go to China early in the morning!'

'You're *always* going to China!'

'But Mummy, it's my job!' I cried, but it was no use. She'd already put the phone down.

I tried to excuse her behaviour towards me; after all, I'd had many of the opportunities which upper-middle-class convention of her time had denied her. Intellectually, I knew she was a victim of the overwhelmingly sexist conventions of her era and class, but emotionally I found the results hard to manage.

She used to have a folder which she called 'my swank kit', full of cuttings of my work and snippets written about me in other newspapers. Whenever she worked herself into a rage with a tradesman (which was often), she would demand of him, 'Do you know who my daughter is?'

Of course the hapless tradesman usually didn't, and anyway, what difference would it have made? I'd hiss sotto voce to her down the office phone, 'Look, Mummy, *please* stop doing this! There's no way I'm going to write a diatribe about your butcher in the *Daily Express* just because you want me to! And anyway, it wouldn't get printed!'

'What's the point of being such a powerful journalistic name if—'

'But Mummy,' I'd protest, 'I'm *not* powerful!'

' – powerful, *thanks, I may say*,' she'd add darkly, 'to your father and me – and you won't even help me when I need you!' She would then slam down the phone and I would spend the next half-hour shaking with rage.

When a blood relative of hers, the bestselling crime novelist Frances Fyfield, became well known, my mother would say to me: 'Well, at least *my* side of the family has achieved something!' She constantly wanted me to meet this one famous name on her 'side of the family', but I was so resistant to the treacherous maternal undercurrents beneath such requests that I not only refused to meet

Frances, but even to read her books – a fact I confessed to her when, by chance, years later we did meet at a party.

*

Ever since I was obliged as a child to leave the subcontinent I had always longed to go back and in the Seventies, after I'd left the *Express*, I pitched some ideas about India to the editor of the extremely tabloid *Sunday Mirror* who, despite his job, was thoroughly civilized and rather better educated than his readers. 'Forget it, Ann – India is death at the box office.' His readers weren't stricken with post-imperial guilt of course: they just didn't want to read anything about Indians or Pakistanis unless they were served up blood-curdling stuff about how they'd all come here to steal British jobs and put the frighteners on little old ladies.

Luckily *Punch* magazine agreed that if I could get an interview with India's Prime Minister Indira Gandhi, they'd probably print it.

Mrs Gandhi heartily disliked the Western press which, unlike the Indian press, was not inclined to garland its prose with descriptions of her 'stunning beauty' (she was, in fact, rather plain), nor did it appreciate the hubris involved in her renaming her party after herself and campaigning under the slogan 'Indira *is* India'.

Besides, I was a woman, a species which she seemed to believe mostly consisted of drippy whingers. She'd made an exception for Jean 'Glenda Slagg' Rook because, bizarrely, Indira Gandhi was a great fan of romantic novelist Barbara Cartland and Cartland was Rook's friend. Rook did Cartland proud with her descriptions of the Indian Prime Minister's 'huge sacred cattle-soft eyes' and 'water-lily hands' (except when the hands were being 'bird-small'), and bafflingly noted that Mrs Gandhi's tiny size 'clobbers you like the foot of an elephant for which she couldn't provide a toenail'.

Luckily for Rook, amid all this Indo-Saracenic fauna-and-flora imagery, she did not make much of the fact that Mrs Gandhi was a woman. The Indian Prime Minister loathed being reminded of this unfortunate truth: in Washington on her first formal visit in 1963 she was asked by an American feminist reporter whether her gender had been a problem with Indian voters. She coldly replied, 'I do not regard myself as a woman.'

So on both counts – gender and profession – I was bound to be a loser and doubted I'd get the interview.

But I knew the legendary foreign correspondent James Cameron and he'd been very close to Mrs Gandhi's adored father, India's first Prime Minister, Jawaharlal Nehru. 'Indira and I have fallen out somewhat,' said James, 'but I'll write to her to ask if she'll see you.'

And he did. And she did. Which is why I found myself in New Delhi one day vomiting in the private Prime Ministerial lavatory.

The night before my appointment with her I had ordered a room-service curry in my luxury government-owned hotel. I woke up in the small hours racked with pain and bleeding from several orifices.

I couldn't believe this was happening. I never got food poisoning in India, not least because my mother believed in 'building up one's immunities' by getting all our food from the bazaar. American expat children dropped like flies, or ended up in the dreaded 'iron lungs' (this was before polio vaccine was invented), because hygiene-obsessed Moms only fed them imported stuff purchased from the American Commissary. Indeed, as a toddler I was found in the garden eating a dead mongoose and emitting little 'Mmmms!' of appreciation, like a punter on a TV chef's show, and I never even got a tummy upset.

But now I was obviously dying. I crawled to the phone, gasping, 'I must have a doctor immediately! *Jeldi! Jeldi!*' The man on reception told me they couldn't get a doctor to me because Delhi was flooded, but that the hotel pharmacist was stranded in the building and he'd send him up to me. The pharmacist arrived and I pointed out to him, between groans, that I had a very important appointment with the Prime Minister in the morning. He was suitably impressed, went away and returned with a vile-tasting potion he'd mixed up for me. 'Very, very strong Indian mixture, Memsahib. It will bind you up for many, many days.'

Unfortunately, although it did indeed 'bind me up' down below, it also made me vomit uncontrollably. But I made my way to the Government buildings and, eventually, via many a flunkey, into Mrs Gandhi's cavernous, wood-panelled office. The room, once used by her father, had the cheerless dignity of a funeral parlour, with few personal touches. There was a picture of a horse, some yellow roses, and a bronze of Nataraja, the god of dance: 'Not a very good one, I'm afraid,' she said, glancing at it coldly. I tried not to look at the yellow roses or at Nataraja's four waving arms because they made my head swim. Oh, God, I thought, I'm going to faint.

Mrs Gandhi sat behind a monumental desk, a handsome, aloof woman of grave and wintry charm, whose noble Nehru nose, once fractured by a flying brick, lent her the air of a patrician hawk. As she talked, she played with a pencil. Courtiers scuttled in and out like mice for whispered consultations. A photographer buzzed to and fro and, every now and again, ripples of irritation would cross her impassive face. 'No, I don't like having my picture taken. But there are lots of things about this job I don't like.' Such as? 'Oh, having to live in this dreadful heat. I never really wanted to go into politics: I just wanted to go and live in a cold climate!' She looked distant, murmuring, 'Mountains . . . mountains. They are my great love.'

Once, imprisoned by the British for political agitation, she christened her cell after the mountain Chimborazo. 'For some reason at school I was always terribly bored with geography but the names of the Latin American peaks have always enchanted me. Besides, I've always loved that poem – "Romance", I think it's called. Do you know it?'

Before I could reply coherently I found myself gasping, 'I'm so sorry, Prime Minister, but could I borrow your bathroom?'

Five minutes later I staggered, whey-faced, back into her office. Oh, God, she's going to have me thrown out. She was still playing, irritably, with her pencil. 'Er, Prime Minister, I, er, read that you are basically very shy, which, er, (gulp) doesn't seem likely to me.'

'To tell you the truth, when my father first asked me to act as his hostess I was appalled. It wasn't that I didn't like crowds. I've always been used to crowds, helping my father at political meetings and suchlike. But I'd always been surrounded by people at home, writers, painters, politicians, who were passionately involved in *something*. It was the thought of making small talk about nothing that scared me to death . . .'

We talked about her late husband, a Parsee newspaperman and politician, Feroze Gandhi (no relation to the Mahatma, although the Gandhi 'name magic' certainly did her no harm). The marriage was not, she admitted, 'ideally happy' since her husband understandably 'disliked being referred to as "the nation's son-in-law". He would get upset, and it would take me weeks to win him over. To hurt the male ego is, of course, the biggest sin in marriage.'

But before we could get any further on the subject of the fragility of the male ego in a male-dominated society, I heard myself whimpering, 'I'm so sorry, Prime Minister, but could I borrow your bathroom again?'

When I returned, she made no comment, but still she didn't throw me out. 'What did you have to give up for your job?' I groaned, feeling utterly sunk in humiliation. No wonder she thinks most women are a waste of time. But if she, bizarrely, intended to continue with the interview so, I felt, must I.

'Exercise. I've had to give that up and I miss that terribly. I am getting dreadfully depressed, you know, about my weight, sitting in offices all day.' She was once a keen skier. 'I even started a winter sports club near Simla but I've never had enough time to go there more than twice.' Instead, she started every day at 5 a.m. with a set of yoga exercises. A passion for exercise was hardly typical of Indian women of her class and age.

But then there was nothing typical about Indira Gandhi. I'd been told that she was arrogant, snobbish, utterly unfeeling about people who she considered did not live up to her own high standards. After all, she was the heir to the royal family of Indian politics (her only brother died within three hours of his birth) and had always been in the public eye. 'Even as a student in England,' she told me, 'I was treated as if I were somebody and in India I've been a somebody all my life.'

What happened next belied her icy image. On my third and final despairing trip to the Prime Ministerial loo, I heard a strange sound outside the door. 'Are you all right in there, Miss Leslie?' a voice asked. And then came a keening sound, like Lata Mangeshkar, the great Bollywood 'playback' singer, warbling something which sounded remarkably like an out-of-key Brahms's Lullaby. Oh, God, I'm hallucinating now.

I opened the door: it was Mrs Gandhi. She then led me, shaking, into her office, laid me on a couch and sent for her personal doctor.

She stroked my head like one of the loving ayahs (Indian nannies) of my childhood and said, 'You know I mentioned that poem "Romance"? You remember how it goes?' And she began reciting it to me:

> When I was but thirteen or so
> I went into a golden land.
> Chimborazo, Cotopaxi
> Took me by the hand.
>
> My father died, my brother too,
> They passed like fleeting dreams.
> I stood where Popocatapetl
> In the sunlight gleamed.

She sounded so tired, so melancholy, that years later I wondered whether she had sensed an oncoming doom. Her beloved father had died, her newborn brother had died, her favourite son Sanjay was killed in a flying accident. She herself was then murdered by two of her Sikh bodyguards; and her hapless pilot son Rajiv, obliged to 'inherit' his dead mother's job, was assassinated by a female Tamil Tiger suicide bomber.

*

When the fiftieth anniversary of Indian independence was approaching David English, the editor of the *Daily Mail*, called me. 'Why don't you go back to India for the anniversary and visit your old haunts?'

I determined to do much of the journey in the country by train, because as a child I spent many hours, sometimes days, in those steaming iron behemoths, which emitted long, mournful hoots, belching black smoke, as they crossed the rice paddies, plains and deserts. 'You British created India with the railways,' one long-retired Indian soldier told me. 'Before the British came, if you were a Tamil in the south, you didn't even share the same language as a Punjabi in the north: you ate different food, had different customs, and you didn't feel you belonged together. The railways changed all that, they brought us together, and we came to feel that we, all of us, were Indians.'

I loved the trains which would take me from Bombay or Delhi or Madras to distant boarding schools in other parts of India. I would travel with my ayah loaded up with flasks of *nimbu pani* (fresh lime juice), tiffin boxes and a couple of huge bed rolls. Although there were *chai-wallahs* selling sweet milky tea in tin cups to passengers, there were no restaurant cars on the trains: instead, every station was full of hawkers selling spicy food – and Ayah would alight, haggle, behave with exaggerated melodrama as though she were a Bollywood film matriarch denouncing some *dacoiti* gangster, and return with a delicious meal. Indian stations were small towns in themselves, where whole families would live and die; on the platforms they would wash, pray and defecate with no sense of embarrassment. A need for privacy seemed to have been bred out of their genes, or perhaps privacy was simply another luxury they had to do without.

Sometimes Ayah would order the next meal from the train's steward. He would telegraph ahead to a favoured supplier at the next stop, and amazingly, everything ordered from fifty miles away would turn up. As so often in India, what looks and sounds like unbelievable chaos works remarkably well.

V. S. Naipaul, the Nobel Laureate, a Trinidadian-born Indian, upset India's nationalists deeply when he wrote *An Area of Darkness*, about his first visit to the land of his ancestors. His fastidious Brahmin soul was horrified by its poverty and squalor, its excessive religiosity, its apparent acceptance of 'the beggars, the gutters, the starved bodies, the weeping, swollen-bellied child black with flies in the filth and cow dung and human excrement of a bazaar lane, the dogs, ribby, mangy, cowed and cowardly, reserving the anger, like human beings around them, for others of their kind'.

When I read *An Area of Darkness* in the early Sixties I was almost as upset as the Indian nationalists: Naipaul was stabbing his sharp literary knife into my first love, a love to which I often returned in my dreams. But of course everything he said about India was true. Was it because as a child – and a privileged white Missy Baba – I didn't notice these horrors? After all, I'd grown up with them, regarded them somehow as 'normal'.

But not all my memories of Indian trains are soaked in sepia-tinted nostalgia. One train I travelled on ended its journey soaked in blood.

Chatting one night to an Indian friend in a sultry and sullen Delhi,

I remarked that I thought Nehru's speech at Independence was one of the most moving in history: 'Long years ago, we made a tryst with destiny. . . . At the stroke of the midnight hour, when the world sleeps, India will awake to life and freedom.'

It was, I said, on a par with Martin Luther King's 'I have a dream . . .' My friend sighed. 'But don't forget that as Nehru was speaking, another 20,000 people were being massacred. When we "celebrate our Independence" we should remember the mass murder of our own people, not their "life and freedom"!'

And a dream of that Indian mass murder still occasionally lurches unbidden into my sleep. I was barely six, sitting with my mother on a train which shuddered to a halt, and then after a few seconds the screaming began. I saw bodies covered in blood. My mother clutched me to her, covered my eyes, told me not to be scared, there was nothing to worry about. And there wasn't – not for us. Not for an English Memsahib and her Missy Baba, her freckled little daughter, sitting alone in the shabby first-class compartment of what was to become a 'killing train' in one of the world's largest post-war holocausts. As a child, for many years I wasn't sure whether the events in my dream had really happened. Alas, they had. In an orgy of sectarian bloodletting, up to a million died and at least 14 million people became refugees.

Sir Cyril Radcliffe, a barrister who'd never been further abroad in his life than Gibraltar, was given a mere five weeks in which to carve up the infinite complexity of India – as, with indecent haste, Britain decided to give up its 'jewel in the crown'. By then the brutal sectarian killings were already underway.

Our bearer, our chief servant Yah Mohammed, had (I later learned) rescued me from a friend's garden during what became known as the Great Calcutta Killing in 1946. The city was burning as Muslims and Hindus slaughtered one another: Yah Mohammed, at great risk to himself, climbed over garden walls and hurried down alleys, carrying the little white Missy Baba to safety on his spindly back.

He was a Muslim and had worked for my father even before my parents married; he, his wife and children travelled all over India and Pakistan with us whenever we moved. He was a Pashtun from the North West Frontier, spoke little English and was illiterate, but he was the one constant in my peripatetic life, and I loved him deeply. The only time I remember being beaten by my father was when, yet again, I was caught interrupting Yah Mohammed at his five-times-a-day prayers. And the only time I ever heard my father shout angrily at him was when Yah Mohammed came to him to say that his eighteen-year-old daughter was dying. We paid for the servants' medical treatment but, because our family doctor was a man, Yah Mohammed had not told Daddy about his daughter's illness, and had tried to treat her himself with folk medicines from the bazaar.

My father got her to hospital, but it was too late. 'Why were you so angry with Bearer?' I asked.

'Because there's too much blasted religion in this country! It makes chaps do stupid things!'

Like, of course, killing one another in the name of their gods. Had Yah Mohammed been on that killing train that day, a *kirpan* dagger would have slit his throat; just another Partition statistic. Other Muslim servants of the departing Raj (or Hindu, or Sikh, depending on who was doing the killing) were not so lucky. My parents' friend Alwyne Walford told me about 'a chum of ours who was travelling with his Muslim bearer on one of those trains which got ambushed. He hid him in the private lavatory of his compartment, and when the Sikhs came in they searched the place and said, "We *know* you've got a Muslim with you. Where is he?" Our chum insisted that there wasn't any Muslim there, but a Sikh put a gun to his head and said, "If you don't produce the Muslim, I'll kill you instead!" At that moment, the bearer, having heard all this, unlocked the door and quietly came out. He was of course instantly killed. He really sacrificed himself.'

But in 1997 for the fiftieth anniversary, I went in search of happier Indian memories – to Ootacamund in the Nilgiri mountains where I'd been at boarding school. My mother adored 'Ooty', where she played obsessive games of bridge and sipped many a pink gin in the Ootacamund Club. Was it still there?

Indeed it was – and still determined not to let any riff-raff through its white portals. I had been joined by a photographer from London, but because he was 'improperly dressed', the Club Secretary, Mrs Nargish Patel, refused to let him in.

'Oh, we're still *very* strict here!' Mrs Patel had even thrown out the novelist Farrukh Dhondy. On a trip to India Mr Dhondy fancied a *chota-peg*, a little drink, among the moth-eaten tiger skins and jackal heads of the Club. 'But he was not wearing a jacket and tie!' Mrs Patel informed me. 'He was wearing a *salwar kameez*! So of course I threw him out – even though he is one of my cousins!'

As virtually all the members of the Ooty Club, including its charming President Mr Siasp Kothavala, were now Indians, I would have thought that a well-laundered *salwar kameez* would be acceptable dress. But no: the Ooty Club's rules were the rules of the Raj – and that's the way its Indian members liked it. I met the last surviving British member, seventy-seven-year-old tea planter Bill Craig-Jones, who told me: 'Many of them like to be more British than the British – that's why they belong!'

After ejecting my photographer companion Mrs Patel repeated firmly, through a cloud of cigarette smoke, 'At the Ooty Club we still like to maintain our traditional standards!' She handed me a warming brandy-and-hot-water. Ooty may be only 11 degrees north of the Equator, but at 7,400 feet above the baking plains of southern India, it can be so cold that my Raj era hotel, the Savoy, had log fires in its cottage bedrooms.

Mrs Patel was quite shocked that I should imagine that standards might have slipped since Independence: just because the Raj disappeared fifty years ago that was no reason why the Ootacamund Club – once the most prestigious institution in 'Snooty Ooty', the 'Queen of the Hill Stations' – should change its ways! Perhaps it never occurred to the Club that one day it might have to.

After all, to men like Viceroy Lord Curzon at the beginning of the twentieth century Britain's glory was tied up with the eternal ownership of India. India was 'the strength and glory of England'. There was 'no nobler purpose than keeping the cords that hold India to ourselves . . . To me, the message is carved in granite, hewn in the rock of doom: that our work is righteous, and that it shall endure.'

But, of course, it did not. Astonishingly it lasted a mere 130 years in total, only eighty-nine of which were formally under the control of the British Government. However, the Club still clings to its Raj past; a 1954 photograph of the Queen Trooping the Colour still hangs on its wall, as does a board listing the past sporting achievements of its members (a Miss Heatherbell Irwin won the Ladies' Point-to-Point in 1902). The Club itself was founded in 1841 and the rules of snooker are said to have been drawn up here in 1884.

I looked up at the old portraits of Masters of the Ooty Hunt adorning the dusty walls: there they sat, these large, blue-eyed burra-sahibs with walrus moustaches, gazing confidently out through the ears of their horses at Ooty's undulating Wenlock Downs: they must have thought that this way of life would never end. India was theirs, Ooty was theirs, the everlasting Empire was theirs.

The Sahibs and their Memsahibs had busily set about creating an eternal England-in-India dream. Just as in Granny Ming's days in the Treaty Ports of China, the English had rapidly established churches, tea rooms, promenades, tombolas, theatres, sewing circles and ballrooms amid the vast sea of poverty-stricken peasants.

Many in Ooty, especially women and children, died of the plague, typhoid and 'jungle fever' as they struggled to create Cheltenham in an alien land. Their Indian graves and memorials are still there in the grounds of St Stephen's Church (the teak columns of which were looted by the British from the devastated palace of the defeated Tippu Sultan of Mysore). Like the grave of Georgiana Wroughton who died in 1847 'aged 30 years, leaving her husband and 7 children to deplore their irreparable loss'. They, and so many young men, were all sacrificed to the sacred cause of Empire – and, whatever one now feels about our subjugation of millions of people round the world, these individual imperial tragedies remain intensely moving.

British soldiers, whose fever-destroyed corpses so often filled these graveyards of Empire, called cemeteries like this 'Padre's *godowns*' (warehouses). The Padre of St Stephen's was now an affable young Indian, and his *godown* of forgotten Sahibs and Memsahibs and their innumerable children was crumbling into oblivion.

But the Ooty Club staunchly prefers to preserve its ghosts, even though, confessed Mrs Patel, 'when I first came here I did wonder whether I could live in a place full of these old dead men, and so many dead animals on the walls'. We ate dinner in the empty dining room attended by an aged waiter in the green and gold Club uniform. Mrs Patel cheerfully downed another brandy as yet another portion of overboiled Brussels sprouts (introduced to India by the British) was served. 'But the Club is full of wonderful old books, first editions of Charles Dickens, the Brontës and so on.'

Perhaps the mustachioed Masters of Hounds felt they'd earned the right to live here in the high Nilgiri mountains for ever. After all, it was the British who 'discovered' them (although the area was home to a now almost extinct aboriginal tribe, the peaceable, toga-wearing and polyandrous Todas – of whom, as a child, I was mistakenly terrified).

Two young surveyors had hacked their way up through miles of mosquito-infested jungle and discovered a paradise of water-falls, rolling grassy hills, butterflies and wild flowers. Soon paradise acquired a railway – a little rack-railway 'toy train' which is still, as in my childhood, pushed painfully up into the cool, blue mountains by one of the last two steam trains left in India. In 2005 UNESCO declared the line and its train to be a World Heritage Site.

The fifty-four-mile journey up through the mountains takes almost four hours. 'Why don't we get out and push?' joked a fellow passenger, a Madras accountant here on honeymoon with his young wife. But the little Victorian engine, gasping and snorting, needs lots of stops to recover, and to avoid sacred cows, or herds of chattering monkeys, or absent-minded villagers wandering along the line.

Once Ooty became the summer headquarters of Britain's Madras Presidency, its hillsides were covered with little gabled and fret-worked Victorian villas, with names like Westbury, Sunnyside and Iris Cottage, which – shabby and stained with monsoon moss – still survive in this now cacophonous Indian town.

Here, apart from the plethora of servants, the masters of the Raj could forget that they were in India at all. They imported plants from England – roses, peach trees, apple trees, gorse bushes, pines, straw-berries. By 1876 the Viceroy Lord Lytton could write ecstatically to his wife: 'Imagine Hertfordshire lanes, Devonshire downs, Westmore-land lakes, Scotch trout streams!' He even loved the Ooty monsoon: 'Such beautiful English rain, such delicious English mud!' By the time Edward Lear arrived here on a sketching holiday (he loathed the journey: 'Oh, beastly row! Oh, hateful Indian travel!'), he declared it was 'so English as to be, I think, utterly undrawable'.

Lord Macaulay, author of *The Lays of Ancient Rome*, began writing the mammoth Indian Penal Code here: he, almost uniquely, knew that India would one day be free, and rejoiced in it. The railway had not yet been built and his large, grumbling frame was borne up to the mountains 400 miles from Madras by sweating 'natives' carrying a palanquin.

By the time I came to school in Ooty, the confident Raj of Macaulay, Lytton and Lord Curzon had died, though Raj habits lingered on. The British Army had gone home, the British civil servants too; at the height of Empire, a mere 1,000 of them administered one-fifth of humankind.

But some of us, like my family, stayed on in the new India. Every Hot Weather, when temperatures rose to 43 degrees centigrade and the plains shimmered and rang like a vast brass gong under the hammer blows of sun, we'd head joyously for the hill stations. Memsahibs of the now-vanished Raj would, like their predecessors, pack their tweeds, their white cardies and their gardening gloves and, in a cloud of mothballs and small children like me, pile into long-distance trains, cooled night and day by tin bathtubs full of ice, and head up into some corner of that foreign field that was forever Esher.

The annals of the Ooty Hunt still adorn the Ooty Club: the hunt was interrupted only once, I noted, in '1857: The Mutiny'. Mrs Patel snorted: 'What you call the Indian Mutiny, *we* call the War of Independence!' As altitude and brandy tended to make her rather excitable, I thought I wouldn't risk mentioning Brigadier General John Nicholson, the man dealing with the 'mutineers', who remarked on arriving several hours late for dinner in the Officers' Mess, 'I am sorry, gentlemen. I have been hanging your cooks.'

To safer ground: the Hunt, founded in 1835, was presumably now defunct? 'Not at all!' my hostess declared indignantly. And she was right. 'We still have seven or eight Meets a year!' said the only surviving European member at that time, Bill Craig-Jones. And who keeps it going? The Indian Army, based at nearby Wellington Barracks. 'Tremendous riders, these chaps. Yes, of course they wear the traditional hunting pink! And we still have the stirrup cup – which is provided by the Indian Army as well.' And the courtly Mr Mahendra Ahluwalia, manager of the Savoy Hotel, lays on the traditional Hunt Breakfast.

But, I thought, why bother? After all, there's nothing to hunt these days – overpopulation and the growth of industry have largely driven the wildlife out of these once idyllic hills. Even the jackals, which the

British hunted instead of foxes, had retreated; there'd not been a 'kill' of anything, apart from the odd rabbit, for years. 'But the Ooty Hunt is part of our tradition!' exclaimed Mr Ahluwalia, shocked, like Mrs Patel, at my assumption that modern India would reject its Raj heritage. The current Huntsman, a tiny, shabby Indian called Mr Pakyanathan, spoke no English, but was still intensely proud of his tattered hunting-pink coat, his tinny hunting horn, and his pack of foxhounds, descended from those imported here in the nineteenth century. Even the hounds' names remained relentlessly English: Albert, Gallant, Unicorn, Amanda.

And, astonishingly for me, my old school in Ooty, St Hilda's School for Girls – once all-English, now all-Indian – carried on as if 'Indianization' had never happened. Same grey uniform, same sixteen-bed dormitories, even the same Sunday breakfast of puffed rice and boiled eggs. Same compulsory services in chapel – even though 90 per cent of the children were now non-Christians. And the same school magazine, the *Clarion*, still issued hearty 'Congrats to Carmichael House for their horse-like stamina that won them the Cross Country Cup! Phew, what a run!' 'Why', asked one of the sari-clad teachers, 'should St Hilda's change just because India is independent?' Why indeed? St Hilda's was then 100 years old – and independent India a mere fifty.

Where once bossy little prefects called Sarah and Penny dished out 'lines' to the juniors, now equally bossy little Sangeetas and Sunetras did the same. Mrs Bessie Collison, the Indian headmistress – who delighted in showing me, 'an old Hildite', around – may have worn a sari, but Miss Hall, my old headmistress, would have felt that she was a worthy successor to Hildite tradition. 'Mind you,' said Mrs Collison, 'I sometimes think the prefects are a little severe: for a very minor infraction, one junior was given forty-seven lines of *As You Like It* to learn, which at her age was a little tough!'

To my further amazement Higginbotham's the booksellers still exists – where, I was told, one can still order a copy of *First Steps in Tamil*, published in 1922 by missionaries, and still reprinted. It contains such memorable 'conversations' as: 'Yonder I see an elephant standing. How did it come here?' Second person: 'It is not a true elephant. It is a monolithic sculpture.' First person: 'My eyes deceived me. The deftness of the hands of the sculptors is something marvellous.'

My own Indian idyll had come to an end four years after Independence because of a panther and a rabid dog. The panther had streaked out of the mossy woods in Ooty where I was taking a friend's small Maltese terrier for a walk. The terrier's lead was dragged from my hand, his little body was never found, and I suddenly felt a terrible sense of foreboding. Not about the panther. Panthers were always eating assorted Fluffs and Fidos, the pedigree dogs so beloved by Ooty's English Memsahibs, and we all had to be very stiff-upper-lipped about these tiny tragedies.

But I'd recently been bitten by a pariah dog in Charing Cross, the centre of Ooty, and had had to endure three weeks of agonizing anti-rabies injections deep into my stomach. After each injection I was given my favourite sweet, coconut ice, and have never been able to eat it since.

I knew that the hungry panther and the rabid dog meant that I would probably now be sent 'home': never to live in India again, never to play with my pet mongoose, never to see the pale gold dust at twilight, never to smell woodsmoke in the night villages. Never to sneak into the servants' compound (forbidden to the Chota-sahibs and the Missy Babas, the sons and daughters of the Raj) to eat cashew nuts with them around the courtyard fires. And rarely to see my parents again, perhaps twice a year at most. And so it came about.

I had been at boarding schools since I was four. But those schools were in India: now I was going 'home' into exile. And my young heart broke. As it broke for so many who, earlier, had had to leave India, and who never felt truly at home anywhere else again. Some even returned, like tea planter Bill Craig-Jones, who had bought a farm near Andover in Hampshire in the Sixties. 'And then one day I told my wife Dorothy, "I'm going to pack now." And she said, "Where are you going?" – and I said, "Home." And she said, "I'm coming too!" Because for us "home" was no longer England, it was India.' And for a moment my eyes filled with tears, because here, in what was left of the old eucalyptus and mimosa-scented Ooty, I knew exactly what he meant.

A reader who had learned that I'd lived in India as a child sent me an anonymous handwritten poem she'd found on a piece of paper inside an old book.

> And those who came were resolved to be Englishmen,
> Gone to the world's end, but English every one,
> And they ate the white corn-kernels, parched in the sun;
> And they knew it not, but they'd not be English again.
>
> They would try, they would swear they were, they would
>   drink the toast,
> They would loyally petition and humbly pray.
> But over them was another sort of day,
> And in their veins was another, a different ghost.

The reader asked me if I knew who'd written it. I didn't, but over the years I'd ask Old Africa Hands and they'd say 'well it's obviously about Africa – the "white corn-kernels" is the clue'; and Old India Hands would declare 'it's obviously about India – stuff about Englishmen and "drinking the toast".' In fact it was written by the American poet Stephen Vincent Benet about the colonization of the American West. But if both old Africa hands and old India hands believe it relates to their own colonizations of a continent and a subcontinent, it may be because the poem evokes someting universal about the colonial experience from the point of view of the colonizers. It expresses a sense of displacement, of loss, of a subliminal ache in the soul.

And although I was a child when I left the land my 'tribe' colonized, to this day I too feel haunted by 'a different ghost'. My ghost is not England; it is India.

4

The Little Flower of Jesus
and the Rustless Screw

My childhood life in India ended when, at nine-and-a-half, I was shipped back to England and deposited in a Catholic convent in Derbyshire. I'd been happy at St Hilda's in Ooty, an Anglican school which, religion-wise, was mercifully undemanding. Not so this ghastly, cold, damp mausoleum in the Peak District, with early-morning Mass before breakfast every day and weekly Confession; 'processions', during which we pigtailed little girls, wearing white mantillas, would trudge round the grounds singing hymns and chanting prayers; and retreats, during which we had to spend days in total silence, reading holy books about the lives of female saints, usually virgin ones.

Unsurprisingly, the nuns were very keen on that sappiest and most sentimentalized of all saints, St Thérèse of Lisieux, also known as the Little Flower of Jesus. She became a cloistered Carmelite nun at fifteen, died of TB aged twenty-four in 1873, never went anywhere, never founded missions, and wrote, 'under orders' from her Mother Superior (who happened to be her sister), a glutinous spiritual memoir detailing her 'little way' of using self-abnegation as a route to sainthood. She made much of her realization of 'one's nothingness . . . leaving to great souls, great minds, the books I cannot understand'.

For someone who apparently did nothing to draw attention to herself during her short life, it did strike me even then as a little odd that the modest, cloistered Little Flower managed to get herself photographed cradling a Baby Jesus statue and doing the convent's laundry.

Decades later in China I came across the cult of Lei Feng, a

Communist 'saint' who instantly reminded me of the Little Flower.
He was a humble squaddie in the People's Liberation Army, whose
only ambition was to be 'a rustless screw in the machine of the
revolution'. Like St Thérèse, this Communist saint managed to keep
a diary and, miraculously, to have a photographer on hand to record
his humble deeds. I saw these 'authentic' photos on display at a
travelling Lei Feng exhibition near Guangzhou: 'Lei Feng doing his
Comrades' washing', 'Lei Feng helping an old lady across the road',
'Lei Feng giving his lunch to a Comrade who forgot his lunch box'.

And, like St Thérèse, Lei Feng died young (he was killed aged
twenty-two when a telegraph pole fell on his selfless head). We at
the convent had to learn from the Little Flower, and Chinese children
still have to 'Learn from Lei Feng'.

Obviously, if you're an icon, whether religious or secular, dying
young is a great career move. The Little Flower, Lei Feng, or indeed
Marilyn Monroe, Che Guevara or Princess Diana would not have
achieved such gibberingly sentimental cult status had they grown
old as we who are left grow old. 'Better dead than wrinkled' should
be the motto of anyone aiming at iconhood, though perhaps Mother
Teresa, Churchill and Mahatma Gandhi are exceptions to this rule.

The Church's Holy Picture industry adored the Little Flower – just
as the Chinese Communists adored Lei Feng and other Red 'saints'
like Iron Man Wong; and as the Soviets officially worshipped the
'heroic' coalminer Stakhanov; and as the nationalist Serbs I spoke to
during the Balkan wars idolized the Christian Prince Lazar who (you
may remember) lost the decisive Battle of the Field of Blackbirds to
the Muslim Ottomans in 1389. (Serbs win at so few things that
they're obliged to worship their biggest losers: Lazar has now been
canonized as a Serbian Orthodox saint and martyr.) All authoritarian
regimes – and I include the Catholicism of my childhood – rope into
their propaganda machines iconic, and extensively fictionalized, historic figures who typify the required selflessness.

However, young though I was then, I couldn't see why the Little
Flower's example was supposed to enthuse us schoolgirls; the message I got from this goody-two-shoes was that stupidity, unnecessary
physical pain and a poor education led to saintliness – which was
great for the school, whose exam results were usually lousy. And so
we at the convent were encouraged to spend our pocket money on

this irritating Little Flower and, especially, on Holy Pictures of the Virgin Mary, which portrayed her as a milk-white, swoony-eyed silent-movie star, surrounded by lush blooms and heavenly rays of light and draped in luxurious silken robes. Her reality – that she was a Middle Eastern, poverty-stricken, tough and enduring working-class mum – was of course never mentioned, and even her Jewishness was glossed over.

It was not many years after the Holocaust, but a whiff of anti-Semitism still lingered in the upper-middle-class British psyche. My father – whose friends included the Jewish Schlesingers (parents of John, the distinguished film director) and the Benedictuses (parents of novelist David) – always used jocularly to refer to a Jewish boyfriend of my sister as 'Mike the Hebrew'. When a very Jewish-looking Jewish girl enrolled in our school, the nuns were cool towards her and we pupils, I'm ashamed to say, bullied her unmercifully. Not surprisingly, she didn't stay long.

The first of many 'cultural shocks' which hit me when I moved from India to an English convent involved the question of knickers. One of my most loved ayahs did not believe in them. Unhealthy. Air should circulate. Knickers give you prickly heat. Or worse. Better by far to keep clean. Knickers, Missy Baba, are an excuse for girls not to wash down there! All this was forcibly conveyed despite the fact that Ayah only spoke pidgin English and I only spoke pidgin Hindi. It was all expressed with clattering bangles, rolling eyes and sign language.

But on arriving at the convent in the Derbyshire hills my resistance to knickers instantly marked me out to the red-faced bog-Irish nun in charge of my dormitory as someone who might be prone to 'lewd behaviour'. This was baffling to me. In India I never, as far as I can remember, thought about sex; but fear that we might be infected by 'thoughts' seemed to obsess the nuns in charge of us. We lumpy little pre-teenagers knew of course that Jesus's mother had 'immaculately conceived' and was therefore a virgin, and we had a vague feeling that all other mothers might be too; we deduced, however, that they probably weren't – because the nuns seemed extraordinarily anxious to warn us about a mysterious process known as Going Too Far. This process was, of course, never defined. So terrified were the nuns of (to paraphrase Dr Johnson) 'exciting our propensities' that they confined the weekly film shown on the rickety projector in the school hall to wholesome Nelson Eddy and Jeanette MacDonald musicals, involving lots of trilling, ribbons, falling petals and rushing streams. The only time it dawned on some of the less sophisticated of their charges that sex might involve the unclothed male body was when Reverend Mother mistakenly hired *Sanders of the River*, starring Paul Robeson. To her horror the film featured a plenitude of rippling, black, half-naked muscles; whenever such a scene juddered into view, she'd slap her hand over the projector lens, monitor the sequence on her palm, and remove it only when the danger-points were past. (Plotwise, therefore, the film proved highly confusing.)

Britain in the Fifties was the era of spam fritters, blonde bomb-shells, Brylcreem, dirndls, Teddy boys, censorship, the Lord Chamberlain, suspenders, the Comet jet, 'waspies', and above all a Crippsian obsession with the rationing of pleasure (I can't remember a more ecstatic moment than the day when sweet rationing ended, and I promptly threw up after scoffing vast quantities of Cadbury's Milk Tray). A Proustian madeleine moment, usually involving a Jaffa cake, can even now bring back the sounds and smells of boiled cabbage, yellow smogs, coffee bars infested with rubber plants and acne, Lonnie Donegan's washboard, the Frankies Vaughan and Laine and that mighty-bosomed diva Alma Cogan belting out 'Never Do a Tango with an Eskimo'.

The nuns may have had rather Talibanic views about incitements to 'lewd behaviour', but of course they were only marginally more extreme than the rest of 'respectable' society. Nudity of course was a Fifties taboo. I well remember the discreet family uproar that occurred when, during a half-term, a clod-hopping bachelor relation, on leave from his Kenyan farm in the Aberdares, was instructed by my grand-mother to take me to the theatre; he took me to the Windmill Theatre in Soho. It was the only public theatre where the censor, the Lord Chamberlain, allowed naked women to appear on stage – as long as they stood stock-still and pretended to be classical paintings. I later learned that boys of my age would furtively seek to acquire copies of *Health and Efficiency*, a relentlessly wholesome magazine intended for nudists which nevertheless had to veil the bits 'down below' with a convenient sprig of shrubbery or with what looked like ectoplasm.

But the social atmosphere in the late Fifties was already changing under its prim and placid surface, even though my parents' generation seemed largely unaware of it. A somewhat uninformed pearl-and-twinsetted relative made the mistake of taking me to see John Osborne's *Look Back In Anger* when it opened in 1956 and remarked loudly during one of Jimmy Porter's rants, 'I really don't understand what that rude young man is so *crawss* about!' Neither did I, and wondered why Alison, the downtrodden wife, didn't clock her ranting spouse with a hot iron.

Osborne had boldly declared that the monarchy was nothing but 'the gold filling in the mouth of decay'. For those of us who'd grown up with tooth-rottingly twee royal hagiographies – our convent dorm was decorated not only with Holy Pictures of a soupy Madonna standing on a cloud, but with photos of our future Queen, the fetchingly pretty 'Lillibet', working as a Land Girl – all this 'crawssness' was deeply puzzling.

The growing anti-Establishment feeling, especially after the Suez debacle in 1956, became much stronger. Lord Altrincham (a Peer of the Realm no less!) complained, with shocking *lèse-majesté*, that the Queen's speaking style was 'frankly, a pain in the neck', and that her 'priggish utterances' were put into her mouth by a coterie of 'people of the tweedy sort'. He was publicly punched in the face by an outraged member of the League of Empire Loyalists, and the Duke of Argyll declared that he should be hung, drawn and quartered.

Being cross about the monarchy, class and more or less everything was, of course, the unique selling proposition of the Angry Young Men – Osborne, Kingsley Amis, John Braine, men who had benefited from the Butler 1944 Education Act, which established state grammar schools and began setting up the new redbrick universities. (We women didn't start getting cross until rather later.) The Angries in the late Fifties were, of course, jolly cross about 'bourgeois' attitudes towards sex. As we know from Philip Larkin, sex didn't really happen till the Sixties; certainly in the Fifties our teenage ignorance about the subject was pretty total.

But apart from occasional visits to relations I had little contact with Fifties cultural life outside the convent walls; even my holidays were largely institutional. I had a younger sister and brother, and for a while my parents couldn't afford to bring more than one child at a time back to India for school holidays: we three therefore had to take turns.

When it wasn't my turn (and this usually included Christmas), I would often be parked at Overdeans, a holiday home for expat children in Hampshire, which was run by a woman we called Auntie Monica and her mother, a cantankerous old biddy we called Gran.

Mysteriously, we were sometimes joined at mealtimes by a tall, limping, tramp-like figure, who was known as 'Uncle'. He only ever seemed to eat boiled eggs and was as cantankerous as Gran, with whom he had constant spats; he wasn't related to any of us, or indeed to Auntie Monica or to Gran.

He was in fact Harold Falkner, an eccentric architect from a wealthy landed family, who built Overdeans – and a slew of other wonkily romantic buildings – out of bits of demolished old houses, and he was the curmudgeonly landlord of our 'home'. Sir Nikolaus Pevsner admired him because they shared a loathing for the clean lines of Modernism, but most people found him a pain in the neck. When a tenant complained about a roof leak, he 'mended' it by installing pipes jutting into the rooms to collect the dripping water. Mere practicality was, he believed, a 'low' consideration compared to romantic Olde England aesthetics: which is why in one of his houses he forgot to build a kitchen, in another installed a bathroom which could only be reached through a door in the inglenook fireplace, and in a third placed French windows on the first floor that opened directly onto a suicidal drop. Not surprisingly he was defeated by Lutyens in the competition to build New Delhi, India's new imperial capital.

He (like his godmother Gertrude Jekyll) was obsessed with gardens, and especially with the Overdeans rhubarb patch: if any of us children, when playing, blundered into it, Gran would shriek 'There'll be hell to pay from Uncle!' No wonder Auntie Monica became extremely tense whenever Uncle, unannounced, wearing his scarecrow felt hat, limped crossly into the kitchen in which Gran lurked.

We expat children rarely had any permanent toys because we were always on the move from boarding school to quasi-children's homes, to our parents' ever-changing bases in far-flung outposts of the former Empire. I only remember one beloved toy: a fluffy blue elephant called Heffalump who, being soft and small, was easy to squash down and pack, and who, from time to time, would be soaked with my homesick tears.

But as the actress Angela Thorne, then a fellow Overdeans boarder, remembers, 'We didn't really feel sorry for ourselves because in those days we expat children had to learn how to be stoic. We didn't question why we had to be separated from our families so much. It was just how it was.'

It was far worse for the expat children of my father's generation. Sometimes they'd be separated from their parents for years. My Uncle Kingsley told me that when his mother, Ming, having spent over six weeks travelling from China, turned up at his prep school in North Oxford to take him out to tea, he didn't recognize her. 'Oh, I thought you were one of the aunts,' he told his stricken mother. But Ming, who was criticized for putting her duty to her husband in China above her duty to her children in England, was very firm about her priorities: in her view, husbands must always come first.

My fellow boarder Angela loved Overdeans but remembers: 'You always struck me as rather lonely. When Auntie Monica took us all to Cornwall on a trip, I remember you just sat on the rocks, reading a book.' True, I always escaped into books; even now I get hysterical if trapped in an airport for more than half an hour without something to read. When I was young the written word, rather than human companionship, was always my consolation.

My mother loved poetry, and some of my happiest childhood memories when I was about eight are of long, somnolent afternoons in our shabby East India Company mansion overlooking the Bay of Bengal in Vizagapatnam. The house had a pillared 'elephant porch' which enabled the British nabobs, some of whom were on the portly side, to get into the howdah on top of the elephant without too much effort. My mother and I would lie on string-bed charpoys on the verandah, with the punkah fan slowly clunking above our heads, soothed by the smell and sound of the sea, while the sunlight outside would flicker lazily through the slats of the bamboo blinds. Mummy would intone to me, like some ancient ritual priestess, lines from Yeats, Masefield, Keats, Elroy Flecker: '. . . the hidden sun that rings black Cyprus with a lake of fire . . .'

Immersed in romantic poetry at an early age, I always hated writing, and still do, because I knew I could never match those siren voices from my childhood. I was so self-conscious about my own lack of skill that I stolidly labelled a secret scrapbook which contained my own poetic efforts 'Boring Things, Very'.

5

A Shrimp and Two Peas

My parents' social life, while busy, was a little short on international glamour, so that any celebrity who landed however briefly in their milieu inspired intense, if somewhat stiff-upper-lipped, excitement. One of my father's colleagues had once been engaged to a Hollywood musical star, which brief event in itself seemed to endow him with ersatz fame for evermore in their expat circles. 'He's *so* glamorous – you know, he was once engaged to Ann Miller!'

No wonder then that the other Memsahibs greatly envied my mother when they learned that she was about to play hostess to a genuine celebrity. Her famous guest was Douglas Bader, the RAF pilot who lost both his legs in a crash, and then, with two new tin ones, climbed back into the cockpit again and went on shooting down German enemy planes. His life had been the subject of the film *Reach for the Sky*, starring Kenneth More. Bader was a colleague of my father in Burmah Shell, and on a visit to Karachi came to spend a weekend with us in our ramshackle wooden beach house on the edge of the Sindh Desert. We children loved the beach house, especially when the giant turtles lumbered on to the shore to lay their eggs, which we'd protect from the land crabs; then in the moonlight we would ride the mother turtles, glittering with phosphorescence, back into the Indian Ocean.

I felt that Bader didn't much like our beach house. And, to my teenage disappointment, he didn't seem at all like Kenneth More; he was loud, overbearing and never stopped talking. His downtrodden wife Thelma barely uttered a word. My father said later, 'Yes, I know he's a bit of a pain in the neck, but you couldn't survive what he's gone through without being extremely bloody-minded and egotistical.'

But once I got to Oxford it seemed to me that you could hardly throw a pebble in a quad without hitting a passing celebrity, usually an academic one. W. H. Auden was Professor of Poetry and I was greatly star-struck by him. When he came round one day for tea and biscuits with a small group of undergraduates in my all-female college, Lady Margaret Hall, I blew my chance to quiz him on exactly what inspired him to write 'New Year Letter' . . . Soon after I'd begun solemnly reciting his own lines to him, he turned his great ruined-wedding-cake of a face towards me, and said, 'Where's the Gents?' I told him, he left the room, and none of us saw him again. He didn't even nibble one of our biscuits. Perhaps, as a homosexual, he found being surrounded by so many earnest young blue-stockings too much to bear.

One of my friends, a tall, thin, redheaded young man, was an obsessive collector of 'experts', and of course Oxford and its environs was knee-deep in them. At one point he became obsessed with entomology, so he took me to see the Hon. Miriam Rothschild, then the world's greatest expert on fleas. She was a scarf-draped eccentric, a teetotal vegetarian who never wore make-up and always wore leather-free shoes – moon boots in winter and plimsolls in the summer. It was plimsoll season when we went to see her. Naturally, once we were there, my friend and the Hon. Miriam ignored me completely, being too wrapped up in their mutual fixation with fleas.

His next obsession was with archaeology. He informed me one day: 'I've been invited to have tea with Max Mallowan – like to come?' I knew that Mallowan, a renowned archaeologist, was married to Agatha Christie. So, er, would we meet Agatha Christie? My friend replied, 'S'pose so, if she's there,' but he clearly regarded my interest in a mere crime writer (albeit one who was no mean archaeologist herself) as an example of what he always told me was my 'lack of seriousness'. At the Mallowans' cottage Agatha Christie, a rather chaotic-looking old lady who resembled Margaret Rutherford's Miss Marple, kept beaming and pouring out the tea and I kept saying, 'Thank you, Mrs Mallowan,' feeling obliged to pretend that I had no idea who she was. And, of course, to my obsessive friend she wasn't the celebrity, it was her husband. Once again, as at the Hon. Miriam's, he took no notice of me – or indeed of Agatha Christie. He just sat there talking Scythian pots with Max.

Living in Oxford, with all its irresponsible pleasures, meant that I was more or less constantly short of money, and my father thought I should get some paid work during the long vacation to ease my budget deficit. Through a neighbour he'd got me a summer job at an advertising agency in London. I was of course paid a pittance, and commuted from Abney via the little local puffer known as the Marlow Donkey to catch the mainline train to Paddington.

The agency was renowned for being 'progressive' and 'innovative'; but it was a hot summer, the kind of summer where no one – least of all 'progressive' and 'innovative' types like the account executives and copywriters – wished to drain their creative juices toiling in a stuffy office and dealing with products they despised, like Eno's Fruit Salts and Bird's Custard. So they went to lots of 'meetings' out of the office; they were in fact conducting progressive and innovative affairs with each other.

I was the dogsbody who was left back in the office to do the work and write the ads for extremely lucrative campaigns; I sometimes wondered whether the Yorkshire mill owners of Kosset Carpets ever guessed that the person writing copy featuring the famous white Kosset Cat was an exhausted, fed-up undergraduate whose only qualification was that she was dogged and could touch-type. In that heatwave, when I'd arrive at work every sweaty morning, I very soon came to hate that smug, fluffy creature.

But one day a postcard arrived at Abney from two Oxford friends, Giles, a law student at Trinity College (now an Old Bailey judge), and his girlfriend Maxine, whose family home was a beautiful aristocratic pile in Oxfordshire and whose father was a Master of Hounds.

The postcard had been sent from a remote fishing village in Catalonia, telling me how wonderful it was there, how they were paying peanuts to rent a small village house with no running water, living off 'tomatoes stolen from the fields!' and it was such *fun*, so why didn't I join them? So, I thought, to hell with the Kosset Carpets cat.

Nowadays it's so easy to get to Spain, but it was rather less so then. Under Franco's fascists the country was backward, enclosed, suspicious, isolated, dirty, superstitious. Giles and Maxine had no phone (phones were then quite rare in Spain outside towns) and I had no address for the 'small village house', so couldn't warn them that I was coming. Never mind, they'd told me they'd be there for the rest of the summer.

After a long series of ferries, trains and peasant buses full of chickens, vegetables and old, headscarved women looking like characters out of Lorca, I eventually arrived in the village, Cadaqués.

The place was full of 'small village houses', but none contained my rich Oxford chums. They'd simply decided to move on somewhere else. This left me somewhat in the lurch as I had spent my money just getting there and I was now hopelessly broke with no means of getting home. In my state of self-pity, lines from *The Great Gatsby* floated into my mind: 'they were careless people, Tom and Daisy' (apologies to Giles and Maxine), 'they smashed up things and creatures and then retreated back into their money and their vast carelessness'.

Suddenly gripped by fear at being stranded penniless in this withdrawn, alien country where I didn't speak the language, I went and sat on the small shingly beach, gazed out at the fishing boats, and wept.

A beautiful young woman with long blonde hair came skipping up to (what looked to me) a very old man sitting near me on the pebbles and kissed him. They spoke in English!

I went up to them. 'Do you happen to know where a couple of English friends of mine called Giles and Maxine live? I'm supposed to be staying with them.' The beautiful blonde woman replied, 'Oh yes, they've gone off. To Greece, I think. Poor you! Oh, let me introduce you – this is Man Ray.' The 'old man', already legendary as the master Surrealist photographer, nodded to me. 'Hi,' he said in a gravelly American accent. Oh, my God, I thought, I've just met *Man Ray*!

The beautiful blonde, Suzanne Phillips, then married to a wealthy Canadian artist, took pity on me and drove me on a winding dirt road up the mountain to the romantic, decrepit old monastery building in which they lived. I could stay as long as I liked.

Thus began what Reverend Mother would undoubtedly have described as my 'descent into mortal sin'. Indeed, I was surrounded by nothing but 'sinners', Surrealists like Marcel Duchamp and Man Ray himself, assorted Bohemian aristocrats from faded European dynasties, stoned starlets and rich visiting hippies. The hippie movement had not really got going in America, and had certainly not reached Britain, but it was undoubtedly already under way in Cadaqués during that hot, indolent, guiltlessly decadent late summer.

Life in the old monastery, dizzily perched above a blazingly beautiful sea, seemed to me to be one long open-house party, everyone smoking 'weed', drinking rough local wine, giggling, nibbling the grapes hanging from the terrace pergola, and lazily fornicating amid the wild rosemary to the sound of cicadas.

Tim, Suzanne's painter husband, heir to a Canadian tractor-company fortune, was a mild, vague, kind man who'd worked as an assistant to Salvador Dali and hero-worshipped him. Tim liked to paint in the nude and I'd go for long walks with him, clambering over the rocks where he would set up his easel. 'Have you tried sea urchins?' he asked, levering the prickly bomblets off the rocks, breaking them open and feeding them to me alive and dripping in brine.

Being fed raw sea urchins with their musky taste off the hot, steaming rocks seemed very sensual, even sexy, but Tim never showed the slightest sexual interest in me; his mind was on higher, spiritual, painterly things. In fact I got so used to him in the nude that I took little notice of his nakedness myself and took happy-snap photos of him, the rocks and the ferociously indented Catalonian coast.

(Unfortunately, later back home the local chemist developed the film and reported me to my father. There ensued a daughter–father conversation – 'Honestly, Daddy, I really was just photographing the rocks!' Perhaps because my father had, unknown to me then, certain adulterous secrets, he was mostly just amused. 'But I won't tell your mother and I hope the chemist doesn't either!')

One afternoon Tim announced we were all going to see Dali (no one ever called him Salvador), who lived in a warren of seven whitewashed fishermen's cottages at Port Lligat next to Cadaqués. They were all linked together above the tortured, light-splashed ochre rocks which feature in so many of his paintings.

We met him on his sunset-bathed terrace: Dali wasn't sitting in one of the giant broken-topped egg sculptures from which he liked to greet visitors, but with his bulging eyes and huge waxed moustache he was an arresting sight nonetheless. He theatrically summoned – in an almost incomprehensible mixture of French, English and Spanish – a lissom boy servant to bring pink champagne.

I'd already seen photographs of the famous Mae West lips sofa and the giant, bejewelled stuffed bear that adorned his house, but what mesmerized me that first evening were the candelabra made from driftwood. Now a cliché of retro interior design, those driftwood candelabra were so exciting, so utterly unlike anything I'd seen before, that they totally entranced me. I felt like collecting some Catalonian driftwood and Tim's sea-urchin shells and taking them back to Abney to relieve the pompous Edwardian chinoiserie with which Granny Ming had filled it.

Gala, Dali's Russian-born wife, who'd left the poet Paul Eluard to run off with him, sat looking stony-faced under the olive trees. The only time his muse and grasping business manager seemed to spark into life was when Dali repeatedly summoned the lissom boy for more champagne: with her oddly masculine, extraordinarily plain Slavic face, she'd coldly indicate to the boy that he could take the bottles back where they came from. Gala's lifelong motivations were sex and money, and allowing pink champagne to be liberally sprinkled among us was clearly considered an intolerable drain on the Dali household budget.

She did not, of course, address a word to me: for a start, I was not male. Later I learned that, a dedicated nymphomaniac, she would cruise Cadaqués with Dali looking for lithe young men to pick up and take back to Port Lligat: Gala to perform, Dali to watch. (One of their pick-ups many years later was the then young art critic Brian Sewell, presumably not for Gala but for Dali, who wanted to photograph him masturbating in some artistic brushwood – and Brian obliged.)

That first evening Dali turned his moustaches like radar spikes towards me and again, rather incomprehensibly, asked me whether I wanted to see the Egg Room. Of course, I said. He took me up some stairs into a beautiful, almost bare, ovoid room. 'Oh, how *divine*!' I gasped. 'Now: would you like to see the divine Dali?' said the voice behind me. I turned round.

Dali's trousers were on the floor. There is no more comical sight than a man with huge waxed whiskers displaying his 'divinity' with his shirt rucked up and his trousers round his ankles. I tried not to giggle, but after I'd swiftly left the room and gone back down the stairs, I exploded with laughter to the other guests: 'You wouldn't believe it – Dali just flashed me! He asked me if I wanted to see the divine Dali. Not much of a "divinity", I have to say. Just a shrimp and two peas!'

And of course they laughed, but then I noticed the laughter dying: Dali was now standing behind me, no longer trouserless. I was appalled: you don't laugh at Spaniards, I'd been told. Particularly not about their 'manhood' or, in his case, their 'divinity'. But to my relief, he too was laughing, his pointed moustaches leaping upwards towards his grubby hair like an insect's claws.

Later, back in the monastery, one of the vague and beautiful young male hippies said to me: 'He knows he's got very little down there; probably impotent. I never know whether that bothers him. That's why he's a voyeur.'

'Is he a virgin?' I asked.

'Dunno, don't care. He's a great artist, that's all that matters,' he replied before drifting off in an aromatic cloud of weed.

Whenever we visited Port Lligat thereafter Gala was never present; we were a money-and-time-wasting lot as far as she was concerned. Once Dali was driven up to the monastery; I sat in the back of the car with him as we negotiated the hair-raising road. He would whinny with fright at every bend, clinging to the door handle and uttering wildly exaggerated prayers to the Holy Mother for his continued survival. 'Yes, he's very deeply Catholic,' Tim solemnly informed me. 'Even though he never goes to Mass. It's the iconography, I think'.

One day Dali told me he wanted me to sit for a sketch for a massive painting of the Resurrection which he was then planning. He asked me to show my neck, pull down my blouse. By now I'd been doing quite a lot of pulling down my blouse and showing my neck, and occasionally other parts besides. But Dali's weirdness awoke the remnants of my own staid Catholicism (and a vision of Reverend Mother) so I demurred. Nevertheless, many years later someone I knew who'd visited the Dali Museum in Figueres told me he recognized me in a tiny piece of the huge painting.

It was in Cadaqués that I was introduced to drugs, especially mescaline. Cannabis had little effect on me until much later in California where, alas, I learned to inhale and thereafter became addicted to nicotine for life.

Mescaline was different. Only half a dozen years earlier Aldous Huxley had published *The Doors of Perception*, the title inspired by Blake's line 'If the doors of perception were cleansed everything would appear to man as it is, infinite.' He'd recorded his (supervised) experiment with mescaline, a drug derived from the peyote cactus, common in Mexico and used in local Indian religions to induce a mystical psychedelic state.

At school I'd studied the poetry of Gerard Manley Hopkins (the nuns approved of him as he was such a good, devout Catholic) and his theory of *haeccitas*, 'this-ness', inspired by the visions and writings of the thirteenth-century Scottish friar Duns Scotus. None of the nuns could explain the term to me beyond saying, 'Well, dear, 'tis all very spiritual, all about the love of God's creation.' Huxley said that mescaline could reveal the 'this-ness' of the world – and not necessarily in terms of the cramped and cabined God of the convent. And here, in an old monastery above a then remote Spanish fishing village, among what would now be termed rich 'Euro-trash', this magical drug was opening the 'doors of perception' for me to the secret of *haeccitas*.

The first time I took it I was terrified. Half an hour after drinking the potion I looked at my hand, and instead of freckles and sunburn I saw the red cat's-cradle of veins pulsing over the bones; looking in the mirror I saw, like Webster, 'the skull beneath the skin' – and, horrors, the skull was wearing mascara.

Gazing at a mere flower arrangement, Huxley had described how he felt that 'I was seeing what Adam had seen on the morning of his creation – the miracle, moment by moment, of naked existence.' In this magical place of sea, rocks, olive groves and twisted hillsides, which already had a shimmering, surreal intensity about it, the effect was literally mind-blowing. Oddly enough, I felt totally in control; some tiny rational part of my brain was, in a sense, taking notes.

Which meant that one day at the monastery, worrying about a Middle English poem called *Sir Gawaine and the Green Knight* about which I was going to have to write an essay on my return to Oxford,

I drank another dose. I'd found all that holy knights and holy quests stuff in *Gawaine* deeply boring; I loathe allegory. But now, full of mescaline, I suddenly saw the trees writhing with energy and life, the leaves glowing with lapidary brilliance, the dark stones pulsing like atomic particles and, 'taking notes', my mind began to relate to the poem on a mystical level that I would never have believed possible.

After my eventual return to Oxford I submitted the essay to my tutor, a joyless, spinsterish woman who disliked me and who'd already decided that I had 'an essentially trivial mind'. She read the essay and to my amazement told me, 'I never thought you'd ever come to grasp the allegorical mind of the fourteenth century.'

She went so far as to submit the essay for a prize, which it won. But I confirmed her opinion of my 'essential triviality' by spending the money I won, not on an academic tome on i-mutation in Old Norse, but on two very pretty, very silly cane chairs for my college room which I have to this day. I could never, of course, admit to anyone that my brief *Gawaine* brilliance had been wholly inspired by a mind-expanding drug.

Since I never took it again I have probably remained the rather prosaically unimaginative and matter-of-fact person that I really am, and thus never became gripped by New Age mysticism.

Later, when I came across mescaline's darker sister LSD in California, and covered the savage murders by the Manson Family and the disintegration of all that happy hippiness, I was glad I never succumbed to its seductions. 'Mescaline is gentle, acid is not,' a man utterly destroyed by LSD told me.

*

Tommy, one of the rich hippies at the monastery, told me he had to go to Zurich to deposit some money in his Swiss bank account. As his wife Rehlein would be staying on in Cadaqués, would I like to come with him? I would. I had a crush on him. And I was thoroughly flattered.

Rehlein, a German actress, would lounge on the herb-scented monastery terrace in a barely-there bikini, filling me with envy; her beauty, her lithe, bronzed, suntan-oiled body, the perfect legs and breasts, were something that I, solid, freckled, pale, could never achieve.

We set off for Switzerland. Tommy was heavily involved with the avant-garde troupe the Living Theatre and was a friend and fan not only of Dali, but also of 'beat poets' like Ginsberg and Ferlinghetti, who were so angrily, but exhilaratingly, unlike my beloved Keats. Tommy drove an Aston Martin and had the carelessly confident air of the very rich; despite his hippie hair and garb we never had any trouble getting tables in Michelin-starred restaurants, or suites in some of Europe's most famous hotels.

I knew one should never go to bed with a married man, but by now that sort of bourgeois rectitude didn't seem to apply. Besides, as a repressed convent girl of nineteen, I found the whole idea of hippy wealth, the Aston Martin, the Swiss bank account, wildly glamorous. I thought of us as a devil-may-care Kerouacian couple, and I revelled in it all. It was thanks to the 'depravity' of Cadaqués that I 'committed mortal sin' by losing my virginity in the Hôtel d'Europe in Avignon.

We stayed vaguely in touch when I went back to Oxford and he, eventually, to Canada. Rehlein's son by an earlier marriage was a nice, polite, dark-haired little boy called Jay. Tommy and Rehlein wanted Jay to go to an English boarding school, so Tommy and I leafed through school prospectuses and eventually chose an appropriately avant-garde establishment called St Christopher's in Hertfordshire.

His stepfather and I delivered him there and I felt so sorry for this pillar-to-post little boy, wondering how he'd eventually turn out. In fact he turned out pretty well and became a second-rung Hollywood star, specializing in cowboy roles. Whenever I see him now, a middle-aged man playing the tough guy on television, I remember that sad, crumpled little face as Jay entered the school gates. Perhaps it reminded me of the times that I, too, had been 'abandoned' by those I loved and blithely delivered into the hands of strangers in alien schools in an alien land. I got used to it, of course, and learned to be emotionally self-reliant and even perhaps a little flint-hearted.

6

Fragile Sunlit Girls

It was at Oxford that I met Michael . . .

It is a truth universally acknowledged that a pretty woman who goes boyfriend-hunting must be in need of a plain girl by her side. My friend Elizabeth, the stepdaughter of the first telly-don, the archaeologist Sir Mortimer Wheeler, was not just pretty but ravishingly beautiful, with a tinkling-waterfall laugh, gold-painted eyelids and a Garbo profile. One blink of the golden eyelids and strong men quivered and slumped adoringly at her dainty feet like felled bison. This did not tend to happen with me.

But boyfriend-hunting at Oxford in those days was relatively easy since men outnumbered women by about eight to one. We female undergraduates were housed in five all-women colleges on the outskirts of the ancient heart of the city. The University had always been a bit funny about women, classifying them along with Drink and Bad Company as part of an evil trinity designed to lead young men astray; blame that, perhaps, on an ancient folk memory of the days when all Oxford undergraduates were monks or minor clerics to whom the naughty nunnery at Godstow proved an irresistible temptation.

On the surface Oxford was all very Bridesheadian. In the summer fragile sunlit girls would trail their silvery fingers in the Cherwell as they were borne off in punts to distant meadows filled with dragon-flies and buttercups, from which one could occasionally hear the muffled sounds of male undergraduates struggling with pneumatic nurses amid the shimmering cow-parsley. (Nurses and girls from local non-university establishments made up some of the female shortfall.)

But come curfew time, the fragile sunlit girls would have to climb onto their rickety bikes and, whatever the weather, pedal off through the copper beeches of Victorian North Oxford to the gaunt buildings, redolent of dry rot and Jeyes fluid, in which we women were corralled.

Our romances were conducted in our rooms over *intime* tea parties for two (no wonder Fuller's Walnut Cake figures so heavily in my erotic memories). If trying to persuade some man on whom one Had Designs to be chivalrous and walk one back to college, some of us at Lady Margaret Hall would invoke the 'threat' we faced from the Norham Gardens Flasher, a tiny, harmless man who lurked nightly among the laburnums.

At the beginning of each term Elizabeth and I would plan our boyfriend-hunting strategies. Male undergraduates would huddle together in like-minded herds, each with their own habitat, distinctive cries and appropriate plumage. One of our friends in college who was extremely skilled in this field told us one day, 'The Marxists are the sexiest men here but the only way you can get within unbuttoning range of them' (in those days, fly-buttons, rather than zips, were the norm) 'is if you've read Marx's *Eighteenth Brumaire*.' She was right about the Marxists, who were either moody, lofty, acne-ridden, usually chippy grammar-school boys, or old Etonians trying to assume 'Mockney' demotic in order to conceal their public school background. But somehow the Marxists, wreathed in Gitanes smoke, seemed madly sexy to 'nicely brought up' convent girls like me and Elizabeth.

So we both read *The Eighteenth Brumaire* and the other sacred texts, but after a while snaring a Marxist or two struck us as being way too much like hard work. We even tried the college sportsmen, but neither Elizabeth nor I was temperamentally suited to standing ankle-deep in mud cheering on assorted 'rugger-buggers'. So we went for the university acting fraternity.

One day we sauntered into the golden-stoned back quad of Queen's College to audition for parts in Chekhov's *The Cherry Orchard*. It was there, in a smoke-filled room, that I first saw Michael, a scruffily dressed, dark and dourly handsome Heathcliff in blue jeans. 'I'll have him,' I thought. But within seconds, like every other man in the room, he'd fallen victim to Elizabeth's golden eyelids.

'Come and have tea,' he murmured to her afterwards. 'We'd love to,' I said firmly. He looked at me sourly and perhaps in revenge took us both to the tackiest caff in town, paid for three cups of repellent tea and to our fury left us to pay for our slices of Dundee cake. Clearly, as he'd only invited one of us to tea, he felt under no obligation to pay for two – and cake as well.

'You can have him,' hissed Elizabeth whose beauty had always previously ensured that she never had to pay for anything.

But I, not Elizabeth, got the part of Chekhov's seventeen-year-old Anya, with Michael playing my swain, the student Trofimov. I proved to be a hopeless actress and was eventually sacked from the production. By then I'd got Michael to dispose of his current girlfriend and we became a couple. But somehow I never thought I'd become a wife and a mother.

Particularly the latter. After all, my own mother had never been very keen on children. With this neurotic, embittered and needy maternal role model, I wasn't sure that I'd be very good at being a mother myself. But Michael began pointing out to me that one day I would regret not having children. 'But *your* life won't change! Mine will!' I'd snap. 'You can't be a woman foreign correspondent and have children! It'll be the end of my career!'

The female foreign correspondents I most admired in those days were perpetual nomads, who either never bothered to get married or, if they did, didn't encumber themselves with children. Clare Hollingworth, whose first scoop was reporting on the German troops crossing the border into Poland in 1941 – and who covered the desert campaign in World War II and worked in Vietnam, China and the Middle East – did get married. But she never wanted children who, she believed, would obstruct her spectacular career.

The legendary war correspondent and legendarily promiscuous Martha Gellhorn famously – and fairly briefly – married Hemingway, but again, there were no children to cramp her style, possibly because she'd had too many abortions. At the age of forty she did adopt an Italian orphan but the attempt at motherhood proved to be disastrous for both of them and eventually she rarely saw him.

She used men shamelessly, especially when trying to get access or accreditation. She started an affair with the World War II American General Gavin despite the fact that she said she couldn't see what all the fuss was about sex: 'I daresay I was the worst bed partner in five continents.'

When Andrew Marr wrote *My Trade*, a wonderfully readable book about the press, he remarked that one definition of a journalist is someone who looks and behaves like one. 'This is a boy thing mainly, though a few great female journalists, Martha Gellhorn or Ann Leslie, have a certain unmistakable and raffish style.' (But Andy, I was *never* as 'raffish' as Martha.)

The formidably glamorous and fiercely competitive Anne Sharpley of the London *Evening Standard* (who reminded me of Rosalind Russell, the ace reporter in *His Girl Friday*) was never happier than when being shot at during the Cyprus troubles or being tear-gassed in Algeria. Like Gellhorn, she had numerous affairs (possibly including one with her employer, Lord Beaverbrook, who was fifty years her senior), but she never married and told me firmly that it was 'madness' for a female foreign correspondent even to contemplate 'indulging herself' by having children. Like Gellhorn, too, she believed that men were to be used quite ruthlessly. The novelist Lawrence Durrell told me she'd slept with him when he was a British official in Cyprus: 'I'm sure it was only to get some information out of me!' Her advice to me on becoming a foreign correspondent was: 'First sleep with the resident Reuters correspondent, and then with the Chief of Police. That way you'll pick up stories before anyone else.' I told her that (having met a few Chiefs of Police and Reuters men in my time) I somehow didn't fancy laying down my body for my career. 'More fool you!' Anne snapped.

Of course attitudes have now changed among female journalists who decide to become mothers: if they no longer feel guilt-ridden about leaving their children behind, and as long as they have selflessly supportive partners or husbands like mine, many of them do now cover wars. But at the time when Michael was nagging me to have a child I didn't believe that was possible. Just as I never wanted to be a journalist, and never wanted to 'dwindle into a wife', I also never wanted to be a mother. Helen Gurley Brown, founder of *Cosmopolitan*, famously declared that women 'can have it all', and I didn't believe her.

However in the end, as always, I gave in to Michael. I'd even had a bit of a struggle with him (and he with me) over the issue of whether we should get married in the first place. Altogether our 'courtship' lasted about seven years. On and off for four years I'd propose to him and he'd say no; and on and off for another three years he'd propose to me and I'd say no.

In between times we both received proposals from other people and we'd both say no – well, at least on the issue of marriage – to all of them. One of those who proposed marriage to me was James Mason.

I'd fallen for him not just because he was highly intelligent, a Cambridge graduate with a passion for Shakespeare, but mostly because he was extremely sexy (I described his voice in a daftly purple-prose profile as 'sounding like soft footfalls in the dark'). Besides, he'd once saved me from professional disaster.

The *Express* had flown me to West Berlin to interview him on the location of his latest film. Despite having shorthand, I thought I'd try out a newly introduced gadget, a cassette tape-recorder. I decided to use the 'pause' button to cut out my questions; unfortunately when I came to transcribe the tape I discovered I'd cut out all his answers. I couldn't remember a word he'd said as I'd been gazing too besottedly at him as he talked. I clearly couldn't reveal that fact to my employers and I obviously couldn't fly back to Berlin to interview him again. I managed to get hold of him on the phone and, with much trepidation, I explained the situation and threw myself on his mercy. He was not only still a major star but also had a reputation for being extremely moody and treating those whom he considered to be incompetent as irredeemable clod-hoppers. I would clearly come into the latter category.

But in the event he was enchanting and gave me another inter-view on the phone which I suspected was actually better than the first one. Ours was mostly an epistolary affair as he was always working abroad, which is one of the reasons the relationship eventu-ally fizzled out. I do remember one depressing occasion when he invited me to meet his elderly parents who lived in a large, dark Victorian house in the old mill town of Huddersfield. His mother kept looking beadily at me and making slightly minatory remarks like: 'It's *so* sad, as you know James has this terrible skin condition called psoriasis. Sometimes, when it erupts, his sheets get *covered* with flakes of dead skin.'

He went on to marry someone else, and I went on – reluctantly at the time – to marry Michael.

When I was working for *Queen* magazine I was asked to go on a round-the-world working trip to Thailand, Australia, Fiji, Tonga and California, producing articles from each place. I would obviously be away for some time. Michael, a man who is slow to make up his mind, but thoroughly obstinate when he has, decided that we would get married before I left. If we didn't, he told me, he would not be there when I returned. So we agreed to get married, but I told him I didn't want to know anything about the event. He was to fix everything and not bother me with any of the finer details, such as date, time and place.

Unknown to me, Michael wanted to get married in a tiny 900-year-old Anglican church in the pretty village of Compton in Surrey, which for various reasons at the time required a Special Licence from the Archbishop of Canterbury's office. He forged my signature on the form (a skill he's maintained on my behalf for the thirty-nine years of our married life).

Canon Howard, the vicar of the church (and father of the political commentator Anthony Howard), became a mite concerned at Michael's refusal to allow him even to meet me, let alone include me in any discussions about the wedding arrangements. Perhaps fearing that Michael might be in the white slave trade, the saintly Canon rang my father to seek clarification. He told the Canon that 'my daughter can be rather eccentric', but assured him that the wedding would be legit.

It took place on a bright, snowy February morning with only our immediate families present. There was a sudden flurry of snowflakes outside and as I looked up at them through the stained glass of the tiny church window I thought to myself, 'I'm having this annulled for a start.'

The honeymoon did not greatly improve my mood. Michael had booked a fortnight's skiing in Klosters. On my third outing on to the slopes I fell down the mountain, ripping ligaments in my knee. I was then imprisoned in plaster and had to spend my days lying on a sundeck wearing a protective nose-beak, alongside ghastly old mink-coated socialites who had a thing about Communists and seemed to own most of Peru. I had of course assumed that we'd curtail the honeymoon, but Michael who, having paid for a skiing holiday, was going to have a skiing holiday, spent much of the time schussing down the slopes surrounded by carolling girls. After a row about this I hobbled into the hotel television room and watched my old swain James Mason emoting and smouldering in a black and white movie dubbed into German. Ah, what might have been . . .

But when I finally agreed with Michael that I would become a mother, I discovered to my fury and complete surprise that I couldn't conceive. I assumed the reason I'd never got pregnant before – these were the years before the Pill and legalized abortion – was simply that I'd always been 'careful'. Others weren't of course, and on more than one occasion I'd driven pregnant girlfriends to a well-known illegal abortionist, a rather seedy-looking but efficient and clean little man, who 'did' them in exchange for a large wad of cash in a net-curtained semi in Ealing.

Just as I was determined that I would become a journalist, despite my initial reluctance and my first news editor's determination to stop me, so I became equally determined that I would become a mother, despite my initial reluctance and my body's obstinate refusal to allow me to conceive. Thus began the slow, humiliating business of investigations into our apparent infertility. First there were the weeks of taking my temperature daily to ensure the optimum moment: 'Sorry, darling, I know you're at work but you've got to come back home immediately because we've got to do it *now*!'

These days doctors have, I trust, learned to be 'sensitive' about the feelings of couples who can't conceive. Not then. In my local hospital, the infertile women had to share a waiting room with pregnant mothers and I began bitterly to resent their complaints. 'Can't believe I've bleedin' fallen pregnant *again*!' 'Oh, I know, terrible – mine won't leave me alone either!' They'd then chortle merrily and rub their tummies with what I, increasingly paranoid, felt to be a display of smug fecundity.

The rather deaf woman doctor investigating whether I was killing Michael's sperm one day bustled into the waiting room full of swelling bellies, and shouted at me, 'Mrs Fletcher? Tell your husband they're dead! All dead!' And bustled out again.

An acquaintance of mine, in the same situation, experienced the same doctor shouting out like a fairground barker: 'Mrs Limpkin? Tell your husband his sperm count's okay, but he's certainly no Hercules!' This of course caused much merriment in the roomful of swelling bellies. Fertility investigation and treatment can put a tremendous strain on any marriage, but mine – and hers – managed to survive it.

Eventually, stuffed full of fertility pills, I conceived. I went on working at full tilt; four months pregnant, I flew out to what was then Rhodesia (now Zimbabwe) under the white regime of Ian Smith. I managed to persuade the authorities to let me go on a rather dangerous patrol into the almost impenetrable bush with the Royal African Rifles, the black army contingent which fought on the side of the whites against the 'munts' and 'terrs' of Nkomo and Mugabe.

I was told I had to carry a Rhuzi submachine-gun (the Rhodesian copy of the Israeli Uzi). Fearful of stumbling and inadvertently shooting off my tiny 'bump', I held the Rhuzi at arm's length like a daffodil. 'No! Not like that! And stop waving it around! It's not a *bleddy flower*!' shouted the sergeant. Had I confessed I was pregnant I might well have been accused of irresponsibly endangering his unit.

And perhaps I was being irresponsible by thus endangering my 'bump'; I'd initially been refused fertility treatment because I had early signs of cancer, 'and pregnancy can cause it to accelerate', I'd been told. I insisted on going ahead because by now this 'unmaternal type' was so obsessed with having this child that I was willing to take the risk.

But there were complications in the pregnancy and I was hospitalized for the last month. Because I was 'an interesting case' the consultant would sweep into the ward followed by a shoal of medical students. He never addressed a word to me and one day, riled by this lack of courtesy, I wrote in lipstick on my enormous belly: 'Good morning! My name is Mrs Fletcher.' Tired of having my privates probed by a cast of students from Britain, Egypt, Malaysia and, for all I knew, the Trobriand Islands, I snapped, 'If I were a stately home, I'd charge an entrance fee.'

Later, I repeated the remark to the cartoonist Michael Heath. 'I'm stuck for a cartoon idea for the *Guardian* Women page, and that's a good one!' The resultant cartoon was, I thought, rather funny. But unfortunately the *Guardian*'s Women page in those days was staffed by a cabal of almost stereotypically humourless feminists who didn't get the joke: they immediately declared they would go on strike if Heath, the creator of this 'demeaning and sexist' cartoon, was ever employed on the *Guardian* again.

In his defence Heath pointed out that 'it's not sexist against *women*! It's against chauvinist gynaecologists!' But unfortunately he also said, 'In fact it was a woman, Ann Leslie, who gave me the idea!' This made matters worse: *Guardian* women had long ago decided that, because I occasionally mocked the 'whining wimmin' of political feminism, I was obviously a right-wing tool of male chauvinist oppressors. Mercifully for Heath, the Women Page editor had more sense than her silly sisters and his job was safe.

It was while I was in hospital that I first heard the euphemistic medical phrase 'precious baby'. 'Is the "precious baby" in Bed 6?' I heard some junior doctor mutter to a nurse. As I was in Bed 6, I asked the nurse what the phrase meant. 'Well, it means the mother probably won't be able to have another one. A "precious baby" is her last chance.'

For the complicated delivery a large medical team was assembled. At one point an emergency began and I gasped to the Registrar in charge, 'Have I lost it?' He almost shouted, 'I've never lost a f***ing precious baby yet, and don't f***ing intend losing *this* precious baby!'

And finally the 'precious baby', Katharine, was born. She would be our only child, and the moment she bawled her blood-smeared way into the world I instantly loved her with an almost primeval ferocity which initially I found almost too overwhelming to bear. Even today, thirty years later, remembering the Registrar's expletive-filled outburst, I find my eyes brimming with grateful tears.

7

Youthquake and Meteors

The editor of the *Daily Express*, Bob Edwards, having rescued me from its Manchester office and installed me in Fleet Street, reluctantly agreed that I could stop writing my column and get out of the office to do interviews instead.

Someone I didn't want to interview was a youth of barely seventeen who'd turned up in the lobby of the *Express* demanding to see me and insisting that he wouldn't leave until I came down. The receptionists in the lobby were all disabled male war veterans whose huge chests clanked with rows of campaign medals (Beaverbrook believed that 'our brave boys' should always be able to find a perch in his Lubianka). These battle-worn blokes may have been missing a leg here, an arm there and an earlobe or two, but they'd successfully seen off the beastly Hun on many a foreign field. Yet they proved totally helpless in the face of this bespectacled, spotty, gingery public schoolboy's charm offensive. He was not at the time old enough even to vote or get married without Mummy's and Daddy's permission. And yet, when I interviewed him about a student magazine he was trying to flog, I somehow took him seriously. I told my Features Editor, 'I've just had a chat with an extraordinary teenager who could either end up in jail or become Prime Minister or a multi-millionaire – possibly all three.' I think it was the first national newspaper interview given by the future Sir Richard Branson.

The so-called Swinging Sixties were then underway, and to chronicle that fact a twenty-five-year-old journalist called Jonathan Aitken, the Old Man's great-nephew, wrote a book entitled *The Young Meteors* about how we, the golden youth of the capital, were becoming extraordinarily successful – and apparently appallingly sinful – at a very early age. 'London', Aitken declared somewhat prissily, 'is now widely alleged to be the sexiest city in the world, the mecca of permissiveness, promiscuity and perversion. These are strong words, but they have been well-earned.' Strong words indeed from a clever, ambitious young man who went on to become a Tory Cabinet Minister, was renowned for his numerous affairs (including with Carol Thatcher, the daughter of his boss), fathered an illegitimate child, and eventually ended up in jail for perjury. As one of his friends put it, Jonathan 'couldn't lie straight in bed'.

I was one of his 'Young Meteors'. 'Turning to the top young female writers, one who stands out is Ann Leslie, twenty-six, a star of the *Daily Express* specializing in show business features. She is probably the highest-paid woman journalist in Fleet Street.' Meteoring away with me in this vapid book were the likes of Michael Caine, David Bailey, David Hockney, Terence Stamp, Twiggy, David Frost, Mary Quant, Terence Conran, Melvyn Bragg.

Some of Aitken's 'meteors' simply burned out: the Beatles' gay and tortured manager Brian Epstein committed suicide and the disco king Kevin Macdonald, soon after declaring, 'It's the greatest, happiest most swinging ball of the century – and I started it!', jumped to his death from the top of a building in Chelsea. Many of the Swinging young things who strutted around photographing each other in Day-Glo boots and giving cocky interviews to the marvelling scribes of *Time* magazine are now utterly forgotten.

In fact those of us 'meteors' who did survive that giddy period did so because, despite the huge amounts of fun on offer, we all actually worked very hard. In between interviewing film stars and dashing off to cover stories like the murder of an old lady by an eight-year-old, or the Mods and Rockers riots in Clacton, or attacking the Postmaster General (the then Anthony Wedgwood Benn) for his dotty ideas about the phone system, I scarcely had the time or the energy to indulge in the 'promiscuity and perversion' that Jonathan Aitken had so disapprovingly described.

Of course, the Sixties didn't swing in Hull or Gravesend. In reality, outside a small geographical section of London – which was still pockmarked with World War II bomb sites, in one of which I used to park my car – Britain as a whole remained as purse-mouthed, frugal and dyed-in-the-wool conservative as ever.

Express readers frequently reminded me of that fact whenever I wrote trendy 'Voice of Youth' comments on such events as the anniversary of the Battle of Britain and the publication of a British Medical Association pamphlet which stated that all seventeen-year-olds should be in bed by 10 p.m. I told the BMA that they were nothing but fuddy-duddy 'old squares' and that this was 1965, not 1865, and quoted Bob Dylan at them about how the times, they were a-changin'. En masse, our 'old square' readers in the provinces flooded the Letters Page denouncing my views and calling for a return of the birch. One father informed me that if his seventeen-year-old daughter stayed out after dark without his permission *or* an approved chaperone, 'She'd get a good tanning on her return, and be all the better for it!'

But by 1968 the voices of blokes who thought their daughters should be 'tanned' if they came home after dark were being drowned out, media-wise, by *les événements*, the sit-ins, the anti-Vietnam War protests, and riots in Parisian streets which in turn inspired sit-ins in British universities and the riot outside the American Embassy in Grosvenor Square. That exciting, but to me rather childish, crusade against the Marcusian 'repressive toleration' committed by bourgeois daddies everywhere – especially the biggest bourgeois daddy of all, the United States – filled the airwaves. Mind you, the 1968 'revolution' was largely a male thing: girls were mainly there to paint the posters and provide R and R for their hairy young warriors, who readily concurred with the view of Black Panther Eldridge Cleaver that 'the position of women in the revolution is on their backs'. (Incidentally, Cleaver died a signed-up Republican and a born-again Christian.)

That staple of youthful bedsitter-land, Van Gogh's *Sunflowers*, was ousted; in came that beautiful, murderous poster-boy of the Cuban revolution, Che Guevara. My copy of *Venceremos* (still, alas, unread) was always on prominent display when some Maoist self-styled *enragé*, complete with revolutionary pimples and dirty hair, came round to discuss Sartre and, sometimes, my 'frigid', 'class-ridden', 'petty-bourgeois' reluctance to open my legs whenever he happened to be in the mood. 'Oh well, okay,' many of my generation of women sighed in weary compliance, before our 'sisters' in the subsequent feminist revolution told us that we didn't have to, and that we didn't have to wash his disgusting smalls either.

The *Express* had sent hordes of reporters down to Grosvenor Square to report, in suitably horrified tones, the rioters' behaviour. (Our readers were very pro 'our boys in blue', so police behaviour was not much criticized; what seemed to upset readers most was the plight of the police horses.) One of my girlfriends at the paper was sent to the Square and, somewhat surprisingly, came back to the office a starry-eyed convert to the slogan 'Be Realistic – Demand the Impossible'. The look in her eye seemed to indicate a longing for a spot of revolutionary violence and, if possible, a noisy 'We Shall Overcome' sit-in at the *Express*. Not surprisingly, her career at the paper didn't last long and neither did the affair she was having with a prominent, and married, MP.

But I was far too busy earning a living to become a romantic revolutionary and perhaps by nature I lacked the required propensity for ideological zeal. Besides, a lot of the 68ers' fondness for theatrical political stunts reminded me too much of showbiz silliness – and I knew a lot about that, because by now I was specializing in show-business. Indeed, there was scarcely a star in the worlds of film, books and theatre of the time whom I didn't interview; some weeks I would clock up five interviews in seven days.

Paul Newman, Sophia Loren, Liza Minnelli, Alec Guinness, Arthur Miller, Goldie Hawn, Tennessee Williams, Roger Vadim, Otto Preminger, Yves Montand, Peter Hall, Cliff Richard, Jeanne Moreau, Oliver Reed, Peter Ustinov, Ingrid Bergman, Sean Connery, Peter Sellers, Gloria Swanson, Diana Dors, Tallulah Bankhead, Sammy Davis Jnr, Rex Harrison, Benny Hill, Satyajit Ray, Dirk Bogarde, Dudley Moore, Yehudi Menuhin, Tony Curtis, George Balanchine, Shirley MacLaine, Ralph Richardson, Robert Graves, John Betjeman, Marlene Dietrich, Roman Polanski, Michael Caine . . . Simply typing out a list of names at random takes me back to long chummy chats in plush restaurants or even plusher hotel suites – or at rather less plush film locations on the Yorkshire moors or in gritty Parisian suburbs.

Some of the stars wanted our chats to be rather more than chummy. One in particular was the urbane, witty, sophisticated David Niven, a worldwide symbol of 'the perfect English gentleman'. Whenever he was in London we'd meet up for urbane, witty and sophisticated meals. He would regale me with wonderfully funny anecdotes about what he and his chum Errol Flynn would get up to

in what they christened 'Cirrhosis-on-Sea' and about what happened
when as a young actor he had to perform a clinch with the ageing
movie diva Gloria Swanson, and one of the stays in her corset shot
up into his nostril, and *then* ... And so the endless anecdotes of
Hollywood life would roll merrily on.

One day when he was abroad he sent me a thoroughly obscene
telegram about another columnist. The Post Office clerk, who was a
woman, could scarcely read it out to me (on request they could read
out telegrams over the phone to you in those days), because she was
convulsed in shocked giggles. I told him this – and promptly received
a stream of similar telegrams 'because I think Post Office clerks
deserve to be cheered up!'

After a while I realized that I kept hearing the same wonderfully
funny anecdotes, endlessly repeated and word perfect every time.
One evening over the candlelight and claret I said, 'David, I've got a
wonderful idea: why don't you just talk all this into a tape recorder
and I'll ghost your autobiography? I'll have to clean some of it up, of
course!' He said he'd think about it.

Then, at our next meeting in the Connaught Hotel, where he
always stayed, he asked me, 'Look, do you mind coming up to my
suite for a few minutes? I'm expecting a call from LA.' But calls from
LA do not require to be answered without trousers or underpants,
and in any case the phone never rang: I suddenly realized I'd fallen
for that oldest of ploys, 'Come up and see my etchings.' Making very
urbane, witty and sophisticated excuses, I left. I thought no more
about it.

But then 'the perfect English gentleman' began spreading rumours
about me which ranged from 'Ah, Ann Leslie, always available!' to
'Ann Leslie, typically spinsterish convent girl! Maiden Aunt Annie
I call her!' Perhaps big stars like Niven felt they had a *droit de
seigneur* and were so miffed when the 'maiden' didn't agree they had
that they turned extraordinarily spiteful. And that autobiography I'd
hoped to ghost? It was the massive bestseller *The Moon's a Balloon*,
and I missed out on a small fortune.

In 1983 I went to cover Niven's funeral in the Swiss village of
Château d'Oex, throughout which his widow Hjordis, a former Swedish model, was paralytically drunk. Niven had told me he always felt
guilty about Hjordis: after his beloved first wife Primmie died in a

freak accident (falling down stairs while playing hide-and-seek), he fell in love at first sight with Hjordis and within ten days had married her.

She was fantastically beautiful but utterly devoid of talent, so never became the actress she wanted to be. 'I'm afraid Hjordis is just terribly jealous of my fame,' Niven told me. 'That's why she drinks too much, poor girl.' But he would never leave her for good (and they remained married for thirty-four years) because they'd adopted two adored little girls. 'And anyway I'm to blame for it all.'

As the world's press – and Niven's old friends like Prince Rainier of Monaco, Yehudi Menuhin and Audrey Hepburn – gathered for the funeral, a fellow resident in Château d'Oex, the writer Alistair Forbes, took me aside. 'Rainier's finally persuaded Hjordis to come, but he's very worried. He and I will hold her up at the graveside, but we wonder if it would be possible for you to persuade your colleagues not to point out that she's terribly drunk?'

I assured Alistair that British readers, who loved Niven, would not thank us if we wrote about the boozy behaviour of his widow at his funeral or the fact that she'd had to be persuaded to attend it in the first place. Insiders knew about Niven's drunken and adulterous wife but his fans didn't. When Hjordis threw rose petals into his grave, only Rainier's and Alistair's grip on her arms prevented her from following the petals into the mud.

As I penned sentimental words about how Hjordis, overcome with grief, looked 'pale, smiling with a kind of feverish courage', I knew that as a truthful journalist I should have added, 'Actually, she was overcome by the bottle, not grief, as she has been for years.' And I was thinking crossly, 'David, you don't deserve my telling lies on your behalf, when you told lies about me; but I suppose this isn't the time or place to tell the truth.' One of his sons by Primmie, who knew I'd been economical with the truth about his stepmother's behaviour, wrote to thank me profusely for 'your sympathy and support, in the circumstances'.

Prior to the Niven estrangement, my only serious spat with a major star came early on in the then still handsome shape of Marlon Brando. He had summoned the press to the Savoy Hotel to listen to him make an important announcement to the world. There would be no questions allowed.

He stood on a podium; behind him, a white plaster sculpture of a lady with heavy lids and a small cynical smile. I was soon feeling pretty heavy-lidded and cynical myself. 'Mr Brando', I wrote, 'is here to tell us all that he is going to smash racial prejudice by being unkind enough to insist that none of his films are to be shown in countries of which he disapproves.'

The movie-star arrogance struck me as astonishing: did Brando really think that if he deprived white South Africans of the joys of seeing *Teahouse of the August Moon* they'd all be so grief-stricken that they'd abolish the cruelties of the apartheid system overnight? As if.

And why did he think that mumbling on self-righteously and self-admiringly in a luxury hotel was going to strike anyone as anything other than a vanity-stoking stunt? Was he even stupider than he sounded?

At one point I yawned. 'Er, I see we have some yawns here,' he noted disapprovingly. It was probably the most articulate sentence he uttered. His speech was slow, ruminative and punctuated with endless 'ums' and 'ers'. This, I wrote, was a great help to those respectful hacks present who, unlike me, had no shorthand and 'who, like the lizards in *Alice in Wonderland*, were scribbling away like mad'. Sitting beside him was the critic Kenneth Tynan, pecking furiously at a succession of cigarettes; he understandably left half-way through the mumbled sermon.

I was not nearly as rude about Brando in print as I felt at the time. I expected little or no reaction to the article. I was startlingly wrong. Llew Gardner, a star reporter on the *Sunday Express*, who'd been a fervent Communist until the crushing of the Hungarian uprising in 1956, stormed down to the Features Department on the *Daily* and, in front of everyone in the office, yelled hysterically at me, 'You are a disgrace to journalism! I am ashamed, *ashamed*, to have to share the same building as you!' (Years later Llew became a neighbour and demonstrated, by picking fights with everyone, that he clearly had what would now be called 'anger-management issues'.)

Peter Evans, the Showbiz Editor, got a furious call from Brando's publicist, Mike Baumohl: 'I'm going to *destroy* that girl!' According to Baumohl at least two national newspaper editors had rung him to tell him that, in their view, I was the most disgraceful journalist in Fleet Street. And Brando himself had 'gone crazy with rage'.

What had so infuriated Brando was the fact that I'd 'unfairly' referred to not only his spoiled-brat pomposity but also his inarticulacy. At that time, journalists were too much in awe of the Great Star – any Great Star – to do so; I was thus guilty of unforgivable *lèse-majesté*. In those days showbiz journalism was far more forelock-tugging and, perhaps for that reason, you could usually interview a star without an army of publicists deciding in advance on the 'rules of engagement' for an interview and insisting on copy approval of the piece before it could be printed.

Favours were constantly being done to stars. When one dim and inarticulate starlet had the gall to complain that she never said what had been printed in the paper, the *Express* interviewer was outraged: 'Of course she didn't! But what's she complaining about? I gave her some of my best lines!'

It would be inconceivable these days for a major star like Steve McQueen to be unaccompanied by publicity minders and therefore be free to say, as he did to me, 'Hey, Ann, I hate having to talk about myself. No good at it. Let's go for a drive!' And boy, did we go for a drive. McQueen, who loved fast cars, had been lent a supercharged Mini Cooper and he drove me at terrifying speed up and down Park Lane, mostly on the pavement, with me shouting, 'Steve! Stop it! You're going to kill us both!' Startled pedestrians were leaping for cover and I thought later, 'Well, at least some of them will be able to say "Steve McQueen nearly ran me over in Park Lane!"'

But the Brando row looked as if it might run out of control and Peter Evans knew he had to mollify Baumohl, who handled virtually all the top Hollywood stars visiting Britain at the time. To have him blacklist the *Daily Express* would be a disaster for Peter's department.

Baumohl, a sharp, sardonic American Jew who drove a red Porsche, was the forerunner of Max Clifford. Over a peace-making lunch arranged by Peter, Baumohl and I became great friends; and from then on he'd occasionally take me to showbiz parties and introduce me to his starry clients, while hissing sotto voce: 'If you do a Brando on *her*, I really *will* destroy you this time!'

Oddly enough, I was then quite naive about the wicked ways of showbiz. Years later, when Baumohl was back in America, he told me about the elaborate publicity stunts he cooked up in London. Why didn't he tell me about them at the time? 'I thought you had too much integrity and might be shocked,' he grinned. 'Besides, I was trying unsuccessfully to get you into bed and thought you might hold it against me!'

As with Max Clifford, much of Baumohl's expensive time was spent trying to kill off pictures or stories which, albeit truthful, would enrage his cosseted stars. And one of the biggest stars of the day was Kim Novak who, when making a film in Britain, decided to go swimming in the nude in a lake on a private estate. Unfortunately a freelance with a long lens managed to sneak through the undergrowth and take pictures of the naked Novak. The photos only showed a bit of her cheek, one nipple and lots of back. But although she was a Hollywood sex symbol at the time, she believed that she had to exude an air of sexual mystery. Skinny-dipping in her birthday suit was not, according to Novak, part of the approved script.

'She went absolutely spare and ordered me to get rid of the photos and the negatives, or else.' In exchange for some exclusives, Peter Evans was in on Baumohl's plot and arranged for him to have lunch with a top *Express* executive.

As Baumohl tells it, 'I said to the *Express* man: "These pictures are not of Kim and if you use them, she'll sue." But he remained utterly confident until I said, "I'm afraid we have conclusive proof that those pictures aren't of Kim." "Oh really?" said the still defiant *Express* man. "Kim has a small tattoo on the top of her bum," I informed him. "Enlarge the pictures and you'll see there's no tattoo." The *Express* man's face went white. He then caved in, and promised me I could have the pictures and the negatives, and we'd say no more about it.' Did Novak have a tattoo on her bum? 'I've absolutely no idea! But that little bit of . . . let's call it creativity on my part saved the day!'

When Reginald Maudling was the Tory Chancellor of the Exchequer, Baumohl tells me that he decided to exploit the fact that Maudling had a gorgeous, much photographed (and star-struck) teenage daughter who lived with him at No. 11. He was doing publicity for a film being made starring Dame Edith Evans – not an easy wicket for his particular skills. Evans was old, grand and distinguished and therefore did not, in Fleet Street jargon, 'give good pix'.

So Baumohl informed the daughter that, as she was so beautiful, he wanted her to try for a role alongside the Dame. He fixed up a screen test, and then arranged for her to emerge from No. 11 holding her 'contract' aloft like her daddy's Dispatch Box.

But of course there had been no screen test (unbeknownst to Maudling's daughter, there was no film in the camera) and definitely no contract. The stunt worked so well that the pictures outside No. 11 were used in virtually every newspaper. According to Baumohl, the pictures were then sold to *Paris Match* which hugely enlarged the snaps and discovered that the 'contract' she was brandishing was actually a biography of Edith Evans. Not surprisingly, the *Paris Match* editor thought there was something *un peu* fishy about the story and demanded to see a copy of the 'screen test'.

Baumohl had to scramble. He arranged for the daughter to do another 'screen test' which consisted of nothing but a brief stills session. 'I then rang *Paris Match* to say that, for reasons of confidentiality, they could only see a single frame of the screen test.' The picture editor at *Match*, who knew Baumohl, was not fooled. But, like Peter Evans, he decided – in exchange for a few exclusives – not to rat on him and quietly buried the gorgeous Maudling daughter's fake 'pix'.

So great was my innocence about showbiz in those days that I interviewed Dusty Springfield in 1964 wholly unaware that she was lesbian – as was widely known even then in the pop world's inner circles. Perhaps she had a Baumohl/Max Clifford in her life: she was reported to be having a 'torrid romance' with a now forgotten pop singer called Eden Kane. Homosexuality was illegal then and although lesbianism wasn't (Queen Victoria, whilst agreeing to the criminalization of sodomy, didn't believe that women were capable of equivalent 'depravity'), being outed as a lesbian, even in the Swinging Sixties, would have been the death of twenty-three-year-old Dusty's career.

Were she alive today, how she would envy lesbian singers like Beth Ditto and k.d. lang whose unembarrassed sexual orientation has, if anything, added to their appeal. But it drove poor Dusty to drink, drugs and cutting herself. Although she actually died of breast cancer, her regularly denied lesbianism undoubtedly ended up destroying both her career and her sad, secret, ravaged life.

Even when I knew her she already had a reputation for being 'difficult' (though she wasn't with me), and I had certainly never met anyone who was so successful but who seemed so inexplicably unhappy. 'I feel waves of sadness leaking out of you,' I said. She was silent for a moment. 'I wouldn't be honest if I said I was happy. My mother always says you can't be happy if you're always thinking about yourself. But in this business you have to.' And as for the 'romance' with young Eden Kane: 'It's ridiculous.'

It was a late autumn dusk, and I was driving her to her next appointment. Dusty looked out of the car window and in a small, un-Dusty-like voice murmured, 'Sometimes the loneliness just hits me. When going down streets like this at about five in the afternoon, before people draw their curtains, I look at all these semi-detached houses and see families sitting down to tea together – and I just ache to be like them, and have what they have.' A short silence. I admired her white fur coat. 'It looks good,' she replied sadly, pulling out little tufts of fur like dandelion fluff. 'But – as you can see – it's moulting.'

*

Looking back at that period, I realize how irritating we arrogant young Sixties 'meteors' must have been. We'd not lived through the Great Depression, or World War II, and we behaved as if those who had, had merely earned the right to be mocked.

We were, of course, very much in favour of the working classes, so long as they didn't let the side down by being old, drinking tea, keeping pigeons or clattering their false teeth. Cilla Black, then aged twenty-one, spoke perhaps for many of us when she told me, 'I never want to grow old. I've always said I would shoot myself when I'm fifty.' Cilla now advertises insurance schemes for the over-fifties who, like her, did not shoot themselves on reaching their half-century.

In 1965 I was sent to Paris to interview the top fashion designers of the time like Balmain, but I insisted that I include what I described as the 'two new boys', André Courrèges and Yves Saint Laurent, who died recently. Saint Laurent had worked at Dior, was conscripted into the army, then had a nervous breakdown – whereupon Dior fired him. After a miserable year of unemployment, 'when all I did was walk the streets and visit museums and art galleries, feeling very bitter', he borrowed money to start a new fashion house bearing his name. He told me that he was now getting his ideas from *la rue, la jeunesse.*

Unlike 'the youth' who inspired him, Saint Laurent seemed extremely morose, highly strung and withdrawn. I thought it was just me, but it turned out he was like that with almost everyone. In which case he was rather out of tune with the Sixties which were extraordinarily hopeful times, its young almost naively excited by everything new, including the glamour of space exploration (which didn't lose its popular appeal until astronauts began getting killed and costs grew gargantuan).

In 1961 President Kennedy had declared that America would land men on the moon within a decade. Courrèges, the other 'new boy', was so inspired by that vision that he held a show he called Moonwalk where all the models wore space helmets; his shapes were sharp, pared-down, geometric, his colours space-age black and white; his models strutted about in shiny, toothpaste-white boots.

He claimed to have invented the mini-skirt and told me that, unlike older masters of haute couture like Balmain, 'We work in a different spirit from the others. We are fast and we are young and we don't have five people around when we only want two. Modern life is fast and hard! We create for that spirit!'

Knock-off copies of the Courrèges look began appearing everywhere in the London streets (even I bought a pair of long shiny white boots). No one bothered to do knock-offs of Balmain because he only made clothes for the wealthy elite.

And we were, of course, very anti-elitist, or at least we said we were. Actually we were highly elitist, but the elitism we practised was the elitism of style, of youth, of newspaper colour-supplement triviality. How wildly funny we found net-curtained 'respectability' and the terrified whimpers of 'What will the neighbours think?' emanating from the suburbs.

A friend of mine from the Manchester *Express*, Derek Taylor, was at the heart of Swinging London and its drink, drugs and 'hope-we-die-before-we-get-old' culture. He'd been the showbiz editor in Great Ancoats Street and we adored each other. Derek was a sharp, mordantly funny, kind, generous and wildly romantic Liverpudlian and for a while we had an intense, almost sexual, relationship. Almost, but not quite, because he was married to Joan (by whom he eventually had six children) and I had an absentee boyfriend, Michael, who was living in London. Besides, we were both tortured Roman Catholics, struggling, sometimes unsuccessfully, with what the nuns and priests of our childhood had denounced as 'the mortal sins of the flesh'.

In Manchester I knew that Derek drank a great deal (which led to much guilt-ridden fumbling on both sides), but then we all did. It was when he became the long-time press officer, and close chum, of the Beatles that he also became a druggie. He was something of a pop-music legend himself, having been a co-founder of the Monterey Pop Festival in '67, at the height of the so-called Summer of Love when thousands of dreamy hippies swallowed LSD, nicknamed Monterey Purple. He handled not only the Beatles, but also the Byrds, the Mamas and the Papas and Nilsson, along with other Sixties pop luminaries.

From time to time, once installed in Fleet Street, I'd pop round for a gossip to Derek's office in the Beatles' Apple Corps building in Savile Row, where Derek would sprawl in his peacock chair, drinking champagne – on which he seemed to mainline – and we'd share a spliff or two.

I rarely smoked pot, the popular name for cannabis in the Sixties, because I actually found it rather boring. I had once grown it in my little Hampstead semi, but became so fascinated by the way the plants changed sex in order to achieve gender balance that somehow I never got round to harvesting it. But the main reason why I abjured pot (much milder than it is these days) was that cannabis made you fat. It induced terrible bouts of 'the munchies', an overwhelming desire to gobble up gargantuan amounts of chocolate cake, cream buns and sweet pink wine. Besides, a drug bust – and thus a criminal record – would endanger my American visa.

I never understood how Derek, despite consuming so much pot, managed all his life to remain as skinny as a whip (and witty, even when stoned); I suppose it was the cocaine. When he died of cancer at sixty-five, the tributes from the pop world, especially from his closest Beatle friend, George Harrison, were deservedly fulsome; he was indeed an extraordinarily lovable man. The song-writer Jimmy Webb described him best: 'He was the dapper, mustachioed, trench-coated war correspondent of rock 'n' roll.' For years Derek publicly declared that neither he nor any of the Beatles took drugs – a ludicrous lie which was publicly exposed when Lennon and Yoko Ono were arrested by Scotland Yard in 1968 for heroin possession.

Very occasionally, invited by Derek, I'd go to a party where one or more Beatles would be present but where everyone was always so stoned – all of them smiling idiotically and finding the dullest remark hysterically funny – that I'd usually leave early. I never saw anyone smoking heroin, or dropping acid, but even the druggies knew that that was probably best done in private.

When Lennon was murdered, my phone rang constantly with radio and television producers asking me 'to come on our tribute programme and share your memories of John'. 'But I don't have any! I didn't know him!' I'd protest. Michael, passing my office at home, overheard one of these brief conversations and said, 'What are you talking about? Of course you knew him! You told me about the time you saw him in his underpants!' Oh well, it must have been at one of those stoned parties. . . . Years later I thought, I'm an idiot – people have built entire publishing careers on 'The Lennon I Knew' hagiography shtick, sometimes based on an even slighter acquaintance of him than I had. I could, albeit dishonestly, have really cashed in.

My now sputtering friendship with Derek died in the forecourt of the Savoy Hotel. He told me we were going to have lunch and he was bringing a friend of his, who turned out to be the jazz giant Thelonious Monk, of whom I'd never heard at the time. The taxi arrived to pick me up and as soon as I got in I realized that both of them were catatonically drunk and/or stoned. We arrived at the Savoy and a doorman in top hat and tails opened the cab door for us, whereupon both Derek and Thelonious Monk fell out, face down, limbs flailing, into a disorderly heap on the pavement. I felt so humiliated that I instantly got back into the taxi and told the cabbie to take me home.

The nearest I came to drug addiction in the Sixties was as a result of Lesley Hornby, then a seventeen-year-old model from Neasden who had limbs as skinny as liquorice sticks and a virtually concave chest – which of course most of us hadn't.

We Swinging Sixties women knew that the only kind of female who could wear a mini without exciting ridicule was the kind of child-woman creature epitomized by Lesley, now renamed by her Svengali Justin de Villeneuve (born Nigel Davies) as Twiggy. With her anorexic bones, and bruised-looking eyes, she exuded a kind of blank, soiled innocence, a paedophiliac fantasy of youthful corruptibility.

This child-woman was indeed appropriate for the time. It was after all an era in which adult childishness was elevated into a radical creed: childish politics – 'Never trust anyone over thirty!'; a childish belief that there were short cuts to happiness – 'I want it now!'; a childish belief in irresponsibility – 'Tune in, turn on, drop out!'

The Twiggy Effect panicked hordes of us – actresses, socialites, models, even a 'Young Meteor' journalist like me – into a notorious Dr Feelgood's waiting room in Harley Street where he ran a 'slimming clinic'. We would all hide behind huge Jackie O dark glasses and were never tactless enough to recognize one another openly.

We constituted a high-speed and lucrative production line for Dr Feelgood who'd whizz us into his consulting room, jab a needle containing some mysterious potion through our tights – 'horse urine, I think' one devotee speculated to me – and then eject us into the room next door where his elderly dispenser lurked. She'd shovel scoops of multi-coloured pills out of huge vats and pour them, uncounted, into our plastic bottles; she'd then take our cheques.

The pills were basically 'uppers' which made our metabolisms race so much that we were always high as kites, peed a lot, and scarcely bothered to eat at all. We all got very thin, very fast, talked nineteen to the dozen, and at least one of us ended up having a minor heart attack; a fashion editor friend of mine even had a psychotic episode and was briefly 'sectioned' under the Mental Health Act. It was, of course, all rather dangerous. Dr Feelgood, unsurprisingly, was struck off after a Sunday newspaper exposed him. Even four decades ago super-skinny models – the subject of so much controversy today – were able to influence young, insecure women to do profoundly silly things.

I used to allege bravely that I must have been originally designed to be a sex symbol in Tonga where, I wrote, somewhat facetiously, 'they rightly scorn the idea of the pocket Venus, preferring something more on the scale of a Gladstone bag. The loins of Tongan manhood refuse to stir for anything much under thirteen stone or a 40C cup – and thus it was that working there one summer I found myself sprinting coyly from palm grove to copra factory, and back again, with the flower of Tongan youth in hot pursuit murmuring pretty fol-de-rols from the Song of Solomon.'

Nevertheless, I knew in my heart of hearts that I couldn't stand being large, so I'd truss myself up in rubber panty-girdles which, in hot weather, made one stink like melting tarmac and made a slapping, pinging sound when you tried to peel them off. One day Baumohl said to me, 'Fer gawd's sake, Ann, you're not fat! You're what we Jews call *zaftig* and we like women that way!' But *zaftig* means plump so I wasn't reassured. Which is why, wearing my Jackie O shades and writing yet another cheque, I kept on adding to the size of Dr Feelgood's bank account.

I once returned to Tonga after a crash diet involving starving, smoking, fainting and Dr Feelgood's horse-urine, which had not only removed enough fat to grease a ship's boiler but which also reduced me to an instant non-runner in the Tongan sex-symbol stakes. The flower of Tongan manhood remained quite unmoved, slumped beneath the palm trees, picking its teeth in boredom as my new svelte shape wafted past its sightlines. Alas, I gather that these days even in Tonga slimness is becoming obligatory. And the Song of Solomon is off the top twenty Tongan chat-up lines. I blame globalization.

8

Farewell to the Black Lubianka

In the Sixties I got to know the photographer Patrick Lichfield, more formally the fifth Earl of Lichfield, who was a cousin of the Queen and who took the official photographs of the wedding of Diana and Prince Charles. He was a very amusing, rather sweet and extraordinarily handsome man with bouffant hair and apparently lots of money, and we used to go out together, in a desultory manner, to places like the then Sloaney nightclub Annabel's. When he took a portrait of me he turned me, via air-brushing, into what he clearly thought I should be and what he was used to: a beautiful, dim, debby Sloane.

Dressing up in leathers and riding a Harley, Patrick always liked to pretend he was one of the 'lads' – the iconoclastic, rough-and-ready, fashionably working-class photographers like his mates Terry O'Neill, Terence Donovan and David Bailey. But of course he knew perfectly well how useful his title and his royal connections were. Not least because 'They save me money!' he told me one day. 'I never employ assistants who don't have private incomes – they work for me for nothing because their mothers hope "something might come of it"!' Thus, for example, one of his assistants was an American heiress called Berry Berenson, granddaughter of the couturier Elsa Schiaparelli and great-great-niece of the art critic Bernard Berenson (her sister Marisa played the doomed Jewish heiress in *Cabaret*). In fact Berry went on to marry Anthony Perkins of *Psycho*, but lost her life on 9/11 when the American Airlines plane she was travelling on was flown into the World Trade Center.

For as long as possible, I kept my friendship with Patrick dark from my mother who, like the hopeful mothers of his wealthy assistants, might have deluded herself that 'something might come of it'. Apparently she had never entirely got over the fact that she had not married an alleged admirer who was a Scottish earl. When she did finally learn that I knew an even more exalted earl than her lost swain, she became nervously excited.

'But Mummy, he'd never marry me, even if I wanted him to. Which I definitely don't! He's told me he'll never marry a girl who isn't aristocratic by birth, because non-aristocrats don't know "how things work"!'

And when he did get married in 1975 it was to Lady Leonora Grosvenor, daughter of the fabulously wealthy Duke of Westminster. Many of his former girlfriends, including me (although I hardly qualified), and the actresses Britt Ekland and Gayle Hunnicutt, were guests at his lavish wedding at the ducal estate in Cheshire. His almost compulsive infidelities eventually destroyed the marriage to his Countess, just as infidelity – among other things – destroyed the marriage of Prince Charles to his Princess.

Patrick's wedding was, in its way, a faintly comical affair, involving a special train from London and charabancs ferrying us and assorted Royals to the venues. The streets of Chester were lined with cheering crowds and we in the 'celebrity' charas, wearing our 'celebrity' wedding hats, soon started waving back at them in the bent-elbow style perfected by our own dear Queen, a fellow guest. At the crowded reception I heard a small squeak behind me: I'd trodden on the toe of Queen Beatrix of the Netherlands.

It was Patrick who persuaded me to leave the *Daily Express* and go freelance. He was tired of my moaning about how 'Any time there's an important political figure in the news, I'm only asked to interview his bloody wife! Foreign Secretary? No, his wife! Chancellor? No, his wife!'

My fears about losing a steady income were airily dismissed. He told me, somewhat inaccurately, how his mother, Princess Anne of Denmark, and his stepfather were so angry when he decided, after leaving the Army, to become a mere photographer, that they'd cut him off financially. 'I was so broke I had to sleep on the floor at friends' houses!'

At the *Express* the last straw for me came after I'd told David English, then Foreign Editor, that I wanted to run the New York Bureau; he was enthusiastic. But Derek Marks, the huge, diabetic, half-blind and often slurry Editor – whose daily 'lunch' in El Vino's consisted of up to twelve large whiskies, which he called 'sharpeners' – was shocked by this revolutionary idea. 'But you can't have a *woman* running a Bureau!' This despite the fact that Marks was evidently so alarmed by me that he would ask my permission before he hired another female feature writer, a fact which enraged me. 'Derek, you're the editor, you hire who you want. It's none of my business!' Being frightened of women is usually part and parcel of a sexist man's psychology.

But David was upbeat: 'As soon as I become Editor, Ann, you can have any job you want.'

When English was at the *Express* it was a powerful newspaper interested in foreign news, and he'd been a foreign correspondent himself. He had a slightly spivvy, gossipy and manipulative charm – but, if he lost faith in someone, a terrifying coldness. I, like many of his staff, was both alarmed – he took a gleeful delight in stirring up what he called 'creative tension' – but also thoroughly exhilarated by him.

I remember ringing him one night from one of those flyblown, forgotten, dusty, tumbleweed-littered towns scattered across the more remote parts of America. I was lying in bed in my tacky little chipboard motel, in a place on the Texas/New Mexico border, with only one traffic light to its name, and the local TV news had just told me that there was a 'Tornado Advisory'.

I was reading to David from the local newspaper which, as a matter of course, printed the school meals menu for the week as a front-page story. As I read out the menu to him (shouts of joy at the other end of the line), the approaching tornado was building in ferocity. The wind was forcing crisp packets, special-offer flyers, ice-cream wrappers under the ill-fitting door, and I said that there was something eerie, strangely animated about the detritus of consumerist America – an America unable, for all its power, to curb the ferocity of nature – and how that detritus, like a demon, was creeping and curling slowly and inexorably under the door, invading my room, climbing on to my bed . . .

I suddenly realized that there was silence at the other end of the line.

Fearing that the approaching tornado had downed the phone lines, I shouted, 'Are you still there, David?'

'Yes,' came the quiet reply. 'I just envy you so much. I remember those strange, dusty little American towns, those newspapers which splash on school-lunch menus, and I'm afraid I just felt so moved – and so *jealous* – that I couldn't speak for a moment.'

I became a foreign correspondent largely because David began sending me on foreign jobs and had an unshakeable faith in me – when others, understandably, didn't. Early on, he sent me on a story in the then British Guyana and I blew it. The macho thugs on the Foreign Desk jeered. 'We told you so, David. Girlies can't hack it!' As one such thug later told me ruefully, 'He said to us, "This girlie will be able to hack it. Wait and see!"'

But I knew that David would not get the top job: the proprietor Max Aitken, son of the late Lord Beaverbrook, had a reverse Midas touch when it came to hiring editors (a skill which never left him, thus accelerating the decline and eventual sale of his once mighty newspaper). So I wrote Aitken a cool letter of resignation and was summoned up to his office. I told him why I was leaving: 'Not least among my reasons is the fact that you are not going to make David English the editor, which means that this newspaper will inevitably go down the tubes.' And sadly, I was right.

Patrick Lichfield was a good friend of Jocelyn Stevens, the proprietor of *Queen* magazine. 'I've written to him to say you'd be a wonderful catch for the magazine, detailing all your wonderful skills (well, not those, of course!).'

Jocelyn, the nephew of publishing tycoon Edward Hulton, had inherited a tidy sum from Uncle and, as a twenty-fifth birthday present to himself in 1959, bought a stuffy society magazine called *The Queen*, which catered for the aristocratic and landed classes. But the zeitgeist had changed and Jocelyn decided that he'd target the so-called 'Chelsea Set', which included his chum, the raffish Princess Margaret, cockney photographers, hairdressers, debs, conmen and bright young things who lived on Daddy's trust fund.

So as not to alienate the magazine's existing core readership of nobs and snobs, he went on printing the achingly boring 'Jennifer's Diary', which detailed their social rituals. It was written by an absurd woman called Betty Kenward who, while not a nob, was most certainly a colossal snob. Mere journalists and photographers belonged, as far as she was concerned, outside the tradesmen's entrance. Her hauteur so irritated a young photographer hired by Jocelyn to work for *Queen* that he determined not to invite her to his wedding. 'I thought, "She's been so rude to me, I'm going to punish her." And I really enjoyed her panic when she saw she wasn't on the invitation list!' he told me later. 'She really had to grovel and beg!' The wedding wasn't any old wedding: it was the wedding of the year when the young photographer Anthony Armstrong-Jones married the Queen's sister, Princess Margaret, and became Lord Snowdon.

Like so many wealthy men, Jocelyn could be extraordinarily mean (the oil billionaire Paul Getty told me that *of course* he obliged his house guests to use the pay-phone in his Sutton Place front hall, because 'If you don't look after your money it soon disappears'). Jocelyn once called me from the *Queen* office after hours. I said, 'What on earth are you doing there?' He bellowed in reply, 'What I'm bloody doing here is switching off all the bloody lights because my bloody staff seem determined to bankrupt me by leaving all the bloody lights on when they go home!'

Known to his staff as Piranha Teeth, he was prone to volcanic rages, tearing phones out of the wall and on one occasion flinging an office typewriter out of the window. Helmut Newton, the German fashion photographer whose pictures combined half-naked Amazonian models, sex, surrealism and sado-masochism, was the amused object of one of these rages. He was arranging some layouts and Jocelyn walked into the room. He took one look at the pictures, threw them down and screamed at Helmut, 'What are these masturbating women doing in my magazine, lying on the floor while phallic symbols are exploding outside the window!' Yet another phone was then yanked out of the wall.

I briefly became one of his favourites so was never the object of his ire. 'My dear Ann,' he wrote once, 'It's a great piece, you're a great girl, and I love you. Yours, Jocelyn.' Despite my being 'a great girl' it was extremely hard winkling payments out of him, albeit sometimes with success. 'Dear Ann, I enclose a vast cheque for your article on Muggeridge,' he wrote to me in January '68. 'And I agree a further huge payment of £100 for Princess Elizabeth of Toro. I remain your most admiring employer. Yours impecuniously, Jocelyn.' I kept his letters as evidence because he tended to 'forget' what we'd agreed. (Elizabeth of Toro, incidentally, briefly became Uganda's Foreign Minister under Idi Amin.)

One day he barked at me, 'Go and sit in on David Frost's programme for a week! I want a piece called "The David Frost Phenomenon".'

In 1967 Frost, a Methodist minister's son from Kent, was, at twenty-seven, already wealthy and a huge star on British television. It was not immediately clear to Jocelyn, or indeed to me, why. As I wrote rather pompously at the time, 'Television is the first medium to make an art form of the ephemeral and Frost is the master of the instant, ephemeral effect.' And as the *Sunday Times* critic sniffed, 'He is by no means a fluent master of language, nor a gifted performer in the ordinary sense, nor, so far as we know, a profound or original thinker. He is not even a striking personality.' Malcolm Muggeridge's wife, pondering the Frost Phenomenon, famously proclaimed that he 'rose without trace'.

Frost was not handsome, had a weird pie-frill hairstyle, a nasal accent and rabbity teeth, and a dreadful taste in jokes. So how had he done it? True, he'd been in the first wave of the satire boom along with people like Peter Cook, who liked to boast that he'd once saved Frost from drowning in a swimming pool and had regretted it ever since.

The current affairs TV magazine programme bearing Frost's name went out live with a studio audience three nights a week and is said to have introduced the by now common concept of 'trial by television'.

The crooked boss of the Fire, Auto and Marine insurance company, Emil Savundra, was due to defend himself on the show. He made a severe tactical mistake at the beginning by responding to a heckler from the audience with the words, 'I did not come here to cross swords with peasants. I came here to cross swords with England's bravest swordsman.' Then 'England's bravest swordsman', cheeks quivering with outrage, eyes small stones of fury, launched into him. It was riveting blood-on-the-carpet television, but I wondered how genuinely angry Frost was or whether, as a consummate showman, he knew that the conman Savundra was easy game. The night before, I'd watched him in the studio with George Brown, then

Foreign Secretary, whose susceptibility to booze was legendary: the phrase 'tired and emotional' was coined by *Private Eye* to describe his embarrassing behaviour. Brown – and the Foreign Office – were understandably nervous in advance of the interview. Brown told me, 'Oh, everyone, my family, my colleagues, the Foreign Office, they all urged me not to do it! But I trust David!' And rightly so: the papers next day described the interview as 'the best party political broadcast of the year'.

Did Frost give an easy ride to the powerful and take a tougher line with the small fry? I couldn't work it out. There was – and is – something unknowable about David. Perhaps that's why, although he was always unfailingly affable to all his colleagues – 'Marvellous! Marvellous! Thank you *so* much!' – none of them seemed to like him very much. A lot of it was jealousy of course. Many of them, including Ned Sherrin, were big names in their own right, but even if they disliked him, their professional fortunes were now contingent on this 'whipper-snapper's' talents, energy, nose for a story and complete imperviousness to setbacks. The programme editor, Peter Baker, told me, 'I don't know what David believes, what he cares about, who he cares about. If he ever has secret agonies, no one would ever suspect it. He's just not like a normal human being.'

As a condition of being allowed to sit in on the making of the programme – from planning to transmission – I had to give copy approval. I 'anonymized' some of the more disloyal and spiteful of his colleagues' comments. He read it through, and the only thing he objected to was a line where I noted that his stomach was 'straining through his canary-yellow shirt'. 'Strike that out: I'm not fat.' I then pointed out that none of his colleagues on the programme actually liked him. 'I really don't care, so long as they do their job.'

Over forty years later he is still working, has an even larger fortune, is on first-name terms with most of the world's power-brokers, is married to the beautiful daughter of a duke, and has received a knighthood. And as far as I can see (and I've been on programmes of his several times over the years), he's as affable and as unknowable as ever.

One of the things which profoundly irritated many people at the time was Frost's accent: in those days it was something of a shock to traditionalists when someone on television didn't employ 'RP', the 'received pronunciation' of the ruling classes. I asked him to describe his: 'Mine is yer basic thirty-miles-out-of-London accent really. Bit of yer Gillingham, Kent, a bit of yer Cambridge, and a bit of yer Television Classless.'

Class, an abiding British obsession, has changed its livery over the decades, though it hasn't disappeared, and never will. When I listen to early broadcasts made by the Queen I find it hard to believe that anyone ever spoke in those high-pitched, clipped and/or drawling tones (although I suspect, with embarrassment, that I once did). Frost's unashamed lower-middle-class accent, his early bumptious-ness, his refusal to sound like Noël Coward (lower middle-class him-self) trying to ape the aristocracy, had the effect of making all those ambitious people who took elocution lessons (like several veteran television stars I know) now feel rather foolish. As one of my tele-vision friends, who used to speak pure Brummie, put it to me, 'If I was starting out nowadays, I wouldn't have bothered. Regional accents are now so "in".' When I was young, you never heard working-class or regional accents on the airwaves unless they were actors playing 'amusing' characters like Mrs Mop or villains or comic policemen; such non-RP accents tended to be associated with stupidity/and or criminality. Frost's ubiquity on Sixties TV helped to change all that.

9

Sophia's Nose and the Drug Mule

I'm sometimes asked variants of 'Isn't it a great disadvantage being a woman when working and travelling in dangerous parts of the world?' And I usually reply that the doughty adventurer Dame Freya Stark thought not: in 1934 she wrote, in *The Valley of the Assassins*, that the great advantage of being a woman is that 'one can always pretend to be more stupid than one is, and no one is surprised'. (By 'no one', she meant men.) This particularly applies in macho countries – which are usually the maddest and most dangerous corners of the world. Playing the 'helpless little woman' would be pointless in, for example, Sweden.

When I left the *Express* in the Sixties I decided to go to Mexico and follow the drugs trail which led north from the poppy fields in the mountains into Southern California. Unfortunately two of the most notorious and lawless drug-producing Mexican states were under martial law and I was informed in Mexico City that, before the police would give me permission to go there, I had to carry a gun – and know how to use it. I wasn't keen: Mexicans, especially the kind I'd be dealing with – the drug-running *traficantes* – are born with guns in their teeth. By the time I'd got the gun out of my handbag, either I would have been riddled with bullets or, more likely, would have shot my own toes off.

But, alas, training was insisted upon. At the firing-range, the police marksmen struck me as a very dodgy lot: not only did they smell of tequila, but most of them seemed to have little bits of their anatomy missing – an ear here, a finger there, a nostril there . . . how did these mutilations occur? Such 'flesh-wounds of honour', they told me, strutting with pride, were the result of fiercely fought battles with the *traficantes*. Later, one of them admitted to me that they'd shot off bits of themselves by accident when drunk.

Best to get rid of the gun, I thought, and aim for the totally harmless look, something most women can get away with, but few men. And if men try to, they risk being thought of as homosexual, which is not a safe thing to be in most macho countries.

A month later, in a remote area of Durango province, I was looking for a particular illegal poppy field. As I trudged up the hill, a band of mustachioed *traficantes* leapt into view from behind the cactuses, aiming their ancient Lee-Enfield rifles at me. Then they suddenly stopped in astonishment: nobody, absolutely nobody, had ever come trudging up their gun-bristled hill wearing white gloves, a white-and-yellow Horrocks frock (in those distant days, the epitome of the bourgeois Celia Johnson style), and carrying a white handbag.

Naturally these brave peasant sons of Zapata laughed like drains. I was obviously so mad that I was not worth wasting bullets on. Not only that, but I became a kind of exotic trophy to be shown off to the rest of their mustachioed Lee-Enfield-draped chums. I never had any trouble from the *traficantes* after that.

But after a while I'd had enough of Mexico. Indeed, I suddenly hated the place, hated the flyblown, verminous food, hated travelling on filthy, overcrowded and dangerous local buses where I had to squash in among the vegetables and squawking chickens hanging upside down with their legs imprisoned in twine, hated the gap-toothed old men and the ludicrously macho *mestizos* with moustaches and gold teeth who leered at *la gringa* and constantly tried to touch me up. I hated the dirty little hotels in small broken-down towns, where the taps stuttered and would occasionally vomit forth thin streams of rancid brown water, and where the ceiling fans did little more than stir the humid air like soup.

But even they were preferable to the small, hotel-less villages where I'd cadge accommodation from impassive, suspicious local Indians, who would allow me a corner of an earth-floored hovel in exchange for a handsome fistful of Yanqui dollars. Even if I'd spoken Nahuatl, which I didn't, I knew I'd never get through to these people, descendants of the Aztecs, who had never reconciled themselves to the Spanish conquest of their empire and who turned the Conquistadors' religion – my religion, albeit vestigially – into something stranger, wilder and more alien than anything dreamed up in cruel Old Castile.

Why, I thought, are these Mexican Indians so unlike the Indian villagers of my childhood, who would let me play with their children, roast cashew nuts with them, and whose smiling grandmothers would smudge red paste *bindis* on to my forehead? But of course, I'd remind myself, Mexican Indians aren't Indo-Europeans: they're a different race; 'Indians' was simply the name given to them by the gringos.

At night in the still, cold villages, exhausted and tearful with homesickness, I would fall asleep on a filthy blanket on a dirt floor, with only the howling of stray dogs to disturb me. Mercifully, Mexican Indian babies never seemed to cry at night. I soon realized why they seemed to fall asleep so quickly and so blissfully: they dozed off in hammocks rocking beside a fire of marijuana leaves. They were the most stoned babies in Christendom.

I remembered that my mother once told me she'd had to sack an ayah who was ensuring my sleep by ladling spoonfuls of gin into me from the drinks cupboard. It was said that some Victorian nannies would guarantee similar infant doziness by turning on the gas taps and gently giving their charges a whiff. I thought this rather funny when I first heard about it, but it didn't seem so now. But then nothing did, now. I felt too depressed.

I suddenly felt that I hated all Mexicans, and I particularly hated their endless kitschy celebration of death, especially their Día de los Muertos, the Day of the Dead, during which everyone from grannies to toddlers feasts on sugar skulls, sugar bones and sugar coffins at raucous family picnics held in graveyards.

Of course, we staider Northern European Catholics also 'celebrate' the dead on All Saints' and All Souls' Days. But in Mexico the Day of the Dead struck me as more sinister, more deeply stitched into the Mexican psyche, more pagan, more sexual, more Aztec, more bloody. No wonder Malcolm Lowry set his drunken, hallucinatory novel *Under the Volcano* on the Dia de los Muertos.

The Mexican Nobel Prize winner Octavio Paz once said that 'the Mexican idolizes death – chases after it, mocks it, courts it, sleeps with it; it is his favourite plaything and his most lasting love'. Perhaps this (to me) strange relationship with death meant that Mexicans simply didn't take it too seriously; death produced just another skull, another coffin you could turn into a sugar bonbon. In Mexico City I was chilled by the fact that a local newspaper off-handedly covered the death of fifty-two workers at a union meeting in one 'Just Fancy That' paragraph. (And no, it wasn't the notoriously violent police, just the result of a demarcation dispute.)

In the depths of my homesickness, missing Michael, red buses, clean lavatories, Marmite on toast and the harmless rituals of family word-games at Abney, I had never felt so alienated in my life.

In 1938 Graham Greene (a far more tortured Catholic) had been financed by the Vatican to go to Mexico to report on the savage repression of Catholicism there. His reportage in *The Lawless Roads* was the basis for his novel *The Power and the Glory* about the life and violent death of a 'whisky priest', and he chronicled what he saw as the decay and corruption of Mexican Catholic culture. He too hated Mexico and the 'blank, expressionless brown eyes' which greeted him everywhere.

But despite being permanently guilt-ridden, Greene felt no guilt about what, nowadays, would be seen as his 'racist' views about Mexicans. I, however, did. I was, after all, a young woman who'd osmotically absorbed the Sixties peace 'n' love message and who sincerely believed that 'all human beings are brothers'. Besides, women are pre-programmed to feel guilty, and being a Catholic just imposed another layer on top of my 'original sin'. I've always felt crippling guilt about more or less everything, but by now the over-load of guilt in Mexico was just too much. I'd had enough of the noise of urban Mexico, the grinning, money-grubbing *mariachi* players, the grinding traffic, the thin, smoggy air, the Mexican inability to talk at a normal voice level.

Which is why I suddenly decided to head north to Acapulco.

True, Acapulco was still in Mexico but it was a fashionable coastal resort full of rich, spoiled, glamorous gringos. Gringos who, without guilt, shamelessly indulged in air conditioning, hygienic food, and large yachts which, as they thrummed in the marina, sounded as if they were gargling with gold coins. Besides, I'd heard there was – as usual – a Hollywood movie being shot there. Might be a quid or two in that; by now I was running low on cash.

The movie was called *Sol Madrid*, a crime caper which had the tag-line, 'He's the Only Cop who Can Con the Mafia out of $3,000,000 in Heroin!' It starred David McCallum, a British actor who'd made his name as the international heart-throb Illya Kuryakin in a hit TV series, *The Man From U.N.C.L.E.*

I persuaded the *Sunday Mirror* to finance me in one of Acapulco's most luxurious hotels: 'Cyril, I *have* to stay in the Villa Vera or Las Brisas – if you don't stay where the stars stay you haven't got a chance! And believe me, Cyril, this film is going to be *big*! Not only does it star McCallum, but *Stella Stevens*!' It was the latter name that clinched it: Stevens was a former nude model from Yazoo City, Mississippi (her first major acting assignment was as Appassionata Von Climax in *L'il Abner*, and she'd starred with Elvis in *Girls! Girls! Girls!*). Blonde and bosomy and then in the top ten of the most photographed women in the world (alongside Jackie Kennedy, Monroe, Bardot and Raquel Welch), she would guarantee a great spread in the paper.

And thus it was that, for a deliriously cheering ten days or so, I spent time in the arms of absurd luxury, much of it star-spotting. 'No! That can't be Ursula Andress!' I hissed at a crew member sitting with me by the pool. 'Far too short!' Not for the first time I noted how the film camera adds magnificently to the height of most movie stars.

Mind you, I've always been irritated by famous beauties who allege they're mortified by their ugly knees/skin/height/metatarsals/ earlobes. Like most women, my response is – you should be me, lady. The only star I ever had dealings with who appeared several feet taller than even their screen image was Sophia Loren.

Never before or since have I seen anything more gorgeous in the flesh than Loren. Marlowe's lines could have been written about her: 'Was this the face that launched a thousand ships, and burnt the topless towers of Ilium?'

One day I had to go round to her suite in a London hotel to have her clear a set of contact prints because, routinely, she always insisted on picture approval. Loren, wearing specs, and certainly not in 'burning the topless towers of Ilium' vein, was businesslike. Every one of the contacts showed her looking triumphantly voluptuous, ravishingly beautiful. Peering through her spectacles and a magnifying glass, she began crossing out most of the contacts with a white chinagraph pencil. What on earth made one picture acceptable and most of the other, equally ravishing ones, not?

Chatting about her several decades later with the great portrait photographer David Steen (who joined up with me in Mexico and became a friend of Sophia's), I got no further than repeating the question I put to her when he interrupted: 'It was her nose, wasn't it?'

Indeed it was. Loren had explained to me, 'Look. This one, this one, this one . . . no, no, no. It is my nose. Its tip looks like the beak of a parrot.' It didn't; but her obsession with her 'parroty' nose meant that all approved pictures of her tend to be photographed from below, thus eliminating the alleged defect. But why should I, never hired for my beauty, be puzzled by someone obsessing about her appearance, which after all was an essential element of her job?

One day at the hotel in Acapulco I perched on a stool in a swim-up bar and the Swiss-born Andress – whose image in the first Bond movie as Honey Rider, rising up out of the ocean in a white bikini with a knife in her belt, is now iconic – swam up and joined me. 'Don't drink the ice!' she commanded me like some bossy little suburban shop assistant in a Zurich pharmacy. I responded 'Look, if you'd had to drink what I've had to drink for *weeks* in Indian villages and . . .' Not surprisingly, Honey Rider yawned and swam away.

The only member of the cast who would listen, spellbound, to my not-that-exciting adventures in Mexican *traficante* territory was John Cassavetes, who made his name as the director of pioneering art-house movies like *Shadows*. I told him about my brief encounter with Andress (who, luckily for her, was not in *Sol Madrid*). 'Well, she's got a cute ass, but she's not very smart.'

'You don't have to be smart in Hollywood, do you?'

'No, you certainly don't. In fact being smart works against you – as I know to my cost.'

And then, over endless tequilas (not surprisingly he died of cirrhosis at a mere fifty-nine), John would tell me how much he despised Hollywood, how he particularly despised *Sol Madrid*, how the director Brian G. Hutton (who'd directed Richard Burton in *Where Eagles Dare* and who subsequently directed Elizabeth Taylor in some forgettable movies) was 'complete crap. I mean, you've watched him on set – do you think he has the faintest idea what he's doing?'

'No,' I replied. 'But then I think he's absorbed Raymond Chandler's advice that if you don't know what to do next in a plot, introduce a guy with a "gat" in his hand. Or, in Brian's case, have some torturer burst into the scene.'

It was obvious that *Sol Madrid* was not a happy shoot. The two stars, McCallum and Stevens, seemed surly and distant. I forgave Stevens because, despite the heat and humidity, she was constantly weighed down by a heavy blonde wig like a lump of yellow concrete, but I was less forgiving towards McCallum who behaved, on screen and off, like a petulant teenager.

'He wants us to think he's already a big-screen star, and he's certainly not!' I told Cassavetes crossly after McCallum had refused to exchange more than a few sulky words with me. 'Yeah, well, he'll soon learn!' drawled Cassavetes with a lopsided triumphalist grin.

He and I knew that *Sol Madrid* would be a critical – and probably a box-office – disaster. And we were right. McCallum's career trundled on, but never reached the heights of *The Man from U.N.C.L.E.* Once, watching the American TV show *NCIS*, in which the former heart-throb plays Ducky, a crusty British pathologist, I heard one character ask another 'What did Ducky look like when he was young?'

'He looked like Illya Kuryakin.'

Had *Sol Madrid* been a hit, that humiliating script-line would never have been uttered.

One night, the perennial Latin heart-throb Ricardo Montalban – playing a Mexican gangster – and his wife asked me to join them for dinner at La Quebrada. Cassavetes wouldn't join us, perhaps because he disliked watching poor Mexican boys, the *clavadistas*, performing death-defying dives off the Quebrada cliffs, which they did every night for ooh-aahing gringo tourists, to earn themselves a few pesos. But knowing Cassavetes, I thought it more likely that he wanted nothing to do with any of the cast of *Sol Madrid*. 'I just don't hang out with these people,' he informed me. 'I'm only doing this crap movie to finance my own movies, which of course never make a cent.'

The sad thing was that both the producer Hal Bartlett and his luscious, red-haired movie-star wife Rhonda Fleming *did* sincerely believe, against all the odds, that *Sol Madrid* wasn't just another crime caper: it was *artistic*. I'd learned by now that, contrary to what cynics allege, very few movie producers (other than porn merchants and money launderers) actually set out to make a crap movie. Over long dinners in the languorously warm evenings Hal and Rhonda would expatiate to me about the 'genius' of their director, his 'creative integrity', his 'attention to detail'. The latter, I concluded from watching Hutton on set, consisted largely of endless reshooting of the most inane scenes, perhaps in the hope that dross would turn into gold.

Later I learned that Cassavetes had his name taken off the credits, apparently a habit of his once he'd pocketed the money.

After La Quebrada, Acapulco's most famous attraction was Merle Oberon's mansion overlooking the bay. Tour boats made it part of their itinerary. When I stayed with her for a couple of days I wondered how she could stand the non-stop clicking of cameras and the constant shouts across the water of 'Hi, Merle! Look this way, Merle!'

Actually, she could stand it very well. Merle was only forty-six at the time (to me, at twenty-six, a Methuselah-like age) but entirely wrinkle-free. When we swam in her pool together I'd peer at her hairline hoping to spot a few cosmetic surgery scars. Never did. Besides, she rarely allowed the sun to fall on her face: 'Very bad for the skin.'

(It had certainly been very bad for a fellow guest, Princess Gabriela of Savoy, the daughter of a former King of Italy. Every day the Princess would hobble round the mansion moaning, with her feet swathed in bandages. She'd fallen asleep under the deck canopy of a yacht sailing off Yucatan, the boat changed tack, her feet jutted out and she suffered terrible burns).

But of course Merle had another reason not to go out in the sun. If her skin darkened, her dreadful secret might be revealed. She was, in the dismissive phrase used by the Raj's white overlords, a 'chee-chee', the mixed-race offspring of an English railway engineer and a Singhalese nurse, and had been born in Bombay. When I mentioned I'd lived in Bombay as a child she became very vague. And I suspected I knew why.

I'd once remarked to an old India-hand friend of my father's that I'd found Oberon's Cathy in the film *Wuthering Heights* 'unconvincing'. ''Course it is!' he snorted. 'Where she got this ridiculous name

"Merle Oberon" from I don't know. Her real name is Queenie Thompson. A chee-chee through and through: used to be a regular fixture as a nightclub dancer in London.' In other words the great movie star was, he was saying, in reality Queenie the half-caste slut.

These days, whenever I hear a film star like Halle Berry celebrating her mixed blood, I think back to poor Merle. She'd pretended she'd been born in Tasmania, alleging that all her school records and birth certificate had been destroyed in a fire. Her dark-skinned mother would be introduced to visitors as her maid. When her mother died she commissioned a series of portraits of her, based on old photographs, but instructed the painter to lighten the skin.

I thought no more about *Sol Madrid* until some months later. A parcel arrived for me from LA. I'd lost my camera in Acapulco and this was it, returned. I assumed it had been sent by Cassavetes because I'd given him my address and he'd sent me the odd affectionate postcard. I trotted down to the local chemist to get the film developed.

A week later my father called me in. 'Look, the chemist has developed your film and thinks there are some questionable photographs.' Questionable? Snaps of the 'floating gardens' of Xochimilco and the pyramids at Teotihuacan? They were on the film all right. But so, at the end of the roll, were soft-porn images of Cassavetes and his actress wife Gena Rowlands 'making out', an American phrase I'd only just learned.

I was not only humiliated but also deeply puzzled. Who'd taken those photographs? Who'd decided to send them to me? Was it John, for some drunken reason? Was it his wife, deciding to warn me off? But surely, like so many film stars, and indeed foreign correspondents, she must know the initials D.C.O.L.: it 'doesn't count on location'. But my brief, albeit intense, relationship with Cassavetes had never been more than an *amitié sentimentale*. It wasn't a case of D.C.O.L. Frankly, I wasn't even sure that he'd fancied me. Had I been older, more self-confident, I'd have explored the puzzle a bit further.

But as it was, I just tried to drop the whole issue, crimson with embarrassment. I wanted my father to think I was his wonderful, clever, flawless little girl. It was only years later, when I saw the far more pornographic pictures he'd taken of his assorted girlfriends, that I realized that his 'disappointment' over the pictures I'd taken of Tim Phillips in the nude in Cadaqués, and these showing the Cassavetes husband and wife enjoying themselves, might actually have been increased by his knowledge of his own behaviour. (After his death, his bank manager rang me to say that my father had locked a sealed box in a safe deposit and had told the bank that it should be given not to his widow, but to me.) Now his darling daughter was perhaps going down the same road as him and maybe he felt a smidgen of paternal guilt.

*

I knew I couldn't spend any more sybaritic time in Acapulco. I had to finish the drug-trafficking story and in Durango had acquired a couple of names of *burros*, 'mules', who'd be willing, for a hefty fee, to allow me to accompany them as they smuggled some heroin across the border into California. I met up with a willing *burro* in a whorehouse in the honky-tonk border town of Tijuana.

He'd been a professional boxer in Mexico until the heroin got him; the *traficantes* paid him in the stuff. Before illegally crossing the border into San Diego, he needed a top-up. So, in one of the whorehouse booths, he strapped his arm, heated up some brown heroin in a teaspoon and injected it. 'My God, that stuff looks like Nescafé!' I exclaimed. One of the whores laughed throatily: 'It mostly is!' – and when I saw her Adam's apple jerking up and down I realized that 'she', like the others, was a transvestite.

I decided against crossing the border illegally with the drugged-up 'mule' – but nevertheless felt I'd fallen short in the journalistic courage stakes.

10

'Spies 'R' Us'

One night in 1968 I'd been lying in bed watching my tiny black-and-white TV, which was showing the Warsaw Pact tanks rolling into the Czechoslovak capital, Prague. I had never been to Czechoslovakia, Russia, or indeed any of the Eastern European countries; I had no connections there, and had been immured in my convent boarding school when the tanks rolled into Hungary in 1956.

My knowledge of Communist Party atrocities was limited, although at school there had been a nun who one day told me, 'Stalin has just died. He killed a lot of nuns. Wicked man! But God will forgive him,' she added with pursed lips, perhaps doubting that even God could bring himself to forgive a nun-killer.

Even in 1968 I still cared nothing about ideology. It was hard enough trying to wriggle free of Roman Catholic ideology, let alone concern myself with any other. Alexander Dubček, the Czech leader, had tried to bring 'Socialism with a human face' to his country, but the Soviets preferred Socialism with an inhuman face and sent in the tanks to prove it.

So, lying in bed that night, watching the tanks crushing the 'Prague Spring' was, for me, a kind of epiphany. I felt a sudden, unwonted connection with these people being gunned down in 'a faraway country of which we know little'. I had been born and grown up in a country where people starved, were suppressed, had few human rights, but I'd always remained curiously detached, cocooned by my privileged position as a Daughter of the Raj.

But that night, those grainy pictures of the tanks and the protests made me feel angry and agonized. For too many years 'human rights' meant little to me – it was just a phrase. But now I suddenly felt that the Soviets, by attacking these anonymous but all-too-human Czechs, were attacking all of us.

At the end of the extended News, an announcer appealed for help for a number of Czechs who, during the brief 'Prague Spring', had taken the opportunity to travel abroad and were now stranded. They had no money and no idea what to do next.

Viewers were told that anyone who could briefly house and/or employ these stranded people should 'ring this number'. I did, in tears. 'Look, I don't have a job to offer anyone and I have a very small house, but if anyone is stranded, I could take two or three people in.'

And thus, for a few months, assorted Annas and Josips and Marinas trooped up to my front door. They were all embarrassingly grateful, a fact which could be expressed only in bear hugs and many tearful expostulations. Back home they were teachers, music students, doctors – but here, in a tiny 1930s semi, they were beggars, relying on 'the kindness of strangers'. A stranger who, in my case, became increasingly exasperated by their presence, but who was also acutely aware of how humiliating all this was for them.

The chief problem was language as none of us shared a single word in common. They spoke virtually no English (little more than 'Sankyou! Sankyou!' and 'okay'!), though some of the older Czechs spoke German as a result of the Nazi occupation.

When Milan, an elderly teacher, produced a syringe and – in sign language – indicated that I should inject him in his lower back, I panicked. I'd never injected anyone, had no idea what I was being asked to inject him with. For a moment, remembering the drug 'mules' I'd met in Mexico the year before, I wondered whether I was perhaps turning my semi into a Czech drug den. (In fact they all turned out to be Slovaks who, it transpired, hated the Czechs with whom they were then yoked.)

I rang my then boyfriend Michael, who spoke some German, and he reassured me, after talking to Milan, that it was simply medication. And so Milan would pull down his trousers and each day I'd inject his pale, quivering, humiliated flank.

There remained two problems: food, and the lavatory handle. I had a vague idea that Eastern Europe was full of sheep and cabbage fields, so my refugees would assuredly love lamb with cabbage. I would roast legs of lamb, complete with garlic and home-grown rosemary, and was dismayed to find them merely toying with it, while uttering their by now ritual 'Sankyou!' Turned out they all hated 'sheeps', especially the smell.

'Oh, God,' I'd wail to Michael on the phone. 'They're living with me and all they'll eat is cabbage! They'll starve!' Mercifully I found a wonderful Slovak priest, Father Babik, who'd been tortured and imprisoned and now lived in exile in north London, who was able to guide me in Slovak culinary tastes and much else. It was wall-to-wall pork thereafter.

But the lavatory handle was a more intractable problem. All 'my Czechs' (as I rather patronizingly, and inaccurately, thought of them) were very modest, very devout, even – to my mind – excessively prudish Catholics. Especially a long, thin, Kafka-like former priest called Vaclav. The lavatory handle had a will of its own; sometimes it would work, but often you'd have to coax it with soft words and sudden deft movements into doing its flushing duties. 'You have to understand its *moods*, Vaclav!' I'd shout helplessly and pointlessly at him through the door.

Whenever Vaclav went to the loo, the lavatory handle would become mulishly obstinate. Preserving his sense of propriety to a maddening degree, he would never leave until it had flushed. This meant that Vaclav would be immured for long stretches of time, thereby preventing anyone else in the house from using the loo. I even found myself peeing under the apple tree in the garden out of desperation, or nipping along to the pub.

Once again I realized that the only thing I could do was ring Michael. He would shout instructions to Vaclav down the phone in German while I held the earpiece against the keyhole and at long last, thank goodness, there came the victorious sound of a flush, and Vaclav, eyes down, pink with shame, would finally emerge.

This being 1968, the year of violent street protests against America, my temporary refugees from Communist Czechoslovakia were, Father Babik told me, baffled – and rather hurt – by the absence of mass street protests in the West against the Warsaw Pact's suppression of their countrymen. But in those days the dictatorships of the Soviet Union, Cuba, North Vietnam and China were, stupidly and cruelly, much admired by many of the proudly ignorant and obstinately ill-informed protesters.

Most of 'my Czechs' eventually returned home because they'd left behind families who'd believed, as they did themselves, that they were only going to the West for a short holiday. But their excessive gratitude remained.

The following year Michael and I went on holiday to Austria and in Vienna got a tourist visa to cross the border into Bratislava in western Czechoslovakia. 'My Czechs' (who by now I realized were 'my Slovaks') had insisted we come and stay with them so they could return my hospitality. We drove into the city at night, and instantly got lost.

Our little white Triumph Herald convertible glowed in the deserted, ill-lit streets as if declaring, 'I am a capitalist car containing imperialist, fascist, bourgeois spies – come and get them!' Naturally the police arrived within minutes, and, naturally, took Michael away for questioning.

I was left in the car, speaking no Czech, in a gaunt and silent city which seemed infused with a strange miasma of gas-like chemical smells, wondering what on earth was going to happen next. We'd agreed we would not mention our friends and would try to give the impression that we were just two daffy young tourists; and using his hesitant German Michael managed to convince them.

There followed three rather scary days for us. Our friends, two of whom did speak some English, insisted on cramming us into a decrepit Skoda and driving us into the High Tatras, the mountain range of which Slovaks are very proud.

On our lengthy drive to the east of the country we saw fields full of Soviet tanks. Our friends would lean out of the windows and yell in English, 'Go home, Ivan!' I kept thinking to myself, please, please, don't do that! We're the only real English speakers in the car and we'll get arrested! And then I felt ashamed of myself: the worst that would happen to us would be that we'd probably spend a few days in jail, the Foreign Office would have 'discussions' with the Czechs, and then we'd get expelled. But for them, yelling 'Go home, Ivan!' might even be classified as a 'counter-revolutionary' crime, for which people got shot.

The worst moment for us came on departure. Our friends – and other Slovaks whom we'd never met before – asked us if we would smuggle out letters addressed to contacts in the West. What should we do if the border police searched us? One of our friends told us firmly, 'In that case, you must eat letters. Authorities must *not* read them!'

I felt that even the stupidest border guard might find his synapses sparking with suspicion if he saw two Western tourists suddenly gobbling down wads of paper. But we didn't feel we could refuse to do this when our anti-Soviet friends took many more extreme risks every day of their lives.

Between Bratislava and the Austrian border we stopped the car and, amateurish to a degree, decided to hide the letters under the carpets. At the border post we joined a lengthy queue of Austrian-registered cars. And to our horror saw that every one of them was being meticulously searched. 'My God, they're even removing the hub-caps!' I quivered to Michael. When the border police eventually reached us they made a thorough search of our luggage, removed the hub-caps, looked underneath the car but, eventually, waved us through.

It was only when we were back in Vienna that we found out the reason for the hub-cap removals. Pork chops were very cheap in Czechoslovakia, but not in Austria. So Austrian pork-chop lovers were heading across the border on day trips, buying up the chops and hiding them in suitcases and hub-caps. Presumably the border police assumed that you couldn't hide a load of chops under a car carpet, so didn't bother to rip up ours.

Back in London, as I posted the letters, I felt a huge swell of anger about a political system which was so cruel, so utterly pointless. Over the next few decades I got to know both victims of Soviet Communism and their victimizers. But such are the complexities of human nature that sometimes a victim can also be a victimizer – just as abused children can often grow up to be abusers themselves. As, for example, in the case of a small, nervy, chain-smoking Soviet friend of mine called Igor, who always (atypically for a Soviet Communist) wore a white ice-cream suit.

The only remotely spy-like behaviour Igor ever displayed to me in London was to use the name 'Mr Brown' when making restaurant reservations for us. Why? 'Because Russian family name too difficult.'

'Nonsense, Igor. Your family name, Kuzmin, is very easy for a city which has thousands of "difficult" foreign names.'

I enjoyed teasing him. 'Igor, you're a spy, aren't you?'

'*Nyet! Nyet!* How can you, my friend, say such terrible thing? I am journalist like you!'

But of course Igor *was* a spy and in 1989 he and a slew of other London-based KGB and military intelligence men, masquerading as diplomats and journalists, were expelled for 'activities incompatible with . . .'

On the evening of the explosive announcement of the mass Soviet spy expulsions I was on BBC TV's *Question Time*. At the end of an answer to a question about Anglo-Soviet relations I looked towards the cameras and said, 'Bye bye, Igor, it was good to know you.'

He rang me the next morning. 'I saw you on BBC last night! Is completely unjust! I am not KGB agent!' I replied: 'Well, Igor, as a friend I'm hurt: as you know, Michael and I are building a new kitchen and we've run out of money and I know from my sources in the security services that you've been running around with suitcases stuffed with cash and frankly we could have done with some of it!'

Having previously worked in the Soviet Union, I'd already suspected that Igor was a spy, not least because of the structure of its bureaucracy. He was number two at the state news agency Novosti in London, and the number two official in virtually every foreign-based Soviet institution then was a KGB man tasked with spying, not only on foreign imperialists, but also on his fellow employees, lest there be any ideological 'deviationism' in the ranks.

Many years later a Russian journalist friend of mine who had worked with Igor in Canada told me how bitter he was about him. 'I was always careful to behave myself in an ideologically correct manner – but Kuzmin knew what I really felt, and he denounced me as a "counter-revolutionary" and I was ordered back to Moscow. It ruined my career.'

But frankly (and selfishly) Igor's KGB activities didn't bother me. His connections made him useful. When the reforming Mikhail Gorbachev came to power in 1985, this new, young, energetic General Secretary – '*Davai! Davai!* Let's get on with it!' – instituted a policy of allowing Western journalists, if they had official permission, more access to ordinary Russian life.

That was certainly not the policy in 1974 when Michael and I had joined a small tour group visiting Moscow and Leningrad (now St Petersburg). Leonid Brezhnev was in power and the Soviet gerontocracy, 'the wooden overcoats' and 'concrete heads' in the Kremlin, presided over a vast, decrepit, corrupt, shambolically incompetent and heavily armed empire covering eleven time zones – which, by then, was only being held together by the glue of fear.

Communist ideology as a quasi-religious faith had long ago died in the crushed citizenry's hearts (although it still showed signs of extremely vigorous life in the West among those whom Lenin had called the 'useful idiots' of the Left). In its Russian heartland it only existed in bombastic Party slogans on red banners plastered over public buildings: 'Let Us Make Moscow the Model Communist City!' 'Let Us Celebrate the Triumph of the Proletariat!' 'We Will Drive Mankind Forcibly Towards Happiness!'

Those in power during that 'era of stagnation' seemed to have completely lost the power of original thought and tended, out of systemic inertia, simply to repeat what was already written down on a Party document. One underground joke from that time described how Brezhnev, on hearing a knock on his door, reached into his pocket, took out a slip of paper and dully intoned the words written on it: 'Come in.'

The *nachaltsvo*, the big cheeses, were insulated by their Party-awarded privileges from the dour reality of what life was like for the *narod*, the masses. They had special hospitals, and special stores full of luxury, hard-currency goods (one such store was housed, as I discovered and secretly photographed, in an anonymous-looking building near the Kremlin called 'The Bureau of Passes'). Their salaries were small by Western standards but then of course their living expenses were low: the State supplied and paid for their homes, cars, chauffeurs, servants and luxury dachas. All they had to do was keep their noses ideologically clean and, as there was no free press, no one publicly exposed the Party's comfortable racket. Their complacency was of course reinforced by the routinely fulsome tributes of their grovelling underlings.

One of these was a young, ambitious provincial Party boss in Stavropol in the Caucasus whose final, much praised, essay at school was 'Stalin – Our Combat Glory. Stalin – the Elation of Our Youth', and who declared: 'Leonid Ilyich Brezhnev has revealed a talent for leadership of the Leninist type! His titanic daily work is directed towards strengthening the might of our country, raising the well-being of our workers and the strengthening of the peace of nations. Communists and all the workers of Stavropol are boundlessly grateful to Leonid Ilyich Brezhnev!'

Michael and I, in common with most of the Soviet Empire, let alone the world, had never heard of that obscure provincial Party boss. A decade later we would. He was of course Mikhail Sergeyevich Gorbachev.

In 1974, despite the party banners urging it to celebrate its 'triumph', the proletariat seemed to be in far from celebratory mood – except insofar as being drunk might be misconstrued as being so. Indeed, if we attempted to ask a member of the 'triumphant' proletariat for directions – say to Dyetsky Mir, the vast toy shop in central Moscow – not a single person would reply, or even look at us. An informer might be watching, might report them for fraternizing with foreign imperialists; best to keep their heads down.

I'd read so much pre-Revolutionary Russian literature, full of passion, romanticism and high-flown, often doomed, but always extravagant idealism, that I felt that these sullen, enclosed, suspicious people trudging wordlessly, heads down, along the snowy streets, would be unrecognizable to Tolstoy, Chekhov or Pushkin.

The only member of the proletariat who actually seemed to go out of her way to 'bump into' us was a large, chatty Russian woman with good English who kept turning up, standing behind us if we were queuing in a shop or trying to buy a cup of coffee, always in different parts of the city.

'What wonderful coincidence!' she'd cry every time. 'Let me buy coffee!' Er, okay. '*Pozhalusto*, please, favour for me your Russian friend!' Er, what favour? 'Soviet brassieres not good. Can you send me some from your famous Jewish shop Marxi Spencer?' True, Soviet bras then were constructed like World War II bomb casings, but the increasing intrusiveness of this Marxi Spencer bra fan's questions, her extravagant praise for us and requests for 'favours' began to look to us like an absurd KGB set-up and we took to scampering out of sight whenever her vast bulk hove into view. If she was KGB, she clearly wasn't the most skilled of operatives, but then Michael and I, two young English tourists, were very small fry in the Cold War's ideological struggles so probably weren't deemed worthy of the attention of someone higher up the espionage food-chain.

At one stage during that '74 trip I collapsed with pneumonia. We were in Leningrad and I was informed by the tour group's Russian minder that I had to go to hospital. *'Balnitsa nyet!'* I groaned in my extremely limited Russian: I would not go to a Soviet hospital, which if it was anything like their 'best' hotels – decrepit, dirty, with surly, drunken staff – might have meant death. Possibly from starvation.

In those days even hard-currency tourists like us found it remarkably difficult to get anything to eat. Granny Ming in Moscow in 1930 noted that she met an American couple who, dazzled by the idea of this brave new Soviet society, had come to witness its joys at first hand. They were due to stay a month but 'confided to me that they were obliged to leave after ten days, "driven out by hunger"'.

Perhaps Russia had an excuse for food shortages in 1930: it had endured two revolutions in 1917, a comparatively brief involvement in the Great War, and by 1918 had embarked on four years of social and political upheaval and a devastating civil war. But by 1974 there was no excuse: food shortages were due almost entirely to stifling Party centralization, military spending and grotesque economic mismanagement. There was even less excuse in the mid-80s when I started going there regularly and still found it virtually impossible to get food.

State food shops, *produkti*, were largely bereft of any 'products'; besides, to buy anything you had to queue three times: first to choose whatever was available – usually not much more than jars of pickled cucumbers and sausages bulked out with sawdust; secondly to pay for it; and finally to collect what you'd bought. Russian women always carried an *avoska*, a just-in-case string bag, just in case they came across something unexpected they might want to buy, or which might be useful for barter. It was estimated that Russians spent an average of three hours a day queuing – with dire consequences for productivity.

There was a handful of restaurants open to foreigners, but as an individual foreigner you had to ask Intourist to make a reservation for you at one of them, whereupon you had to collect an official confirmation slip. You'd arrive at said restaurant with your piece of paper confirming your reservation. More often than not, the door would be opened and the restaurant manager would declare, 'Reservation incorrect. Restaurant full,' and would then slam the door shut.

Over the shoulder of his stained jacket you could see that the restaurant was in fact completely empty.

If there was anything Russian restaurant staff disliked it was customers. They might actually eat the food, such as it was. It usually consisted of little more than *kotleti*, fried chicken breasts which tasted of brick dust and sump oil or, alternatively, 'Georgian Flattened Chicken', a burnt, sharp-edged discus with which, if flung with sufficient force, you could decapitate a passer-by at ten metres. Food was not for customers, it was for the staff – either to eat or, more usually, to sell on the black market.

As for the hospitals: in my fevered haze in '74 I remembered what had happened to Granny Ming when in 1930 she travelled to London from Tianjin, via a series of trains through China – where on more than one occasion she and other passengers had to get out and help shovel coal into the boiler – then through Japanese-held Manchuria and on through Siberia and the Urals. She was taking with her her youngest son, six-year-old Tony, who'd broken his leg in an accident.

In Moscow where, yet again, they were changing trains, Ming and some travelling companions decided on a brief spell of sightseeing and hired *droshkys*, Russian open-air horse-driven carriages. The *droshky* drivers were, as usual, drunk.

The driver of Ming's *droshky* was killed instantly when the equally vodka-sodden driver of a lorry, driving down the wrong side of the road, hit them and reduced their 'old carriage to matchwood'. Tony was flung out on to the side of the road and, in a coma, was rushed to the Botkin Hospital, which had once had a relatively good reputation. But when Ming and Tony were admitted, it was clear the Botkin had degenerated into a flyblown slum where the slatternly nurses used the bedpans to wash down woodwork and sinks would be left full of dirty crockery for days. Ming herself suffered concussion, was heavily bruised and for weeks endured a great deal of pain. Tony recovered, but never entirely. And had Ming not had friends in the British Embassy, who brought in some food for her, she would have starved.

So of course it was definitely '*Balnitsa nyet*' as far as I was concerned. The compromise was that I was ordered not to leave my room in the Evropeyskaya and a nurse would visit me every day to inject my bottom with God knows what.

The Evropeyskaya was a huge nineteenth-century Tsarist era hotel. In its heyday it had been the height of *Jugendstil* luxury: famous guests included Stravinsky, Turgenev, Debussy and H. G. Wells. Tchaikovsky spent his wedding night there. By 1974 it was dilapidated: now state-owned, the only reminders left of its former magnificence were the high, crumbling-plaster ceilings, some cracked and dusty mirrors and in our room – inexplicably – a grand piano, decorated with paintings and mother-of-pearl. When Michael tried to play it he found that some of the strings were broken and it probably hadn't been tuned since the Revolution.

Olga the nurse, looking like a sofa on wheels, would bustle in with a huge horse-doctor's syringe and jab it into my bottom. After a while my bruised and swollen bum resembled purple-sprouting broccoli and I was in agony. Whenever I uttered a squeal of pain, Olga would slap my bottom hard: a typically soft imperialist lackey, I clearly lacked the required Russian quality of uncomplaining stoicism.

One day I could take no more and asked Michael to tell her I wasn't there, but it was no good. Olga found me hiding behind the grand piano, yanked me out, flung me face down on the bed and, perhaps to punish me for my insubordination, injected me in what she could see was an especially painful set of bruises.

In those days, no ordinary Russians were allowed through the Evropeyskaya's doors, unless they had staff passes, were medical personnel like Olga or were the omnipresent prostitutes, the *putanas*, who, of course, paid off the staff and were in any case part-time hookers for the KGB. Incidentally, the hotel, completely restored and magnificently refurbished, is now the luxurious – and fiendishly expensive – five-star Grand Hotel Europe, owned by Orient Express.

On coming to power in 1985, Gorbachev instituted the policy of *glasnost*, openness.

In 1986 I took him at his word and went to the Novosti office in London, told Comrade Igor Kuzmin that I wanted to explore the lives of ordinary Russians and asked him if he could arrange an interview with a typical young couple in Moscow. Of course he could.

Communist societies always liked to produce 'typical couples' for the foreign media. Such couples were always – surprise, surprise – good Party members whose 'typical' flats somehow always seemed to be atypically well equipped, and who dutifully uttered 'unre-hearsed' remarks on the lines of 'Thanks to our socialist system, our rents are very low,' and 'Unlike capitalist societies, we do not have much criminal activity because the masses have been educated in socialist morality.'

In fact the whole Soviet system, from top to bottom, was riddled with 'criminal activity'. That murderous old monster Lenin had described the Party as 'the mind, the conscience and the honour of our epoch', but its conscience had long since rotted, if it had ever existed.

When we became friends later, Sveta, one half of the 'typical couple' Comrade Kuzmin had produced for me, admitted to me that everyone in the Soviet Union had to become criminal, just to get by.

Education and health care, for example, were supposed to be free but, as Sveta explained, 'to get proper treatment, you have to secretly pay the doctors and nurses, and if you want your child to get good results in examinations, you have to produce "presents" for the staff and the examiners. It can all get very expensive. Poor people suffer most under our socialist system.'

Marx had said that under capitalism the elite would inevitably amass ever more power and privilege and the gulf between the elite and the masses would grow ever wider. That is an exact description of the allegedly 'egalitarian' Soviet system under Communism. Today, unfortunately, thanks to the gangster brand of capitalism, the gap between the 'New Russian' rich and the Russian poor has become grotesque. As one of the jokes circulating about those vulgar high-spending 'New Russians' in the Nineties put it: 'A New Russian is in a car crash. Climbing out of the wreckage, he wails, "My Mercedes! My Mercedes is smashed!" "How can you worry about your car", asks a passer-by, "when your arm is ripped off?" The New Russian looks at his stump and howls, "My Rolex! My Rolex!" '

The habit of criminality became so ingrained in Soviet life that, once Russians were free of the Party system, the sharper of them (including virtually the entire Soviet *nomenklatura* itself) took to gangster capitalism like fish to water. And I wasn't in the least bit surprised.

I've always felt a mixture of disgust and pity for 'typical' couples like Sasha and Sveta. Whether I'd met them in Eastern Europe, in Cuba or here in the Soviet Union, they struck me as totalitarianism's performing seals, barking only according to the zoo-keeper's script.

At times I've even felt rather ashamed at conniving with the totalitarian zoo-keepers. As, for example, in China in 1979 when two specially selected 'Model Communist Sweethearts' were obliged to endure an interview with me in Canton (now Guangzhou) at the Canton Heavy Machinery Plant. The performing seals in question were twenty-eight-year-old lathe operator Comrade Yang and his lathe-operator fiancée Comrade Lu, whose shy, rosy-cheeked prettiness was not flattered by her shapeless shirt and trousers, her plastic sandals and her approved hedge-trimmer hairdo.

To ensure that the couple never deviated from 'the correct line', these two unfortunate performing seals were accompanied by no fewer than six Party officials. Officially to admit that young Chinese Communists did 'incorrect' things like falling in love, when 'the correct line' was still that the only permitted love was love for the dead Chairman Mao ('the never-setting Red Sun in our hearts'), was in itself a startling development. The Party wished to demonstrate that it was now more 'liberal' than when I'd been there two years earlier.

'It was, er, you know, very hard for a young worker to get the correct line on this, er, subject,' stuttered Yang nervously. 'This subject' was love, sex, and, er, all that, and Yang's little toothbrush moustache was quivering like a gerbil's with wild embarrassment. 'Until recently, you see, the, er, love theme was condemned as a petty bourgeois instinct. So it was very hard for us young workers to receive correct guidance on how we should select girlfriends.' After all, Mao (whose own promiscuous and enthusiastic sex life was then, and still is, a state secret) had declared that 'not to have a correct political point of view is like having no soul'.

(Mind you, the film *The Sound of Music* was still banned in China on the grounds that it was 'yellow', i.e. pornographic. In reality it was probably because the film shows a family fleeing from fascist oppressors and living happily ever after. Even today the government has warned Chinese net-surfers on YouTube that it will no longer tolerate the broadcasting of 'degenerate thinking', and has warned providers of internet shared-video services that in future they must be licensed, so that they can only broadcast material 'which serves the people . . . and abides by the moral code of Socialist morality'.)

So how had the 'Model Communist Sweethearts' met? After all, there were then no bars, no nightclubs, no dance halls or discos. Most young people at that time seemed to meet at the compulsory political meetings with their interminable slogans, which included 'Let us strenuously attack the Ultra Leftist sabotage of Lin Biao and the Gang of Four'. In fact, the couple had fallen in love over their lathes. Said a stricken-with-embarrassment Comrade Lu: 'I was very grateful to Comrade Yang for his correct advice on how to improve my lathe-operating techniques.'

I sometimes think of those 'Model Communist Sweethearts', now middle-aged, when I go back to booming Chinese cities, with their trendy bars, boutiques and nightclubs with 'decadent' names like 'Tango', and wonder whether, when looking back on their youth, the couple feel that they were cheated (thanks to all that 'correct line' rubbish) of the youthful good times now being enjoyed by today's 'petty bourgeois' New Chinese.

Of course, when in 1986 I sought out a 'typical' Soviet couple in Moscow it was the early days of *glasnost*, and the Party zoo-keepers had by now recognized that Western journalists like myself were deeply allergic to the 'typical couple' syndrome. So Comrade Kuzmin assured me that Sasha and Sveta were truly chosen at random: 'They are not even Party members!'

Sasha was a psychiatrist (I later learned he was under a cloud because he'd refused to certify a dissident as insane) and Sveta a sociologist. Unfortunately she, too, had a mark against her: she was ethnically a Jew (albeit non-observing) and that fact was stated on her internal passport; anti-Semitism is buried deep in the Russian psyche, so having that recorded had not been helpful to her career.

Even Gorbachev's glamorous and pushy wife Raisa, who was deeply disliked by the jealous *narod* for her relative stylishness, was always being described to me by her enemies as '*evreika*', a Jewess: 'Only Jewish women behave like she does! Only Jews, who control the West, want to destroy our great nation!' In fact Raisa Maximovna was not Jewish, but the Soviet press agency, obviously aware of these 'denigratory' rumours, pointedly described her at the time of the

Washington Superpower Summit in 1987 as 'an ethnic Russian, born in Siberia'.

A couple of years later, when we'd become friends, Sveta told me, 'These Kremlin people have wonderful private hospitals for the *nomenklatura* only, but those hospitals are not allowed to employ Jewish doctors. But everyone knows that Jewish doctors are the best, so these *nachalstvo*, big cheeses, employ Jewish doctors privately and get the State to pay, while still forbidding Jewish doctors to work in the best hospitals. What hypocrites!'

A Jewish friend in London, a highly paid and successful private doctor, has a large clientele of Arab patients, particularly from those countries which publicly denounce Israel and Jews in general. When Yasser Arafat was dying, the Palestinian leader was flown to France for medical treatment. One of the team of elite surgeons who tried to save him was not only Jewish but a supporter of Israel. The French government refused to confirm the doctor's identity: 'This is too sensitive an issue.' As we all know, hypocrisy in high places is always 'a sensitive issue'.

When Igor Kuzmin told me that Sasha and Sveta, the Russian 'typical couple', weren't Party members, he was telling the truth. But of course the couple weren't in a position to refuse an order. 'We didn't want to give you an interview, because we were very nervous that we might say something wrong. But equally we'd have been in trouble if we'd said no,' Sveta told me later.

After Igor's expulsion from London as a spy I didn't expect to see him again. One day, to my astonishment, I suddenly saw him walking along Gorky Street. He was still wearing his trademark white ice-cream suit, sadly no longer pristine. Perhaps Soviet dry cleaners weren't as good as those in Kensington where he, his wife and their two sons used to live.

'Igor! I thought you'd now be cleaning out boilers in Novosibirsk!'

'Oh, Ann, you are so unfair! My news agency knows I am not KGB, so I still have my job.'

But he never seemed to have to do any work for his employers; perhaps he was still under a cloud for having botched his KGB assignment in London. He was therefore free to work for me as my fixer.

Together at intervals over several years we charted the start of

'Gorbymania', when Gorbachev was still popular, and then his decline. And the rise of that piggy-eyed Siberian peasant drunk, Boris Yeltsin – and *his* subsequent decline.

One day, when the country was in the grip of hyper-inflation, I talked to an American tourist and his daughter in the bar of my hotel. They were on a cycling trip through Russia. He told me they'd run out of loo paper, couldn't buy any, and so instead used rouble notes to wipe their bottoms. He even lit his cigarettes with roubles which were by now virtually worthless.

Right. 'Igor, can you find me one of the mints which are printing so much useless money?' And he did, although they were of course secret establishments. Because of his KGB background Igor could find virtually everyone I wanted to see and every place I wanted to visit. In those days maps of Moscow were (if available) full of deliberate misinformation, doubtless to confuse 'foreign spies'. Once when Igor was ill (probably from nerves) and I had to find a particular street, I noted that the locally purchased map I'd got hold of was a fantasy. Luckily I also had a CIA-produced map (which of course I kept hidden) which enabled me to reach my destination.

Moscow phone books did not exist. Apparently they did once – but, like most things, they were now unavailable. I remember the triumph of a BBC colleague who, on a working trip to the Caucasus, found an elderly Moscow phone book in a market. We all pored over it as if we were archaeologists who'd just discovered the Rosetta Stone.

'Igor, there are rumours that around two years ago one of the factories in the middle of Moscow poisoned the locals with a chemical leak, but no one can tell me which one it is. Can you find it for me?' Of course he could.

It was the Red Rosa silk-dye factory in the centre of Moscow, named after Rosa Luxemburg, the German 'red martyr'. The sign on the factory gate proclaimed that it had won an 'October Revolution' award: a huge red star containing a picture of the battleship *Aurora* whose guns in 1917 signalled the start of the Bolshevik putsch. This 'October Revolution' award-winner had stored all its chemicals in the open air in rusty drums; not surprisingly, the rain got into the drums and caused a disastrous chemical reaction which made the air, filthy at the best of times, even more dangerous to breathe. The accident had of course received no publicity and was denied by the authorities.

As, indeed, was the far more catastrophic accident in May 1986 at the Chernobyl nuclear power plant. I heard Gorbachev, when the news emerged from nuclear monitors in Sweden, stoutly denying that there had been anything other than 'a fire' at the Ukrainian facility, and declaring that 'certain Western politicians' were trying to spread horrific rumours 'in order to defame the Soviet Union'.

Nowadays the long-deposed Gorbachev roams the world denouncing nuclear power, and telling us that the Chernobyl disaster was a 'wake-up' call for him; it certainly hadn't been so at the time. Incidentally he now poses for ads for Louis Vuitton luggage and recently gave a speech in London's most expensive mansion to celebrate an anniversary of one of the capital's most 'high-end' estate agents.

Of course Soviet industry, in 'over-fulfilling its norms' (and faking the statistics), had been steadily poisoning and killing its own people with impunity for many decades. Even when Gorbachev first came to power, Soviet newspapers had to abide by the 'Index of Information' which banned publishing anything about, among other things, air crashes, fires, military accidents, explosions and even earthquakes.

Since all enterprises then were state-owned, the same secrecy applied to them. Moscow, thanks to the huge concentration of dirty industries in residential areas, must have been the only capital city in the industrialized world where average life expectancy had been falling over the previous decade.

Alcoholism had been contributing to the loss of life expectancy, and it still does, particularly among men, whose life expectancy is now just over fifty-eight years. But in those early days of Gorbachev's ascendancy it was only alcohol that was seen as a threat to health and well-being. Indeed Gorbachev, not a drinker himself, had earned the nickname 'Lemonade Joe' because of his crackdown on alcohol consumption. He had distilleries dismantled and vines destroyed in the wine-producing southern republics like Georgia. (Not surprisingly, the Georgians never forgave him.) The only effect, apart from a sudden dive in Gorbachev's popularity, was a nationwide shortage of sugar which was being hoarded to make *samogon* (moonshine).

Back at the Red Rosa factory Igor and I had tracked down its rather shifty deputy manager. The West was now offering technical aid to Russia but Red Rosa's director, as Party factory bosses were wont to do, refused to admit that his factory needed any Western help.

'Everything excellent here. Accident not typical. We have best modern machinery here now – no one should worry about our enterprise! Is completely safe!' Two surreptitiously stroppy women in the outer office were scornful about their boss. 'He said that, did he? Huh!'

A couple of workers we spoke to were certainly not anxious to spit on offers of Western help. One blue-overalled man with indigo-dyed hands told me, 'Until our factory was allowed, under *perestroika*, to earn its own hard currency, our machinery dated from the 1930s and some even dated from before the Revolution.

'Recently we have been able to buy wonderful new machines from Italy and Japan. We have machines, but we workers are disappointed because we do not have technical experts from abroad to show how to use them. Perhaps the factory has run out of hard currency to pay experts to come to explain them to us, so maybe our enterprise's future will be very dark.'

Once again memories of my grandmother's train journey through Siberia surfaced. She'd written: 'One of the strange sights which caught our attention was the quantities of new agricultural machines lying idle, as if just arrived and awaiting delivery, while no farm machinery was visibly in use in the fields. Any active farming we saw was being done laboriously with hand implements, in centuries-old style. It transpires that, under this First Five Year Plan, machinery was being manufactured and distributed before the necessary instructors could be trained to explain them!'

Full-scale famine as a result of Stalin's forced collectivization of agriculture had not yet occurred (that started two years later, resulting in many millions dead), but Ming could already see how poor, dirty and hungry the Siberian peasants now were. 'Our experienced fellow passengers told me that only a few years ago the trains were

My fearsomely tough grandmother 'Ming' marries my grandfather Norman Leslie on Shameen Island, China, in 1913. Grandfather looks wary, as well he might.

My uncles and aunt with my father holding my mother Theodora aloft at Abney House in 1935.

My parents with me aged two, in Delhi.

My younger sister Alison and brother Michael with me and our father
in the Fifties at the family beach house at Baleji, Pakistan.

World War II hero Douglas Bader with his downtrodden wife Thelma at the family beach house at Baleji, Pakistan; a teenage me is acting as waitress.

My parents with their chief guest, Pakistani military dictator Ayub Khan, at the Caledonian Ball, Karachi.

A teenager in Karachi, by then I'd discovered make-up and was aiming to look at least thirty.

1962: my first News Editor,
the moustachioed Tom Campbell
of the *Manchester Daily Express*,
carousing with his 'young lions'.

Making friends with a
Lancashire cow when covering
an agricultural fair in 1962.

Swinging Sixties arrogance:
Daily Express poster.

1962: my 'Youthquake' page,
Manchester Daily Express.

As a 'Young Meteor' in Fleet Street: 'fag-ash Lil' in 1965.

Michael, in mean, moody and magnificent mode, Sixties.

Our wedding, 1969.

Abney House,
the family home
on the Thames in
Buckinghamshire.

Michael and
three-year-old
Katharine beside
the Thames at
Abney House.

Playboy's 'European Photo Correspondent', late seventies. Portrait by legendary Hungarian snapper, Tom Blau.

An early 'new technology' convert: at home with the BBC B computer plus its black box modem – and yes, I could touch-type at speed even with those fingernails.

At Stanley airport,
Falklands, 1982.

In the bleak
and beautiful
Falklands, 1982.

met by prosperous-looking peasants who had for sale quantities of cooked chicken and market produce. But in 1930 supplies for sale were few and the roomy market stalls empty. Once or twice we bought eggs. But usually the vendors would only exchange their eggs for cigarettes. How distressing for them, the shortage of tobacco.'

Fifty-six years later the situation vis-à-vis tobacco had not changed. Soviet ideologues had decided that capitalism's multi-supplier, free market system was 'not rational'. The huge single-supplier cigarette factory in the then Soviet republic of Azerbaijan burnt down and suddenly there were no cigarettes to be had the length and breadth of the land. Russians are slow to riot, but whenever there's a severe cigarette shortage these inveterate nicotine addicts do.

In one of these periods of cigarette starvation in Russia, I used to calculate the cost of transport in Moscow in terms of whether it was a two-pack or a three-pack Marlboro ride. I no longer bothered to look for taxis or trudge through the slush to the Metro: I would just stand in the street, shake my capitalist bracelets, wave a duty-free red-and-white pack, and dozens of Zhigulis, moonlighting as unofficial cabs, would rattle to a stop, eager to do business. Naturally, if you have to carry so much of this alternative currency around with you, it's very hard not to smoke it from time to time.

Even in the then difficult-to-corrupt Stalinist Albania, the Marlboro pack could work its magic. (Although Albanians, being fiercely patriotic, would after pocketing the proffered pack inform you proudly that Albanian 'Partizani' are much better: 'much stronger!' True about the strength: 'Partizani' tasted like a bomb in the throat – one puff and the resulting coughing fit almost levitated you across the Corfu Strait.)

In China post-Tiananmen, I found that a fondness for Marlboros was a signal of defiance: smoking one proved you were either a secret dissident or, alternatively, a member of the plain-clothes PSB (the Chinese KGB) hoping to fool dissident-hunting foreign journalists like myself by blowing 'bourgeois liberal' smoke into their eyes.

*

In the summer of 1991 Michael and I were holidaying in a tiny village in the Bavarian Alps. As my husband considers me to be a news junkie, who must occasionally be ordered to go cold turkey, on holiday he doesn't allow me to read newspapers in a language I can understand or watch television or tune in to the BBC's World Service. He's even been known to confiscate my short-wave radio from our luggage.

Despite all this, I happened to spot a newspaper which told me that Kremlin hardliners in Moscow had just mounted a coup against Gorbachev while he and his wife Raisa were on holiday at their seaside dacha in the Crimea.

Once Michael knew I'd heard about the coup, he also knew our holiday was over. He agreed I had to get to Moscow straight away, a city with which I felt emotionally involved. But how to get in? I had no visa, and back then Soviet visas often took weeks to obtain.

As so often, sheer luck worked in my favour. This was in pre-internet days, but Michael happened to have an airline timetable which included flights in and out of Basle/Mulhouse, a rather distant airport on the French/Swiss border, from where there turned out to be, surprisingly, a direct flight to Moscow by Aeroflot once a week – and it was flying that very day. We drove there at high speed and I rang Igor from a phone box. On the crackly line he said, 'Get on plane and at Sheremetyevo Airport go to room where you get deported. I will see what I can do.'

At Russian passport control, the immigration police, surly and suspicious at the best of times, frogmarched me roughly up some stairs into a smoke-filled room. Assorted armed border guards barked incomprehensibly at me. Igor had obviously failed. Equally obviously, I was going to be bundled off to jail prior to deportation.

And then I saw a young man, not in uniform, sitting in the corner, smiling at my plight. After several minutes enjoying the sight of this gabbling woman sweating in her Alpine mountain gear in a small, hot room, he stood up: 'Mrs Leslie, your driver is waiting for you outside.' The 'driver' was Igor. The young man told me he was working for Boris Yeltsin at the White House, the Russian Federation's headquarters in Moscow, and that Igor had ordered him to go to the airport to help me. Clearly, as a KGB officer, Igor had pulled rank on the airport immigration police, who were controlled by the KGB. It was then that I sensed that the coup would fail, and that the KGB was itself divided.

The coup collapsed in farce, Boris Yeltsin took over, and the humiliated Gorbachev and his beloved Raisa (who never totally recovered from the trauma of their imprisonment in their Crimean dacha) were booted out of power. Not long afterwards the Soviet Union itself collapsed.

I was due to fly later that week to China with the then Prime Minister John Major. But Major had announced that he was going to divert the flight to Moscow so that he could congratulate Boris Yeltsin in person for facing down the plotters. 'Stay in Moscow and join Major's flight there,' the office suggested. 'No, I've got to get back to London for twenty-four hours,' I replied. I needed a change of clothes: red socks, woollies and walking boots were not suitable for midsummer Moscow, let alone Beijing. But mainly I decided to fly back for Igor's sake. He'd told me how depressed his two sons had been by the family's expulsion from London and how they were now acting up, resenting their father, hating the deprivations of Moscow.

I knew the sort of food Igor's boys missed and back in London I stuffed a spare suitcase full of their favourites. Unfortunately those favourites included Kellogg's Corn Flakes. If packed, the flakes would've been crushed to dust, so I'd have to carry them. Lugging huge panniers of cornflake packets, I staggered up the steps of Major's plane waiting at RAF Northolt. The Prime Minister exclaimed, 'What on earth are you doing taking cornflakes to Moscow, Ann? Going to sell them on the black market?'

'No, Prime Minister, they're a present for one of the KGB spies you expelled.'

Once gangster-capitalism had become established, glitzy shops opened, Gorky Street was renamed Tverskaya Street (Gorky had been a favoured Soviet writer, despite spending much of his life on Capri), restaurants appeared with abundant food where the staff seemed delighted to see and serve you, and decrepit old hotels where you used to have to bring your own bathplug were refurbished and now sported bathplugs aplenty; they also became cockroach-free, dazzlingly glamorous and dazzlingly expensive. And dazzlingly attractive to protection gangs, who had no compunction about having the odd inter-gang gunfight in the newly marbled lobbies.

'What's the *krysha* for the hotel I've been booked into?' I'd asked

Igor on the phone before coming to Moscow. *Krysha* means 'roof' in Russian – code for 'protection', in the Mafia sense.

'Yes, that one okay. Chechen Mafia has established its *krysha* and other Mafias too scared of Chechens to dispute it.'

Then one day in Moscow Igor told me nervously, 'I want you have dinner with me in the Metropole tomorrow night. We must be alone. I have something to tell you.' The hotel's baroque dining room had been used for meetings of the First Communist International in 1919, and a vast, idealized mural commemorating the event, featuring Lenin, his Bolsheviks and their allies, still adorned its wall.

By the time we'd eaten our starters of Beluga caviar, blinis and smetana (*kotleti* having mercifully vanished from menus) I knew I'd have to push Igor into saying what he wanted to say. Which was: 'Ann, you my friend. You my friend for many years. But for many years I have been deceiving you.

'I am Lieutenant Colonel in KGB. My superiors want to promote me to full Colonel. But I have resigned. If I become full Colonel it will be almost impossible to leave the service. I have now received permission from my superiors to tell you the truth.' I tried to look astonished by his confession. He was now going to be working as a highly paid 'security expert' for some *biznismeni*, wealthy New Russians.

But, he insisted, we must still be friends and he'd be happy to work as my fixer on future visits. Except that, from then on, he rarely seemed to be available. 'Ann, sorry, but I have to go to Bishkek.'

'You're *always* going to Bishkek, Igor!' Bishkek, the capital of the newly independent Kyrgyzstan, has, I believe, its charms, but it was principally famous then for being an entrepot for the drug-smuggling business.

*

I was working in Moscow in 1998 when the by now President Boris Yeltsin was up for re-election; he seemed utterly unaware that he was likely to lose. Enter 'Rasputin' Berezovsky and his billions. Berezovsky and a handful of tycoons – the so-called 'oligarchs' who had become stunningly rich gorging on the broken body of the Russian economy – were beginning to panic. It looked as if the resurgent Communist Party might defeat Yeltsin and the oligarchs feared that, once the 'Reds' were back in power, their own often dubiously acquired gains would be confiscated.

Once a humble mathematician, Boris Berezovsky was now listed by *Forbes* magazine as one of the richest men in the world and controlled a vast financial and industrial conglomerate (picked up for a song in the botched privatizations). By then he was probably the most unpopular man in Russia. Anti-Yeltsin demonstrators – old Communists, their chests clanking with Great Patriotic War medals, pensioners who were now forced to sell their grandchildren's toys and their own paltry household goods in order to survive, miners from the Arctic Circle who hadn't been paid for months – all would tell me that the country had been 'stolen' from the decent, patriotic *narod* by 'Jewish thieves' like Berezovsky.

'Stalin would have dealt with crooks like Berezovsky! He would have shot them!' an old lady shouted at me on the pavement near the Bolshoi Theatre. She was holding up her grandson's battered teddy bear for sale. She didn't believe in *demokratia* – 'It is nothing but *kleptokratia*! Our great motherland needs a *vozdh*, a strong leader, like Stalin!'

No wonder Vladimir Putin became revered as a *vozdh*, not least because he had driven most of the hated oligarchs abroad, and confiscated the oil tycoon Mikhail Khodorkovsky's businesses and sent him to Prison Camp No. 13 in Siberia, where he remains to this day. Now, thanks to Putin's ruthless and bullying anti-Western use of the 'energy weapon', Russia's vast oil and gas reserves, wages and pensions are actually being paid, and he is adored by the *narod*. Because of the Constitution, which forbade him to run again for President, he's now Prime Minister, but still de facto President behind the scenes. It's only we in the West – and the small but thoroughly divided cohorts of Westernized Russian liberals – who deplore his slow crushing of *demokratia*. We mocked his phrase 'managed democracy', but no wonder it became popular in Russia in view of Yeltsin's years of mismanaged democracy.

During the Yeltsin gangster-capitalism years there were frequent murders, especially among so-called bankers, whose 'banks' were mostly criminal front organizations. One day I rang Michael from Moscow and told him that several dozen Russian bankers had been murdered in contract-style killings in 1995 alone. 'Don't be silly, darling, those figures can't be right – you can't have that many murders of *bankers* without it making worldwide headlines!'

'But this isn't Britain or America, this is a Russian Wild West without a functioning sheriff!' I retorted – and I was right.

Back in 1998 before the Presidential election, oligarchs like Berezovsky had found it impossible to get access to Yeltsin: his inner court of corrupt drinking partners and cronies, fearful of losing their power over him and their own little scams, blocked the tycoons' way.

'It was just like a medieval court!' Berezovsky said as we talked in the Tsarist era Smirnov mansion, one of his many sumptuous berths around the world. His heavies forbade me to park my car near the building; a few months earlier a bomb, placed under one of Berezovsky's heavily armed Mercedes, had exploded, leaving the oligarch himself unscathed but decapitating his chauffeur.

He told me he finally got to meet up with the drunken President through his adored daughter Tatyana, a greedy and scheming woman nicknamed by Yeltsin's enemies the *Tsaretva*. 'We were very open and frank with her about the position in the country.' She needed little convincing that her father was doomed unless a new, slick, modern, high-profile re-election campaign was launched – with shedloads of robber-baron money behind it. The door to the 'Tsar' was opened. But when Berezovsky and his men got in to see him, even they were astonished to realise how completely out of touch he was with what was going on. 'He said to me, "I'm only getting 6 per cent in the polls? I don't believe it! Those figures must be wrong!" The people around him never told him anything, and he spent 90 per cent of his time with them and only 10 per cent of it with his Prime Minister. He was very upset by the news, frankly. But the very next day he took action: even I was quite shocked by the speed of his response.'

'But why,' I asked Berezovsky, 'would Yeltsin trust his political destiny to you, given your reputation in Russia as the archetypal Machiavellian robber baron?'

Berezovsky smiled. 'Of course he didn't trust me as such. He didn't trust anyone except Tatyana. But we convinced him we were sincere in our offers of help. In fact I said to him, "We don't care about you personally, Mr President, we care about us. If you are defeated we have serious doubts about our future!"'

And of course the wily old *muzhik* Yeltsin won. But when it became clear that Russia's President, a sick man, would have to relinquish power, he named – under self-interested guidance from the oligarchs – an obscure former KGB operative from St Petersburg called Vladimir Putin to be his successor. A deal between the two was suspected: for Yeltsin's support Putin, when he came to power, would not prosecute the Yeltsin 'family' (which included more than his immediate relatives) on corruption charges.

Igor had told me, during Putin's rise to power under St Petersburg's 'reformist' (but corrupt) Mayor Anatoly Sobchak, that he was astonished that this short, nondescript, martial arts fan and teetotaller had managed to get so far. 'Volodya and I were both in the KGB in East Germany, and because he had no personality we hardly noticed him.'

(When the Berlin Wall fell, back in 1989, Igor had panicked: 'I am still allowed to travel to Socialist countries, but if East Germany becomes capitalist, I will be forbidden there! I will never be allowed to visit the West again!' His identical twin brother Alexei, also in the KGB, had not yet been banned from capitalist countries. 'Should I pretend to be him?' I told him that, if that was his plan, he'd better get a move on because the whole of Communist Eastern Europe would soon become capitalist and Igor's 'window to the West' would then be completely closed.)

The next time I saw Boris Berezovsky was in London – he now lives in Britain in luxurious exile. For years Putin's government has been asking the British to extradite him to stand trial for corruption; and because we refuse to do so they, in turn, refuse to extradite another former KGB man, Andrei Lugavoi, suspected of murdering Alexander Litvinenko – yet another former KGB man, and an ally of Berezovsky – with radioactive Polonium 210. Anglo-Russian relations are now at a very low ebb.

Berezovsky employs as his PR Lord Bell, who once served Mrs Thatcher in the same capacity. The exiled oligarch now does his best to destabilize Putin's regime. 'I *made* this Putin!' he informed me bitterly in his office one day. 'Without me he would not be where he is today!'

As for Igor, I lost touch with him but, because I'd been fond of him, I tried to track him down whenever I went to Moscow. Particularly when, in 2001, on the tenth anniversary of the failed hardline coup, I interviewed the plotters, including Igor's old boss, Vladimir Kryuchkov, the former head of the KGB.

The nominal leader of the coup had been Vice-President Gennady Yanayev; Russian television, then controlled by reformists, kept focusing on his shaking hands. I already knew Yanayev was a drunk because Sasha, my psychiatrist friend, had secretly told me that he'd tried, unsuccessfully, to treat him.

'I was *not* drunk at that press conference ten years ago!' Yanayev insisted to me. 'This allegation of drunkenness is one of many myths put about by my enemies, the so-called "democrats", to blacken my name! I am a typical Russian man and it is natural for a Russian man to enjoy his drink – but I have never even had a hangover! Look at my hands now – they're not shaking, are they?' Across his office desk in Moscow, he stuck out his hands for inspection and yes, I agreed, the hands looked pretty steady to me.

'But if you weren't drunk,' I asked Yanayev, 'why were your hands shaking so much?'

'Because I was very nervous. We'd announced that Gorbachev was "ill" and would resume his duties when he recovered, because for legal reasons, we wanted to retain him as a figurehead. That was our biggest mistake, incidentally, because he has been proved out of his own mouth to be a traitor to the Communist Party, the Soviet Union and above all to the Soviet people. But the fact was that we had no medical evidence to prove his illness – because of course he wasn't ill. I even delayed that press conference for seven hours so that I could perhaps get some medical documentation to back up our claim. I wasn't taking part in some trivial circus, I was taking part in a vitally important attempt to save the country from collapse!'

One his co-conspirators, Marshall Dimitri Yazov, then head of the 3-million-strong Red Army, told me that anyone in Yanayev's position would be nervous: 'Imagine, your Queen of England hears that her crown *and her whole country* are to be abolished tomorrow – as the Soviet Union was about to be – well, wouldn't *her* hands shake too? But you wouldn't accuse *her* of being drunk, would you?'

One of the reasons the coup failed was because the hardliners like Yazov didn't mow down the demonstrators. But perhaps there were more racist reasons for Yazov's restraint – his contempt for non-Russians was evident throughout our interview, especially for Jews, Americans and blacks. Of course, Russian troops could always be counted on to kill non-Russian opponents, but perhaps, I said, he feared his troops might not be so obedient when ordered to fire on their own kind.

'Absolute rubbish!' he informed me in his loud Siberian baritone. At great length he asserted that any killings of allegedly unarmed people that his men might, possibly, already have committed in the rebellious Soviet republics occurred only in self-defence, under severe 'provocation', and were tacitly instigated by 'the West's hero' Gorbachev.

And most of the killings in places like 'the Baltic states which you seem to love so much' (he growled at me sarcastically) were opposition set-ups. 'For example, in Vilnius the Lithuanians were killing other Lithuanians, in order to blame us. They wanted blood, any blood, in order to further their aims.' In Baku, Azerbaijan's capital, the separatists, he alleged, even dug fake graves to inflate the numbers of dead in order to fool the world into believing tales of Russian brutality.

This burly, unrepentant Communist did not like even mildly challenging questions, or indeed interruptions of any kind. A couple of times he growled at me, a somewhat threatening smile on his rugged features, 'You sound more like a criminal investigator than a journalist! You ask questions like a spy.'

As a teenage soldier Yazov was wounded in World War II and still hero-worshipped Stalin. 'He was a genius – the wisest and most brilliant man in the world. He won the war – in which your people and mine were allies!' I pointed out that Stalin might have won the war rather more easily had he not stupidly purged much of his own officer corps in the midst of the conflict.

But, oh dear, here we go again: Russia's obsessive anti-Semitism raised its head once more. The extent of Stalin's purges, said Yazov, were 'exaggerated' by his enemies, largely Jews, and anyway it was all Trotsky's fault (he was a Jew) who, as an enemy of Stalin, had infiltrated his own people into every institution. I sighed wearily.

Yazov soon got extremely irritated by my perverse refusal to grasp the importance of the 'Jewish problem' in Russia, past and present. 'How many Jews are there in your Prime Minister Blair's Cabinet?'

he barked at me. No idea, I replied. Besides, why does it matter? 'Of *course* it matters! Jews always have their own agenda! I've nothing against Jews, they're talented people, but why should they be allowed to exploit the Russian people?'

Earlier that year I'd been seriously ill, had several operations and spent months in hospital. The trouble is that even when you feel well again, you tend to obsess on your innards. Which was, unfortunately, the case when I perched on a velveteen sofa in an old Politburo flat talking to Vladimir Kryuchkov. This one-time head of the KGB had been the mastermind of the coup and showed absolutely no contrition. Not surprisingly, he was full of praise for the then President Putin: 'All we true Communists have an extremely high opinion of him!' (And neither he nor his fellow conspirators served the expected long sentences for their destabilizing plot.)

The Comrade was a bit rocky on his legs ever since he'd had a spinal operation. I found myself indulging in a bizarre bout of medical one-upmanship with him about our assorted ailments – 'You see, *my* operation lasted . . .' 'Well, I've had *three* operations, which . . .'

I reminded myself of all those thousands of innocent lives that this cold, cruel Stalinist had utterly destroyed in his long KGB career, and suddenly thought how grotesque it was to be actually sympathizing with this aged monster.

As I left I asked him, 'By the way, Comrade Kryuchkov, do you happen to know the current whereabouts of Igor Kuzmin, one of your former agents?' No, he didn't. And neither did any of the other ex-KGB men to whom I relayed my query.

So, as I said all those years ago on television, 'Bye bye, Igor, it was good to know you.'

11

Storm-tossed with
Mikhail and George

'You weren't on the Press Bus! Where the hell have you been?' a
journalist on the rival *Express* demanded suspiciously.

'Oh, I missed it. I was held up having coffee with Gorbachev in
his suite, having a girly chat with Raisa about her party frock, you
know, that sort of thing,' I replied nonchalantly. 'Anyway, anything
going on here?'

'Here' was the Press Centre in a storm-swept Valletta in Malta
during the 1989 Superpower Summit between the Soviet President
Gorbachev and the then American President George Herbert Walker
Bush (the father of George W.).

Now obviously I couldn't be telling the truth. Mere hacks like us
were always nobodies at these summits; posses of Soviet and American security men with wires in their ears and guns in their waist-
bands made sure that we always knew our place – which was well
behind the rope lines. The most we rope-line folk would get would
be a few futile shouts at the passing 'Principals': 'How are the talks
going, Mr President?' And the most we'd get in reply would be 'Very
well, thank you!' For all you knew, the 'Principals' had actually spent
the last few hours foaming at the mouth and upending each other
on the Axminster like a couple of maddened Sumo wrestlers. The
only semi-confirmation of that would be a diplo-speak statement
that there'd been 'full and frank discussions'.

But actually I *was* telling the truth about where I'd been, so I
retailed it to people back in the Press Centre because I knew none of
them would believe me.

As with so many minor scoops (mine, anyway), it all happened by
accident. And if a trio of pushy Italian journalists hadn't been so

unpleasant and racist to my friend Patsy Robertson, who is black, and who was in charge of pool ticket arrangements, it wouldn't have happened at all.

At Superpower Summits, one third of pool tickets would be reserved for American journalists, one third for Soviet, and one third for the Rest of the World. Which meant you'd have to join a lottery with hordes of Libyans, Malaysians, Australians, Samoans and, indeed, Italians.

In her customary charming, efficient and unflappable way, Patsy told the Italian trio that unfortunately there were no more pool tickets available for the next meeting between Gorbachev and Bush. They unleashed a stream of invective, much of it centred on the colour of her skin. She didn't respond of course, except to repeat that pool ticket allocations, of which there were only 100, were now full. (There were 2,300 registered media at the Summit.)

If Patsy, ever professional, was not going to respond to this racist crap, then I would. And I did, rather forcefully. (I'm not sure now, but I've a dreadful feeling that I may have cracked that old, equally racist, joke, 'What's the shortest book in history? *The Italian Book of War Heroes*'.) When I'd seen off the Italians, Patsy whispered, 'Thank you!' and slipped a pool ticket into my jacket sleeve. 'I always keep one spare for emergencies.'

Trouble was, I didn't want it. The meeting was on Saturday and I didn't work for our sister paper, the *Mail on Sunday*. But because I knew Patsy had, briefly, modified her professional code, I thought that out of gratitude I should at least use the precious pool ticket.

As I waited for hours in the cold and freezing rain to get through security, I wished I hadn't. We were queuing to get on to the Russian cruise liner which housed Gorbachev and the Soviet delegation, the *Maxim Gorky*, which was tied up alongside a dismal scrap-metal yard on Marsaxlokk Quay. President Bush's 'White House' was an American warship moored nearby.

By the time we'd been herded like rabid cattle into the bowels of the *Maxim Gorky*, with the KGB and the American Secret Service peremptorily whipping us back behind the rope-line, we were all drenched and mutinous. We then waited for President Bush to arrive. And waited. And waited.

The Soviet choice of the *Maxim Gorky* as a combined Kremlincum-hotel (it saved spending precious hard currency in Malta) might not have been, for a congenitally superstitious people, an entirely wise choice: the omens were not good.

The ship once starred in *Juggernaut*, a disaster movie about a cruise ship and a terrorist bomb – but luckily, on that occasion, Omar Sharif saved it from catastrophe. It hadn't been so lucky six months prior to the Summit: bearing its more usual passenger-load of German tourists, it managed to hit an iceberg while cruising in Arctic waters. One thousand rich and elderly passengers had to scramble to safety on passing ice floes.

By now my teeth were chattering and my fingers were turning blue. I had to get some hot coffee or I'd die of hypothermia. The *Maxim Gorky*'s current captain, a huge man called Vitaly Grishin, loomed into view behind the rope-line. (After the iceberg mishap, the ship's previous captain was now doubtless peeling spuds in some Soviet NAAFI in darkest Murmansk.)

Would Captain Grishin be susceptible to a spot of flirting from a capitalist lackey like me? Gazing up the vast, bemedalled cliff of his chest I decided, *à la russe*, to eschew subtlety. What a *fantastic* compliment it must be to his skill that he and his ship had been chosen out of the *entire Soviet Navy*, with all its *glorious* history, to host this world-shakingly important event!

Captain Grishin succumbed immediately. He had, he told me proudly, temporarily and patriotically given up his creature comforts for the sake of world peace. 'My quarters are now being occupied by President and Mrs Gorbachev. My quarters, they are very nice – six rooms, bathrooms, a, how you say, barber, and a nice little dining room – but only space in dining room for two people!'

I told him how cold I was, how I longed for some hot coffee. 'Unfortunately,' said the suddenly gloomy face above the medals, 'the KGB is now in charge of my ship. If it was me, I would invite you up to the Volga Bar.'

'But Captain Grishin!' I expostulated, shocked. 'A Captain is always the captain of his ship! If there were to be an accident to this ship, who would be responsible for saving the passengers? The KGB? Of course not – it would be *you*, Captain Grishin!'

He rallied and gave me directions to the Volga Bar but said that he had, temporarily, no authority to take me there. I joined Hella

Pick, the *Guardian*'s Diplomatic Correspondent, who was standing nearby and who was as cold and fed up as I was.

Hella is very tall and naturally imperious. I am rather short, but can do imperious when the situation demands. We strode up the stairs in the direction of the Volga Bar. Assorted KGB and Secret Service men would waylay us, but we'd do the imperious bit, invoke the name of Captain Grishin, and finally emerged in the vast Volga Bar.

I've always believed that if you behave as if you have an inalienable right to be wherever you wish to be – and simply cannot understand how anyone could question it – most minions and even the KGB tend to lose their nerve long enough for you to proceed in the direction intended.

Indeed, such imperiousness got me where I wanted to be at Emperor Hirohito's funeral in Tokyo. The international press were corralled by the deeply conservative Imperial Household Agency into a freezing tent about half a mile away in a muddy field. I wanted to get into the Kings' and Presidents' area at the Imperial funeral, not least because I wanted to see whether the Duke of Edinburgh, the Queen's representative at the event, would bow deferentially to Hirohito's coffin, thus enraging former Japanese prisoners of war back in Britain.

Security was tight, not only because of the presence of so many world leaders, but also because of bomb threats by Japanese left-wing groups. Police choppers constantly clacked overhead.

'Where's your pass?' I was asked by various Japanese security officers as I marched through the mud towards the VIP tent. 'Oh, don't be so silly,' I'd say firmly but with, hopefully, a certain Grand Duchess charm, as I swept on by. As the Japanese all look alike to Westerners, I presumed that all Westerners would look alike to the Japanese, and that they might therefore be nervous of dropping a diplomatic clanger.

I ended up standing in the same row as the then President George H. W. Bush. I'd once interviewed him, when he was Vice-President, aboard Air Force Two on his Presidential campaign and I realized, as he kept peering at me, that he was thinking, 'Have I met this woman before?' Perhaps just in case I was the queen of some minor European country whom it would be crass to offend, Bush kept giving me slow, slightly puzzled, lopsided smiles of 'recognition'. Needless to say, had I had an AK47 stashed under my voluminous fur coat, I could have wiped out most of the world's leaders in two minutes flat.

But back to the *Maxim Gorky*. Hella and I ordered coffee from the sole barman in the cavernous and empty Volga Bar. Then the place suddenly filled up. President Gorbachev, wearing a smart pin-striped suit and a maroon silk tie, strode in. To our astonishment he joined Hella and me. 'Soviet coffee, very good, yes?' he twinkled.

He may have been short and stocky, with the large, disfiguring birthmark on his forehead (in official portraits it was always air-brushed out), but I'd always found Mikhail Sergeyevich rather sexy. Indeed, earlier I'd made the mistake of saying so to our own distinguished Diplomatic Correspondent who, like my censorious tutor at Oxford, condemned me for my 'triviality'. 'How can you use the word *sexy* in connection with the second most powerful man in the world?!'

'Oh, very easily, John, very easily.'

Our Diplomatic Correspondent was a dapper gentleman who always wore a red carnation in his buttonhole. Unfortunately, due to the storm (locals said it was the worst since St Paul was washed up on Gozo), flower buttonholes were in short supply in Malta. Remembering John's distress, I surreptitiously nicked a carnation head for him from the floral display in the Gorbachev suite. When I later presented it to him as a peace offering, John snapped crossly, 'It's the wrong colour, this is *pink*!'

As Gorbachev swept into the bar, there was his interpreter, there were all his aides, minds and pencils sharpened for the second bout of Superpower fray, there were his military experts ('Ah, Comrade Karpov!'), there were his foreign policy advisers ('Dreadful storm, Comrade Dobrynin!'), there was his feline foreign affairs spokesman, Gennady Gerasimov, drawling, 'I still have hopes,' there were the serried ranks of the American Secret Service and the KGB, and there was the magnificently uniformed figure of the Soviet Navy's Marshal Sergei Chernayev.

There, indeed, was virtually the entire Soviet military and political establishment, roaming the carpeted acres of the Volga Bar.

All had been set for the next 'historic breakthrough' in Superpower relations at this Summit. But (to echo the Democrats' campaign jibes at Bush the previous year), 'Where was George?' Stuck on a boat with a broken ladder, that's where. Couldn't get off his warship for his meeting with the Soviet President. 'What are we going to do? What are we going to do?' barked Gorbachev in irritation, darting accusatory glances at harried aides and a clutch of deeply embarrassed American officials.

At that point he should have been an hour-and-a-half into talks in the liner's card room with the missing George – and instead found himself reduced to talking about Bush's broken ladder and his rotten Navy to Hella and me. 'Is *your* Navy so unreliable?'

How had the meetings gone so far? 'The meetings have been fine!' Will there be another one tonight? He looked at me levelly and gave a sardonic, almost flirtatious, shrug. 'Depends. If President Bush arrives.' Then, eyes glittering with mischief, he added, 'But if I have to – I'll swim over there myself!'

'Over there', a mere 400 metres or so away across the heaving Maltese waters, lay the *Belknap*, the flagship of the US Sixth Fleet, bristling with armaments and the best telecommunications equipment dollars can buy, but now transformed into an armour-plated prison for an incommunicado American President, who was at that moment desperately trying to keep down his lunch.

In fact it was Mikhail Sergeyevich who had provided the lunch, and mercifully for Bush, a medicated anti-sickness patch managed to preserve the lunch's presence in the Presidential tummy.

Why, Gorbachev was perhaps asking himself, had Bush insisted on leaving the safe confines of the *Maxim Gorky* in the first place? Because, it was said, after their first meeting the President wanted to 'rest and confer' in the tiny 'electronic bubble' room on the *Belknap* which shielded all secrets from Soviet eyes and ears – doubtless including the now not-very-secret fact that the American President was feeling as sick as a parrot.

Perhaps, I thought, as I watched Gorbachev move round the room discussing the hapless matelot George's plight, Bush would be forced to semaphore his Arms Reduction Proposals to us on the Soviet ship?

Or was there an intrepid pigeon on board the *Belknap* which could be launched towards Mikhail, bearing in its beak George's latest *feuilleton* on the Jackson–Vannick Amendment? (The Amendment meant no country was allowed to be granted 'most favoured nation' trade status if it restricted, as the Soviet Union did, the free movement of its citizens.)

Would a despairing Secretary of State James Baker finally have to strap the President to the fo'c'sle and let him signal the American position on Nicaragua to the Soviets with flashing mirrors?

Or would the two Superpower Presidents, having come all the way to confer in person in a ferocious Mediterranean storm, now have to conduct their negotiations entirely by phone just as if they were back home in Moscow and Washington?

I wrote: 'What, Americans may ask, is the point of having the most sophisticated navy in the world if, at the first spot of bad weather, it manages to reduce their President to the status of an incompetent weekend sailor who's lost his paddle on a trip round the lighthouse?'

As American aides hurried up to deliver the latest news about the stranded Bush across the water, Gorbachev's expression varied mercurially between irritation and amusement.

'It's the starboard ladder . . . got broken somehow . . . much too dangerous to try to get the President off . . . helicopter can't fly . . . weather forecast getting worse . . .'

'*Da, da!*'

As Gorbachev moved away from Hella and me several Soviets around him looked almost preternaturally poker-faced: perhaps, like me, they were biting their cheeks to avoid bursting into incredulous laughter at the increasingly bizarre situation.

The Soviet Foreign Minister Eduard Shevardnadze walked over to us and made jokes about the uselessness of the American Navy. 'Is your Navy as bad?' We toyed with alternative methods of getting the two Presidents together, short of allowing Gorbachev to leap overboard and do a suicidal breast-stroke towards the *Belknap*. Perhaps we could do a parachute drop! Or perhaps you could send a submarine, we suggested. 'Ah, good idea!'

If only the massed ranks of the US Navy could finally mend the President's ladder, the Soviets were willing to welcome him aboard as an overnight guest; Presidential spokesman Gennady Gerasimov was apparently quite willing, in the cause of world peace, to doss down in the Volga Bar lounge. 'I have offered President Bush my cabin to sleep in tonight!'

By now Captain Grishin had also turned up, eager again to do his bit for world peace. 'I have zees two large boats, very big, very powerful, very strong. No, not my lifeboats. Tenders for taking passengers ashore. Perhaps we lend you one to try help you fetch your President?'

An American official, whiskers twitching like an alarmed rabbit, gazed up the vast expanse of Captain Grishin's chest towards his huge and amiable potato-face. 'Er, well, sir, that is very kind, very kind! But, er, I think we may come back to you on this but, er, at the moment . . .'

Perhaps he knew about Omar Sharif or the Arctic iceberg, or both.

Margaret Tutwiler, the State Department's spokeswoman, was declaring in her ringing Suth'n tones: 'This is a *mess*!' So, indeed, was she: the usually elegant Ms Tutwiler (inevitably nicknamed by the White House press corps 'Queen Tut') had clearly abandoned all hopes of a stable hairdo in the face of the Force 8 gales. Shortly after that she disappeared, and mysteriously re-emerged in a plastic mac and hood: perhaps she, too, remembered Omar or the Arctic ice floes and wanted to be ready, just in case.

Suddenly, I heard a high-pitched voice trilling at me behind my back: 'Good afternoon! Good afternoon!' It was Raisa Gorbachev, looking ravishingly sexy in her bright red party frock. 'I have put on dress for no purpose! Is big shame!' She headed past us to join her husband in the depths of the bar and the couple sat down at a little table, smiling and nodding, and began to drink coffee. Coffee over, we asked Gorbachev as he came back past us, 'How are you enjoying Malta?' Laughing, he replied, 'We're still trying it, we're still trying it!'

Raisa's pretty party frock had been donned in vain: the talks and the dinner party on the *Maxim Gorky* were to be abandoned for want of one crucial but stranded guest. 'Oh, look at the storm!' Raisa trilled, as indeed she must have been doing for the preceding twenty-four hours. Clearly Bush's wife Barbara, by refusing to countenance this madcap sea-borne Summit, had scored over Raisa by staying away.

For more than an hour, I thought incredulously, Hella and I had been allowed to stroll about the inner sanctum of Gorbachev's floating Kremlin, chatting to him, his wife, his foreign minister and his entourage – despite helpless pleas of '*Pozhalusto*, please! Please move away!' from various bewildered and equally incredulous KGB men. What price 'ring-of-steel' security clichés now?

Later, back on the rain-lashed quay, we flagged down a US Defence Department car. As we drove through the darkness towards Valletta, the two officials in the car, clutching large metal boxes on their knees, were trying to put a brave face on the fiasco. Wasn't this terribly embarrassing for you Americans, I asked.

'No, we, er, don't see it that way. We kinda think the embarrassment is about equal on both sides. You see, the Soviets couldn't get on to the *Slava*, their accompanying warship, either. So we think their Navy is about the same as ours, in that respect.'

'Ah, but their President was not stranded out at sea like yours!'

'Yes,' they agreed sadly, 'that is, er, unfortunately very true.'

Back in the Press Centre a Norwegian journalist was studying a press release about the postponed talks. 'Can you believe this? The President of the country with the most powerful Navy in the world can't get off his ship just because there's a bit of a wind blowing – we in Norway have much worse storms, and we are transporting men to and from oil rigs every day!'

But, I pointed out, to lose a Norwegian oil-rigger or two might be unfortunate, but to lose President Bush in the same way might prove catastrophic: 'It would be Hail to the Chief – President Dan Quayle'. The Norwegian paled. 'Oh, my God – I hadn't thought of that!'

Bush had hoped (he'd said) not to 'do something dumb' at this Summit; obviously, he'd failed. The moral of this tale, I concluded, was that God, despite rumours to the contrary, does have a sense of humour. Clearly He decided that both men, their Navies and their Superpower pretensions needed puncturing: and what better way to do that than to zap them with a violent storm, thus rendering them helpless in the face of a brilliantly timed meteorological joke from on high?

12

The Wall Comes Down

Night after night in 1989 television news around the Western world was showing huge, peaceful demonstrations against the East German Communist government in the grimy industrial city of Leipzig, with the crowds chanting, '*Wir wollen raus!*' ('We want out!'). David English, the *Mail*'s Editor, rang me at home: 'What do you think is going to happen next over there?'

'Well, the East German Politburo ultimately only has two options,' I told him. 'The first is the "Chinese Solution" – which is to gun 'em down, like the Chinese did in Tiananmen Square four months ago. But they daren't do that because they know that the Soviets, under Gorbachev, won't give permission – because if he allowed a massacre to take place that'd give the lie to all his West-sweetening rhetoric about *perestroika* and reform. He's already given warning to the East German government that he's not going to come to their rescue. And their own troops are outnumbered by the 390,000 Soviet troops based on their soil. This isn't East Germany in '53, Hungary in '56 or Czechoslovakia in '68. Stalinists in the Soviet satellite states are now out on their own.

'Option Two? Well, in one way or another, they're going to have to bring down the Wall.'

'So when can you go?'

'Well, I'm a bit tied up at the moment. Look, I don't think any of this is going to happen immediately. Nothing happens that fast under Communism!' I pronounced confidently. 'I'll go in about a fortnight's time, once I've rejigged my diary.'

And, in a fairly unhurried way, I did rejig it. I'm appalled, looking back, to think I might have dawdled too long and thereby missed not only one of the most exciting stories I've ever covered, but an event which changed the world for ever.

There was, however, a slight problem. I'd been before to the German Democratic Republic, as the East German Communists called it, and after writing a fairly anodyne, if mocking, piece about the 'triumphs' of what they called 'real, existing Socialism', they'd refused me another journalist visa. One should never underestimate the pressure on journalists who are desperate to get a visa and, once in the country, not to get expelled; it does tend to put a dampener on any tendency towards uppity criticism.

Oh well, no matter – all I had to do was go to West Berlin and cross over to the East on a tourist visa. But my previous fixer seemed to have gone to ground, possibly because I was already persona non grata. In West Berlin a contact suggested I get in touch with an East Berliner called Wiebke Reed.

'She's a lovely girl, speaks perfect English and was once married to Dean Reed'. Dean who? An inexplicable question to anyone in the Soviet bloc at that time. Reed was the Denver-born son of a respectable, conservative family who'd tried to become a pop star in America. He once briefly got into the bottom of the top 100 in the charts.

Desperate to salvage a fading career, he began touring Latin America where he discovered Marxism and declared, 'I have become a revolutionary!' Although he couldn't sing very well, his good looks and the fact that this was a Yanqui-bashing Yanqui made him a huge hit. He even sang at the Marxist Salvador Allende's presidential inauguration in Chile, and was to repeat his triumphs in the Soviet bloc.

Russia's Khrushchev and East Germany's then dictator Erich Honecker decided that Dean was their answer to the capitalist Beatles, whose music was dangerously infecting their local proletariats. As Honecker's successor, Egon Krenz, ruefully put it long after Reed's death, 'I was sure we had got ourselves a Hollywood star!' The East German authorities spread the lie that his song 'Our Summer Romance' had reached No. 2 in the US billboard charts. Elena, a friend of mine in Moscow, told me, 'In my teens I absolutely worshipped Dean. We all wanted to marry him!'

Unfortunately, or (in the event) fortunately, for Elena the adored Dean met and married a beautiful young teacher with strawberry-blonde hair from Dresden called Wiebke, even getting special permission to do so from Honecker himself. Their marriage broke up when Reed left Wiebke and their daughter for a well-known East German actress. By the Eighties an increasingly restless populace in East Germany had tired of their Red Elvis; he was a 'salon Bolshevik' who, unlike them, was able to travel the world and lived in comparative luxury in a lakeside villa provided at a peppercorn rent by the state. His relentlessly Marxist down-with-capitalism message now bored and annoyed them; belief in Communist ideology had collapsed long before the states which promoted it finally themselves collapsed. Reed's continued defence – 'it's still necessary' – of the Berlin Wall (officially called 'The Anti-Fascist Protection Rampart') added to his former fans' disillusion.

He committed suicide aged forty-eight. He had grown to loathe the regime himself, and had taken refuge in alcohol. Now that Steven Spielberg and Tom Hanks are planning a bio-pic on the 'Comrade Rock Star', Dean Reed may eventually achieve in death the fame in his home country which eluded him in life.

Of course, someone like Wiebke who'd got high-level permission to marry such a 'national asset' could not, I thought, be anything but a Stasi 'asset' herself. We in the spoiled West forget now how the Stasi, the secret police, infiltrated every corner of East German life. At its height the Stasi greatly outnumbered (per head of population) Hitler's Gestapo, and around one in five of all East Germans were either employed directly by the Stasi or were 'IMs' – *Inoffizieller Mitarbeiter* (unofficial co-workers) – who spied on their neighbours, their colleagues, even members of their own family. The German film *The Lives of Others* (which won an Oscar in 2007) portrays the atmosphere of fear, paranoia and betrayal that infected the whole society.

But even though I suspected Wiebke, I certainly wouldn't have blamed her if indeed she were an 'IM'. After all, she had to survive in this society which, as far as she knew at the time, would never change. Erich Honecker himself had proudly proclaimed a mere nine months before I arrived in East Berlin that 'the Wall will survive for fifty or even one hundred years'. Would I, in Wiebke's situation, have acted any differently? If, in order not to be bothered by the Stasi, she wrote bland reports about my activities, well, so what? The worst that would happen to me was that I would get expelled.

Besides, it's not always a bad idea to employ a fixer who you suspect may have a formal or informal 'arrangement' with the state. Some of my best fixers – who are much more than mere interpreters – have been people with 'arrangements' of this kind: Igor, the KGB man in Russia; the woman who came from the same Montenegrin town as Radovan Karadzic and was a family friend of the Bosnian Serb leader; the Chinese driver/fixer who had 'access' to a curtained Politburo car which enabled me to get through checkpoints near the North Korean border; the man who was an employee of the Iranian government but who, when he suspected I had also secretly hired someone more independent, did not choose to betray me: he was 'just doing his job', and he knew I was just doing mine, and he trusted me enough to know that I would do my best to protect him in the event of any 'misunderstanding' when my articles were published.

In my view, there can be no greater crime as a journalist than betraying one's fixer, even if only out of carelessness. A journalistic team who subsequently employed my Iranian fixer committed that crime, and this good and brave man ended up in solitary confinement for weeks in Tehran's notorious Evin prison. He lost his job and his family was reduced to near-penury.

Too many foreign correspondents choose to gloss over the essential role of the fixer, preferring to strut about posing as lone gunslingers. The fact is that, without the ingenuity and courage of knowledgeable fixers (who naturally charge a sizeable wodge of cash for their services), most of these gung-ho chaps would be stumbling about in an alien landscape like blind men without a stick.

The advantages of using someone who has some sort of 'arrangement' with the powers-that-be is that he or she is someone with invaluable contacts, someone who knows (sometimes in the biblical sense) the man or woman in charge of special passes, or who can borrow an 'official' car that will ensure no jobsworth dares stop you, or who is the cousin of the woman who is sleeping with the married police chief and who therefore may be able to exert some useful pressure.

Ideally, a fixer should also have a sense of humour, otherwise – in times of privation and danger – the strain can get to both of you. A spot of gallows humour, especially from someone who knows the madness of his own country well, is a great releaser of tension.

Once, in the coup-ridden Congo, I stood on the river bank and pointed to a huge clump of water-weed floating by. 'What exactly is that stuff?' I asked. My Congolese fixer thought for a moment, then threw his head back and laughed uproariously: 'Probably the last Minister of Education!'

In East Germany Wiebke Reed, whatever the truth about her previous activities, struck me as potentially an ideal fixer. And so she proved. (And, contrary to my suspicions, she was not an IM, and won a libel suit against an author who alleged she'd been 'put into Dean's bed' by the Stasi.)

When I arrived in East Berlin in that first week of November 1989, I checked into one of its better hotels, a dreary concrete 'workers' paradise' establishment with chipped paintwork, brown furniture, hectically patterned carpets and sullen, unhelpful staff. Dusty rubber-plants, so beloved of all Communist regimes, dotted the lobby.

The hotel, like the rest of East Berlin, stank of cheap petrol, pickled cabbage and lignite coal fumes. Unlike the hectic Western half of the city, the dour Eastern half went to bed early; the few cars on the streets were Wartburgs and Trabants, the only two makes available to ordinary people, and then only after many years on a waiting list. I soon learned that the two-stroke Trabi, fashioned out of waste cotton and resin, inspired endless surreptitious jokes: '"Comrade Schultz, you will get delivery of a Trabant in ten years' time on 20 February." Schultz: "Morning or afternoon? I have a plumber coming in the morning."'

All oppressed peoples, if they have enough energy, tend to crack political jokes, which are in themselves tiny explosions of popular rebellion. These jokes would mysteriously mutate and spread like some air-borne virus across distant borders and, since they are never printed at the time, no one could quite explain exactly how that happened.

Five months before my arrival in East Berlin I'd been in Beijing, shortly after the massacre in Tiananmen Square. The man who'd ordered the massacre was the Chinese Premier Li Peng. My undercover Beijing fixer told me the most popular political joke currently doing the rounds in the capital. 'There's this man walking round the Square with a huge placard saying, "Li Peng is a pig!" The PSB, the security guys, arrest him and charge him on two counts. One, for holding an illegal demonstration. And two, for telling the truth.'

When a young East Berliner told me the self-same joke, albeit substituting the East German Communist boss Egon Krenz's name for Li Peng's and the Stasi for the PSB, I didn't have the heart to tell him I'd already heard it before in China. Just as I didn't have the heart to break it to a young Muscovite three years earlier that I'd heard his joke before in East Germany, only then it was about Erich Honecker. 'There's this long queue outside a shop and one man in the queue suddenly shouts out: "I'm totally fed up! I'm now going off to murder Gorbachev!" Several hours later he returns to the same queue. "What happened? Did you murder Gorbachev?" "No," says the man. "The queue was too long."'

That first night in East Berlin when I looked out of my grimy hotel window I thought, my God, this glum city is popularly supposed by people in other Communist regimes – especially in the Soviet Union – to be virtually Western in its wealth, style and sophistication! But then they'd never been allowed across the nearby border into the Western half of the city, never seen the lights of the glittering Ku'damm, West Berlin's equivalent of Bond Street, or stayed in the luxurious Kempinski Hotel, or visited the huge Ka De We department store whose food hall was stuffed with, among many other things, *fresh fruit and vegetables*! East Berliners dreamed of one day being able to sink their teeth into a banana. The lack of this everyday fruit also inspired a slew of surreptitious political jokes: 'Question: how do we know that East Germans cannot be descended from apes? Answer: because no ape could have gone forty years without a banana'; and another Trabi joke: 'How do you treble your car's value? Put a banana on the back seat.' I sometimes wondered why East Germans weren't riddled with scurvy from the lack of vitamin C.

I woke up the next morning to a bombshell. The entire East German Politburo had resigned. With Wiebke I went to see Marianne Birthler, a tall, rangy woman wearing earnest steel-framed spectacles, in her makeshift office in a Lutheran church which overlooked a railway line in a working-class district of the city. The church's youth group had been organizing anti-government demonstrations: 'Two weeks ago,' Birthler told me, 'those of us in this human rights group prepared all our papers and wrote letters for our children, in case the worst happened. We were really afraid. The "Chinese Solution" seemed a real possibility.'

But now she was wildly elated by the news of the Politburo resignations: 'Wonderful! Wonderful! But we still have Egon Krenz, and Krenz must go too!' He'd been the leader of an internal Politburo 'putsch' which had just ousted Honecker and was now General Secretary.

I wrote at the time: 'Suddenly, in the heady atmosphere of East Berlin today, even the departure of Krenz seems possible. As Birthler put it, shaking her head in disbelief, "Everything here is happening so fast now, every day something astonishing happens!"'

Of course, the hated Krenz and his Communist cronies would never have been seen dead in this shabby district. As Wiebke told me, 'They live in another world which we've nicknamed "Volvograd" because these old Stalinists are all driven around in curtained Volvos, and I think, until just now, they didn't physically see or hear what the people were saying. They had totally cut themselves off from reality.'

Like the Soviet leaders, they lived in special compounds, had state-supplied domestic staff, had the use of special private shops stocked with luxury foreign goods unavailable to the 'workers and peasants' they ruled, and had their illnesses dealt with in state-provided special hospitals. They even hunted in special private forests, stocked by the Party with furred and feathered game and (a favourite of Honecker's) wild boar. A vast tract of the 2.7-million-acre Brandenburg Forest was sealed off for their private pleasure, as were whole stretches of the Baltic beaches.

The reason they favoured Swedish Volvos instead of Mercedes or BMWs was because they were not built by 'fascist' West Germany. The bosses of the 'workers and peasants' party of course made sure that the workers and peasants themselves never had access to any such goodies.

But even these protected Communist bosses couldn't shut out the sound of the swelling street demonstrations for ever. They'd tried to disassociate themselves from the reforming Gorbachev, banning Soviet publications like the magazine *Sputnik* which had been shining an unwelcome light on past Communist malpractice, including murder. The magazine had even unearthed evidence that the pre-Nazi Communist Party in Germany had refused to join an alliance to stop the rise of Hitler. The entire credibility of this so-called 'Anti-Fascist State' was thus at stake.

But until he was ousted the aged Erich Honecker, who'd been in power for eighteen years, remained obstinate. He'd even had the cheek to tell Gorbachev that his *perestroika* (reconstruction) policy was completely unnecessary in East Germany because the German Democratic Republic was already pretty well perfect. The 'concrete heads' in the East German Politburo had hoped that Gorbachev would be overthrown and that the Soviet Union would 'return to its senses'.

They looked towards China which, in their view, had successfully destroyed the 'counter-revolutionary traitors' in its midst by unleashing the Tiananmen massacre. I'd actually been in Beijing on the day when the visiting Egon Krenz, his sallow, vulpine face wreathed with what his countrymen called his 'Dracula smile', publicly congratulated the Chinese leadership for its murderous actions on 4 June. As I'd seen at first hand the tank tracks in Changan Avenue and the dried blood in crevices on the walls, Krenz's statement made me feel sick to my stomach.

Alas for East Germany, its 'Socialist brother' Hungary had already been infected by Gorbachev's 'madness' and had begun opening its borders with Austria and the West. Thousands of East Germany's best, brightest and youngest loaded up their coughing Trabis, which then chugged like rusty lawnmowers into Hungary, and from there on into Austria. They then applied for asylum in the West. The GDR was bleeding to death.

By now everyone I met – even the normally taciturn cleaners in the hotel lavatories – was talking so openly that I decided to try to get official press accreditation. I went round to the Information Ministry and admitted that I was in the city 'illegally' but said that I would like an official press pass. The woman in charge, a hatchet-faced Party functionary who looked like Rosa Klebb, the slab-sided killer in a Bond film, merely shrugged: 'Well, this place is going completely mad. So I don't see why not.'

Which is the only reason I was at the press conference that Thursday night. It was to be given by the Berlin Politburo boss,

Günther Schabowski, and promised to be intensely boring. I merely wanted to test my new press credentials and intended to leave early on because the conference was billed as being about 'the forthcoming Party plenum'. Yawn.

Which was exactly what every other journalist present felt; by now we were all so exhausted that several press people used Comrade Schabowki's droning announcements to have a spot of shut-eye. The ITN man beside me kept having to shake himself awake.

And then, at 6.57 p.m., three minutes before the scheduled end of the conference, Schabowski fished out a piece of paper and said, with an air of slight surprise, 'Oh, this might interest you.' He then read out a convoluted statement which implied that East Germans would now be able to travel freely to the West. One reporter called out: 'When?' Schabowski, looking confused, peered at a piece of paper and said that, as far as he knew, '*Ab sofort*', with immediate effect.

Pandemonium. Comrade Schabowski then fled into the Gents, pursued by a bunch of pressmen demanding clarification. But the press conference had been broadcast live and I knew that millions of East Germans would fasten on that '*Ab sofort*', rather than any bureaucratic 'clarification'. It emerged that Schabowski had blundered; the announcement was a draft and, in any case, wasn't supposed to be announced until the next day. Some suspected he was drunk, an allegation he indignantly denied.

My heart pounding with disbelief, I rushed out to go to Checkpoint Charlie. It looked the same as it had done for the last twenty-eight years: floodlights, concrete blocks, heavily armed Vopos, border guards, muffled up in greatcoats, blowing on their fingers, their breath hanging like steam in the freezing night air; a clichéd scene from endless spy movies.

Apart from the Vopos, Wiebke and I were the only people there. When I asked the guards if they'd heard the news, they looked uncharacteristically confused and nervous: one young officer's spots seemed to be erupting with fright as I spoke. I wondered whether he feared being lynched by a vengeful mob – which, at that point, seemed unlikely to turn up.

A more senior guard replied slowly and carefully, but without the usual cold dismissiveness – perhaps he and his colleagues knew in their heart of hearts that all those years of imprisonment, torture and murder of innocent people in the cause of 'Real Existing Socialism' had been utterly pointless. 'Yes, we heard Comrade Schabowski's statement on the radio, but we do not know what is happening. We have not been given any new orders. We cannot get through to our superiors.' (At least one of the superiors, oblivious of Schabowski's blunder, had gone to the opera.) 'But, as you can see, there are no crowds here.'

I began to feel as if I'd dreamt what I'd heard at 6.57 that evening. Wiebke and I raced round to another border checkpoint at the Friedrichstrasse railway station. Same largely deserted spy-movie scene. But Schabowski's casually spoken '*Ab sofort*' had lit a fuse which was now slowly and steadily burning. It led to an explosion which, with remarkably few deaths, would destroy the entire blood-soaked Eastern European Communist empire in a mere six weeks. It inspired the 'velvet revolution' in Czechoslovakia, the ousting of Todor Zhivkov in Bulgaria and of the Ceausescus in Romania – and, eighteen months later, the collapse of the Soviet regime itself.

The Cold War which had dominated my generation and divided the world ended not with the nuclear bang – which we all sub-consciously feared – but with an almost banal whimper, a stupid blunder, and the sound of thousands of little household hammers battering their way through the high concrete Wall.

But at first the initial absence of crowds that night unnerved me. I'd obviously got it wrong: East Berliners were evidently too cautious, too afraid to take that '*Ab sofort*' literally. I turned away from the checkpoint, intending to return to my hotel. And then suddenly I saw in the distance a vast tsunami of young East Germans: they were heading slowly, inexorably towards me and the border with the West.

As they drew closer I saw in the vanguard a daring little group of young people, giggling nervously among themselves. Wearing cheap Turkish leather jackets and stone-washed jeans, they began to queue with German orderliness when they reached the checkpoint. They just wanted, they told me, 'to go over to the West for twenty minutes, just to see what it's like!'

And then, astonishingly, that first hesitantly lapping wave of youngsters at the border turned into a torrent of 'Ossies', East Ger-mans, pouring unhindered through the barriers. The once-deadly border guards were utterly helpless and, I suspected, deeply afraid. 'We Are the People,' the demonstrators had chanted in the weeks before. And the people were now taking over.

As the crowd built up, Wiebke decided to go home. Years later she told me, 'I was so afraid, I thought this will not end peacefully, there will be shooting. So I'm so sorry, poor Ann, I left you alone!'

That night East Berlin was delirious; Trabis and Wartburgs, belching exhaust fumes and coughing with joy, raced up and down the streets honking their horns, flashing their headlights. Watching them, I felt that the cars themselves had grown skittish and, like their owners, were frisking noisily through the night streets like puppies suddenly let out to play.

However, not every journalist present at Schabowski's press conference thought it was a big story. One rather self-regarding and pompous Foreign Editor had declared to his colleagues, 'I'm going to bed. Nothing will happen until tomorrow when the new travel regulations come into being.' He not only slept through the whole chaotic night but missed the story of the first 'Ossie' baby to be born in the West (a heavily pregnant mother gave birth on the Ku'damm). 'Never mind, John,' one of his cheekier underlings remarked next day. 'So you missed the "first baby" story, but with any luck you'll be there in time for the first stiff. I'll bet there'll be lots of Ossie heart attacks in the West today.'

In the early morning, Wiebke and I drove in her red Wartburg through Checkpoint Charlie, one of the first East German cars to pass unhindered into the West. As we crossed the Death Strip – the mined no-man's-land separating the 'workers' and peasants' paradise' in the East from the 'decadent bourgeois fascism' in the West, we saw ahead of us vast crowds of 'Wessies', West Germans, who were chanting '*Endlich! Endlich!*' ('At last! At last!').

As I was dressed Ossie-style in jeans and cheap leather jacket, the Wessies thought I was as Ossie as the East German Wiebke – and I didn't disabuse them. We were showered with champagne and small children threw sweets into the car. I was overcome with emotion, tears and mascara ran down my cheeks, and I shouted, 'Wiebke, I love you!' And she yelled, 'I love you too, Ann!'

All night 'we, the people' had been dancing on the Wall, and hijacked mechanical diggers had been biting huge chunks out of the

'Anti-Fascist Protective Rampart'. Because I could not phone my copy over to the *Mail* in London – the few international lines out of East Berlin were totally clogged – I kept having to climb through new holes in the Wall to get to the West, hurriedly write and phone over my copy, and then climb back again into the East. I must be the only person who witnessed the fall of the Wall who was too busy to pick up a chunk as a souvenir.

Over in the West on the Ku'damm, Wessies were handing out free bunches of bananas to their impoverished cousins. A portly businessman in the lobby of the Kempinski was dispensing sheaves of 50-Deutschmark notes to the rubber-necking, dazzled Ossies. 'I just want them to enjoy themselves while they are here,' he told me, almost embarrassed by his own emotional spontaneity. So many Wessies were treating Ossies to extravagant celebratory breakfasts that the city's bakeries ran out of bread, and over that weekend so many filth-spewing Trabis had pumped their fumes into West Berlin's air that the city's authorities put out an urgent smog alert.

West Berlin, geographically isolated within East Germany, had often been described as 'a luxury Alcatraz in a sea of poverty' – a heavily subsidized showcase for capitalism marooned in the Communist ocean. And now it discovered to its joy – though later to its dismay – that with the fall of the Wall the East's 'sea of poverty' came flooding in. It was not to know that, for many years after Chancellor Helmut Kohl had predicted that the East would become a 'blooming landscape', this Eastern sea of poverty would still be there, crippling the rest of the German economy.

But while it lasted, the honeymoon between Ossies and Wessies was ecstatic. This Prussian city became almost Latin in its emotional exuberance: everyone was kissing, hugging and weeping with joy on everyone else's shoulder. As indeed I was.

I suspected, and told David English on the phone, that perhaps my copy went a bit over the top. I also moaned that by now, having had little sleep for days, I was completely exhausted. He replied, 'Stop complaining, woman! I shouldn't be paying *you* – you should be paying *me* for enabling you to be present at one of the greatest moments in twentieth-century history!' And of course he was right. He also reassured me, 'I'll tone down your copy if it's necessary.'

Unfortunately he didn't, thus inspiring Craig Brown, *Private Eye*'s cruelly funny parodist, to gleeful mockery. 'Award-winning Jill Shrill begins her Berlin Wall piece with the words: "The mascara is puddling down my cheeks. My lipstick is smeared in myriad patches over my nose and chin. My clothes are drenched with exhilaration and joy. I cannot believe this is happening. I forgot to take off my clothes before turning on my hotel shower." Yes, I admit I did use the 'mascara puddling' phrase.

Surprisingly, few of the Ossies I met in that delirious week actually wanted the reunification of the two halves of Germany. The dissident Marianne Birthler told me, 'I don't want it and I don't think about it. I love my country, and I want to stay here. I just want it to behave in a more humane and civilized way.'

Mrs Thatcher, always suspicious of Germany, didn't want reunification either. In an interview in No. 10 I challenged her on her foot-dragging over the Wessies' plan to absorb the Ossies: 'You don't trust a powerful, united Germany, do you?' Her brisk and glittery-eyed reply was: 'I think it would be *quite wrong* to ignore the realities of the past! It was because people thought that after World War I there could never be another world war that they let down their guard!'

In the event, a reunited Germany did not, as Mrs Thatcher envisaged, revert to its old warmongering habits. On the contrary, it became almost stereotypically pacifist. But in those heady days after the Wall fell, few imagined how difficult the subsequent reunification marriage would be, how expensive it would be for the Wessies, or how miserable it would become for the Ossies. The Ossies lost their jobs in factories which for years had produced little that anyone wanted to buy, lost their cheap (if meagre) health care, free child care and low-cost (if grotesquely inadequate) housing. Some became very rich, but most remained very poor.

At the Friedrichshain Hospital in the week before the fall of the Wall, I'd interviewed Professor Harry Randow, a Party apparatchik and the hospital's deputy medical director. He gave up trying to defend the regime and told me: 'I don't think any of the East Germans who've gone to the West will come back. Those who do return will be those who know they'll be failures in the West. And we do not want any more failures. We are now a country full of failures.'

Few then realized how internalized that sense of failure had become in East German minds. It resulted in a corrosive resentment towards the Wessies; the briefly joyous Ossies came to believe that they were being shoved aside by the 'elbow society' of ruthless and arrogant Westerners, who'd once thought that handing out free bananas to their liberated cousins would earn undying love. And few foresaw how irritated the Wessies would become by what they came to see as the ingratitude of the 'lazy' Ossies who, they felt, were accustomed to living on hand-outs and couldn't hack it in a global economy.

Even today there are East Berliners who tell me that, after that initial excitement, they now never venture across the vanished border into West Berlin. There is still, as one Berliner put it to me, 'a Wall in the head'.

And even on the day after the fall of the Wall some people suspected that the honeymoon expectations of the night of 9 November would be disappointed. One of whom was Wiebke, who scornfully described her fellow Ossies as 'believing in a fool's paradise: they think that roast chickens will now fly into their stomachs without them having to do anything but stand on the pavement and open their mouths!' One Wessie businessman told me, 'I'm very glad they're free, but I hope they'll all go home soon. I think if they do all come it will cost us too much trouble in the future.'

Despite the current fashion among Easterners for 'Ostalgie' – nostalgia for the Good Old Days of 'real existing socialism' – I do not believe that the majority of Ossies want a full-scale return to that ugly, cruel and corrupt past. Nevertheless, embittered Ossies now vote in large numbers for the reconstructed Communist Party or, more worryingly, turn to fringe parties of the extreme, neo-fascist right.

A week before the Wall fell, I had met a friend of Wiebke's, Karin Wiesner, a young doctor, who said that so many people were leaving East Germany that 'soon all we'll have left here will be the very old and the very young'. Her prediction has now largely come true. Whole villages and even medium-sized towns are bereft of working-age people. They've all gone West in search of jobs.

Dr Wiesner had told me: 'All my life I have had dreams in which the Wall had come down, but I couldn't go through to the West because I was on duty; and when I got off duty, I was too late – because the Wall had gone up again.' The first part of her dream came true; she now runs a private clinic in the West.

Marianne Birthler, who didn't want to leave her country and didn't want it to be reunited with West Germany, now heads the federal commission which investigates the Stasi files. Before the Ossie crowd ransacked their headquarters, the Stasi went on an orgy of file-shredding and, when the shredders broke down, set fire to as many of the documents as possible. Sixteen thousand black bin bags full of shredded files are still being pieced together by Birthler's staff.

And what of Günther Schabowski, the man whose blunder on the evening of 9 November brought about the fall of the regime? Ten years after the event, I hunted him down.

'Ah, you were at the press conference, were you?' he growled with a wry smile as he welcomed me into his two-storey flat. No need of course to specify which press conference. He told me he had been haunted for years by what his *grosse Maul*, his big mouth, let him in for that night.

Now awaiting the outcome of appeals against his three-year sentence for his role in the old regime, Schabowski was still living in the same flat as when he was the all-powerful Berlin Party boss. The once heavily guarded apartment block used to be nicknamed by fearful East Germans the *Bonzensiedlung*, or 'bosses' colony', stuffed as it was with Politburo chiefs. Others had moved away from Berlin, but not the bluff, obstinate Schabowski. 'I came to Berlin when I was only four years old and my heart belongs to the city' – the city which, of course, his regime had divided and terrorized for so long.

How strange it felt to me now to be able to walk into the slightly shabby lift of the old 'bosses' colony', wander down its characterless corridors without let or hindrance, and then to be greeted affably by a once feared, now despised, old age pensioner and his much loved but noisy grey parrot.

'The parrot's ten years old, and they can live to the age of forty!' Schabowski informed me with gruff affection as the bird and I introduced ourselves. The former Comrade's television in the corner of his book-cluttered study was blaring out some old romantic movie, and for a while it was hard to hear oneself speak above the sound-track and virtually non-stop parrot squawks. Having at my request silenced the parrot by putting a cloth over the cage, Schabowski told me he'd had time to reflect on his own role in Berlin's tortured post-war history.

'I don't look back on my life and say I wasted it exactly, but I did follow the wrong policy,' he said with an honesty rare among his former Politburo colleagues. 'People like me were convinced that we'd devised a good system, a policy which was for the people, for the common man, and we couldn't understand why the people rejected it. Obviously, they didn't reject it because of propaganda from the *Daily Mail*' (a heavy-lidded smile), 'so, if you've got any brain at all, you have to ask yourself *why* they rejected it.

'They rejected it because this wonderful system for the common man just didn't work. The fact is that our system in the GDR was politically bankrupt, as well as economically bankrupt. When I say this I'm accused by my former colleagues, who are still Communist, of being a traitor. But the leaders of the PDS, the reconstructed Communist Party, are being dishonest: it annoys me that they blame all the social and economic troubles among Ossies on the federal government, when it was our system – the system in East Germany – which created the problems in the first place.'

Did he believe that he deserved to go to jail? A resigned shrug. In the event he only served a short portion of his sentence. The lawyers for those charged argued that it was unjust to prosecute these men for 'crimes' which, at the time they committed them, were perfectly acceptable under East German law.

In 2007 I tracked him down again for a BBC documentary on the fall of the Wall. He and his Russian wife no longer live in a privileged 'bosses' colony' apartment: their cramped, book-lined flat is in what his regime used to denounce as 'fascist' West Berlin. The parrot is still with him, still adored.

'How do you feel now about having gone down in history as the man whose blunder brought about the fall of the Berlin Wall?'

'*Was ist* "blunder"?' It was *not* a blunder, he insisted, even though his former Politburo colleagues all blamed him for it. He was of course rewriting history, as so many do.

But even though he'd initially seemed reluctant to see me again (and only on condition that I paid him 100 euros), in the event he seemed anxious for me to stay and talk with him for hours about those pivotal days. It reminded me of Albert Speer, Hitler's architect and close colleague, whom I interviewed in Heidelberg when writing a series about the children of the Nazis in 1973. I wanted to interview his son Albert, also an architect, and this visit to Speer was merely a courtesy call on my part. But the man who spent twenty years in Spandau prison for his use of slave labour as Hitler's Minister for Armaments seemed, like Schabowski, eager to rewrite history and have me stay and listen to him. Was Speer just old and lonely? Or did he, like Schabowski, somehow miss being in the limelight, even though that limelight only served to illuminate his leading role in a grotesque regime? Perhaps, as the saying goes, it's better to be wanted for murder than not to be wanted at all.

These days, most Berliners have lost interest in old, ill, defeated men like Schabowski. Yet the symbols of Berlin's grotesque history, under both fascism and Communism, are impossible to escape.

Just up the road from where Schabowski used to live in his 'bosses' colony' apartment lies the restored Hotel Adlon, once the most glittering hostelry in the Weimar Republic – the Germany of *Cabaret*, of ruinous hyper-inflation, of Dietrich, of 'divine decadence'. Next door to it, the Brandenburg Gate and the restored Reichstag, the symbols of Prussian triumphalism; a ten-minute walk away, two grass- and rubbish-covered hillocks, the remains of Himmler's 'SS City', the Gestapo headquarters. And below Schabowski's window, the grandly rebuilt Potsdamer Platz, where Hitler made his last stand in his underground bunker and where he committed suicide. 'Yes, Hitler's bunker is down there, but there's nothing to see. It's just a small mound.'

Berliners, not surprisingly, have constantly wanted to destroy evidence of their city's murderous past; and there is now very little left of the Wall which once so cruelly sliced through its heart.

13

The Star, the Slave and the Stiff

'Have you seen the Wow Room yet?' I was asked by Mrs Ramos, the wife of Filipino Army General Fidel Ramos who'd sided with most of the population against Ferdinand Marcos, the dictator of the Philippines, and his wife Imelda, thus bringing about the fall of their larcenous regime. No, I said. I'd interviewed Imelda Marcos here in the Spanish-built Malacanang Palace, when she was still First Lady – but she'd never shown me any 'Wow Room'. What is it? 'Come with me!' Mrs Ramos said, seizing my arm and twinkling with merriment.

She opened a door at the top of some stairs leading down into a basement. 'You go first, Miss Leslie!' So I did – and when I saw what the room contained I gasped, 'Wow!'

'*Now* you see why it's called the Wow Room, because that's what people say when they first see it!'

This was of course the Aladdin's Cave in Imelda Marcos's private quarters which contained, among many other extravagant goodies, the soon-to-be legendary 3,200 pairs of shoes. Before the People Power revolution overthrew the Marcoses, their subjects knew of their First Lady's spendthrift ways, but no one suspected her obsession with footwear. 'Look at these! Aren't they ridiculous?' said Mrs Ramos, holding up a pair of the matronly Imelda's disco shoes which had battery-powered electric lights in the heels. The vast majority of the shoes, as far as I could see, were still unworn.

What is it with dictators and, very often, their spouses? For example, what did Hitler want those boxes of military insignia *for*, asked baffled visitors to Hitler's underground bunker after the war. Why would anyone, fighting for his and his country's survival, waste much-needed space on boxes full of these useless pieces of metal? Perhaps they were like magic charms, there to remind Hitler of his once great power; perhaps, against all odds, they might restore that power.

And why did the Soviet Union's Leonid Brezhnev bother to acquire his vast collection of flashy foreign cars? As the Soviet leader he had unlimited access to official cars like the hefty armoured Zils; obviously he couldn't be seen by the proletariat being driven in any of the capitalist Cadillacs, Mercedes and Rolls Royces that he collected with such dour passion. After his death it was found that many of his exotic motorized 'toys' had scarcely any miles on the clock, just as Imelda didn't get round to actually wearing many of her shoes.

Not long after my visit to the Wow Room, the shocked and baffled slum-dwellers of Manila trooped through it and must have asked themselves, 'What could she *do* with all these clothes, these shoes? And what woman needs to own 1,000 pairs of knickers?'

The answer of course is that she didn't. Any more than, on a practical level, Hitler needed boxes of Iron Crosses in his last days of life, or Brezhnev needed those secret Cadillacs. Or Lenin needed his capitalist-imperialist Rolls (and he had nine in the course of his career – one of which I saw in the Moscow Museum. The grumpy guide told me, 'Our Russian cars are much better: I do not understand why Comrade Vladimir Ilyich needed this capitalist car').

Did Saddam Hussein need all those palaces, or did the Romanian dictator Ceausescu need a 1,100-room, twelve-storey 'House of the People' into which, of course, the people were forbidden to enter? But the 'Imelda Syndrome' is not about the practical needs of practical-minded people: it's about the psychological needs of dictators.

The fact is that these collections of cars and fancy footwear did not exist for mundane utilitarian purposes: instead, they were like some medieval pasha's vast harem which, hidden from public view, existed primarily to serve as a symbol of the pleasures and privileges available only to potentates. Imelda Marcos's collection consisted of objects of adornment, almost as though they were religious tributes to a beloved goddess, who was of course herself.

She never gave away any of her clothes because, a deeply superstitious woman, she feared that her enemies could use them for black magic. It's easy to see how such a superstition could arise:

even 'normal' people tend to regard clothes as an extension of themselves. 'It's not me,' we'll say of something which doesn't suit us, and any woman who's been burgled and had her clothes destroyed or stained feels herself to be in some way violated. But with Imelda the feeling that 'I am my clothes' seems to have become pathological. Why should that be?

Perhaps it's because it was her husband who had acquired the real power for himself. Imelda hadn't, and perhaps in her heart of hearts she knew it. So she invented for herself a strange ideology of 'beauty' which she hypnotized herself into believing that her people shared. Her own beauty had given her power in the first place by ensnaring Marcos: perhaps by serving her beauty she could acquire even greater power and ensnare a whole nation of Filipinos.

And to do so she collected countless objects to preserve and project that beauty: anti-wrinkle cream by the ton, thousands of jewels, frocks, shoes, furs, gallons of expensive, seductive scents, girdles to rein in that billowing waist. Her vast collection of underwear and beauty aids had become amulets whose mere existence, rather than their use, conveyed some kind of supernatural power.

I once asked her how she would counter criticisms in the foreign press about her extravagance. (The Filipino press were of course unable to express anything other than adoration of her.)

She replied, 'Oh, foreigners completely misunderstand Filipino culture! Filipinos are obsessed with the desire for beauty. If you show them a building or an object, the first question they ask is not, "Is it technologically sound?" or "'Does it work?" or "Is it very expensive?" or even "Is it useful?" No! What they ask is, "Is it *beautiful*?"

'Frankly, I have to tell you that the most tedious part of my life is having to get dressed up. I am not at all vain because all my life I have been beautiful – so I've taken it for granted, I don't have to be obsessed with my looks like plain people tend to be. No, the only reason I get dressed up and make myself look glamorous is because of the Filipino desire for beauty. As a soldier for beauty, I have to do it for them, out of respect for their sense of the visual ecology.'

Like the Mad Collector who kids himself that he steals Old Masters 'for the sake of posterity', Imelda Marcos had convinced herself that her plundering of the Filipino Treasury in order to preserve her own 'visual ecology' was done 'for the sake of my people'. And if this sacred 'visual ecology' necessitated collecting thousands of pairs of shoes, bras and panties, why should the 'beauty-loving' Filipinos complain?

Never have I met a vainer, more self-deluded woman than Imelda Marcos: this former beauty queen truly believed that her power, her wealth, her sumptuous lifestyle were, as she put it to me one morning in one of her almost trance-like states of self-adoration, 'an inspiration to the poor! They need a Star to reach for! I am both a Star and a Slave! I must be a Star, something beautiful and inspiring for the poor to reach up to. And I must also be a Slave – so that everybody in the gutter can be lifted up, by my work and my example, to be a Star too!'

For two hours I'd listened to this drivel, perched beside her on a tapestried sofa in her windowless music room. The windows had all been replaced by huge mirrors which reflected her to herself and kept the outside world at bay. 'Oh, my beloved music room! You see how I am, Miss Leslie – I must always be surrounded by beauty, by harmony! It is this beauty and harmony that I give to my beloved people!'

Outside, the approach roads to the humid, orchid-filled grounds surrounding the Malacanang Palace were sealed off by a series of armed guards. Imelda may have believed that her people adored her for the 'beauty and harmony' of her lifestyle, but neither she nor her husband was taking any chances on letting them come close enough to express their 'gratitude'.

I was one of the last European journalists to interview her before she fled with her husband into exile. I had been half expecting to encounter the tough, shrewd Iron Butterfly persona she'd invented for herself: 'I am strong as iron, and beautiful as a butterfly!' Instead, I found a plump, puffy, exquisitely coiffed and painted doll, out of whose pink satin mules peeped heart-shaped painted toenails, and out of whose dewy-pink rosebud mouth poured an unstoppable stream of sentimentality, stupidity and self-love. Perhaps power not only corrupts: too much of it for too long (judging by this Filipina Lady Macbeth) may actually addle the brain, had there been much brain to addle in the first place.

The vast edifice of power and wealth this woman had built around herself in twenty years as First Lady had apparently deprived her of the ability to see or hear anything which contradicted her delusions. At one point I managed to fling a question into her unstoppable Niagara of narcissism: 'The Shah and Empress of Iran, who were your great friends, believed their people loved them – but the people rose up and threw them out. Don't you feel, insulated as you are by power and wealth, that perhaps you may be making the same mistake?'

'*What* mistake?' she snapped, momentarily abandoning the Patience Strong stream of consciousness. 'The Iranian people *did* love the Shah and Empress! But no matter how much your people love you, it is very hard for Third World countries who have a crisis of identity to resist outside pressures, outside subversions from super-powers and super-ideologies who spend *billions of dollars* trying to confuse them!' But in Iran's case, I pointed out, it wasn't the Western powers (who tended to support the Shah) but the ordinary people in the mosques and bazaars – the poor who allegedly loved their rulers – who rose up in 1979 and threw those rulers out.

'Yes!' Her eyes flashed imperiously. '*But who orchestrated them, who financed them?* That revolution did *not* arise spontaneously from the hearts of the people!' President Jimmy Carter, she said bitterly, should not have abandoned the Shah in his hour of need.

However efficient and ruthless the Marcos intelligence machine may have been, I don't think that the First Couple ever understood or believed the depth of hatred that they – and especially Imelda – inspired. To this day Imelda is angry that the American government abandoned them as it had the Shah and his Empress.

During my time in the Philippines, before the final crisis which toppled the regime, I heard endless Imelda rumours swirling through the squatters' slums and even the mansions of the rich (many of whom knew long before the Marcoses that the party would soon be over, and who were already smuggling their fortunes out into foreign bank accounts).

One Army man, at that stage still a Marcos loyalist, told me, 'We'll support President Marcos because we believe that, if we don't, we'll have a Communist take-over. But the First Lady!' He rolled his eyes. 'Her whole way of life is an incitement to Communism!'

That way of life included commandeering planes from the national airline for shopping trips to Europe (I was bumped off one flight for precisely that reason), and throwing endless parties in which Imelda, a restless insomniac who craved an audience like a junkie his fix, would turn night into extravagant day, dancing and singing Cole Porter and Tagalog love songs, knowing that none of her guests dared yawn or creep off to bed before she wished it.

She certainly had one character trait which she shared with her fellow countrymen: every Filipino, like every Welshman, is convinced that he or she has unique musical ability. Which is why, alas, many an evening in the Far East has been blighted for me by a Filipina *chanteuse* confidently launching into an off-key rendition of 'My Way'. Anyone who's endured Imelda in song-thrush mode knows how hard on the eardrums that can be.

When I interviewed the First Lady at 11.30 one morning she had only just got out of bed. 'Oh,' she sighed. 'I am so cruel to myself. I scarcely sleep because I am working so hard for my people.'

Part of Imelda Marcos's stupidity lay in not recognizing that she had no power-base outside her marriage certificate. It was her husband who made her Governor of Metro Manila and Minister of Human Settlements, a vast, money-gobbling housebuilding programme (her opponents alleged that much of the money it gobbled ended up, not in houses for the poor, but in real-estate deals for the Marcoses in America).

She told me with a roguish laugh, 'I always say, half-jokingly, that my family were never poor but when I met Marcos, I hit the jackpot!' But like that other deluded dictator's wife, China's Jiang Qing, the screechy-voiced 'White Boned Demon' widow of Chairman Mao, Imelda never grasped that once her husband's power crumbled, hers would too.

Imelda had alienated everybody, including the rich, by dunning them for 'voluntary donations' to her ludicrous prestige construction projects like a mansion built entirely from coconuts, and her pet enthusiasm, the Manila Film Centre, which she described to me as 'my crazy little Parthenon' (crazy indeed, since it cost over £11 million and thirty-five lives and ended up showing porn movies).

She'd alienated the middle classes too because they felt ruthlessly excluded from the crony-capitalism that enriched so many Marcos insiders. One well-born Filipina insisted that she could only talk to me in the middle of a hotel swimming pool – 'Here, the listening devices in the hotel don't work! People like me hate the Marcoses because we none of us can rise above a certain level in our careers because of the stranglehold they have on power and influence. I hate the Communists, but one day I may be driven into their arms!'

And as for the poor on whose 'love' Imelda relied: well, they eventually showed what they felt with their 'People Power' revolution. Why, I asked her, did her Ministry of Human Settlements not build them the millions of homes they needed, instead of the handful of 'model settlements' she displayed so proudly to the press?

In a hurt little-me voice she replied, 'But who am I to build a million homes for the poor? I may not build the kind of homes they like! All I can do is show them examples and then let them build their *own* homes, according to their tastes and needs. I believe in letting them have the freedom to choose where and how they want to live.' (But when poverty forced them to 'choose' squatter slums, in the interests of 'beauty' Imelda had them bulldozed as the eyesores they undoubtedly were.)

My last memory of Imelda Marcos when she was still in her heyday as the First Lady, was of her prattling away on her little chaise-longue wearing a long evening gown at noon, in that closed, wood-panelled, flower-filled music room, which resembled a sumptuous coffin. The whole air of luxurious unreality, cut off from the seething crowds of Manila, had made me feel I'd fallen into a time-warp where a Hollywood star of the Fifties still held court, oblivious of the fact that her fans had finally abandoned her.

It was in Nigeria's capital, Abuja, that I first heard the phrase 'Villa Sickness'. This is the syndrome which affects leaders who may start out well intentioned and moderately sane but who then move into Presidential Palaces (or indeed Downing Street) and gradually lose touch with the people who've elected them. Or, of course, who haven't elected them: the worst victims of Villa Sickness tend to be dictators who've seized power and kept it without asking permission from the voters.

The syndrome is named after the vast Presidential Villa which shelters under a huge rock in Abuja; it was built by German contractors as an impregnable bunker in a heavily guarded and fortified compound by a previous military dictator, Sani Abacha. Such lavish Presidential Palaces exist all over poverty-stricken Africa.

When, during Tony Blair's visit to Nigeria in 2002, I entered the Presidential Villa I was astounded, not just by its vastness and luxury, but by the way it was designed to insulate its owner from the ugly realities of the world outside. It was lined with mirrors, dotted with servants scuttling between its sumptuous black leather sofas, its walls were panelled in dark wood, and its picture windows were shielded from the sun and prying eyes by permanently closed brocade curtains. The then President Olesegun Obasanjo never needed to emerge from this fortress except to get into his limo and, with a screaming motorcade escort, zoom to Abuja International Airport and board his private jet for yet another wastefully expensive jaunt overseas.

Its decor, its mirrored walls, curtained windows, coffin-like panelling and heavily guarded seclusion all reminded me of the Marcos palace. The First Couple of the Philippines suffered from the delusionary effects of 'Villa Sickness' to such a degree that they were astonished to discover, shortly after my visit, that they had an unstoppable revolution on their hands.

Imelda had handed me a present of flowers made from sea-shells. 'I cannot live without flowers – because flowers remind me of the smiles of my people. Sometimes I am asked, "Madame Marcos, what is the basis of your country's economic index?", and I reply, "It is the smiles of my people!"'

*

It was when I next met her, six years later, that Mrs Marcos – now fallen from power – insisted to me that she was not into shoes. Goodness me, no. 'Shoes aren't even my particular weakness,' she simpered, the light from the privately chartered jumbo-jet window glinting on the black gob-stopper pearls in her ears.

Her husband Ferdinand having died, his widow was returning to Manila, without permission, after the years of exile. The journey home may have looked like a typically grotesque and extravagant piece of mischief-making against the then President Cory Aquino's government, but to Mrs Marcos it was a deeply spiritual journey made by a holy widow risking her freedom and, possibly, her life so that she could answer God's call (if no one else's) to be 'the mother of the nation'.

Across four time zones, from the icy winds of New York, to the sunshine of Hawaii, to the sauna-like heat of Manila, she tried to fend off talk of The Shoes. How distressingly earthbound, indeed shoe-bound, the hordes of pressmen travelling with her proved to be. She wished that we would be more spiritual! Her spirituality could not be in doubt – after all, her preferred reading on the ten-hour flight from New York to Honolulu was an uplifting work called *Too Busy to Pray – Slowing Down to Be with God*. (I know this because it was artfully arranged on the seat beside her for a photo opportunity.)

She fingered a rosary with a diamond-encrusted crucifix and, just in case we still didn't get the spiritual aspect of Imelda's home-bound flying circus, she was accompanied everywhere by a tiny Filipino courtier lugging a three-foot-high statue of the Virgin Mary in a pearly crown. 'Eet ees very heavy!' the tiny Filipino had gasped as he staggered in Mrs Marcos's mink-coated wake at JFK airport at the start of the journey in New York. When not lugging Madonnas round the world for Imelda, his other role in life was, he told me, 'Marketing Manager for Landwealth Securities Inc.'.

For the previous four days, while talking of 'mothering the poor' as she waved a huge black-pearl-and-diamond ring worth, at the least, a terraced house in my area of north London, the 'Iron Butterfly' had been emitting clouds of spiritual squid-ink. But we piranhas of the press didn't want talk of God, we just wanted to talk shoes.

Finally, in Honolulu she relented and, in the garden of a rented mansion, posed with A Shoe, held aloft for the photographers – and, oh, by the way, she pointed out, she does *not* take a whopping size eight-and-a-half: 'My size is eight!' A fact which might have come in useful for those of her myriad well-wishers who had apparently spent two decades lovingly lobbing shoes at her in tribute to the beauty not only of her size eight feet but of her size twenty-eight soul.

The way poor, misunderstood Mrs Marcos told it, shoes, apparently unbidden, kept flying through the air and landing in her cupboards and oh, how maligned she'd been on account of all this misleadingly luxurious footwear. Those pairs which she did acquire herself were, of course, purchased in order to promote the Filipino shoe industry (although how the mass purchase of the products of the Italian and French shoe industries was supposed to help the Filipino one is puzzling). And now, alas, no one remembered her years of self-sacrifice. Even one of her lawyers (she had four travelling with her to Manila) conceded in a New York court that she was a 'world-class shopper', but we evidently did not realize that this world-class shopping for personal jewellery was all in the line of duty to improve the 'visual ecology' of the Filipino people.

The former First Lady's shoe mountain was, she told me in her habitual martyred tones, a particularly shocking example of the continual propaganda which alleged 'that we were thieves, that we were criminals!' In the Honolulu garden, one of her Filipino admirers knelt before her and begged to be allowed to buy a sacred pair. 'Oh, you won't be able to afford them,' she tinkled regally down at him. 'They cost up to 10,000 dollars a pair!'

The Mount Pinatubo earthquake which devastated the Philippines was, she said, a punishment from God. If President Aquino had not denied Imelda the right to bury her late husband in his native soil, the earthquake might never have happened. Why a merciful God should choose to devastate the lives of thousands of innocent people simply to satisfy the familial wishes of the Marcos clan was beyond me.

Marcos died in exile in Hawaii, and Imelda wanted to visit his refrigerated coffin, which was draped in a Filipino flag and lay in the Valley of the Temples Memorial Park on the island – where, the previous year, she'd held a birthday party for his corpse, declaring that she changed his shirt every so often 'so that he keeps looking good'.

Imelda had launched a War of the Widows, and she was Widow No. 1. Widow No. 2 was President Cory Aquino whose husband, the then opposition leader Ninoy Aquino, was assassinated eight years earlier as he stepped off the plane at Manila airport after returning from exile. (The murder is widely believed to have been ordered by the Marcoses.)

Widow No. 2 was understandably eager to get her government's handcuffs round Widow No. 1's bejewelled wrists – or at least to get the handcuffs on the billions the latter had allegedly siphoned off from the national treasury. The reason the Widow Marcos was taking this risk was simple: if she didn't return before 27 December she would lose all claims to her disputed assets.

Wasn't it possible, I asked her on the plane as we headed over the mountains of North Dakota, that she might be assassinated on arrival at Manila airport – just as Mrs Aquino's husband had been. 'I hope not, but I think death is destiny; when it's your time, it's your time.'

The Widow Aquino (whom she derided as 'frumpy' and thus someone who did nothing for the visual ecology of the Filipino people) is a 'feudal lord' and 'completely lacking in heart' in refusing to allow her to bring home 'my late husband's mortal remains. I pray for her. I cannot understand this. It is truly shocking and inhumane that we not only persecute the sick and dying' (I think she meant her husband), 'but continue to persecute and imprison the souls of the dead' (this time I knew she meant the corpse awaiting us in the Hawaiian freezer).

The Widow Aquino who, unlike Imelda, was short, saintly and looked as if she put her make-up on in the dark, had by now lost her original Housewife Superstar status among the people as a result of the corruption and incompetence of her government. She was said to fear that the Widow Marcos might use the funeral as a showcase to rally her diehard supporters in a Marcos bid for the Presidency – either by herself or with her son, Ferdinand 'Bong Bong' Marcos the Second, one of the Philippines' most notorious playboys, who had just been arrested after his surprise return to Manila.

Back in New York the flying circus had begun in typically extravagant and farcical style. I arrived late on a Wednesday afternoon at Mrs Marcos's five-storey town house to find it in uproar. The chartered 747 flight had been cancelled! Twelve charter companies, on hearing that the Widow Marcos was to be the chief passenger, refused to handle this jewel-encrusted hot potato.

'Maybe they thought we'd be shot out of the sky!' shrieked Mrs Sol Vanzi, Mrs M's small and excitable press aide. One charter airline in Iowa had agreed to take her on, but got cold feet on receiving a telex from Cory Aquino's government telling them that five of the party – including Imelda's maid, the chap 'who waters her plants', her personal photographer and the pilot who was to fly the plane – all had warrants out for their arrest.

'How can the pilot be expected to fly the plane if he's going to be arrested, for what we don't know, on arrival – or, worse, shot!'

A further message arrived from Manila. Mrs Vanzi waved a photo-copy at me: 'Look at all these restrictions. They say they won't grant landing rights if there are any human remains on board!' This meant that the former First Lady could not transport any corpses back to Manila, one of which was that of her late husband's butler. 'Not even the butler!' (Perhaps the Widow Aquino feared that the Widow Marcos would switch corpses in Hawaii.) But by midnight the flight was on again.

During the many hours I spent in the house being buffeted by exasperated TV newsmen, excitable Filipinos and assorted hangers-on (including an Italian who told me, 'I am very famous producer and my aunt was Ingrid Bergman', and his handsome male friend), I had plenty of time to read the numerous Humanitarian Awards to Mrs Marcos adorning the wall. There was an eclectic choice of statues in the mirrored hall: a large wooden Boy Jesus, a huge white porcelain Chinese goddess and a massive green jade Buddha. Mrs Marcos clearly believed in hedging her spiritual bets.

On Thursday morning, the pavement was being piled high with cardboard boxes and Louis Vuitton cases and we were seriously behind schedule: the superstitious Mrs Marcos refused to leave the house until every piece of luggage was out of it. Suddenly she emerged and headed, through a struggling ant-heap of cameramen, towards the black stretched Cadillac; its number plate, IRM 77, consisted of her initials and this numerologically obsessed widow's lucky number. Seconds later, still covered in cameramen, she went back inside again: someone had lost the car keys.

By now, the entire street was blocked by the six limousines and six vans of her motorcade, and New York's none too patient drivers and cabbies were expressing their irritation with a cacophony of honking and expletives and, in one case, by actually wrenching the door off the Japanese TV crew's limo.

And then our Star re-emerged, preceded by her miniature courtier lugging the three-foot Madonna, which was manoeuvred, like the Star, with some difficulty into the back seat of IRM 77. Alas, we were still not on our way to the airport: Mrs Marcos wanted a quick crawl-and-pray (she always crawls up to altars) at St Patrick's Cathedral.

All the while she was playing her 'sad but happy' role to perfection: her luscious blackberry eyes constantly quivered with tears, but somehow Imelda's tears never managed to smudge the make-up which, unlike ordinary mortals', seemed to be shellacked to her hamster-like cheeks. Either that, or 'it's one of the miracles she's always talking about', a Filipino journalist, well versed in her ways, told me.

We were over three hours late for departure, but life is never dull in the Marcos camp. There was the constant entertainment provided by the running feud between the Filipino entourage and the ten-strong team of American bodyguards hired to protect Imelda, should God forget to do so.

The security men all had expressionless boiled-egg eyes and walked as if they'd got piles; they had still not grasped the fact that Imelda *wanted* the press around her, and therefore spent much of their muscle-bound time trying to beat them up.

The chief feud was between press aide Mrs Vanzi and a mus-tachioed gentleman from Iowa who was described as 'the travel co-ordinator', and who was distressingly prone to making remarks like 'I'm into big bucks here!'

'Big bucks! I'll give him big bucks!' shrieked Mrs Vanzi. 'After this job I'll make sure he won't get hired to co-ordinate the travel plans of a piece of chewing gum!'

None of this made the progress of Imelda's flying circus any smoother. But finally we made it to Hawaii. Once there we visited the Corpse and then had to wait five hours (the Widow is of course never punctual); we thus had time to note that the white-painted hut, on a hill overlooking the lawns of the Memorial Park and the crumpled green mountains of Oahu, was as much a shrine to Imelda as to her late husband.

Outside it was adorned with vast photographs of Ferdinand scrawled with love messages to his wife on the occasion of his birthday in September '84 when she was abroad on 'a diplomatic mission', aka shopping: 'To my beloved Imelda, I shall bear my loneliness when you are away. But I cannot bear this pain too long.'

His tardy beloved eventually arrived, today wearing the Filipino national colours, and, after kissing the ebony coffin, told a handful of cheering members of the International Friends of Marcos that 'I said to my husband that I'll be bringing him home soon! Perhaps tomorrow!'(Which was the day our flight was due to arrive in Manila.)

'Is she really going to haul the stiff in the freezer out of that crypt and cart it off to Manila?' cried an incredulous American journalist. 'What if she does – and the Aquino government hears about it?'

What indeed? Would we be refused landing rights? Shot down? Would our 747, full of quarrelling Filipinos, Iowans, a hundred or so media folk, the three-foot-high Madonna and the Widow Marcos – and not least the aforementioned 'stiff in the freezer' – be doomed to roam the air lanes of the Pacific seeking some country that would let us land? And if we did land, what then?

Wisely, Imelda eventually decided to leave the body in the freezer behind, and fly on to Manila without it.

Nowadays, constantly and unconvincingly pleading poverty, she has taken to flogging the 'Imelda' line of costume jewellery on a TV shopping channel. Doubtless she'd describe this tat as part of her continuing battle to improve the 'visual ecology' of her 'beloved' people – who sensibly now seem to have lost interest in this supremely silly woman.

14

They *Do* Do God

Everything in America, from murder to religion (especially religion), can be turned into showbiz. The marketing of God can be an especially lucrative business. Travellin' preachermen had long been a feature of American culture, but they usually plied their snake-oil business in revivalist tents, set up in fields outside small towns across the Bible Belt, among poor folks like themselves. But as their congregations got richer, so did the preachermen, and scandals – like those which engulfed Aimee Semple McPherson and Sinclair Lewis's fictional but fact-based Elmer Gantry – inevitably followed the money.

The Eighties were the boom time for America's holy-roller scandals. The evangelist Jimmy Swaggart denounced his rival Marvin Gorman on air for fornicating with a member of his congregation, whereupon Marvin hired a private detective who discovered Jimmy was fornicating with a prostitute. Soon everyone seemed to be denouncing everyone else for fornicating with women who weren't their wives. Oral Roberts announced that God had told him that, if his followers didn't send him $8 million, He was going to 'call me home' and if his followers wanted him to hang around on earth, they'd better stump up quickly. The target was not quite reached but – surprise! – God allowed Oral to go on living, despite the shortfall of funds.

But there's scarcely been a bigger holy-roller scandal than that of 'Gospelgate', involving Jim and Tammy Faye Bakker. Before their downfall, Jim and Tammy Faye had turned their 'Praise the Lord' television ministry into a Christian entertainment colossus with assets of $172 million. In the process they rewarded themselves with six luxury homes (complete with gold-plated taps and an air-conditioned kennel for Snuggles, Tammy Faye's pet pooch), a houseboat and a fleet of expensive cars.

How on earth, I wondered, do these fat-cat preachermen (and women) exert such power over the minds and wallets of this rich, sophisticated nation? The answer lay all around me as I drove through Bible Belt country, where the Bible is believed to be literally true and the theory of evolution to be a godless lie. Here religion is an ecstatic, emotional business, and 'pointy-headed intellectualizing' a Satanic plot. Ahead of me, a Cadillac adorned with bumper stickers urged me to 'Honk for Jesus!' At the gas station where I stopped, a slack-jawed youth was listening to a Christian rock group bawling about a boy called Johnny: 'They teach him 'bout evolution, they teach him every day. They teach him 'bout Marx and Lenin, but they don't teach him to pray! Shame, shame! Shame, shame!'

Of course the words of that song – if songs were themselves permissible among the fundamentalist Islamists I've talked to in the Middle East – could have been repeated word for word by jihadists. But there is no moral equivalence between Christian fundamentalists and Islamist fundamentalists: on the whole Christian nutters do not threaten to destroy, culturally and physically, the entire Western world's way of life. And, despite paranoid utterances on the left about George Bush's alleged millennialist tendencies, the holy-rolling Christians simply do not have the power to damage all of us – as, we fear, their Islamist equivalents do.

But what is common to both groups is the way in which self-proclaimed 'leaders' can rip off their gullible and emotionally needy congregations. One day in Ramallah on the West Bank I remarked to an Islamist preacher who was a spokesman for Hamas, 'I notice that none of you, while urging "martyrdom missions" on your followers, ever volunteer to blow yourselves up or urge your own sons to do so.' He replied soulfully, 'If Allah does me the honour of calling me to a martyrdom mission – or any of my family – we will of course obey him. But so far Allah has not issued that call.' Oh, how *very* convenient, you smug hypocrite, whose slew of offspring also know that, happily, they themselves will never be 'called'. You know that your teachings guarantee your people's continuing poverty and despair, but you seduce them by promising endless joy, wealth and fornication in the next world.

And no, I did not say the last bit to him because the atmosphere was already getting dangerously heavy; he and his grim-faced bodyguards had accused me of being a Zionist spy, and my Palestinian fixer thought we should skedaddle. There are, I'm afraid, times when I don't feel like fulfilling an unasked-for 'martyrdom mission' on behalf of readers.

At least no Christian fundamentalist (and I've interviewed several) has ever made physical threats against me. And at least the Bakkers promised their followers wealth and joy in the hereafter (and the present) without requiring them to commit mass murder first. It was of course as fraudulent a promise as the Hamas spokesman's, but obviously less destructive of the innocent (albeit damaging to their wallets).

And, let's face it, there are fewer laughs to be had from the Islamists. The minute the baggage porter outside North Carolina's Charlotte Airport heard me asking the way to Heritage USA, I knew he'd have a 'Gospelgate' joke to tell me. After all, Heritage USA, a $100-million no-smoking, no-drinking, no-fornicating Christian theme park in the Deep South, was at the centre of the bizarre God-greed-and-sex scandal which was rocking the lucrative world of America's TV evangelism – and sending a seismic wave of laughter through virtually everyone else.

'Y'all heard the one 'bout how Tammy Faye Bakker was baptized by full immersion in Maybelline?' the porter chortled. Yeah, I'd heard that one – I'd heard 'em all. In the previous few months Tammy Faye, the sobbing and simpering Barbie-doll wife of the disgraced millionaire preacher Jim Bakker, had spawned a nationwide joke industry. (Try that among the Islamists, as the Danish cartoons furore proved, and you'll be rewarded for your 'sense of humour' with arson and murder.)

Most Tammy Faye jokes concerned her baroque taste in cosmetics: fly-swatter eyelashes, gravity-defying wigs and pan-stick so thick it resembled the peanut butter fudge on sale in Heritage's Heavenly Fudge Shoppe.

Before her spectacular downfall Mrs Bakker told the 13. 3 million devout fundamentalists who regularly watched the *Jim and Tammy Show* that when she was young she believed that wearing lipstick was a sin – but then the Lord revealed to her that lipstick was God's work, so now she even wore God's work in bed!

No doubt further inspired by God (who always seemed to inspire the Bakkers to do what they wanted to do, particularly if there was money in it), Mrs Bakker had even marketed her own brand of Tammy Faye cosmetics. I drove down the Billy Graham Parkway through the 37-degree C Southland summer heat towards Jim and Tammy's 2,300-acre Heritage USA just as the 'Gospelgate' saga was reaching a new climax.

For weeks rival evangelists had been noisily accusing Jim Bakker of greed, fornication, homosexuality and fraud – and the Bakkers had been fighting back with counter-accusations of lies, hypocrisy, theft and blackmail. And if some of the faithful felt that perhaps Mrs Bakker, who became known as the Imelda Marcos of evangelism, was 'a tad flamboyant', it apparently never seemed to occur to them that it was their donations to the Praise the Lord Ministry that she was being flamboyant with. Besides, as Tammy Faye soothingly explained, shopping wasn't a frivolous exercise for her, it was 'therapy' – doubtless for her self-confessed addiction to prescription drugs.

And then disaster struck. An enemy evangelist discovered that Jim Bakker had not only 'fornicated' seven years earlier with a secretary called Jessica Hahn but he'd also paid out $265,000 of Praise the Lord money in order to hush the shapely Miss Hahn's mouth.

Bakker, suspecting a plot to steal his ministry, had turned to the oleaginous Reverend Jerry Falwell and had asked him to caretake the Praise the Lord business for him. But horrors! Betrayal! The plump, sleek and wealthy Reverend Falwell, founder of the Moral Majority and one-time adviser to President Reagan, was now refusing to give the empire back – on the grounds that he had evidence that Jim Bakker had been having a homosexual affair with a terrorized Praise the Lord employee.

All sides were now consulting lawyers (the week before I arrived the Bakkers were hiding out on the appropriately named *Adequate Reward*, the yacht belonging to their millionaire attorney Melvin Belli). The tax authorities had set up an investigation office at Praise the Lord (or, as cynics now dubbed it, 'Pass the Loot'), and the whole financially secretive world of TV evangelism was now in the national spotlight.

As I drove towards Heritage USA I entered another America. Beyond the dreary tract-housing, the nail parlours, the neon-lit hamburger signs, there lay another, to Europeans, utterly foreign land – the one we rarely hear about, where poor rural folk, both black and white, live out hardscrabble, arthritic lives in shabby clapboard houses with broken fly-screens on rotting porch doors. This was the 'sub-prime' world which spawned Jim and Tammy Bakker. Before television, evangelists like the Bakkers shared the stoic lives of their flocks, and preached a Gospel that promised rewards not in this world, but in the next.

But when the flocks began watching television they soon yearned for a few of the earthly rewards they saw other, less godly souls enjoying so guiltlessly on the screen. Please, Lord Jesus, is it so wicked to long for a new fridge, or one of them fancy Winnebago camper-vans? Yes, they sadly concluded, it is.

And then along came the Bakkers and Praise the Lord Television, and millions of small, sad, hard-pressed people saw the Reverend Jim's godly, clean-cut countenance and his endearing 'aw-shucks' grin, and they heard him say that it *wasn't* wicked to pray for earthly health, wealth and happiness!

Jim and Tammy told them God *wanted* His born-again children to get rich, same as godless folks did! 'If you pray for a camper-van,' Jim roguishly urged his flock, 'be sure to tell God what colour!' He made God sound like a celestial mail-order magnate – but instead of sending your savings or your welfare cheques to heaven, you mailed them to Jim and Tammy Faye Bakker. And if the fridge never came, if the Winnebago camper remained an impossible dream (not least because you'd been sending your money to the Bakkers) – well, that wasn't Jim and Tammy Faye's fault. It was yours: you hadn't believed strongly enough!

After all, as the Bakkers constantly told their flock, wasn't their own success proof of what can be given unto poor folks if only they had enough faith? Why not come, they urged, to Heritage USA and see for yourselves the miracles that Jim and Tammy Faye's faith hath wrought.

And lo, l6 million people did just that, making Heritage USA the most popular theme park after the two Disney operations. At the entrance to the Heritage enclave a pertly uniformed Suth'n belle handed me an Activities Program, which offered such 'wholesome, inspirational' delights as a guided tour to the great preacher Billy

Graham's childhood home, a Passion Play, a visit to the vast Praise the Lord Television studio, and a Teaching on Healing Seminar in 'The Upper Room' (an alleged replica of the room where the Last Supper was held). 'Have a nice day and praise the Lord!' she trilled through her glossy Tammy Faye lips.

I checked in at the registration desk of the 500-room Grand Hotel, whose florid red, gold and white interior, with stiff bouquets of fake flowers dotted around, made it look like a cross between a snazzy funeral parlour and a requisitioned bordello. Otherwise, at first sight, it resembled any 'normal' luxury hotel. At second sight, it definitely didn't. Over the registration desk, the words 'Jesus Christ Is the Lord' were emblazoned in brass; the receipt for my Jim Bakker Thick Crust Pizza Special had 'Praise the Lord' stamped on it; there was no cocktail bar and no ashtrays – and in my room, the 'Checkout time is 11 a.m.' note gnomically urged me to consult Matthew 7:12 to discover why God wanted me to vacate my room on the dot.

I joined the holidaying Christians strolling down 'Main Street', an indoor shopping mall which re-created a mythically idyllic small town of yesteryear. The Christians were smiling. Under a perpetually blue neon-lit 'sky' these good, dim and decent folk felt content. This was America as it should be: in Heritage's Main Street, unlike the real Main Streets of America, there were no litterbugs, fornicators, drug-dealers or sodomites. Oh, Praise the Lord indeed!

Here their kids could spend their pocket money in Gift Shoppes which only sold 'uplifting' toys – like the Samson doll which, its makers promised, has 'Fully Programmable Action with Real Hair and Includes Authentic Costume and Jawbone!' But did Heritage's Main Street shoppers still support the disgraced preacher who'd made all this possible?

'Sure do!' declared forty-year-old Mrs Mary Ell Gort as she waddled out of the Heavenly Fudge Shoppe, her mouth full of Divinity Pecan Drops. But what about all the ungodly things Jim is supposed to have done? 'Lahs! All lahs!' she insisted, her mountainous bosom heaving in righteous indignation beneath her 'I'm Nuts About Jesus' T-shirt. 'This whole business is the work of the Great Deceiver who couldn't bear for to see all those souls bein' saved by Jim and Tammy Faye!'

The Bakkers' flamboyant mismanagement had allegedly plunged Praise the Lord into a $72 million debt: 300 staff had been laid off already. Down by the wave pool in the $10 million water park I found PTL employee Marjorie Deceglio playing with her baby daughter. She seemed remarkably unworried: 'We've been through crises before and we've survived. I know God wants this ministry to survive.' (All evangelicals here seemed convinced – somewhat presumptuously I'd have thought – that they knew from moment to moment exactly what God was thinking.)

However, this calm assumption of survival was not the stuff with which to regale the watching millions – might lull them into hanging on to their wallets – and if there's anything a TV preacherman hates, it's people hanging on to their wallets.

I joined the audience at the recording of the daily PTL television programme, a prayer, song and schlock show presided over (in the unavoidable absence of Jim and Tammy) by a glittery-toothed young preacher in a sharp suit called Gary. It began, of course, with an appeal for funds by the Reverend Falwell (who commuted by private plane). The beautifully lit Reverend leaned towards the camera. 'We need, right now, as sacrificial a gift as you can afford. Join the Resurrection Committee by mailing today 1,000 dollars or more – it's tax-deductible! We will send you, as a special token of our appreciation, a free copy of my autobiography – the leather-bound edition – with your name embossed in gold. And, inside, I'll write a personal note!'

Big deal, I thought crossly. 'Isn't the Reverend Falwell wonderful?' murmured the grandmother from Illinois sitting beside me. She thought the following turn – the one in which 'Uncle' Henry, the announcer, did his usual sobbing number – even more wonderful. Uncle Henry, an old chap in a Val Doonican sweater, was ensconced in a peach-coloured velvet armchair in the 'living-room' section of the elaborate set.

'Director, please stay with me a moment!' he pleaded, quite unnecessarily, as Uncle Henry's sobbing solo had been precisely timed and was accompanied by a suitably tear-jerking musical threnody. 'In the wee hours of this morning . . . .old friends . . . employees terminated . . . my heart will burst . . . please help us . . . I'm not crying wolf . . .' Oh yeah? It was all too much for me and I crept out of the studio, leaving the Illinois grandmother dabbing her eyes and sighing, 'Oh, poor Uncle Henry!'

It seemed to me incredible that, barring Mary Ell Gort and others, Jim and Tammy Faye Bakker could have any followers left. I was wrong, according to Don Hardister, who was Bakker's bodyguard for seven years. 'Remember Guyana – when all those disciples committed suicide because their leader Jim Jones told them to? Well, I never could understand that till now. But since all this happened I've met people, right here in PTL, who just don't *care* what the Bakkers did: they just want them back! And, yeah, I think they'd even drink poisoned Koolaid for them!'

All preacherman cults seemed obsessed with denouncing 'fornication' while of course secretly 'fornicating' like rabbits. By contrast, the Esalen Institute at Big Sur, California, founded in 1962, saw no philosophical problem at all with it – in fact fornicating, if done with consideration and with sincerity, could be part of one's holistic healing, of exploring one's full 'human potential'.

The religious instinct in the American psyche runs deep, and Esalen became known as the 'Religion of No Religion', and as such was denounced by the preachermen and right-wing zealots like the John Birch Society. Of course it wasn't *anti*-religion (this is America, after all), it just liked a pick 'n' mix approach to spiritual traditions. You wanna bit of shamanism? A sliver of Eastern mysticism? A soupçon of Freud? A touch of parapsychology? A sampling of hallucinogenics? You into space aliens? After all, a belief in visiting aliens who rape you or take you on day-trips to Venus doesn't in itself prove that you're nuts. On the contrary: according to one earnest Esalen stalwart, extra-terrestrials represent 'the human soul exteriorized into three-dimensional space as a religious experience'.

'Esalen isn't all about sex and nude bathing you know,' said a defensive Michael Murphy, who owned the place, when I called him. 'Both are *entirely* optional.'

'Of course, Mr Murphy,' I said.

'I mean, it's not *all* massage and jumping in and out of bed with people. Just so long as you *realize*. I mean, the way we get written about, you'd think, well . . . So you've got to join a weekend workshop before we'll allow you to write about it.'

'Yes, Mr Murphy,' I said meekly.

'Just so you realize . . .' he repeated.

Thus it was I found myself one Friday night in the late Sixties, wide-eyed with terror, driving a neurotically over-sensitive Mustang convertible up the unlit corkscrew roads leading from Monterey along a lonely stretch of the Pacific coast to the Institute, the most famous, beautiful and controversial temple to hip psychology in the world.

Its most notorious resident psychologist was the German-born Dr Fritz Perls, inventor of 'Gestalt' therapy, an unashamedly randy seventy-five-year-old. He was frequently to be seen pottering naked around the Esalen sulphur baths that were perched on the edge of a vertiginous cliff, happily pawing equally naked female passers-by. Scorning the bloodlessness of academia, Perls, when asked on one occasion to submit a paper on the language of existentialism for a symposium, sent in a cheerfully obscene poem instead which ended with the words: 'I am a scoundrel and a lover of arts. / I am what I am, and I screw when I can. / I'm Popeye the sailor, man.'

He never pawed me because I was never naked. Whenever I was urged to take off my clothes I'd reply firmly that 'Mike Murphy told me that nudity is *optional*!' My reluctance to strip off was partly because the women – mostly rich, narcissistic hippies who regularly strolled around in the nude – all had perfect, bronzed bodies.

I do not tan so instead slather myself in summer – or in California – with the bottled stuff. One night, with a couple of male 'workshoppers', I strolled down to the sulphur baths, lit by guttering candles, and, when no one was looking, stripped off and climbed in. Unfortunately the hot baths, fed by springs, are extremely hot and I realized I was going to faint. By now we'd been joined by other 'workshoppers' who had upped the candle power. I had to climb out of the bath, realizing with horror that the excoriating effect of the sulphur had stripped off the fake tan and, while from the shoulders upwards I was the required Californian nut-brown shade, from thereon down I was as white as an asparagus root. Mercifully my fellow workshoppers, while looking startled, did not obey the Esalen rule which stated that concepts like 'politeness' and 'consideration of others' are simply cop-outs meaning dishonesty, hypocrisy and cowardice. They sweetly chose not to comment.

I loved my long weekend at Esalen, all the sobbing, screaming and embracing during marathon encounter groups; and I even loved the food, although it did tend towards the healthy-groats end of the culinary spectrum. Besides, Murphy's 150-acre estate is situated in one of the most beautiful places in the world, where you feel stoned simply by breathing in the sparkling sea air and the piny scent of the redwoods, or watching the seals and the otters below the cliff cavorting joyously and sunning their tummies in the achingly blue Pacific. The Esalen Institute still exists, but its glory days as the Vatican of the 'Human Potential Movement', when it housed the likes of Aldous Huxley, Joan Baez, Ansel Adams, Arnold Toynbee, Timothy Leary and Hunter S. Thompson, are long gone.

But if it is no longer the trailblazer, its ideas, once considered so wacky and way-out, have now permeated modern culture: 'sensitivity' courses, group therapy, management 'training' weekends (where you pretend to be a teacup so you can learn to emphathize with your company's mission statement), and even – and especially – the beauty business.

There can't be a luxury spa in the world today which doesn't have something of Esalen in it. Every time I heard that Cherie Blair was into 'crystal therapy' and other New Age idiocies, or listened to 'lifestyle gurus' like Carole Caplin wittering on about 'holistic' well-being, I blamed Esalen. The 'Religion of No Religion' gives mentally lazy, self-regarding people the illusion of spiritual virtue without ever having to do much to earn it, other than to worship their own bodies. Unsurprisingly, I began to feel a certain nostalgia for the austere saints of my long-lost Catholic childhood: at least they had to endure a bit of selfless suffering on behalf of others in order to win their spiritual awards.

I became friendly with Mike Murphy, who told me he actually disapproved of many New Age ideas because 'they lack intellectual rigour', and we'd meet up when he came to London. As he was into parapsychology and UFOs, he asked me to join him on a trip to Warminster in Wiltshire. This small town is a magnet for, if not visiting aliens, at least for UFO obsessives, one of whom Mike wanted to meet. 'He's done some interesting work.' We spent many an earnest hour with a small, skinny fellow who'd once been a respected astronomer but who now worked on UFO-hunting in a shed lined with tin foil full of home-made Heath Robinson equipment. 'What do you think?' I asked as we drove away. 'Well of course, he's obviously totally nuts,' said Mike.

15

'A nice little media war'

Foreign correspondents will talk, and even write, at length about the gear they need to do their jobs. What they rarely mention is the phenomenon of the Press Hotel, unless the one they happen to be staying in at the time gets blown up.

But the fact is that in every hot spot there's always one hotel in which the international media congregate. This is not mere herd instinct, a chance to drink in the bar with their mates. The press hotel becomes an essential clearing house for news and rumour, and it's the crowded haunt where the local 'spooks' – Mossad, Sigurimi, CIA, Shik, Stasi, Tonton Macoutes, MI6, KGB, FSB – hang out in the bar (they grill us while we grill them). It's also the place to which brave but frightened local people will often try to come if they want their stories to be heard, hoping that the presence of the inter-national press will protect them.

Old Indochina, Middle East, Balkan, African or Central American hands have all got fond, and sometimes less fond, memories of cockroach-infested press hotels they've known. (And although I dis-like cockroaches, especially when they scuttle into the bedsheets, I've become quite tolerant of the rats who've sometimes shared a room with me. In order to keep the local wildlife out of guests' beds, in the Sixties the press hotel in Georgetown, Guyana, placed the bed legs in tin cans full of insecticide, though unfortunately a small band of lizards and giant spiders took refuge overnight in my handbag instead.)

Press hotels tend to be the ones that are closest to the scene of the story, are passably well equipped and, above all, have good communications, which in the past usually meant little more than a room telephone that worked. (Ideally they also have enterprising, and sometimes brave, staff.) Examples of famous press hotels over

the years include the Holiday Inn in Sarajevo, the Palestine and the
Al Rashid in Baghdad, the Ledra Palace in Cyprus, the Hyatt in
Belgrade, the St Georges in Beirut, the Intercontinental in Kinshasa,
Meikles in Zimbabwe, the American Colony in Jerusalem.

In El Salvador the press hotel was the Camino Real.

Neither my newspaper nor my family wanted me to cover that
particularly nasty civil war. But I was already doing a story in Honduras, a short flight away from El Salvador, and it was tempting to
nip over there.

The Honduran story in itself had not been that interesting – but
it did involve a beautiful, high-born English Sloane who used to
share a flat with an ambitious young Austrian woman called Marie-
Christine who eventually became Princess Michael of Kent (thereafter dubbed 'Princess Pushy' by the Royal Family). Beautiful blonde
English aristocrats in exotic places, especially if they're in some
danger, go down a treat with readers. Chuck a soupçon of royalty
into the mix and you're away.

The beautiful Sloane was now married to the faintly sinister,
charming and Machiavellian American ambassador and the couple
were living with their adopted Honduran daughters in the scruffy
little capital, Tegucigalpa. At the time John Negroponte was a towering hate figure for whole swathes of the international left, who called
him Uncle Sam's Central American Pro-Consul. (He most recently
became George Bush's security 'tsar' and is still a hate figure.)

Central America was always heavily addicted to coups, invariably
mounted by right-wing, deeply corrupt blue-chinned generals who
employed death squads to bump off their enemies. And of course
their enemies – Marxists, Maoists or simply local peasants fed up
with being exploited – tended to answer in kind. Central American
ditches had a distressing habit of filling up at night with dead and
mutilated bodies.

This was during the Cold War when America and the Soviet
Union fought proxy wars all over Africa, Asia and Latin America.
Uncle Sam and Pro-Consul Negroponte were determined that their
neighbours to the south of the Mexican border should not turn
Communist; after all, Castro's Cuba was doing its best to spread its
own anti-Yanqui revolution to countries like Nicaragua, Guatemala,
Honduras and, especially, El Salvador.

I checked in late at night at the Camino Real in San Salvador, the capital. 'Nice little media war, this,' an American embassy official told me the following evening over a Cuba Libre in the bar. 'Small country, lots of bang-bang – you guys can drive out into the war areas and with luck get back in time for dinner! Yep, a very nice little media war . . .' Except, of course, some people never did come back, for dinner or for anything else. In the small hours of my first night there, my hotel room phone kept ringing. Every time I picked it up I heard nothing but odd clicks on the line. Bloody Salvadorean telephone system!

Except it wasn't. Scratchy with sleeplessness, I descended in the morning to the restaurant which was full of foreign correspondents of many different nationalities. One of them was Paul Ellman, an old friend who worked for the *Guardian*; I'd last seen him when we were both covering the 'liberation war' in Rhodesia, now Zimbabwe. His mood was gleeful: 'Hi, Leslie! You've come at the right time! Some really good stuff going on here.'

He and I knew that the reason we were both in El Salvador was because there was, in terms of copy, 'some really good stuff going on here'. Even though our readers, especially mine, didn't share our obsessions, we both felt it was our obligation to make people living in 'normal' countries care about what we cared about.

Paul's gleeful greeting makes him sound heartless. But he wasn't: he cared passionately about the victims of that vile little war. And he was willing to risk his life to cover their fate, even though he knew that scarcely anyone in Britain (except Guardianistas and revolutionary cells in Walthamstow bedsits) gave a toss about that tiny, beautiful, troublesome country.

I complained to him about my malfunctioning room phone. He laughed. 'Nothing wrong with the phone – that's the usual "welcome" from the death squads to any newly arrived foreign correspondent, warning you not to write "slanders" about them. The clicks in your earpiece were their usual clicking on and off of the safety catch on a gun!'

I almost felt sorry for the booby on the other end of the line who'd had to sit up all night clicking his safety catch, to little effect. Out of fairness to him I really should have mugged up on local death-squad etiquette in advance so that he could, as required by his job description, suitably terrify me. Whereas, poor lamb, he'd merely irritated me.

The military were much better equipped (by America); but the rebels had a steady supply of arms which were smuggled in from the Soviet Union via Cuba and Nicaragua. Between the lot of them, the warring sides had already forced one fifth of all Salvadoreans to flee the country.

Soon after my arrival in El Salvador a rumour swept through the Camino Real; I was laconically informed by some members of the press corps, veterans of Vietnam, that 'a hundred Gs are supposed to have been greased by an air bombardment near Las Perasas'. 'Gs' were the leftist guerrillas who controlled large areas of the country-side, and in 'nice little media wars' like this, a massacre – or 'greasing' – of a hundred Gs by the American-supplied planes of the Salvadorean Government might make a 'nice little story', especially for the *Guardian*. A handful of us decided to investigate; after all, we should, like the embassy man said, be back for dinner.

True, a Dutch television team had been travelling on the road we were about to take and had been kidnapped. Shortly afterwards, their bullet-riddled bodies were found – murdered (as official announcements in El Salvador so often put it) by *desconocidos*, unknown assailants. Nevertheless, we set off in two jeeps into the rebel-held territory of Chalatenango province.

'We should start smelling the bodies by now. Don't see any vultures yet though,' said Ellman, with the practised nonchalance of a man who had seen many such *matanzas* (massacres) before. I was slightly alarmed that, as our departure from the hotel had been observed by those who might like to kill us, we might end up in a mini-*matanza* ourselves. As I now knew from my 'malfunctioning' room phone, foreign journalists were much hated here: they did not tell *la verdad* about El Salvador, at least not 'the truth' that the death squads wanted the world to hear.

On the main roads constant roadblocks and lounging teenage soldiers cradling M16s and eating watermelons proclaimed that the government was, just about, in control. Eventually, a slogan scrawled across a tiny white church in a little red-tiled village which said 'Long Live the Military and Economic Programme of the FMLN!' told us we'd reached rebel-held territory.

'Ah, vultures!' Ellman exclaimed, pointing at the flocks wheeling ahead of us. 'We must be getting near!' The symbolism in his words was uncomfortable: perhaps we too were like the vultures, excited by the prospect of feeding on death. No wonder people hate journalists who flock to scenes of death and disaster, and call us 'vultures'; we do indeed, alas, have much in common with those scavengers.

'Hell, we forgot to bring a white flag!' shouted Ellman. Do we really need one? 'You'd better believe it! Up on those hillsides there are hundreds of watching eyes. Without a white flag on the aerial one tends to wind up dead. Haven't you anything we can use?'

All I had was a Marks and Spencer's petticoat, which I yanked off: Ellman looked witheringly at this absurd frou-frou covered in rose-buds and lace and was full of contempt. Having fixed it to the car aerial he said, 'Mind you, having this thing fluttering up there in a macho country like this is asking for trouble! Want to be dead *and* raped?'

The possible rape didn't hugely bother me. The only time I came near to being raped was in the early Seventies when I was working with a French TV team in Abu Dhabi; a highly civilized Palestinian, whose wife and children I knew, suddenly decided to use a knife to 'persuade' me of the seriousness of his 'amorous' attentions. I was so enraged by his presumption that I thumped him in the groin and escaped with only a few knife cuts on my back. I didn't report him to the police: although he worked for the government, he was stateless, and his wife and four young children would have been expelled. I didn't see why I should render his innocent family shamed and destitute when I myself had scarcely been harmed.

And one of my colleagues who'd been raped repeatedly during the civil war in Angola told me that, while extremely disagreeable, rape was certainly not a 'fate worse than death'. You can, with dif-ficulty, get over rape. You can't get over death. Besides, my raped colleague and my own non-raped self come from cultures where our families won't automatically reject us because of the 'shame' and 'dishonour' such violation would bring upon them.

An angry Ellman subsequently yanked the petticoat off the aerial, and we drove on until we reached a village called, in Spanish, Sweet Name of Mary – a straggle of shabby houses, a few black pigs, a vast poinsettia bush and one old man in a sombrero. Yes, there'd been bombardments from the air: 'Boom! Boom!' But no massacre here – it's over that hill. He told us that some other *periodistas*, journalists, had come through here ten minutes earlier. Also, a couple of hours before them, about 500 guerrillas: look, there are their bootmarks in the dust.

The old man was upset: the 'freedom fighters' had taken his cows and refused to pay for them. We sympathized, but were more worried about our fellow *periodistas*: 'We should be able to see their dust from here. Hope the Gs haven't got 'em!'

As we lumbered on I tried to concentrate on the heart-catching beauty of this wild and tragic land – lush, flower-filled valleys, sapphire lakes ringed by sleeping volcanoes, yellow butterflies flickering above streams where peasant women washed their clothes, brilliant parakeets overhead. The original inhabitants called this the 'Land of Pretty Things'.

If only one could forget the miasma of death that hung over this 'Land of Pretty Things'. Almost a tenth of the population had been obliterated by the war, 30,000 people lived as refugees in their own country and, after gastroenteritis, violence was the commonest cause of death.

At one point I looked into the wing mirror and in a moment of alarm saw the spectral shape of a pickup truck looming up in the cloud of dust behind us. Anyone who'd been in the surreal nightmare of that country for more than a few hours would understand my reaction – and my relief when I saw the truck taking a turning off. Pickup trucks driven by *desconocidos* had become harbingers of sudden death in El Salvador.

A Cherokee Chief truck with *desconocidos* was seen following the Dutch journalists along this road shortly before they were kidnapped and killed; a Toyota truck with *desconocidos* was seen near where four American mission workers had recently been murdered; a pickup was always seen roaring away from a pile of half-naked bodies dumped by the side of a road, or in a ravine, or even in the parking lot of the luxury Camino Real.

A pickup full of *desconocidos* was always part of the despairing stories I'd been told by the Mothers of the Disappeared and Assassinated Ones in their refuge in a temporary hut in the grounds of the Catholic Archbishop's offices. (His predecessor had been assassinated during Mass.) Woman after woman would open what looked like ordinary family snapshot albums, and inside, in a grotesque parody of happy family pictures, I'd see photographs of mutilated bodies, bodies crawling with worms, bodies with the faces burned out by acid. And then the women would intone in a dreadful litany, 'A pickup truck came one night and *desconocidos* took away my husband/my brother/my son/ my daughter . . .'

After a while, Ellman and I no longer saw the vultures or, indeed, the dust trail of our colleagues' jeep. Ellman was furious with me: 'It's all your fault! We've lost the others because of you faffing around with that stupid petticoat!'

'What do you mean, it's *my fault*! I've only just arrived and it was *you* who neglected to come with a white flag *or* a *La Prensa* sign on the jeep!' He was also furious that we'd found no evidence of a *matanza*; not surprisingly, because it eventually emerged that there hadn't been one.

We headed back on to the main road, scarcely speaking to each other. Our way was barred by an Army roadblock: these had of course been set up to stop independent witnesses like us going into the area of the alleged massacre. The soldiers were baffled: what were we doing the wrong side of the roadblock? 'You were too slow!' we jeered, turning up the car radio fortissimo in childish mockery.

Back in the capital, the armed forces issued a statement about their non-existent 'success' in the air bombardment. 'One hundred and nine *subversivos* were killed in Chalatenango province . . .' Propaganda and lies were, of course, a favoured element of any '*solución*' in El Salvador – as they are in most conflicts.

On our return to the hotel, we learned that our colleagues who'd been in the jeep ahead of us had been kidnapped by the *subversivos* whose bootmarks we'd seen in the dust. 'F***ing Leslie, if only we'd been kidnapped, we'd have got a story! It's all your fault!' I told him that, on the whole, I preferred *not* to get kidnapped, particularly in view of what had happened to the Dutch team. (Fortunately, our colleagues were released unharmed after a fortnight's incarceration.)

It was with relief that I checked out of the Camino Real; my own '*solución*' was just to leave this stifling, misbegotten land. Exhausted, I fell asleep on the evening cab journey to the airport. After a while a pothole shook me awake. The darkness was suddenly rent by the sound and sight of white-haired women screaming out prayers at an evangelical prayer meeting in a street-side slum. And then – coffins! Row upon row of coffins, brilliantly illuminated by the surreal blue-neon glare from a coffin-maker's window.

Hysterical prayers and shining coffins: fitting symbols for El Salvador, whose Spanish name means 'The Saviour'. The Saviour Himself must have looked down upon those thousands of unshriven bodies in his namesake land, and turned His eyes away in disgust.

*

In Albania the press hotel was the Rogner Europapark in the capital, Tirana.

In March 1997 we'd gathered there because chaos had engulfed that desperately poor, former Stalinist country after the collapse of a pyramid-banking scheme. One dark, velvety night, five hours into a government-imposed curfew, gunfire crackled through the hitherto morgue-like silence of the street outside the hotel.

Oh, my God, I thought wearily, here we go again! Here I was in the midst of yet another baffling and bloody Balkan mess, and I'd covered a few of them. Did my readers care that this was 'essentially' – according to an American expert on Albania dispensing ethno-graphic wisdom in the lobby – 'about the rivalry between the Ghegs of the north and the Tosqs of the south, divided by the Shkumbin River'? More to the point, should I break the curfew and go and investigate the gunfire? No, I yawned to myself. Seemed a silly reason to die, just to prove that another bunch of Albanian government goons (largely Ghegs, apparently), fresh from firebombing the offices of an independent newspaper, murdering opposition figures and beating up journalists, had been loosing off fusillades from their Kalashnikovs at 1 a.m.

Why did they do it? Perhaps just for the sheer, Gheg-ish fun of shattering the nervous sleep of the hapless citizens of the shabby, dust-choked little capital of a tiny country which seemed to be on the brink of civil war. These blokes, with their extravagant mous-taches, clad in cheap nylon anoraks, dirty trainers and T-shirts, were being described by pro-government (and heavily Gheg-ish) sources as 'noble citizens' who were allegedly 'defending democracy' against 'Red terrorists'.

These 'noble' Albanians were, of course, employees of the euph-
emistically named National Information Service, or SHIK, the predic-
tably grotesque secret police, and thus the only people allowed to
roam the city at night in unmarked cars, loaded to the gunwales with
weapons. Was it something, I wondered, in the *water* round here
which makes the Balkans ungovernable by anybody, including – and
often especially – themselves? Ah, said my new Albanian friend Altin
Rraxhimi, 'Is old Albanian saying: is easier for two stones to become
one, than for Albanians to unite!' (Why are *all* 'old sayings' in the
Balkans so melodramatically *glum*?) And why were Albanians so
stupid as to indulge (as Pashtuns and Arabs often do) in bouts of
'happy fire' where, in celebration of something or other, they fire
streams of bullets into the air. After all, bullets which go up tend to
come down, thus slaying the odd passing goat and a granny or two.

Albanians are not of course inherently stupid people. Even under
Stalinism, when I first visited the country nine years earlier, the
small, dark, secretive Albanians made me suspect that beneath their
sullen poverty they might prove to be extremely sharp. I wrote then:
'Give the Albanians an inch of freedom, one suspects, and they'll
take an extremely entrepreneurial mile and will generally get up to
no good.' But no one had told Albanians what capitalism really
meant: they were, when it came, easy meat for capitalism's sleaziest
sharks; inevitably mayhem and lots of 'unhappy' fire commenced.

After all, the late 'Beloved Leader' Enver Hoxha – the murderous,
thick-lipped Stalinist who ruled this hapless land for over forty years
until his death in 1985 – had sealed Albanians off from the outside
world, pockmarking the countryside with gun-bunkers known as
'concrete mushrooms'. (The current government has decided to
paint them in fondant ice-cream colours to make them look jollier.)

Albanians, secretly tuning in to Italian television across the water,
dazzled by its game-shows and stripping housewives, had no idea
what the realities of finance and banking were. Under Hoxha and his
successor there were no banks, and no private property; shops, all
state-owned, displayed little more than limp pink knickers, dusty jars
of pickle and slabs of yellow, slightly gritty soap. Albanian television news (even three years after Hoxha's death) contained long
sequences of old film of the Beloved Leader congratulating heroic
olive-growers on exceeding their norms. The only Western movies

allowed starred Norman Wisdom, promoted as a proletarian hero fighting bloated capitalists. Norman Wisdom and Lord Byron (one of the few figures in history who had nice things to say about Albanians) were virtually national icons.

When I'd first visited the country, no private cars were allowed. Salih, my government guide, had smoothly explained to me, 'We have learned from the traffic problems you have in the West. So, to prevent them, we have banned private cars.' Sorted.

Salih had told me that Albanians were not the least bit interested in Western television: 'They find it boring. They much prefer ours.' Not true, Comrade Salih, as well you knew. Although Albanian radios were locked on to regime frequencies and reception of foreign broadcasts was forbidden, the naturally duck-and-dive Albanians, by dint of pieces of bent wire on rooftops and elsewhere, managed to tune in to overseas stations and were fully aware of Western consumerism.

Why, I wondered, do such regimes always try – in the end, always pointlessly – to keep their citizens in ignorance of the outside world? Even today, in China and parts of the Middle East, regimes try to keep the 'corrupt' West at bay (in order to preserve their own corruption from being 'corrupted' by ideas of freedom), but in the end human curiosity will always prevail.

The Albanian capital smelt of the fifteenth century, all cabbage and wood smoke, and an eerie pall of silence hung over it, as though some strange nerve gas had drifted down from the surrounding hills. Stick-like figures, huddled inside grimy overcoats and mufflers, crisscrossed the huge Skanderbeg Square, looking like survivors of some catastrophe.

The only spots of colour in the square came from the gigantic golden statue of the late Beloved Leader, complete with flapping overcoat and huge Elton John shoes, and the ubiquitous red banners declaring 'Long Live the Party of Comrade Enver Hoxha!'

Hoxha, who spent 20 per cent of Albania's pitifully small GDP defending it against invasion from an utterly indifferent world, once declared, 'Do not forget that, together with the Chinese, Albanians make up one quarter of the world's population.' Even the shiny, hard lavatory paper in the decrepit government hotels was stamped with the words 'Property of the People's Republic of China'.

Then suddenly in 1992 poor little Albania emerged from its hermit-crab shell, toppled the Communists and the giant Elton-John-shod Hoxha statue, and started to embrace the outside world. Thanks to massive Western aid, she began enjoying herself, disco-ing, smuggling, voting, and merrily filling the streets with Mercedes nicked in Germany. (Judging by their insanely insouciant driving, the one human right I believed Albanians should have been deprived of was the right to own a car.)

One day in 1997, in the early evening, a group of young Albanian journalists decided to seek safety in our press hotel; one newspaper office had been burnt down and opposition journalists were being rounded up, threatened and in some cases beaten up. Suddenly, I and three human rights activists – Frances D'Souza, then of Britain's Article 19, the Albanian-speaking Fred Abrahams of America's Human Rights Watch and Thierry Cruvellier of France's Reporters Sans Fron-tières – found that we had a minor asylum-seeking crisis on our hands. We made hurried, secretive and fruitless calls to embassies, trying to calm the kids (all in their early twenties), but with the curfew drawing closer their hysteria was mounting by the minute. The lobby was full of filthy 'Partizani' cigarette smoke and, of course, Shik secret police.

'Okay, so we'll have to shelter them for the night.' 'How do we smuggle them into our rooms?' 'Some of them will have to sleep in our baths, or on the floor'. 'If anyone knocks on the door at night *pretend you're asleep* – don't open it, whatever you do!' 'Surely they won't drag them out of our rooms, not with the world's media here?' 'Er, I'm not so sure!'

Suddenly finding myself co-opted as Den Mother to Albanian dissidents, I herded the trembling flock into our press hotel dining room. The Shik goons followed us. I kept having to count my charges, in case the Shik managed to lift one of them when I wasn't looking. If one of them went to the loo without telling me I was furious: 'Where's Enton gone? Why have we only got *seven* here instead of *nine*! Where are the others?' Another of 'my kids', a terrified girl called Mimosa, despite being hungry, said she was much too fright-ened to eat. 'Mimosa!' I ordered, in best Den-Mother style, '*Eat up your dinner now!*'

Earlier, I'd appealed to other Western journalists in the hotel to help out with accommodation overnight. All were embarrassed and said no. The reporter from a left-wing French newspaper was particularly dismissive of my appeal on behalf of 'my kids'. 'You are an idiot, *absolument!* Why do you want to get yourself in trouble by involving yourself with dissidents? You'll do yourself no good at all.' Maybe I wouldn't, but all our terrified charges survived the night, calmed down and got home safely the next day.

That French reporter, always vocal about American abuse of human rights, didn't choose to lift a finger on behalf of human rights in Albania if it involved even a smidgen of danger to himself. When I next bumped into him five years later, I icily reminded him of that fact.

Actually, I was quite glad he was still alive: whenever someone had seriously annoyed me I used to say to my husband, 'Well, I've marked *his* card,' and that applied to the Frenchman. I stopped uttering the phrase when two people whose card I'd marked suddenly dropped dead. I now take a more slow-burning Bedouin line. As my old friend Abdel Bari Atwan, editor of the pan-Arab newspaper *Al Quds al Arabi*, once put it to me: 'The Bedouin say a man is hasty if he waits forty years to take revenge.'

*

The Rogner in Albania, being a new, bland business hotel, was quite unlike the press hotel in Haiti, the Grand Hotel Oloffson, in the capital, Port-au-Prince. Ever since I'd read Graham Greene's novel *The Comedians*, a morality tale set in that impoverished, insane little country under the grotesque François 'Papa Doc' Duvalier, I'd wanted to go there and stay in the Oloffson which, in the book, he called the Trianon.

The chance came in 1993 in the aftermath of yet another coup which two-and-a-half years earlier had ousted a bug-eyed, manic-depressive little priest called Father Jean-Bertrand Aristide – 'Titid' – who'd become the first democratically elected President in Haitian history. Various black emperors, psychotic generals, voodoo dictators, and the kleptomaniac playboy, 'Baby Doc' Duvalier, were among his predecessors. After seven months the slum-dwellers' beloved 'Titid' had been overthrown in a military coup.

Which is why Britain had sent a frigate to join an armada of American, Canadian, French and Dutch warships on their way to Haiti to enforce a UN oil and weapons embargo and thereby 'restore democracy'.

The Haitian military insisted that the little slum-priest was 'a Communist', a 'psychopath', 'anti-American' and a 'cannibal', and wouldn't have him back.

My immediate problem was trying to persuade the Oloffson to accommodate me. From London I rang the manager, a dreamy Haitian-American called Richard Morse who was pro-Titid and also ran a voodoo band.

'Do you have a room?'

'Depends,' he said cautiously. Since I knew that Haiti's once glamorous little tourist industry had long ago collapsed, I found this puzzling. The Oloffson's glory days were long gone, when the likes of Mick Jagger, John Gielgud and Truman Capote used to turn up on the marijuana-scented wooden verandah of this eccentric ginger-bread mansion.

Never mind. I'd get into the Oloffson somehow.

At the shabby little Port-au-Prince airport, there were no cabs. Riots tend to be bad for the taxi business. I met a helpful Canadian missionary who told me he had a truck outside and he'd give me a lift but I'd have to sit in the back as the passenger seat was full of medical supplies he was ferrying to a slum clinic. (Haiti, once the richest country in the Caribbean, is now the tenth poorest in the world.) So I climbed into the back and was transported along with a lot of gunny sacks to the Oloffson. The Princeton-educated Richard, in bare feet, watched me arrive, and evidently decided that I was his sort of guest.

The building's original owner was a former President (who was dismembered bit by bit by a mob through the railings of the French legation in which he'd taken refuge in 1915). A misinformed pro-Titid mob had turned up not long before I arrived to burn the hotel down, but had changed its mind; now it was the anti-Titid military who were said to be considering setting fire to the place, which would have been a doddle since it was mostly built of wood. No wonder some of the more nervous flak-jacketed American newsmen wouldn't come near it, and instead holed up, along with the few remaining UN staff, in a fortified luxury hotel more securely located on top of a hill.

What we Oloffsonites scornfully nicknamed 'the Independent Republic of Hotel Montana' on the hill might have been a safer berth, but nothing was as redolent of Haiti as the Oloffson.

Richard's only protection for the hotel was voodoo. From time to time the Oloffson guests would be rounded up to march round the building scattering mysterious liquids and chanting. The message went out that the voodoo spirits would be deeply offended if anyone tried to bring harm to the Oloffson, and since voodoo is the unofficial but prevailing religion, these precautions were, thus far, effective.

And so, night after gun-punctured night, I would lie in my bed in the ghostly Grand Hotel, gazing on a portrait of the black Emperor Jean-Jacques Dessalines in his Napoleonic tricorne hat, and listen, as Graham Greene once listened, to the distant staccato sounds of the poor killing the poor in the interests of the rich.

From the filigreed verandah of the decaying Oloffson (beside an area of the capital called Lower Not Very Much), I couldn't actually see HMS *Active* patrolling the blue-green waters off Port-au-Prince. But I knew she was still there, and I could therefore justify my own continuing presence in this beautiful, mad hotel in this beautiful, mad land.

Mostly you never had to leave the Oloffson verandah to find out what was going on. Indeed, the eccentric Caribbean correspondent of the *Guardian* couldn't understand why I ever did. 'But everyone who's everyone on all sides comes here every evening!'

Among them would be Monsieur Aubelin Jolicoeur (Mr Pretty-heart), a wildly camp father of six, who'd prance across the Oloffson verandah in his white suit with his silver-topped cane, a foulard scarf tied Nöel Coward-style round his black neck. 'A-a-ay am Mistair Haiti . . . A-a-ay am like ze bee to ze flower . . . D-d-darling, you are s-s-so beautiful!' he'd stutter joyously as he deposited a courtly kiss on the palm of some sour-faced female hack.

He was always bumming free meals off the Oloffson. Aubelin was the man on whom Greene based his character Petit Pierre, the Haitian gadfly gossip columnist and police informer, in *The Comedians*.

'Ah, President Duvalier was like a father to me!' Aubelin gabbled ecstatically. 'A-a-ay did not wish to help him run the country – but four times President Duvalier saved my life, telling those who wished to kill me: "Aubelin Jolicoeur is my son!"'

Aubelin was still a columnist (although, alas, 80 per cent of Haitians couldn't read), but these were very bad times. One evening Richard Morse dreamily mused, 'Perhaps I should change sides. It would be *so* nice to be on the winning side for once!' But the Oloffson verandah set just drank another rum punch, smoked another spliff, and equally dreamily concluded that things weren't yet *that* bad.

And perhaps the ubiquitous presence of Aubelin Jolicoeur was in itself a talisman for survival. By alternately flattering and excoriating the powers-that-be and the powers-about-to-fall, Aubelin, in a land of so many undeserved deaths, was the one great Haitian survivor.

When it looked as if the slum-priest would survive in power, Aubelin was an enthusiast: 'Such a time of *hope*!' Now, Aubelin's finely tuned antennae had concluded that Titid's UN-backed return was a dead duck.

'Aristide blew it, darling! He deserved to be ousted! He is a m-m-monster! They are all monsters! A-a-ay *love* my poor little country! But the problem with the Haitians is they are all irresponsible people – Aristide is no different!

'Let me tell you, my darling, he is now living the life of a *nabob* in America! Do you think he would care to come back to Haiti now? No! He just wants to stay away and *p-p-punish* us all with this terrible embargo – while he's having a b-b-ball!'

One day a group of 'Oloffson set' journalists headed off in a truck into a nearby slum. We came across two dead bodies; lying like a scarf across the neck of one of them was a strangled newborn kitten and a dead rat which, through its astonished eyes, gazed up at us and the blazing Haitian sun.

Another dead rat peeked out of the crotch of the second man, whose arms had been tied behind his back before he'd been shot. 'The animals? For voodoo!' explained a ragged youth as he and a small, nervous crowd gathered round the men's bodies, dumped on a rubbish heap in La Saline, one of Port-au-Prince's most foetid slums. I couldn't see the bullet holes in the dead men's skulls: their heads had ballooned into black cauliflowers thick with buzzing bluebottles. The bodies had lain there amid the rotting orange peel for over twelve hours; no one had dared come forward to claim them.

And no one, of course, would investigate their deaths. After all, 'everyone' knew who'd done it. Sweet Mickey's men. Sweet Mickey's so-called *attachés*, the name now given to the re-emergent Tonton Macoutes (the 'Uncle Knapsacks' in Creole fairy-tales who steal naughty children at night). The Macoutes who once terrorized Haiti for voodoo dictator Papa Doc now terrorized it again for his political heirs.

Illiterate black men from the slums, these armed plain-clothes thugs fanned out from their favourite haunts, like the Bar Normandie off Burial Street, and roamed Haiti's streets at night in their trucks, killing their fellow illiterates for a handful of dollars from on high. And all because Sweet Mickey, his greedy military chums and the mulatto millionaires nibbling Lobster Thermidor in their mountain mansions willed that it should be so.

No point, of course, in sending for the police to investigate these two particular grisly, if commonplace, deaths: you see, Sweet Mickey *was* the police.

Ah, Sweet Mickey, Sweet Titid, sweet Haiti, sweet smell of money, sweet smell of death.

The embargo may have been causing 1,000 extra deaths a month among the poor – but hell, it was causing much worse than that in Kenscoff, the mulatto millionaires' haunt up in the cool, mauve mountains: it was actually blighting the luxury restaurant business. *Dommage!*

An exasperated US ambassador had once described the tiny top layer of mulatto and Arab families who owned around 97 per cent of the country's wealth as the Morally Repugnant Elite, or MREs. The initials were a play on the US military's rations which are called Meals Ready to Eat. The top six families were nicknamed the BAM BAM, from the initials of their surnames; 'Bam bam' in Creole, the language of 95 per cent of Haitians, also means 'Gimme! Gimme!'

And thanks to the embargo even Jean-Guy Barme, the smooth Frenchman who owned La Souvenance – the MREs' favourite res-taurant in Pétionville – was now feeling the pinch. True, the military coup leader General Cedras still popped in for a bite with his fierce wife Yannick, but the others . . . 'No gasoline. Anyway, it's not very safe going out at night these days,' Monsieur Barme told me sadly over a dinner of *brochette de langoustines à l'ail*.

Malheureusement, Monsieur Barme had recently lost two of his regulars. One, the Aristide-appointed Justice Minister, had been assassinated the previous month. 'A very *charmant* man,' sighed Monsieur Barme elegantly. The other, a millionaire who'd 'betrayed' his class by backing the Little Priest, was dragged out of Mass and shot in the head by Sweet Mickey's *attachés* (who went on to kill thirteen in all in that single spree). 'Another very *charmant* man,' Monsieur Barme sighed again, contemplating the gradual decimation of his clientele. '*Hélas*, business is very bad these days.' Well, murder does tend to put a dampener on a Haitian gourmet's pleasure.

Monsieur Barme's mulatto French-speaking clientele traditionally left politics, otherwise known as murder, to the black thugs down the hill. In exchange, of course, for being allowed to go on doing what they'd always done – shamelessly exploiting the poor. And, of course, topping up their wallets with a spot of contraband, plus huge drug-smuggling dues.

My fixer in Haiti was Colson Dormé, whom I'd met on the Oloffson verandah. He was an opposition radio journalist who'd recently been kidnapped and beaten for a week by the military, but who still insisted on helping me. One night, when an Oloffson regular gave him a lift home after a day with me, the *attachés* were waiting for him; she turned the car round, screeched away at high speed, and took him into hiding overnight.

'Oh, that happens every three weeks or so!' Colson told me next morning with a wry grin. 'But I'm not afraid. I believe in liberty and democracy! Anyway, I have this wonderful voodoo potion which means I can face the *attachés* without fear!'

Colson noticed that every time I got up from a chair I winced in pain. 'Yeah, I have a back problem which no one, not even the top specialists in Harley Street, seems to be able to fix. I just have to stuff myself with pain killers,' I sighed.

'You must see my *houngan*! He saved my wife from death and zombification.' It was like I was back in north London getting tips from a chum about their favourite chiropractor.

A *houngan* is a voodoo priest. Well, I thought, a chap who can save a wife from zombification could surely cure my back problem. And so we went to visit Monsieur Henri Avry Fritz, Colson's affable *houngan*, in a filthy dirt-floor 'temple'.

On the way Colson told me that the ritual to save his wife from zombification 'took nine hours! But your problem is just back pain so it shouldn't take as long as that.' On our arrival the 'temple' filled up with an instant congregation of friendly Carrefour slum-dwellers.

'Monsieur Fritz,' explained Colson, 'will now go into that shrine and when he comes out he will be possessed by the spirits'. Which spirits? 'The spirits of Gedé, the god of Fertility and Death.'

'But Colson, I'm not too keen at the moment on either fertility *or* death! Couldn't I have another choice of spirits?' No. It turned out that voodoo spirits, like grouse, have seasons – and this was Gedé's – so I'd have to lump it.

'Colson, will there be people biting off the heads of live chickens? I'm not too keen on that either.'

'No, no, chickens are only for serious problems, not for back pain.' Besides, he added, people were now so hungry that there weren't that many chickens to spare these days for voodoo. 'Certainly not for back pain.' So that's all right then.

The next problem came when, amid much hollering and singing and lots of pimiento-flavoured rum, bonfires and chants from the congregation, Colson told me that the spirits of Gedé had commanded me to take off all my clothes.

Ah.

I muttered under my breath, 'No nudity please, I'm British.' But I'd already been there for almost three hours and it seemed churlish to pull out now. Colson went into a huddle with Monsieur Fritz, apparently informing him in Creole that Madame Leslie would take everything else off but wished to keep her knickers on. The spirits of Gedé conferred among themselves and mercifully agreed that hanging on to my knickers would be acceptable.

Their spokesman Monsieur Fritz, having received their verdict, then smeared my body with some noxious liquid in the course of a spectacularly long and noisy ceremony. And then suddenly it was all over. Monsieur Fritz snapped free of his 'possession', gave me a huge bottle of the same slime-green stuff, told me to drink it three times a day, and politely asked for his fee, just like any private doctor in Harley Street, although, by their standards, his charges were absurdly small.

I dressed, bade farewell to my fellow congregants, and returned to the Oloffson with my 'prescription'. Which I then sipped. The verandah regulars, who included world-music DJ Andy Kershaw, were horrified. 'You're mad!' First, for going to Carrefour where I might have been murdered. Second, for having a voodoo *houngan* deal with my back. And third, 'for drinking that stuff! It'll kill you!'

It didn't. True, as a result I did get a bout of amoebic dysentery a week later (a great way of losing weight). But I haven't had a twinge of back pain since.

I've never returned to the termite-infested Oloffson or to mad, spirit-haunted Haiti. I wrote then that I suspected that 'Haiti will remain, perhaps for ever, a tiny black empire of the doomed; a Haitian black comedy without end.' And, judging by the continuing chaos and murder, that has, sadly, proved to be true. Titid, the Little Priest, did return to power, but made a mess of it; Sweet Mickey's *attachés* were replaced by Titid's *chimères*; the Little Priest was ousted yet again and fled into exile in South Africa; and Sweet Mickey, on Titid's return, had fled to the Dominican Republic next door. His *attachés* were responsible for the deaths of at least 4,000 Haitians, and the Americans tried to have him extradited on the charge of smuggling 33 tons of heroin and cocaine into the US from his private airstrip. Unfortunately, he is still free and living in Honduras.

Greene's 'Petit Pierre', Aubelin Jolicoeur – he of the camp stammer, outrageous gossip and famous silver-topped cane – died aged eighty, in penury. Someone had even stolen his cane.

And poor dear Colson, my brave friend, found that while his voodoo potion saved him from Sweet Mickey's *attachés*, they could not save him from Aids. He, like so many HIV-positive Haitians, is now dead.

16

War Junkies

Why do some wars attract little attention, whereas others become instant honeypots for swarms of foreign correspondents? If you want your country's war to be noticed (other than by its victims) then frankly it helps if your country is small (like El Salvador or Israel) and easily accessible (both for getting into and getting out of); and if possible it should be one which lends itself to easy characterization: this armed lot over here are the goodies, that armed lot over there are the baddies. Unfortunately, as I know so well from my own experience of wars and civil conflicts around the world, the divisions between goody and baddy are very rarely clear-cut. But such ambiguities can be exasperating for journalists and, worse, extremely confusing for their readers and viewers.

It's easier, for you and your readers, if you keep the storyline simple. For example in the early days of Israel's struggle for survival, most of the Western media were passionately on the side of 'plucky little Israel' and passionately anti-Arab. Now the journalistic position has been almost completely reversed. The problem is that it's hard to hold an audience if you just wring your hands and say 'there is good and bad on both sides' – which of course there always is.

This applied to the Balkans when Yugoslavia was breaking up. Very soon the herd instinct of the journalists who covered it meant that the Serbs were declared to be the irredeemably black-hearted villains of the piece, and the Croats and the Bosnian Muslims were usually classified as victims. Thus only Serb-committed massacres would get huge coverage. The Bosnian Muslims were relatively poorly armed: to compensate for this lack of military matériel, they needed, and got, international public opinion on their side. So the Bosniaks were extremely helpful and would even lay on an 'atrocity bus' to ferry hacks in besieged Sarajevo to view the latest proof of Serb wickedness.

The Serb leaders, being a stupidly pig-headed lot, did the opposite by being thoroughly unhelpful, blocking access, occasionally putting some of our number under house arrest, and generally making it extremely difficult for us to cover anything. The Serb ability, propaganda-wise, to shoot themselves in the foot meant that few in the West cared to listen to stories about the murder of innocent Serb civilians. It spoiled the unambiguous storyline.

But I did listen. I worked quite a lot on the Serb side of the lines and I knew about, and had seen the results of, massacres of Serb civilians, which never aroused the slightest interest back in London. The one-sidedness of Western news stories about these Balkan massacres so irritated me that I decided to open one of my reports with the words:

Mrs Malenka Ristic was too old and weak to run away when her village was 'ethnically cleansed'. So the sixty-five-year-old grandmother and fifty-eight of her elderly neighbours in the village of Skelane were all murdered. Mrs Ristic was tortured, all her fingers were cut off while she was alive; death finally came when they slit her throat. Radosava Kovacevic was seventy-eight when they murdered her: 'Look, you can see the knife wounds on her hands where the old lady tried to defend herself!' sighed the pathologist, Dr Zoran Stankovic. At twenty-six Radivoje Mitrovic was of fighting age, but he was disabled. Couldn't move, couldn't flee, couldn't fight. Like the old ladies, at whose broken naked bodies I had to force myself to look, Radivoje was utterly harmless, no conceivable threat to anyone. Nevertheless, they went ahead and slaughtered him as though he were just another pig in a peasant's backyard.

After giving several more examples of this hideous cruelty and these degrading deaths, I continued:

The wimpish West must stop dithering, stop making empty speeches, stop uttering empty promises. These grotesquely grinning gap-toothed bullies (and I've spent enough time with them to detest them all) must be taught a lesson they won't forget! Men who delight in torturing and killing harmless old ladies, young girls, disabled and helpless men, must not be allowed to get away with such barbarism any longer! Surely those innocent Muslim lives must be avenged!

'But there is one problem,' I pointed out.

None of these massacre victims *were* Muslims. They were all Bosnian Serbs. The men who killed them were Bosnian Muslims or Bosnian Croats; in many cases, the killers' names are known, and one in particular – responsible for some of the worst horrors I've seen – has been decorated by the Bosnian Muslim government.

(Rather late in the day, he was sent to the War Crimes Tribunal in the Hague to stand trial.)

Later in London one rather drunken Balkan-specialist reporter attacked me for that piece: 'The Serbs deserve whatever they get!'

'But these were innocent civilians!' I pointed out.

'They're not innocent – they supported Milosevic!'

'You don't know whether they did or not.'

'I don't care – they're Serbs!'

Which is more or less the same excuse today's jihadists give for slaughtering British and American civilians: 'They deserve death because they voted for Bush and Blair!' And even if they didn't, 'they're all *kuffar*' – just as Mrs Kovacevic, who may or may not have supported Milosevic, 'deserved' death merely because she was a Serb.

All sides in the Balkan War behaved atrociously. The main difference was that the Bosnian Serbs were the best armed and were well supplied by their instigators and sponsors in Serbia proper, and therefore had more of the wherewithal to create murder and mayhem.

'They're all psychopaths,' was the simple journalistic shorthand to explain the behaviour of the Serb leaders. A defining characteristic of psychopaths is that they are abnormally self-centred and have no ability to distinguish between right and wrong. But the Serb leaders I met knew the difference only too well. They were complex, deeply conflicted human beings who unfortunately tried to find a kind of healing for their own psychological scars by inflicting scars, and death, on others.

One such was Nikola Koljevic, the bookish, bespectacled scholar who had been a Professor of Literature and Critical Theory at Sarajevo University, spoke perfect English and loved Shakespeare. Yet he supported the bloody ethnic cleansing of Muslims and Croats, and this lover of books signed the order for the shelling of his own former university's library. When challenged about it he'd make self-satisfied academic jokes as though joshing with colleagues in a cloistered senior common room. (The poet Goran Simic in Sarajevo wrote about the burning books: 'Set free from the stacks, characters wandered the streets/ Mingling with passers-by and the souls of dead soldiers.')

How could the Professor rejoice in all this? Perhaps his twisted behaviour dated from the death of his only son, killed in a climbing accident. He became severely depressed, turned for solace to mysticism, but also began drinking deep from the poisonous cup of Serb ultra-nationalism. One evening I asked him, 'Which of Shakespeare's plays most closely parallels the situation here in Bosnia?'

'Oh, *Macbeth*, obviously!'

But we all know *Macbeth* ends in tragedy. 'Of course. Which, I expect, will happen to us here too.' Indeed it did, particularly in his case. In 1997 the lover of Shakespeare committed suicide with a gunshot to his head.

Even his leader Radovan Karadzic was more complex than the murderous clown portrayed in the non-Serb media. He too fancied himself as an academic, wrote poetry (quite well), played the *gusle*, the one-stringed lute (rather well), and became a clinical psychologist working in Sarajevo. He'd been born in a stable in a mountainous village in Montenegro, and according to one of my Serb fixers, 'We both come from the same place and when we both lived there, the locals saw him as a big star. He went to Sarajevo taking it for granted that he'd be a big star in the big city, but he wasn't; if anything he was laughed at as a provincial peasant who wore old-fashioned shoes with pointed toes. The humiliation made him very bitter about the Sarajevans.'

Not that I managed to get many words with Karadzic because the few times I met him, this 'provincial peasant' was too busy having his proudly bouffant hair blow-dried and styled by his multi-bosomed daughter Sonja.

The latter insists she didn't know where her father was when, after the Bosnia war ended, he went on the run for over a decade. When he was finally arrested, on a Belgrade bus, in July 2008, he now sported a different, but even more startling, coiffure: a long, white bushy beard and long, white 'hippy' hair; he now passed himself off as 'an alternative medicine healer' and gave lectures on 'spirituality' and 'humanism'.

His daughter was in charge, not only of her father's hair-do, but of the foreign press in the small town of Pale, then the capital of the so-called Republika Srpska, which was perched on a mountain overlooking Sarajevo. She dressed as though in a seedy provincial nightclub, and took a particular interest in young, fit and ambitious American journalists. One of them was so terrified of her power and her obvious carnal intentions that he told me he was thinking of making a risky dash down the mountain to Sarajevo and along the so-called Suicide Alley to escape her predatory bosoms. 'Hey, keep cool,' I told him. 'Just lie back and think of the Pulitzer.' The casting-couch trap sometimes applies to men as well.

The massacres committed in the former Yugoslavia shocked Europeans far more than did those committed in Africa: after all, these people were seen as being our neighbours. Journalists who've witnessed the aftermath of massacres very often find that memories of what they've seen can disturb their dreams for many months, even years, afterwards. My only recurring dream, bizarrely (even banally), involves a corgi dog in Bosnia.

Before reporting on the aftermath of a massacre, a journalist automatically assumes a forensic state of mind – you mentally prepare yourself for the carnage you're about to see. But I wasn't mentally prepared for a trivial incident involving the dog. I'd been up at the frontline near a so-called UN 'safe haven', full of terrified Muslim refugees who were under siege from the Serbs. I was now being driven through yet another burnt-out village back to safety, and a sniper seemed determined to 'slot' us on our way out.

I'd already escaped death by 'slotting' about half an hour earlier. I'd got out of the car, which we'd parked behind a high, broken wall, to make a note of some bloodthirsty graffiti. A sniper on a hill started shooting at me: not, I guessed, initially to kill me but to make me jump like a cat being tortured by a sadistic schoolboy. He was aiming his shots like a sword-thrower in a circus. But I knew that he'd end his amusing game by shooting me dead.

I should, of course, have been terrified. Instead I was, unexpectedly, simply consumed with incandescent rage. I had a deadline, the nearest satellite phone was miles away across the mountains in Pale, and this sniper nonsense was holding me up. I turned towards where the sniper seemed to be and unleashed a stream of obscene invective. I doubt he understood English, but perhaps abusive obscenities don't need much translation. He was clearly so astonished that he stopped shooting just long enough for me to run to the car and get away.

And now, as we drove out of the village, a corgi dashed out of an abandoned bullet-ridden house into the road, joyfully wagging its tail. What on earth was a pedigree dog like this doing here? A corgi isn't the usual peasant dog so it was presumably a highly prized pet. (I found myself speculating later that it might even have been a gift from some Yugoslav working in England who knew that corgis were the Queen's favourites and had given one to his mum on a visit home; East Europeans, despite having overthrown and/or assassinated their own royals, were often extraordinarily sentimental about ours.)

Unfortunately for the dog, our car hit him; I turned round to look back at him: he was lying yelping and jack-knifing on the road. But this was a war zone: there was no way we could stop to save him or to kill him cleanly. Another small, innocent life pointlessly, and agonizingly, brought to an end in this appalling war.

How could I possibly mourn the death of some abandoned family pet when so many human beings were dying in the town I had just left behind? Nevertheless tears came into my eyes at the thought of my part in his slow death. And I still wonder about the dog's owners. If they'd survived, did they – despite what they themselves had suffered – mourn his passing? I suspect that they would have, as I still do.

I've never called myself a war correspondent, although others have, including my own newspaper; I've never sought out wars as such, and prefer to describe myself as a foreign correspondent specializing in international politics. Of course, I've worked in countries where politics often involve violence and sometimes war – as in the Balkans, Central America, Africa and the Middle East. I have seen the bodies, have interviewed the survivors and those who had tried to rape or kill them; and, over the years, have narrowly escaped death myself from rioters, drunken checkpoint thugs, snipers and suicide bombers.

To be a professional war correspondent means, in my view, that you have to be a certain type of person – often, but not always, addicted to danger: you can become psychologically hooked on the adrenaline 'hit', the camaraderie, the black humour, the furious anger with those who inflict such suffering on others, and the fierce bursts of exhilaration when you escape official obstruction or, indeed, death. All of which affords the addict an emotional high that ordinary life can rarely provide.

The hit is so powerful (and I've experienced it myself) that coming home to gas bills and school concerts and all the mundanity of normal life can feel like going cold turkey. You can become tetchy, impatient, unable to deal with a child's problems at school – because you've been somewhere where you've just interviewed the mother of a child who has been repeatedly raped, or someone who has been forced to become the killer of a loved one, or someone who is dying in a shack, covered in flies.

Perhaps that's why many war correspondents I know often have disastrous personal lives, with frequent broken relationships and alienated children. As a colleague once put it to me, 'My wife says I'm a "war junkie" and she's left me because she can't understand why I regard her everyday domestic concerns as "trivial". But, compared to what I've seen, they *are*!'

The fact is that war junkies really only feel at home with fellow junkies. Whatever their gender, race or class background they form a freewheeling, nomadic tribe which speaks the same language, shares the same experiences, and feels the same instant, if often competitive, affinity with one another. And so long as danger is present, they are never bored.

Paul Ellman, my friend from the *Guardian*, was typical in that he left Zimbabwe, where we'd both been working, out of sheer boredom when the war and the ethnic killings had ground to a halt. 'Nothing going on here. It looks like it's becoming a "normal" country,' he'd told me morosely over a farewell scotch in Harare.

The fact is that countries which are, or become, 'normal' do not attract journalists. And in 'abnormal' countries you must be very careful who, or what, you believe. As Louis Heren, a famous veteran correspondent, once put it, a journalist must always at the outset ask him or herself, 'Why is the lying bastard lying to me?'

You have to start with the assumption that no one – neither victimizer nor victim – ever tells the unvarnished truth. The only way to discover where the truth lies is to have journalists who are willing to go there and try to find out at first hand what has, or has not, happened.

It was on this issue that I once had a slight falling-out over dinner in Jerusalem's press hotel, the American Colony, with Channel 4's Jon Snow, an idealistic, rather romantic left-winger who does not share my politics but whom I like and respect.

At that time a radical Palestinian refugee camp at Jenin, a hotbed of suicide bombers, was being attacked by the Israelis. The Israelis weren't letting in journalists, humanitarian workers or even the Red Crescent, the Muslim equivalent of the Red Cross. Yet newspapers and television in Britain were reporting that the Israelis were massacring Jenin's trapped civilians. The Palestinian leader Yasser Arafat declared that henceforth 'This atrocity will go down in history as "Jeningrad!"' In the streets of Arab East Jerusalem I was told that 'At least 6,000 civilians have been killed so far!' How do you know? 'We know it as a *fact*!'

A few Jenin residents who had escaped told terrible stories about how 'even disabled people were just being dragged out of their homes by the Israelis and murdered!' They were not necessarily telling us conscious lies: people under extreme stress often want to believe what they are saying. Jon Snow waxed furious over dinner about Israel's appalling brutality in the camp. 'But Jon,' I protested, 'none of us has yet been able to get into the camp to find out the truth!'

And, when journalists finally did get into the camp, they discovered that only fifty-two Jenin residents in a camp containing 14,000 people had been killed, of whom only twenty-two were civilians – who, as so often in battles, had been caught in the crossfire. The rest were Palestinian gunmen shooting it out with Israeli soldiers.

Even Yasser Arafat's own Palestine Liberation Organization had to agree with these figures. This was no 'Jeningrad', merely another grim and bloody episode in the ongoing Israel/Palestine conflict. Only one newspaper journalist, as far as I know, apologized in print – having learnt the truth about Jenin when he got in there – for having 'talked up' the supposed Israeli massacre of helpless civilians when he himself had not yet found out the facts.

I know why so many war correspondents, many of them friends, explain their often awe-inspiring courage purely in terms of altruism. 'The story needs to be told/You owe it to the people who are suffering/If we didn't do it, no one will ever find out what's really going on.' And, yes, all of that is absolutely true. But the fact is that most war journalists do the job also because – in the words of one self-confessed war junkie speaking to me in the Balkans – 'It's awful to admit it but, in its own weird way, war can be a helluva lot of fun.'

And unlike booze and drugs (to which many professional war correspondents fall prey when they are no longer able to do the job), this kind of 'fun' can actually do some good. It can indeed open people's eyes, expose war crimes, give comfort to hitherto unregarded victims, and awaken in those who live staidly comfortable lives, far from war zones, an empathy with those who suffer beyond our shores.

Of course, none of the war junkies I've known who have been killed in war (and I've personally known six) ever 'asked for' their deaths, and they certainly didn't 'ask for' the misery their deaths have caused their loved ones. Oddly enough, like adolescents, they don't really believe that death can happen to them. Intellectually they know the risks, but they're willing and brave enough, or get enough of a kick out of it, to take them.

One young journalist friend of mine who is gay and who never saw himself as likely to become a victim of 'manly' bursts of testosterone admitted to me, shamefacedly, that when recently in the Congo he saw a man being beaten to death he had felt a terrible sense of excitement, even a kind of blood lust.

I warned him that, for the sake of his own sanity, he must not –

as many have – become addicted to that feral instinct in the presence of violent death. And, I told him, he must never show off about his own courage. As all of us who have been involved in dangerous situations know, the real courage belongs to those who help us, the fixers, because they are people who have to go on living in their desperate, war-ravaged countries; whereas we, if we survive, can get on a plane and fly back to the safety of our homes.

There is of course something slightly mad about war correspondents. No one forces anyone to do the job. As a columnist or a studio-based newsreader you can earn much more money and acquire much greater fame, without having to risk your life in some benighted corner of the world. The most dangerous thing that columnists and newsreaders have to face professionally is an inconvenient computer glitch or the autocue breaking down.

On-screen war reporters can achieve fame especially if they're unfortunate enough to be wounded. (I was somewhat miffed when Granada TV's *What the Papers Say* once named me Feature Writer of the Year, when I hadn't written a single domestic feature that year. 'Why didn't you give me Foreign Correspondent of the Year?' I asked.

'Sorry, Ann, but you didn't get yourself shot.')

Of course war coverage has never been exactly safe, but in recent years it has become even more dangerous. Wearing a press badge used to be an advantage because, rather than kill you, both sides in any conflict tended to want you to tell their side of the story. These days the internet does that for them, so now a press badge can be an invitation to murder, often with a bounty reward attached. And yet there is no shortage of volunteers for this dangerous trade. So why do they do it?

Which is the question I asked an American friend of mine over dinner in London the night before he flew to Israel to cover the Six Day War in 1967. He was baffled by the question: 'Because it's my job of course!' Actually, no. It wasn't his job: it was his vocation. He'd already won awards as a war photographer – he had nothing left to prove in terms of skill or courage. The day after he arrived in Israel he was shot dead. Probably no one outside his grieving family remembers him now. But I do. And I still ask myself, 'Why do they do it?'

17

War-criminal Kitsch

One of the problems when interviewing war criminals is trying not
to laugh – and, of course, to get out alive. Not only do they have an
addiction to murder, they also have a dreadful taste in interior decor,
as though a mad Laurence Llewelyn-Bowen had been let loose on
the premises with yards of MDF, eye-popping paint and what Hilda
Ogden in *Coronation Street* called 'murials'. Plus they take offence
very easily. I've met examples of this deadly, yet absurd, species all
over the world.

Take Eugene Terre'Blanche, the leader of the Afrikaner Resistance Movement in South Africa (*Afrikaner Weerstandsbeweging*,
AWB for short). He was a stout, bronzed and bearded figure in khaki
fatigues who had, I was told, a tendency to fall off his horse after
imbibing. I interviewed him in his Transvaal office in early 1990
(shortly after Mandela's release) where he sat, backed by ridicu-
lously over-the-top Nazi insignia, swastikas and 'murials'. He looked
at me with small, cunning eyes and informed me levelly that he had
never threatened to kill Nelson Mandela. 'It has never been our
official policy to kill specific individuals. We are not racists.' He
tapped out his pipe. 'Of course, what frustrated and angry Boers
may do in the name of the AWB is not something we can be held
responsible for.'

Like hell, I thought, remembering the 'Hang Mandela' banner
at an AWB rally in Pretoria which I'd attended and which he'd
addressed. A white man had heckled Terre'Blanche and had been set
upon and beaten up by the crowd. The white police had arrested the
blood-covered man, but not those who'd beaten him up. 'What are
you doing arresting *him*?' I protested to a cop.

'None of your business, madam. F***k off!' was the response.

At that rally Terre'Blanche's followers had waved banners portray-

ing the visiting American black civil-rights campaigner Jesse Jackson
with the words 'Target Practice! Yankee Kaffir Go Home!'

Terre'Blanche ('My name, you know, means "White Earth"') and
his followers were now openly committing themselves to their own
'armed struggle' which, they promised me, would make the ANC
look like amateurs. He had informed my contact that he would only
speak to me in Afrikaans and not in 'English, the colonial language'.
In the event he abandoned the Afrikaans-only edict and spoke to me
in perfectly good 'colonialist' English.

'This release of Mandela is the beginning of the total capitulation
by our white Judas government,' he informed me. 'And we will not
allow it. Believe me, the world will know when the Boer *Volk* take up
the armed struggle. You can be bloody sure of that! We will fight in
the name of the same God our forefathers fought for and died for.
We promised this land to Him at the Battle of Blood River' (at which
the Boers defeated the mighty Zulu *impis* in 1838). 'God alone can
be the master of the Boer nation: he is the King of the *Volk* – we
cannot give away the land which we paid for with our Boer sweat
and our Boer blood.'

Race, blood sacrifice, the land, the heroic myth of the *Volk*
battling against all odds under the guidance of a Calvinistic and
implacable God – these were the intoxicating elements which
inspired Terre'Blanche and his followers in their attempt to keep the
flame of Afrikaner nationalism alive in, to them, catastrophic and
apocalyptic days.

Terre'Blanche's followers were drawn largely from the ranks of
debt-ridden farmers in the *platteland*, poor whites in decaying suburbs who saw successful, middle-class blacks driving BMWs and
moving 'shamelessly' into officially whites-only rich areas which they
themselves, though white, could never afford; others, more worryingly, were drawn from sections of the trigger-happy white police.

Above all, his support came from white gold miners who were the
backbone of this by now tottering economy and who saw the *kaffirs*,
in alliance with English-speaking capitalists, eating away at their
white, God-given differentials. Afrikanerdom was, in fact, and always
had been, both an industrial and a rural working-class phenomenon.
Ironically, the South African Communist Party, which now supported black liberation, was once a champion of the Boer working

class. It was in this 'suffering proletariat's' interest that apartheid was invented.

'Do we have enough weaponry to fight Mandela's ANC to the death? Believe me, we have enough!'

Unfortunately, Terre'Blanche's career as the stern and godly guardian of the *Volk* had received a severe but alas not yet fatal setback when he was involved in a farcical sexual scandal occasioned by a flamboyant blonde columnist from 'godless' Johannesburg, involving a video, green underpants and carnal cavortings on the steps of the Paaderkraal, the sacred Afrikaner monument to the Boer War.

When I mentioned this episode, the Afrikaner Führer spotted a smirk on my face and, reaching for a weapon, barked threateningly, '*Nobody, nobody* laughs at me!' Er, no, *Meneer*, I'm not laughing, I muttered soothingly, it's just . . . er . . . a bit of spinach in my teeth.

Of course, it was easy to laugh at him and his Nazi-inspired street theatre when eating crayfish *à la Nantua* at dinner parties in what he saw as the depraved Sodom and Gomorrah of the liberal cities. Somehow he seemed less absurd, and rather more dangerous, when seen in his heartland of the Transvaal. Ventersdorp was then a small, shabby, God-fearing (no cinemas allowed) farming town, two-and-a-half hours' drive out from flashy Jo'burg.

'You English-speaking liberals can keep that city: when we have our Boer State we will put borders round it and Johannesburg can be an independent city state like Hong Kong.'

Ventersdorp is approached through mile upon unrelentingly flat and empty mile of maize farms, dotted with lonely silos and small groups of black labourers bent double. I felt that if I kept on driving I'd fall off the edge of the Earth: no wonder the Boer President Paul Kruger believed to his dying day that the world was flat.

There were no '*blankes slegs*' (whites only) signs in Ventersdorp: there didn't need to be. Solomon, my black driver, laughed at my suggestion that we should go into the only hotel for some lunch. 'You want to get me killed, madam?'

'In the bar here the white boys won't drink from a glass handled by a black because they say it's bound to be dirty,' the manageress told me sadly. 'But I must say Mr Terre'Blanche is a very charming man: he even gave me permission to open a blacks-only disco here!'

As evidence of the arsenal in the hands of the white farm boys here, she told me that when one of 'her' Africans challenged a group of whites loitering suspiciously near the blacks-only disco he was attacked by a volley of tear gas canisters.

Terre'Blanche told me that his 'Boer State' would not include the whole of South Africa, just the Transvaal, the Orange Free States and Northern Natal – almost a third of the country. But even here, I pointed out, 'You Boers will still be outnumbered by blacks.'

'Why do you keep calling them "blacks"? Are you a racist, like the ANC? I am not a racist: I believe that every true nation has a right to a homeland. The Zulu nation, the Xhosa, the Sotho, the Tswana and the other nations here all have their homelands, which we gave them. They do not belong in *my* homeland, any more than the French belong in your homeland of Britain. Only a nation can have a claim on land. The ANC is not a nation and therefore has no rights: it is just a frustrated, multi-racial conspiracy financed by international Communism to steal other nations' land.'

For 'nation' substitute the word 'tribe'. The Afrikaner is the only white tribe in Africa; its language, derived from Dutch, German, Huguenot French and even stray bits of Arabic, is the only Indo-European-based language originating in Africa. The Boers did not have British, Dutch, German or French passports tucked into their back pockets: they were no longer European.

But the world, I told Terre'Blanche, will never accept the existence of an all-white Afrikaner state. He smiled the dreamy smile of a visionary. 'It is only a matter of time. Look at Eastern Europe! You now accept that the small nations there have a right to exist in freedom, free from foreign domination. Why not the Boer nation? Why do you hate a small, brave, Christian nation so much? Why do you condemn us for extremism when we say we will fight to the death for our existence? I cannot believe that you will not, one day, grant us the same rights as you give now to Eastern Europe.'

But then Terre'Blanche, like his hero Kruger, still believed that, in political terms, the world is flat. His independent and internationally recognized Afrikaner *Volkstaat* has never materialized and Terre'Blanche has, with his cartoon Nazi regalia, disappeared into bitterness, drink and political oblivion.

His sometime ally 'General' Ferrus Munro, who was obsessed (like most nationalists) with God, dates and maps, told me a year later: 'There's going to be a huge explosion in this country – but there's no way on earth that the Boer is going to lose! Our first principle is to stand up for our God – and when He is on your side, you cannot lose! The Boer will never accept a black government. The black people cannot rule themselves. It was at Blood River that God told the Boer people . . .'

I wondered how long it would be into the conversation before we got to that great sustaining myth of Afrikanerdom: that God and the Boers 'gave' South Africa 'to each other' at Blood River (so named because the river was stained with the blood of 3,000 Zulus; a mere four Afrikaners were wounded).

The AWB's 'General' Ferrus Munro 'blood-rivered' on, sitting beneath a lurid eagle-and-swastika painting and stubbing out his ciggies in a pottery skull. The 'General' was a former city pharmacist who, like many working-class and lower-middle-class whites, had lost his job; God and the force of arms would, he believed, restore the 'Boer nation's' pre-eminence.

The General's blue eyes looked watery as he gazed reverentially towards an ox cart in his office. This forty-five-year-old 'storm-trooper' suddenly struck me as being neither threatening nor comic, but oddly pathetic. (Mind you, not being black, I wasn't a natural target for the *Volk*'s '*kaffir*-hunting picnics', where they'd take pot-shots at the odd unarmed *kaffir* in the nearby township of Tshing.)

'In those ox carts the Boers lived, gave birth and died for the Boer nation!' He paused, the bombast momentarily fading. 'If we must, we Boers will live and die here, in the same way, for the same cause.'

Such Afrikaners, who were never 'Boers' in the strict sense (the word means 'farmer'), still heard the distant ox carts of Boer myth rumbling through the *platteland*, bearing their Calvinist God who would help them conquer the '*kaffir* Communists', just as He once helped them to conquer the black unbelieving 'Canaanites' at Blood River.

This was my second visit to the AWB headquarters. Their 'God's Soldiers' had taken to beating up foreign correspondents like me, so this time I'd approached their HQ with some caution. The unheroic-looking single-storey building was now surrounded by a 5-foot-high maze of sandbags; guarding the door under a swastika flag – made out of the sort of fluffy materials you find in Essex bathrooms – was a spotty youth armed with a hunting rifle and a pump-action shotgun. He spoke no English, but indicated that he was ready to use both weapons on me; I swept past him, resisting the temptation to ruffle his hair and tell him to grow up. He shambled after me, tripping over the shotgun, and looked ready to burst into tears. Poor lad, yet another battle lost to the godless forces of evil.

For over 300 years Afrikaner mothers would scare their naughty children with the threat '*Die kaffirs kom, kinders, die kaffirs kom!*' – 'The niggers are coming, children, the niggers are coming!' Well, the 'niggers' have now '*kom*' and the Boers have finally lost.

*

And it was God, maps, dates, Nazi kitsch and history once again with Vojislav Seselj in Serbia. He called himself 'the Red Duke' and was the leader of the paramilitary Chetniks who had laid waste to much of Bosnia. In his office in Belgrade, a bronze icon of Christ and a vast and lurid oil painting which seemed to consist largely of people strangling each other while tumbling in and out of blood-streaked clouds. Once again there were swatches of fluffy Essex-bathroom material as there had been thousands of miles away among the neo-Nazis of South Africa.

The Red Duke – in reality, a large and paunchy former philosophy lecturer at Sarajevo University – rearranged his floppy blue cardigan, smiled and fixed me with his cold, pale eyes. 'Yes, I agree – I have been named by the UN and the US as a war criminal. And I am *proud* of that title! It was first awarded to me by that great American liar James Baker who said that I and my men killed 3,000 unarmed Muslims and Croats. You realize of course that when Mr Baker was US Secretary of State he was paid millions of dollars by Arab lobbyists in order to protect Muslims?'

Yes, he admitted, he had said that the best way to punish your enemies was to scoop their eyes out with a rusty spoon. 'But it was a joke. Have you English not got a sense of humour?'

The Red Duke then began barking interminably on (as his ilk – whether Afrikaner, Serb or Arab – are wont to do) about the endless sufferings of his people throughout history: '. . . so, in the tenth century . . . then in the fourteenth . . . the battle of . . . massacred by the Turks ... 1389 the Battle of the Field of Blackbirds ... Austro-Hungarian empire ... Croats' genocidal attacks ... Muslim complicity ... betrayals ... World War II ... Ustasha atrocities ...' And as every date and place of Serb martyrdom was once again enthusiastically rehearsed, I was inevitably reminded of Hannah Arendt's famous phrase, 'the banality of evil', inspired by Adolf Eichmann. It certainly characterized this failed academic sitting in front of me in his ludicrous floppy cardie, just as it did the paunchy ex-pharmacist 'storm trooper' in the *platteland*. Seselj looked like what he once was – a squabbling don with poor eyesight from a minor provincial university. He did not radiate demonic charisma; you could not see his horns. And here in Belgrade he and his fellow Chetniks' fascistic fancy-dress props – skull-and-crossbones shoulder badges, long beards, skull-crushing boots and bombastic *noms de guerre* – looked like nothing more than a kitsch re-enactment of Mel Brooks's 'Springtime for Hitler' routine.

Actually the Chetniks' taste for fancy-dress uniforms proved to be useful for me. My Serb driver Cvetko (married to a Croat whom he'd sent to Croatia for safety) wore the full works – long bushy beard, boots, leather jacket – and drove a clapped-out Skoda. He knew where all the Chetnik-manned road blocks were and as we approached them, driving through the self-styled Republika Srpska, he'd tell me to get into the back, lie on the floor and cover myself with a filthy blanket, and he would deal with the road-blockers (whose skull-and-crossbones regalia were, I learned, very often clotted with drink-related vomit).

Naturally these Serb 'patriots' mistook him for one of their own, possibly en route to murdering the odd Muslim or two, and would cheerily toast him on the 'sacred mission' ahead. Had they known that Cvetko was actually an extremely kind, gently hippie, non-boozy, devotedly vegetarian peacenik – who was obsessively concerned with my careless drinking of the local water ('Ann, this is very dangerous to the health!') – they'd have probably shot him on the spot.

The clapped-out Skoda was also useful because, although it frequently broke down on roads potholed by mortars, Cvetko could effect instant repairs involving a 'tool box' which contained, among other things, an assortment of women's tights, chewing gum and hairpins. You could not hire a car in Belgrade if you were heading for the Bosnian war zone: you had to buy it outright for cash (thanks to sanctions no international credit cards were valid). And there was, of course, no insurance, let alone a local AA. Rich but naive international TV teams and journalists (especially the Japanese scattering suitcasefuls of yen) would buy top-of-the-range automatic Toyotas – which would instantly break down on hitting the first pothole. We passed at least two of these stranded and expensively useless metal hulks on our way to the Bosnian Serb 'capital', Pale.

In Belgrade it was easy to laugh at the absurd pretensions of Red Duke Seselj's Greater Serbia dreams. As, indeed, the cult radio station Radio B92 constantly did, pouring out to its small but sophisticated audience mocking references to 'The Land of Serbia – from the Cape of Good Hope to Canada!'. 'We even had a map' (I was told by B92's editor Milica Kuburovic) 'on which we marked the "autonomous regions" of the Chetniks' future Greater Serbia – the "Serbian Autonomous Region of Belgium", the "Serbian Autonomous Region of East Anglia", and so on!'

In his ridiculous neo-Nazi office I had told Seselj of the Muslims I'd met in the refugee camps who insisted that it was his Chetniks who had 'cleansed' their villages, killed many of their neighbours and sent the rest to concentration camps. 'I don't expect any of those you met admitted to the fact that they were war criminals!' he retorted.

'War criminals? Young teenage girls? A girl like Mediha who told me that your men snatched her from the street in Prijedor, took her to the Trnopolje camp and repeatedly raped her?' (The camp was filmed by ITN.)

'Girls like that are talked into telling you they've been raped, and various other propaganda fairy-tales. I'm not denying that individual Serbs may have committed atrocities and rapes – but there were never any mass rapings, and there were no orders to commit atrocities.

'The Muslim men in the camps were captured on the front line, they weren't civilians and there were no women and children in the camps.' But Mediha *was* in Trnopolje camp; indeed, she became part of an official prisoner exchange.

Absolutely unabashed, Seselj replied, 'Trnopolje was not a camp. It was just a place where Muslims went voluntarily.' But why should they 'volunteer' to go there? 'Because in the Prijedor region, during the Second World War some of the worst "cleansing" of Serbs by Croats and their Muslim allies occurred. And so when the war in Bosnia started the people of this area felt insecure because of what their forefathers had done in the past. Naturally, even if they had no reason to fear the Serbs, they felt frightened and preferred to move to where they were surrounded by their co-religionists. The Serbs had no reason to bring those Muslims to Trnopolje – they went there entirely of their own free will.' So all those refugees were lying to me and the world's media? 'Of course.'

I longed to say something which might shake him, so chose to query his precious 'ethnicity'. Is it true, I asked, that there's evidence that you are not, in fact, an ethnic Serb, but a Croat by origin? This, to a nationalist Serb, was the equivalent of telling Hitler that there's 'evidence' that he is a Jew, or to an Afrikaner nationalist that he has Zulu blood in his veins (the latter actually happened, in some cases, to be true).

'That is an absolute lie, put about by my enemies! Because of this, the Serbian Academy of Arts and Sciences conducted an investigation into my origins and I can safely say that I must be one of the only scientifically proven Serbs in the country!' But what if you *did* discover that your 'blood' was not pure Serb? 'I would not mind if they found French, Italian or Russian blood in me – but I would be very upset if there was any German or Croat blood. Why? Because those two nations are criminal nations!'

But I had another weapon in my armoury. I'd heard rumours that when Seselj had been jailed during a fall-out with Serbian President Slobodan Milosevic, he'd been raped by a Muslim guard – and had enjoyed it. Which is why, when he was released, mocking opposition crowds had chanted, 'Faggot! Faggot!'

It's at moments like this that you have to time your questions judiciously, making sure that any heavies – and there were several low-browed specimens present – are not blocking your way to the exit. I of course feigned ignorance of the meaning of the Serb word for 'faggot': 'I understand the crowds were shouting at you . . .' (and I uttered the Serb word). 'Why? What does that mean?'

He suddenly blushed furiously. 'It is completely untrue! It may seem strange to you in England, but this allegation is the worst possible insult my enemies could throw at me!' Worse even than being called a war criminal? 'Much worse – because *no one* in Serbia could be proud of being called a homosexual! But in Serbia you *can* be proud of being a so-called "war criminal".'

The lunatic and bloody Greater Serbia dreams of Seselj – and of Milosevic and Karadzic – have now resulted in the smallest Serbia there has ever been. And it has now lost Kosovo, its proclaimed 'spiritual heartland', since the majority ethnic Albanians who live there have declared their independence. Milosevic died of a heart attack during his lengthy war-crimes trial, Karadzic has been arrested, and the 'Red Duke' Seselj is currently incarcerated in the Hague awaiting his own trial. His Radical Party is now being led, in his unavoidable absence, by a carbon-copy ultra-nationalist who, in recent elections, came within a whisker of winning the Serbian Presidency.

*

If the *platteland* 'storm-troopers' and the Chetnik warlord scored high on neo-Nazi kitsch they were outclassed in the 'naff' stakes by the billionaire property developer Umar Dzhabrailov in Moscow whom I interviewed in 1998. Of course I'm not saying that Umar is a war criminal in the classic sense but if, as Orwell said, 'Sport is war without the shooting,' the commercial battles in Russia during the period of gangster capitalism under Boris Yeltsin did amount at times to war *with* the shooting.

Umar's hero was Napoleon – both men were short, dark, libidinous and had vainglorious aims, albeit that those of the French Emperor's disciple were merely 'commercial'. A vast painting of the Corsican hung in Umar's office. He was also a fan of the Bond movies: in a conscious act of symbolism there lay on his sumptuous office sofa a life-sized white Persian toy cat, clearly modelled on the cat cradled by the Bond villain Blofeld. Its walls were decorated not with *platteland* 'murials', but with a vast and showy collection of swords and daggers.

Frankly these days few people make me nervous, but the then forty-year-old Dzhabrailov did. If Umar got too irritated – with business partners who tried to double-cross him, tiresome rivals or challenging journalists – odd and rather nasty things, quite coincidentally, occurred. 'Accidents', a spot of contract killing, stuff like that. Moscow's Little Caesar was, in the words of one Muscovite friend, 'seriously scary'. Yet he's such a dainty-looking little chap, almost girlish with his long, soft, wavy hair, his equally soft little hands, his tiny hips and feet. Not my idea of what an allegedly notorious Russian Mafioso is supposed to look like, let alone one with an FBI file as long as your arm.

Indeed, if you saw him in some fashionable London nightspot you'd think he was probably an off-duty ballet dancer. Seeing him in his Moscow fiefdom you'd think otherwise. You'd wonder why, for a start, this pretty, dark-eyed, delicate-looking businessman in his impeccable Italian suits and thick silk ties was permanently surrounded by six huge, gun-carrying, distinctly un-pretty bodyguards.

No wonder Frederick Forsyth, when researching in Moscow for his Russia-based thriller *Icon*, decided to base his portrait of the capital's Capo dei Capi on the dainty Umar (whom he calls Umar Gunayev). The evidently star-struck Dzhabrailov was clearly flattered to have featured so prominently in the Forsyth bestseller. But he had some regrets, he told me: 'I'm not sure I should have given permission to Mr Forsyth to use my first name, because he gave readers a very wrong impression about me, saying I'm Mafia and so on. I've left messages on Mr Forsyth's answerphone,' he added darkly, 'but he has never called me back.' People usually do call Umar back. He might get 'irritated' if they didn't. Freddie Forsyth told me later that he'd never received a message from Umar indicating that he was angry with him. But in Russia some very powerful people indeed tried hard not to irritate Umar unnecessarily.

Umar Dzhabrailov originates from the Russian republic of Chechnya which, in an act of criminal stupidity, Yeltsin's army virtually flattened, killing more than 100,000 people; Vladimir Putin earned the plaudits of Muslim-hating Russians when he came to power by declaring that he would 'kill the Chechen bandits in their shithouses'.

Despite the fact that Dzhabrailov is a Chechen – a race despised by Russians as *crni*, blacks – he now controls some of Moscow's most valuable real estate: for example, the hotel I was staying in, the Radisson Slavyanskaya (where President Clinton also stayed). The fact that Russians routinely accuse wealthy Chechens like

Dzhabrailov of being Mafiosi was simply, he told me, 'the result of stupidity. A weakness in the brain.' And certainly he was no common-or-garden thug, no tattooed *vor v zakone*, the traditional Russian Mafioso 'thief-in-law', who has flourished here since Tsarist days and who controlled the thriving black market in Soviet times.

Dzhabrailov and men of his ilk featured in most of the gangsters-and-tarts clichés about life in Yeltsin's Russia. They are now of course establishment figures and have mighty friends in the corridors of power. And one of their mightiest friends is Moscow's all-powerful Mayor, Yuri Luzhkov.

Mr Luzhkov, a former boxer, whose trademark is his proletarian *kepka* (leather cap) lined with bullet-proof steel, at one point considered running for President. Not surprisingly, deceptively pretty little Umar was chosen by the steel-capped Mayor to show Tony Blair around a new underground shopping centre – one of Umar's myriad developments outside the Kremlin walls ('I got a very positive impression of your Prime Minister,' Dzhabrailov told me kindly).

Ironically Blair was in Moscow to sign, among other things, a bilateral agreement to fight the threat posed to international order by the increasingly powerful Russian Mafia. Not, I assure you hastily, that the dainty Umar was at all responsible for any such criminality even if, equally coincidentally, he happened to profit from its results.

He had, of course, nothing to do with the contract killing nineteen months before I talked to him of Paul Tatum, the American manager of the hotel I was staying in, and a business partner of his and of Mayor Luzhkov. Towards the end of his life Tatum declared that he was, thanks to a deeply murky business dispute over control of the Radisson, receiving 'constant threats of physical elimination'. He wrote to the state prosecutor alleging that Dzhabrailov was behind the threats. Tatum tried hiding out in his eighth-floor suite (down the corridor from my room), but one day decided to walk to the nearby Kiev Metro station. As he and his two bodyguards passed under a bridge a gunman emptied his Kalashnikov magazine into him from above, hitting him in the throat and groin. Umar was, of course, questioned and was, of course, found to have had 'nothing to do with the murder'.

The investigation, Umar pointed out to me in bored tones, 'has been going on for a long time now and if I am still here, it means I'm innocent, doesn't it?' Er, if you say so, Mr Dzhabrailov. (Nevertheless, shortly after the murder, the US revoked his visa and President Clinton no longer patronized the Radisson.)

Mind you, being a hotel manager in Moscow, where room rates are now among the highest in the world, was a surprisingly dangerous job. Yevgeny Tsimbalistov, the manager of the Rossiya, one of the world's largest hotels – now demolished – was shot dead in a contract killing, and his predecessor was almost killed with an axe. In November the previous year the manager of the Sovincentr Hotel was also mysteriously gunned down. No one, of course, has been charged with any of these crimes.

When I first accosted Dzhabrailov to ask for an interview, his dark little eyes flickered suspiciously. 'What about?'

'Oh,' I said, 'well, er, stuff about the new Russian tax-code and the IMF loan.' To my astonishment, a man who deeply dislikes the foreign press (he thinks we're in the pocket of the FBI) suddenly – despite much twitching among the gun-laden slabs of muscle surrounding him – invited me to 'come up to my office, now!'

I realized I'd quite inadvertently scored a direct hit on Umar's vanity button. Like so many of Russia's rather shady *biznismeni* of the period, he yearned for respectability, a respectability the Mafia believed it could buy through its then reputed control of 40 per cent of Russia's private businesses, 50 per cent of banks and 60 per cent of state-owned companies. Asking Dzhabrailov about macroeconomics and tax law – instead of who he might have killed and why – was an unwitting genuflection to that longed-for respectability.

A divorced father of two – subsequently photographed 'romancing' the British supermodel Naomi Campbell – he's been described in a *Hello!*-style magazine in Moscow as one of the city's 'most eligible bachelors'.

On a sideboard in his office, covered in kitsch knick-knacks, he gave pride of place to a brick and a damaged mortar shell. 'That brick is from my old school which the Russians destroyed, and the shell is one of many which fell on my family's house in Grozny.' Umar insisted he was not one of those 'New Russians' who had siphoned off the country's wealth and smuggled it abroad. He does however own sumptuous properties overseas and a massive yacht, usually to be found cruising the Mediterranean rather than Russia's Black Sea waters.

Of course, the New Russian gangsters now yearn not for their gaudy, bloodstained Tarantino-style image, but for 'gentleman chic', which is why they like Britain so much and buy up our football clubs and country houses. And why they send their children to British public schools and buy multi-million-pound homes in Hampstead and Kensington. Even their women no longer dress like brassy Vegas showgirls, all cleavage and bling, as they did in the Wild West capitalism of the Nineties. Now it's all pared-down Armani and a look of chicly Parisian-style boredom. If your *attributy*, a Russian neologism which means 'status symbols', are too flashy, you're clearly guilty of *pafosny*, trying too hard.

(Incidentally, it has always puzzled me why the shape of Russian women, let alone that of the prostitutes, has changed so much in the decades I've been going there. In the early Seventies Russian women were short, stout and looked like potatoes in a sack. Now some of the world's top models are Russian: they and Russian trophy wives are now not only exquisitely willowy but extremely tall. Surely, I asked a Russian girlfriend, evolution doesn't move *that* fast: 'There must be a secret factory in Siberia full of mad scientists who are creating these gorgeous creatures in test-tubes!'

'But do you notice', she replied, 'that many of these girls were born in or near the Ukraine? And the radioactive fall-out from the Chernobyl nuclear accident in the Ukraine has, it's said, produced enormously tall rabbits now living in the exclusion zone. So perhaps that's the explanation!' Oh well, it's a thought.)

Of course, no matter how chic these New Russians now are, they're not the slightest bit bothered about the often criminal ways their families acquired all this wealth. Why should they be? After all, no one in Russia, not even the humblest peasant, doorman or factory worker, has ever really believed in the rule of law. Law in Russia has always been an arbitrary diktat handed down from above, whether by a Tsar, a Communist Party General Secretary or the petty bureaucrat down the road. Those with power never seemed to have to obey the law themselves. Outsmarting the law, getting away with as much as you can, was therefore not a habit confined to the Mafiosi – it's a centuries-old Russian survival mechanism.

But when I used the word *biznismeni* to the fabulously rich Dzhabrailov, he suddenly got angry: 'Why do you foreign journalists always use the Russian word for "businessmen"? I used to wonder why until I watched a video of *The Godfather*, and then I knew you were saying that we are all Mafia!'

'No, no,' I demurred nervously, 'it's just, er, a lazy journalistic habit.'

Far from being Mafia, Mr Dzhabrailov insisted he was a Russian patriot, doing what he could to help his country (albeit one whose rulers had destroyed his home city). 'I want to do my business in this country and get rich – and by getting rich, people like me will help this country get rich as well.' But, I asked him, wasn't he afraid that he would himself one day be the victim of a contract killing? He shrugged dismissively: 'Yes, of course I could be killed tomorrow. But there is more to life than fearing death every day. It doesn't worry me. I come from a tribe, Muslims, which believes in destiny. If I am destined to be murdered, I am destined.'

If the *platteland* Boers believed they were 'destined' to regain their power, and the Serb war criminal Seselj believed he was 'destined' to restore Serb supremacy, they were clearly deluded. But the dapper little Chechen Dzhabrailov remains an undeluded winner. He is still fantastically rich, still 'respectable' and, unlike so many of his kind who became wealthy during the days of gangster capitalism, still alive. He may even, thanks to the new Russian fashion for 'gentleman chic', have now turfed the Blofeld cat off the sofa. After all, among Russia's snobbish Armani set these days, displaying Bond symbols would be considered dreadfully *pafosny* – a definite case of 'trying too hard'.

18

Stop the Rot

Robert Robinson, chairman of the long-running BBC Radio 4 chat show *Stop the Week*, was holding forth in the pub which its BBC regulars called the Gluepot, but whose actual name was the George.

His subject was the general uselessness of women as on-air conversationalists. 'Women simply can't do *Stop the Rot!*' (his pet name for the programme).

'Bob, in case you haven't noticed,' I pointed out, 'I'm a woman and I've been doing *Stop* for years!'

He looked at me and remarked dismissively, 'Oh, I never think of *you* as a woman!' Which (as I also pointed out) was not quite the compliment he thought it was.

Stop the Week was a cult programme which ran for eighteen years on early Saturday evenings and, judging by our postbags, all our listeners heard it in the bath before going out for the evening. It was, as Miles Kington pointed out in *The Times*, not a chat show but a soap opera, with the regulars, Laurie Taylor, Professor of Sociology at York University, Milton Shulman the drama critic, and me, the token woman, playing the roles in what Kington christened 'The Skittish Family Robinson'.

Every week we would gird our competitive loins, polish our anxious wits, sweat blood and cross swords for our listeners soaking in their Radox, while we discussed such weighty issues as 'At what point do English seagulls crossing the Channel become French ones?' and 'Is it possible to name six famous people called Stan?' or mused on the fact that, according to the *Sun*, 75 per cent of Belgian men preferred Mrs Thatcher to their own mothers.

Our somewhat eccentric producer, Michael Ember, would then edit the conversation or, as he put it, 'boil off the fat'. Ember – whom Bob would always refer to on air as 'our friend from East Molesey' –

had been a talented footballer in Hungary, and as such was known for his tremendous turns of speed. When the Soviet tanks rolled into Hungary in 1956 Ember put on one of his tremendous turns of speed and ran across the border to freedom and the BBC.

While it was true that most women guests found the Garrick Club atmosphere difficult to cope with – 'You're just a bunch of wankers!' one famous critic pronounced after her own dismal showing – men often found it so too. We did behave like members of an exclusive club, faintly unfriendly to outsiders, each of us extremely possessive about our own particular favourite seat at the table in the cavernous sub-basement studio in Broadcasting House where the programme was recorded. When the distinguished philosopher and womanizer Professor A. J. Ayer came in and confidently placed his bottom on 'my' seat I had to shift him, thereby finding myself startled by the extent of both his irritation and his intense halitosis. One critic said the programme should be renamed 'Meet the Chums'.

Perhaps the biggest postbag I got while on *Stop* was when I remarked *en passant* that my husband Michael (whom Bob always called 'your mythical husband') cut his toenails in the bath and didn't flush them away, so that when I got in I felt like an Indian fakir lying on a bed of spikes. One response: 'Be grateful to your husband, Ms Leslie, because you can then scoop them up and use them as mulch for your roses. Very good for roses, toenails.'

When I once mentioned that lilies are an awful nuisance to grow so I'd stuck plastic ones in my flowerbeds because they were indistinguishable from the real thing, I got grateful letters from listeners who admitted they routinely committed such aesthetic crimes – plastic dahlias in the hanging baskets, plastic geraniums in the window boxes . . .

One of my favourite listener missives came by email from the humorist Dr Rob Buckman who had worked with Billy Connolly and John Cleese, and who, like me, wrote for *Punch* magazine and who, like me, adored personal home computers, which were rather rare in the early Eighties. I'd written about our ancient, clapped-out white Ford Capri (it had mushrooms growing in the boot and the moss on the window frames would actually flower): my husband loved it and it had what the makers called 'a power bulge' on its bonnet (as in, is that a power-bulge on your bonnet or are you just pleased to see me?)

Buckman had moved from London to Toronto: 'I thought I'd just rattle your in-box and see if you're all right or if I could get you anything. Excited, for instance. No, sorry, bad line, didn't mean it anyway, I used to listen to you on *Stop the Week* and you were never allowed to say anything unless it was non-controversial and naff like how you hoovered your handbag, while the Good Old Boys said all those really important wanky things about how they thought pumpkins were middle-class and other major issues of the twentieth century, and I just knew you were really a brilliantly funny person but my goodness stunning and I know you're married and stuff like that but I just want to tell you I'm a fan and I drive a Volkswagen Golf which is a highly non-macho car because my penis is of satisfactory size both of which can be verified I mean the Golf and the other. Mind if I sit down? Oh.'

Bob relished reading out listeners' letters on air, particularly if they were insulting. 'How unkind of your guests to spoil your attempt to speak uninterrupted for thirty minutes.' Another wrote: 'Dear Mr Robinson, I have listened to your programme for five years and it is crap. No offence. Yours sincerely . . .'

At the beginning Laurie Taylor (being tremendously Marxist as sociologists then tended to be) often used to start his sentences with, 'What worries me about our society . . .'. Over time he became less 'worried about our society', perhaps because Marxism and Lacanian semiotics didn't really lend themselves to larky *jeux d'esprit* on the class signifiers of pumpkins or, indeed, what one did with discarded toenails.

Antony Sher, when preparing for his role in the hit TV adaptation of *The History Man*, about a libidinous left-wing sociologist, sat in on Laurie's lectures in York. But Malcolm Bradbury, who wrote the original novel, told me it wasn't based on Laurie as he'd never met him but that, judging by what he'd heard about him, he thought Sher had probably done the right thing.

Milton Shulman would remain silent for much of the programme but would then suddenly remark in a gravelly Canadian accent, 'I remember when Marilyn Monroe told me . . .' Or he would produce another hoary Jewish joke: 'Goldberg and Hymie were stranded in the desert and suddenly a wild animal rushes towards them. Hymie says, "Is that a lion?" And Goldberg says, "How would I know? *You're* the furrier!"'

We all knew his Goldberg jokes backwards, even the more extended ones which took a long time to get through because he kept chortling as he told them. We all loved Milton (as, indeed, we all loved one another) but we would barrack him – 'Get on with it!' – or chant the jokes under our breath. Naturally, some of our listeners thought that we, especially Bob, were being unconscionably rude to him. When Bob was challenged on this issue by a *Times* interviewer he rightly pointed out, 'I'm *not* rude to Milton. I'm not rude to anyone. With people you know, you can say all sorts of things which you couldn't to people you don't.'

Bob, who was also chairman of the *Brain of Britain* radio quiz, excoriated David English, my editor at the *Daily Mail*, by asking 'Why doesn't he get a decent job, like stealing cats for vivisectionists?' I adored David as much as I adored Bob, so I wasn't having that. I remarked coldly, 'Well, we can't all be quizmasters!' Far from taking understandable umbrage, Bob would cheerfully repeat that put-down line to every other person who interviewed him.

It was a programme which inspired tremendous affection and tremendous vitriol, some of it deserved. During a discussion on the Duchess of York's dress sense, I'd remarked that Fergie always looked as if she'd dressed while escaping a burning building. Another panellist retorted by saying that my garb looked as if it were 'composed of electric light bulbs'. One critic commented, 'True enough; I saw Ms Leslie on television, not only wearing a high-voltage sweater but equipped with the most ferocious eyelashes.'

Some listeners hated the programme with a visceral intensity, especially if they'd been a regular panellist who'd been dumped. One of the latter was a dull and self-important little fellow, who claimed he'd co-invented the programme 'acting as an unpaid consultant and confidant to Michael Ember', and accused Bob of the crime of wanting to be Dr Johnson.

When *Stop the Week* was finally axed in 1992 (by a new female head of department who to this day insists she was 'only following orders') most of the newspapers lengthily mourned its passing. But the chippy ex-panellist – who'd been shown the door sixteen years earlier – chose to write a sneery little piece in the *Guardian* about 'the coach trade's idea of a metropolitan dinner party ... I asked myself whether I had given birth to a Frankenstein's monster, a cradle of empty egotism rather than wit, of waffling by the privileged classes rather than insight from all types, of plastic mouths rather than flexible minds.'

It's extraordinary how the memory of the programme still lingers on. Even now, total strangers who recognize my voice will come up to me to say how much they miss it: 'Saturday evening bathtime has never been the same since!'

And the programme did get me a scoop in China – where one wouldn't think conundrums about the nationality of seagulls crossing the English Channel would have much traction. In 1979 I learned that the British embassy had a particular grass-roots source which enabled them to confirm the arrest of the Gang of Four (responsible for the cruel insanities of the Cultural Revolution) before it became worldwide news. The source was not Chinese by birth: he was an English academic who, like so many deluded romantics before him, had gone to China to support Maoist Communism. These left-over 'foreign friends' were some of the saddest people I met in China. They were mostly housed (some might say imprisoned) in dusty apartments in Beijing's Friendship Hotel, distrusted by the Chinese, lonely, embittered, disillusioned, but now unable to return to the lives they'd long since abandoned in the West.

This particular 'foreign friend' did not live in the Friendship Hotel; he lived and worked at Beida University, teaching English. I got his room number and made my way through the warren of buildings and corridors until I reached his door. I banged on it and the man opened it. 'Sorry to bother you, I'm Ann Leslie of the *Daily Mail* and ...' The door banged shut. And almost immediately opened again. 'Are you Ann Leslie of *Stop the Week*?' Yes. 'What's Robert Robinson really like?'

It turned out that his family in Britain, worried that he might by now have lost touch with English conversational eccentricities, would send him tapes of *Stop the Week* and he'd become addicted. He proved immensely helpful with material for the four-part series on China which I wrote for the *Mail*.

Even before the death of *Stop* I'd joined what Michael Ember would witheringly refer to as the 'stage army' of all-purpose pundits who appeared regularly on radio and television programmes like *Any Questions* and *Question Time*. When the late Sir Robin Day chaired *Question Time*, I was devoted to him but also deeply exasperated by him. He indulged in crassly elephantine flirting – poor lamb, not surprisingly he didn't have much success with women – but like most men of his generation he didn't rate women as *femmes sérieuses* or intellectual equals. He was both patronizing towards us and, of course, rather scared of us.

He once told me that he felt thoroughly henpecked as the *Question Time* production team were mostly female. His ideal programme panellists, every week, would have been Michael Foot, Denis Healey, Roy Jenkins and Michael Heseltine. The swarm of production henpeckers would stamp their little feet and point out – to his chagrin – that he could not choose the panellists and besides, the panel had to include a woman. And the only woman he rated was the historian Antonia Fraser (so God knows how much elephantine flirting the beautiful Lady Antonia had to put up with). Shirley Williams was his second choice (Shirley runs late for everything, and *Question Time* was no exception, which always gave the team conniptions).

And, a long way down, his third choice would be me.

He bullied male panellists of course, but he couldn't be bothered to do us women the honour even of being bullied – he just tended to dismiss us and move quickly on. Once he cut me off before I'd managed to finish what I was saying and I snapped back, 'I haven't *finished*, Robin!' He was thoroughly startled – as though some pretty little Stepford Wife had suddenly torn off her pinny and socked him in the face with a home-baked Victoria sponge. After that I got some grudging respect and, in the end, genuine affection – as opposed to elephantine flirting – from him.

To the end of his days Robin bitterly regretted losing *Question Time*, which arose out of a failed power struggle he had with his editor Barbara Maxwell who, not long afterwards, lost her own power struggle at the BBC.

In the late Eighties and early Nineties studio audiences were much more partisan than now, and the left were always far more vocal than the right. David Blunkett, who has been described as the most right-wing Home Secretary of modern times, was amazingly left-wing when he was leader of Sheffield Council (which at the time was dubbed the Socialist Republic of Sheffield). And he was, with some justification, accused of trying to rig the programme by infiltrating as many of his supporters as possible into the audience, on the grounds that *Question Time* audiences were full of 'middle-class professional types' who didn't support the left.

Of course *my* ideal audience in those days would have consisted solely of country solicitors and dear little white-haired old ladies from a village knitting circle who thought that the *Mail*'s star columnist Lynda Lee-Potter or I should be Prime Minister. Instead, I always seemed to get David Blunkett's ideal audience – noisy Trotskyites, militant feminists, left-wing union activists, people with sandals and angry beards wearing CND badges. Blunkett and I were both afflicted by standard panellists' paranoia.

Though perhaps none was as paranoid as Tony Benn on Radio 4's *Any Questions*. He always tape-recorded programmes he appeared on, and often timed the length of each contribution. He once complained to the BBC that it had proved its right-wing bias by allowing me to speak for almost a minute longer than he did.

I never found it easy to be on with either him or miners' leader Arthur Scargill because, when both men were in their prime, audiences would be packed out with their brownshirts. Yes, I know that Tony is now considered a National Treasure but he used to inspire some extremely nasty people.

It was during an *Any Questions* in some grim urban location that Tony's claque started hissing every time I opened my mouth to speak. Hissing is a very effective weapon on radio: listeners at home aren't that aware of it but it's very off-putting if you're trying to talk through it in a hall. I would occasionally share a BBC car with Tony to or from a venue, but I never had a problem with him personally because we were both, like Rob Buckman, obsessed with computers and could chatter amicably for hours to each other about the latest electronic gizmo which had caught our eye.

I first appeared on *Question Time* in 1979 when the programme began, and over the years several *Question Time* 'virgins' have contacted me for tips. One of these was the then rising star in the Tory government, Virginia Bottomley. I told her, 'Say what you really think.' To which she replied, 'It's all right for you. If I say what I really think I'll be accused the next day of having rewritten Tory policies!' And she had a point. One of the many reasons why I never went into politics is that I couldn't bear being told what to say. The *Daily Mail* of course has strong views and, under its two brilliant and forceful editors, David English and Paul Dacre, I've been writing for it for the last thirty-five years. But not once have I been pressured into writing, let alone saying, anything that I didn't wholeheartedly believe.

I'd also tell *Question Time* virgins that if you follow the news you can usually guess what the questions might be, but it helps if you can sit next to the chairman and squint at the upcoming question – it gives you ten seconds' forewarning. The trouble is that sometimes the chairman shuffles the question cards and – if your mind is now racing to sort out what, if anything, you know about an integrated energy policy – you find yourself landed instead with a daffy question about pocket money for the kiddies.

I hated the so-called 'sillies' question, especially prevalent on *Any Questions*. These were usually first addressed to the woman panellist (there was usually only one then) because women are supposed to be good on 'silly' issues. But audiences like these questions, not least because they're sometimes rather revealing. Instead of the 'stage army' panel opining on some major geopolitical issue, we'd be asked, 'What electrical appliance would the panel like to have on a desert island?' I replied to that one, 'An electric chair – because I'd rather die than be stuck on a desert island without company'. Roy Hattersley, then Deputy Leader of the Labour Party, answered, 'An iron.' Turned out that there's nothing this professional Yorkshireman and socialist, goose-killing dog owner likes better than ironing his own shirts. His fellow panellists, and the audience, were agape with astonishment.

The one thing a panellist wants to avoid, if you really have no idea what the question is even referring to, is to get asked first. On the other hand, being last can also be disastrous: the other panellists may already have said all there is to say.

That doesn't bother some people of course. I was once on a TV panel programme with the racing driver Stirling Moss. When the presenter came to him, Moss regularly responded, beaming comfortably, 'I really have nothing to add to what the other panellists have said. I don't know anything about this subject.' If he was asked first he'd simply say, 'Pass!'

In the past, to avoid being asked first, I occasionally used a 'bee-in-the-tights' ploy: I would suddenly look startled, as if a bee had got into my tights, and I'd put my head under the table to disentangle this mythical bee from my underwear. No chairman is going to come first to someone whose head is under the table and thus out of shot.

Sometimes *no one* on the panel knows what the question is referring to. The second time I was on *Question Time* with Tony Blair (then a rising opposition backbencher), we were faced with a question which had purely local significance – I think it was about problems with the county's sewage disposal – and, after a quick dead-eyed pan of my fellow panellists, I knew they were as baffled as I was. I did a quick 'bee-in-the-tights' manoeuvre and so it was Blair who answered – and, I have to say, busked brilliantly, with that slightly insane grin on his face. In those pre-Iraq war days he used to grin far more insanely, and much more girlishly; at Fettes, his Scottish public school, he was nicknamed Emily, and later by his law chambers colleagues Miranda.

Sometimes the location added to one's woes. On one occasion *Question Time* was held at St David's Hall in Cardiff, where this multi-million-pound conference centre's air conditioning wasn't working. It felt as though we'd been sealed in a Turkish bath. We were all, even before the programme started, pouring with so much sweat that the production team provided us with little facecloths with which to mop our brows during recording.

Poor Leon Brittan's brow was a Niagara of sweat – and, cruelly, the director cut to him mopping his brow during some anti-Tory question and made him look as if he was being devious, shifty and sweating with the impossibility of defending the then Tory government in which he was a Cabinet Minister. It was unfair: he was only sweating from the heat because we all were. I don't imagine he was best pleased with that shot.

My worst experience occurred on an *Any Questions* in Scotland where my fellow guests included Robin Cook and the Tory MP and Solicitor General for Scotland, Nicholas Fairbairn. The latter was a Thatcher favourite because of his hair-raisingly right-wing views and, doubtless, his noisily expressed adoration of her. He liked to wear flamboyant Scottish baronial tartan, always carried a miniature (but fully operational) pistol attached to his belt by a chain, showed off about his fondness for snuff, and drank like a fish. One of his mistresses tried to commit suicide by hanging herself from a lamp-post outside his London home.

I was a newcomer on *Any Questions* and, dry-mouthed with fear, had just launched in to the answer to some baffling question about, possibly, Scottish rural landowners' rights, when suddenly I felt a hand forcefully and determinedly groping my crotch. The curtain attached to the table hid this *frottage* from public view. The only person to whom the hand could belong was Fairbairn, who was sitting next to me, but he was looking vaguely into the far distance as if his hand was operating as an entirely autonomous entity. The groping continued on and off for the rest of the programme.

Had that happened in later years when I had more confidence I would have said live on air, 'I'm so sorry, but I can't answer this question – or indeed any other question – until Mr Fairbairn removes his hand from my crotch.' As it was, I blundered on.

After the programme I had to share a BBC car with Robin Cook. I'd never met him before but naturally I assumed that this little ginger gnome, being left-wing and politically correct, would sympathize with me. Not a bit of it. 'You mustn't be so hard on Nicky, he's very in favour of women's rights.' Like the right for women not to be groped by libidinous drunks? Evidently not. I was furious.

Later I recounted Cook's response to my plea for sympathy to another Labour Scot. 'Aye, but that's not surprising. Robin may not share Nicky's politics, but they've got one thing in common: north of the border, Robin's known to be a right little swordsman!' Evidently not only north of the border, judging by the revelations of his former wife – whom he left, pressured by Alistair Campbell, for his Commons secretary.

For a brief period the *Question Time* producers decided that we panellists should not be seen just sitting at the table but should enter – showbiz style – to excited applause, like movie stars on the Parkinson show. We weren't movie stars and we looked extremely silly doing this, and in my case our amateurishness at showbiz strutting led to something rather embarrassing. We had to wear radio mics and transmitters – my transmitter was tucked into the back of my trousers. As I'm always nervous before a programme, I had to go to the loo.

On finishing I pulled up my trousers and suddenly spotted my live transmitter winking up at me from the lavatory bowl. I was instantly and traumatically reminded of the disaster-prone Lieutenant Frank Drebin in one of the *Naked Gun* films, who found, in similar circumstances, that his radio mic had been broadcasting his experiences in the Gents live to a grand gala dinner. Hardly a confidence-building exercise.

Sometimes live broadcasting can prove so chaotic that there's nothing a presenter can do but bite back giggles. For several months in 1996 I presented a live, one-hour weekly magazine and phone-in programme entitled *Britain Talks Back*, on a short-lived satellite channel called Talk TV. I've never met a single person who ever saw either the programme, or indeed knew of the channel, apart from the media commentator Roy Greenslade – and he was a fellow presenter.

On my programme one leading MP flounced out when she discovered that there was no one to do her *maquillage*. 'I have never, ever come across such amateurishness in my life!' The production staff were very young, badly paid and overworked, but they did their best, hurtling to and fro like demented hamsters. As the MP disappeared in an unpowdered huff, one of them muttered to me, 'Don't know what makes her think she'll look any better with make-up – she doesn't need powder, she needs Special Effects.'

The studio was located a couple of floors up in the London Weekend Television building on the South Bank. One day my running order showed that I was due to do a live interview with a breeder of 'zonkeys', zebra and donkey hybrids, and he was going to bring two of them with him into the studio. Shortly before they were due on I heard a frantic squawk in my earpiece: 'The zonkeys are scrubbed! Forget the zonkeys!' The breeder had been trying to push his zonkeys into the lift in the front hall, when some Health and Safety gauleiter spotted him and shouted, 'You can't put those things in the lift! You need a permit for livestock. And get them out of this building!' I gather that both animals thereupon placidly deposited a small pile of zonkey pats at his feet.

There was also a children's programme, presented by a lively young man who at the time was in the process of creating a character whom he initially christened 'MC Jocelyn Cheadle-Hume' – the prototype for Ali G: the children's presenter was Sacha Baron Cohen. 'Respeck!' is therefore due to the long-buried corpse of Talk TV.

One of the joys of having such a varied professional life is the extraordinary connections you find between people whom you've met, interviewed and sometimes got to know well, and who at first you'd think would have absolutely nothing in common.

What, for example, did the dour right-wing politician Enoch Powell, the bullying American drama coach Lee Strasberg, who developed the Method school of acting, and the much-loved Oscar-winning star Jack Lemmon have in common? Bizarrely, what linked this disparate trio was an obsession with the alleged advantages, or otherwise, of a painfully full bladder.

One night I was a fellow guest with Enoch Powell on a live political TV debate. The presenter was Anne Robinson. 'Who on earth is that woman?' asked Enoch, the classicist and fluent Urdu speaker, who was clearly not au fait with contemporary popular culture and equally clearly didn't wish to be. I explained who Annie was and Enoch asked with a slight air of wonderment, 'How is this young woman qualified to talk about political issues?' But before I could fully explain that Annie was very popular with ordinary voters who also were 'not qualified to talk about political issues' in the way that he was, I interrupted myself: 'Sorry, Mr Powell – I'm always nervous before going on air so I have to go to the loo – so please excuse me . . .'

Powell was dressed in his customary funeral director's garb (I was told, by one of his friends, that he always dressed that way, even when going on a family picnic). He turned his glaucous eyes on me and, gripping my arm like the Ancient Mariner, would not release me for my planned run to the Ladies. 'Use it! Use it!' Use *what*? 'A full bladder is an important performance aid. I never empty mine before a speech. The tension it creates in you will prove invaluable for your adrenaline.'

So I took him at his word, and endured the next hour on air wriggling in agony, unable to concentrate on a word I, or anyone else, was saying.

A few days later I was sitting next to Jack Lemmon at a lunch. I described this episode. Lemmon, who'd clearly never heard of Enoch, asked innocently, 'Did this Enoch work at the Actors' Studio?' That, I assured him, was most unlikely.

'I only ask because when I was at the Actors' Studio, our drama coach Lee Strasberg would never allow us to go to the lavatory before a performance. He'd say, "Use it! Use it!" Sometimes those of us who had a bit of prostate trouble or were particularly nervous would actually have slight accidents on stage. But we were so frightened of him that we never disobeyed.'

When many years earlier I'd interviewed Strasberg (who admitted to me that he'd started out as a stand-up comedian and failed), he told me, 'The actor is the most dangerous artistic material there is. They say, "Wassermatter with him? All he's got to do is go on stage and say some lines and go off again." But an actor has terrible personality problems. He has to *become* another person. If he did this offstage he'd be judged insane. Doing it in the theatre can produce real problems in him.' Problems no doubt thoroughly exacerbated by his own implacable veto on the emptying of thespian bladders.

I have never taken Enoch Powell's, or indeed Strasberg's, advice ever again.

The full-bladder issue inspired a small rebellion on my part against Mrs Thatcher. I was covering the 1979 election campaign which brought her to power. In those days campaign buses did not routinely have on-board loos – and I'd given birth the previous year so my bladder was not entirely stoic about having to spend hours out of reach of a public lavatory. I pleaded with her: 'Please can we have more potty stops? I sometimes wonder whether you somehow "vaporize" the stuff, like astronauts. But I can't.' The iron-bladdered Iron Lady looked at me witheringly: 'No one needs to go more than twice a day. I go first thing in the morning and last thing at night, and that's *quite* enough.'

No wonder the world's statesmen found negotiating with this implacable woman so infuriating.

19

'Lift up your breasts and roar!'

Talk about feminism to my daughter's generation and they yawn. Hard for them to imagine the days when women would, for example, be denied mortgages simply because of their gender.

I'll never forget the blinding red mist of rage which engulfed me when a young, besuited, building society twerp refused me one – even though I was the highest-paid feature writer on a leading national newspaper – on the grounds that 'Pretty young women don't need to bother their heads with things like that! Why not find yourself a nice husband and let him deal with it?'

As an article on mortgages in a 1968 issue of *Which?* magazine explained, for a single woman to get a mortgage in her own right was virtually impossible: a handful of 'enlightened' building societies would, reluctantly, lend to a single woman, but only if she was 'over forty, or professionally qualified, especially as a doctor, nurse or schoolteacher'.

I did get the mortgage however, not because I had a right to it, financially or otherwise, but because of another condescending man – the chairman of the building society in question – who was a contact of our Property Correspondent and who told him he admired my work; his suddenly grovelling underling was ordered to grant me the mortgage after all, 'as a favour to this clever girl'! A favour! Pass me the meat-cleaver, sister!

Of course, the sexism young women of my generation endured was very small beer compared to that still suffered by millions of oppressed women in other parts of the world, but it was irritating nonetheless. For example, when I was in my twenties no top hotel or restaurant would admit a woman wearing a trouser suit (one woman, when told trousers were forbidden, whipped them off in front of the doorman, and was told that the police were being summoned to arrest her for 'creating a public nuisance').

El Vino's, one of Fleet Street's legendary hostelries, forbade women to stand at the bar or buy a drink. We were stowed away like toxic material in a back room. Some of the more vocal 'sisters' – all wearing trousers – of the newly emerging feminism mounted a shrieking demonstration against El Vino's, thereby causing much male hilarity.

Admittedly, women journalists – if they were good and had the nerve, both of which applied to me – were paid as well as male journalists, but that was partly because Fleet Street editors were by now very ambivalent about all these women suddenly banging on about their rights. They weren't *against* women, but the type they liked were mini-skirted 'dolly birds', not least because they made good pictures. However, editors also knew that wives made the decisions about which newspaper would be delivered to the family home. So perhaps the 'monstrous regiment of women' should be wooed a little, and maybe female by-lines might help win female readers. The *Mail* asked me to go to the US where the modern feminist movement had really got going – and where big corporations, often more attuned to the zeitgeist there than the newspapers, were making big money out of it.

The Lucky Strike tobacco ads showed tough, sassy, beautiful career women posing fag in hand and boldly demanding of some unseen male, 'Light my Lucky.' But the Virginia Slims campaign, which began in 1968, was pivotal. Who, of my generation of women, can forget the slogan, 'You've Come a Long Way Baby'? It even featured a song, for heaven's sake, which went 'You've come a long way, baby! You've got your own cigarette, baby!'

The suffragettes (of whom my fearsome grandmother so disapproved) had been the first wave of feminism. But the second wave in the Sixties and Seventies liberated us all to get equal-opportunity lung cancer. Naturally, my series was entitled 'You've Come a Long Way, Baby!' And the model wore *trousers*!

I interviewed not only the leading 'sisters' of the new feminist ideology in the States, but also their anti-feminist enemies. In California I went on a course called 'Fascinating Womanhood', run by women who thought all this 'women's liberation' stuff was very bad for women – because men didn't like it. Man's ego was seen as a terrifyingly tender plant, like a rare orchid which couldn't bear the icy blast of women's liberation. To become a Fascinating Woman 'you must learn to be childlike'; become frightened of spiders (even if you weren't); dress like Shirley Temple on the *Good Ship Lollipop*; and boost your man's ego by saying things like (and I quote), 'Oh, will you, big strong hairy man, open this jam jar for little me?' And Faye, our trainer, urged us to repeat to ourselves: 'A feminine woman should never be able to kill her own snakes.'

But I didn't take her advice. After all, I've obstinately been killing my own snakes all my life.

We were told to remember that female charm comes from displaying an air of DRH – Dependency, Radiance and Helplessness. Our class of mostly middle-aged women whose husbands had run off with their secretaries, leaving them with no income and no home, were told that it was all their own fault for not having cultivated DRH.

Faye led us in an exercise in radiant smiling in front of a mirror: 'Open your eyes – wide, wide, wide! And open your mouth – wide, wide, wide!' I told her it made me look as radiantly charming as a toad about to gobble a fly. Faye pursed her lips. I was clearly a women's libber in disguise – particularly when I told her that I objected to being informed that my literary role models should be the drippy Amelia in Thackeray's *Vanity Fair* and Dickens's tiresome Dora. 'Are you married?' said Faye. Yes. '*Still* married?' she asked disbelievingly.

But it was time to move on to the serious business: interviewing the leading members of the Women's Movement. Of course, in no time at all I discovered that the 'sisters' were all at one another's throats and that women were just as obsessed with playing power-games as any man – which was heresy according to the new feminist religion.

Take Betty Friedan. When she published the ground-breaking *The Feminine Mystique* in 1963, she threw a ferocious assegai into the Norman Rockwell image of the idyllic mom-and-apple-pie image of American family life. When Friedan was writing her book, the middle-class white American housewife was, materially speaking, the most pampered woman in history. She could sit all day colour-matching her bathroom towels and devising new ways of cooking meat loaf, while her harried spouse fought frantically in the corporate jungle in order to drag home ever more dishwashers, deep-freezes and barbecues to pile into this spoiled darling's nest. Oh, happy, happy Mom, said advertisers, educationalists, psychologists.

But Mom said otherwise. She discovered too late that fulfilment did not lie in Betty Crocker cake mixes alone. (Because canny cake-mix manufacturers knew that their product made women feel guilty – why aren't I, as a good wife, making cakes from scratch? – the recipes insisted that Mom add an egg, thus absolving her from the crime of housewifely laziness.)

Happiness, said Friedan, did not come dream-kitchen-shaped. Indeed, Mom, trapped in the 'comfortable concentration camp of her home', was a seething snake pit of loneliness, frustration and full-time neuroticism. The book launched a time bomb into the image of the happy white American home, and out of that shattered debris Women's Liberation was born.

Time magazine's cover declared 1975 to be 'The Year of the Woman'. And stated that these pesky creatures 'have arrived like a new immigrant wave in male America'.

Friedan and I met in a fashionable restaurant near the Lincoln Arts Center in New York. My guest arrived at her usual waddling run, her grey locks a little wild, her mother-hen body bundled into a red leather and fur coat. She plopped down, gasping, 'My Ga-ahd what a day!' And downed the first of a long series of whisky sours. Until *The Feminine Mystique* she'd been just another Jewish housewife living in comfortable suburban obscurity with husband Carl in Rockland County, Maryland. Now she lived alone in a forty-fourth-floor apartment in an expensive skyscraper. (Faye would have said that Betty deserved to lose Carl, who must have been longing for some Dependency, Radiance and Helplessness from his stroppy wife.)

I soon became astounded by the virulence of the civil war among the feminists, everyone accusing everyone else of being an agent of, variously, the CIA/the Trotskyists/the Catholic Church/the FBI, the insurance companies and goodness knows who else. I soon lost count of the bogeymen supposedly involved: '. . . I tell you, she's got them to tap my phone' '. . . she's gotta have big business behind her' '. . . she actually tried to strangle me at the last conference'.

Friedan had founded the National Organization of Women but they fell out over 'lesbian liberation' and over the leadership's sharp

left-wing turn. Friedan stabbed angrily with a fork at her steak tar-
tare. '. . . and I said to them, you can't analyse women's liberation in
terms of class warfare. "Man is a class oppressor" – I ask you! You're
just defying psychological, sexual, biological and human reality –
and you're going to alienate the vast mass of women by doing so.'

Then there was the Lavender Menace who regarded any woman
having sexual intercourse with a man to be a sex traitor who'd be
punished in their proposed separatist Amazon state. Friedan, downing another stiff whisky sour, snorted: 'A separate state for women, I
ask you!' She accused the 'lesbian liberationists' of attempting to
'take over' the Movement, 'blackmail' her, and even 'seduce' her.

The lesbians then called a press conference and issued a furious
statement declaring that 'because large amounts of time and energy
in the Women's Movement are being spent trying to shut Betty's
mouth, someone should offer Betty Friedan a muzzle (cameras,
please).'

Said one: 'She's just a bourgeois Old Testament priestess. Take no
notice of her, she's just jealous that she's not the leader of the
Movement any more.' My Gaa-aahd, she was hurt. '*Of course* I'm
wounded. I'm very thin-skinned, all women are. It's the way we've
been programmed, we desperately want to be liked. I'm very brave
about the issues: if I see injustice towards women then nothing and
nobody will deter me. But *personal* hostility, especially from other
women, I find very, very hard to take. I can't cope with it, I'm a
complete coward.'

So why were they so disrespectful to the great feminist pioneer?

'Partly it's due to what I call women's "loser-syndrome". This is
expressed in a really *sloppy* concept of womanhood, which is that all
women are equally wonderful so there must be no leadership.
Unfortunately, underlying all this, I'm afraid, is pathology, the fact
that women after centuries of self-denigration don't trust themselves
to compete and succeed. So rather than face up to this fear in
themselves, they prefer to drag down any woman who can succeed,
who can compete. This way all we wonderful women can be losers
together.'

She then went on to a brilliant analysis of how the in-fighting and
the 'loser-syndrome' were weakening the Movement just at the point
when it seemed to be winning. 'We must stop wallowing in self-pity

and self-hate, and get out and take realistic action where it's needed against economic exploitation . . . social security injustices . . . credit laws . . .' And so on. All very fine, perceptive and rational so far. But then I mentioned the name 'Gloria' – and whoosh! The rational Friedan, arms flailing, hair flying, eyes popping, disappeared into a dust cloud of paranoia, never to return to earth again that evening.

Gloria was Gloria Steinem: Gloria the Legs! Gloria the Golden Girl of the feminist movement, editor and founder of its mainstream mouthpiece, the glossy *MS* magazine. Gloria didn't 'need' to be a feminist – if you consider only plain, embittered man-hating losers 'need' to be feminists. Gloria already Had Everything. That's what was so unforgivable to so many women both in and out of the movement.

A leading journalist and television personality, she was already an established queen of the radical chic jet-set. Steinem's lion's mane hair, Steinem's wit and warmth, Steinem's trendy aviator-glasses, Steinem's scrumptious sex-kitten face were as essential a fixture at the 'in' parties in the shiny penthouses of Park Avenue as the olives in the martinis.

And then gorgeous Gloria in her Gucci shoes and her Pucci pants turned her lovely eyes on the Women's Movement, and the nation's cameras and television crews stopped focusing on fat little Friedan and zoomed in on this beautiful, thin lady instead. My Gaa-aahd, it was so unfair!

So Betty, never averse to a fight (ex-husband Carl was still scarred from a flung mirror), instantly fought back: Steinem was 'ripping off' the Movement for money and fame (of which she had plenty already); Steinem was pushing a 'man-hating' line (patently ridiculous); Steinem was saying *awful* things like 'marriage is prostitution' (which indeed she did, but in the context of a speech on the effects of discrimination on marriage laws). I couldn't help concluding that Betty, so aware of the loser-syndrome in others, had fallen victim to it herself. But alas for Gloria and hooray for Betty: a new twist to the plot. Enter, extreme left of stage, The Red Stockings!

The Red Stockings were yet another feminist splinter group and they'd recently published, with much fanfare, an exposé of Gloria's CIA connections under the title *Agents, Fools and Opportunists*. Now, it's true that Steinem did once run a CIA front organization called the Independent Research Center and travelled under its aegis, and true, you could find yellowing press cuttings in which Steinem praises the laudable aims and liberal thinking of her paymasters. But those were the dear dead days of political innocence before Watergate and revelations of CIA crimes stained the American psyche with paranoia. In those days many bright young men and women (as one of them told me) 'regarded the CIA as just another government agency which seemed willing to lash out bread giving us nice free trips to youth festivals abroad. You were supposed to represent the American way of freedom and write rather jejune reports on the people you met there. Ideologically, it didn't amount to a hill of beans.'

Because Steinem had become rather reticent about her past, the Red Stockings devised a towering conspiracy theory to 'explain the installation of Gloria Steinem as the Movement's "leader" by the rich and powerful'. When I talked to Steinem she chose to behave as if she were above such in-fighting and told me wearily that of course she respected Betty as 'a pioneer'.

One day recently, when I was arguing with an Islamist in the Gulf about whether his version of his faith was oppressive to women, he informed me that Western feminism was actually a Jewish conspiracy (as were most things in his view). 'It was all inspired by American Jews to destroy family life. Look what's happened to Western society now that women can do what they like and neglect their family duties.' Actually, though I never conceded the point, there was in one respect a grain of truth in what he said. Most of the leaders of modern feminism, like Friedan, Steinem, Shulamit Firestone, Andrea Dworkin, Eva Figes, Kate Millett, Germaine Greer, were brought up in one of the great baroque patriarchal religions, Judaism or Roman Catholicism.

The effort involved in questioning and breaking away from these restrictive cultures and faiths emboldened them to question attitudes in the wider society. I know, because I was brought up as a Roman Catholic. As was Britain's version of Friedan, Germaine Greer. A friend of Germaine's once described her as 'just another convent girl run amok'. I can understand that: I too was a convent girl who ran amok, but since I was never as brilliant, showy, iconoclastic or publicity-hungry as Germaine, my amok-running was a somewhat pastel affair.

I had been bowled over by her book *The Female Eunuch*. I was less so when I became acquainted with the author herself. I realized that, like the American feminist trailblazer Friedan, she didn't seem to like women very much. Of course Karl Marx, who promoted the cause of the downtrodden working-classes, actually didn't like them either: they were the lumpenproletariat. But not much liking the people whose cause you promote self-evidently doesn't mean that you can't have a huge influence on their lives.

Like every disappointed disciple, I came to realize that what Germaine really wanted was to be the centre of attention at all times; those who didn't always accept that she was right – at any one time, since Germaine is prone to change her mind rather capriciously – would have the Greer scorn heaped on their hapless heads. And she does do scorn magnificently. Just as in America I became embroiled in a cat-fight between two leading feminists, Friedan and Steinem, so, to a lesser extent, did I in London.

In 1994 I was a regular panellist, along with Janet Street-Porter and the feminist *Guardian* columnist Suzanne Moore, on an all-women BBC2 talk show series, chaired by Germaine. Germaine is a natural bully, and what this great narcissistic and exhibitionist feminist likes to do is bully women. Janet and I were a problem for her: Janet is utterly impervious to bullying; she simply doesn't notice it. I do, but perhaps Germaine suspected I would fight back, and bullies don't like victims who put up a fight. So she fastened on harmless Suzanne who made all of us (except Germaine) laugh by saying, 'Men are good for only two things: DIY and sex.'

Just as Friedan loathed the rise of her younger feminist sister Steinem, so Germaine seemed to think that Suzanne, another rising star, was 'dissing' her own feminist pre-eminence. Besides, Suzanne had two children and Germaine, despite many a struggle, and to her fury, had failed to produce any progeny of her own.

And then sweet Suzanne made a mistake. She casually repeated in an interview the false allegation that Germaine might have had a hysterectomy. Greer shot out of her corner, greying locks a-flying, and poured a gallon of vitriol on sweet Suzanne's head. 'So much lipstick must rot the brain,' she declared, and described Moore's appearance as 'hair bird's-nested all over the place, fuck-me shoes and three fat layers of cleavage'. An understandably distressed Suzanne rang me: 'What should I do?'

'Nothing!' I told her. 'Rise magisterially above it. Leave your friends, like Julie Burchill and me, to do the mud-wrestling.' Which I did. It was a dull week for news, so my phone rang off the hook, not only from British broadcasters but from the States, where Germaine was a big name, and Australia, the land of her birth.

Germaine is one of those people – male and female – who seem to me to be born with an 'extremist gene'. They leap from one extreme to another, their feet never seeming to touch the middle ground in between: from promiscuity to puritanism and back; from Trotskyism to extreme right-wingery (oddly enough, few make that backward leap again); from religious certainty to spectacularly anti-religious polemics – and sometimes back to the beginning again. At least two of my dearest and oldest friends have that 'extremist gene', which makes them tremendously stimulating to be with – but you wouldn't want them to run a chip shop, let alone a country.

Jane Fonda is a prime example of the syndrome. When I first met her she was married to the thoroughly chauvinist, if charming, French film director Roger Vadim, who 'created' Brigitte Bardot and who tried to turn all his subsequent wives and mistresses into Bardot look-alikes. Jane had just starred in his *Barbarella* in which, with her tumbling blonde hair and extravagantly sexy outfits, she was a Bardot clone. When we went shopping for a white cashmere sweater for Vadim's Christmas present, she bubbled over with subservient adoration of her man. Faye of 'Fascinating Womanhood' would have approved of her.

Faye would not have approved of Jane's next incarnation as a rabid, brown-haired feminist without make-up who denounced women who tried to look like a Barbie-doll and who indulged in 'pathetic' attempts to keep young and beautiful by going under the surgeon's knife. And Faye would have been infuriated (as were most Americans) by her 'Hanoi Jane' extreme-left incarnation, when Fonda, the guest of the enemy North Vietnamese Communist government, was 'conned' (she later claimed) into posing on one of the anti-aircraft batteries which were being used to shoot down her fellow countrymen's planes.

She then became the Barbie-doll trophy wife of the media tycoon Ted Turner. She now advertises anti-ageing cream and has suddenly become a born-again Christian; she says her latest marriage broke up because Turner declared, in effect, that religious people were nuts. Fonda's 'extremist gene' must have utterly confused all those, including husbands, who've tried vainly to keep up.

The last time I saw her was in China in 1995 when she was a delegate to the United Nations Fourth World Conference on Women in Huairou. Looking at her, dressed to the nines in rich white feminist 'casual' chic, I remembered that the most sisterly relations I've ever had with activist feminists actually took place ten years earlier at another UN World Conference on Women, this time in Nairobi in Kenya.

I'd been asked by the *Mail* to go there at very short notice so of course the hotels were full. I arrived outside the Hilton to find a huge row being conducted on the pavement between Kenyan officials and dozens of American feminists, led by the extremely noisy, spectacularly behatted Congresswoman Bella Abzug. The sisters, all members of non-governmental organizations, were being evicted from the hotel, despite having booked and paid through the nose for their rooms well in advance. The Kenyan government had suddenly realized, at the last moment, that there were no rooms left for official delegates, so the NGO 'sisters' were being dumped on the pavement.

An evicted group of black Alaskans (until then, I'd never realized there were any blacks in Alaska) had hired a mini-van and, as I didn't fancy hanging around getting earache from Bella, I joined them on a desperate hotel-room hunt. Every hotel rejected us, but our driver knew of one of the fancier whorehouses in town. Mr Chakrabarti, the owner, happily evicted the whores and rented us their rooms at a vast price. The black Alaskans (being thoroughly middle-class Americans) were utterly horrified by the state of the towels, pillows and sheets, so we drove to a shop in our mini-van and stocked up on more sanitary bed linen.

All went well until one morning when a crestfallen Mr Chakrabarti came to me and said that a government official had arrived to inform him that it had now requisitioned his whorehouse to use as accommodation for some lowly official delegates: 'He is coming back this afternoon.' I told Mr Chakrabarti to inform the official that I was a Very Important British Journalist, a good friend of Her Majesty the Queen and of Prime Minister Margaret Thatcher, and that I was now about to alert the news agencies so they could have photographers on hand to record our eviction. 'And tell him he may need troops, as we're not leaving without a fight. Does he want the world to know how the Kenyan government treats important foreign delegates?'

When the official arrived, Mr Chakrabarti relayed this threat to the official, who then slunk away. The black Alaskans and I celebrated our victory; they pinned a walrus badge on me (the walrus, I need hardly remind you, is the State symbol) and later printed in my honour an elaborate certificate which, while not exactly awarding me the freedom of Anchorage, looked as though it might. 'Sisterhood is Powerful!' we chanted, swigging celebratory plonk.

But back to Germaine. One day she informed me that women in peasant India have 'enormous power' (excuse me?) and that she'd noticed that Third World women are 'always smiling' and who are we to say they're miserable and unhappy and must adopt Western solutions to their problems? I told her that she reminded me of the old slave owners who used to say that because the 'darkies' were always singing spirituals in the cotton fields, they were simple, happy folk who didn't want to be freed by meddling outsiders.

I was particularly annoyed when this great feminist took a typically contrarian stance on the issue of female genital mutilation, which has blighted the lives of millions of Third World women. But apparently people like me who condemned the practice were simply indulging in 'cultural imperialism'. According to Germaine, 'looked at in its full context, the criminalization of FGM can be seen to be what African nationalists since Jomo Kenyatta have been calling it, an attack on cultural identity'.

Of course, whether you agree with her or not, Germaine is always entertaining. As were many aspects of feminist propaganda – which was regularly mocked, often by other women. The feminist magazine *Spare Rib* was lampooned by Dawn French and Jennifer Saunders in a TV skit called 'Spare Cheek', which contained the ineffable slogan: 'Lift up your breasts and roar!'

But for entertainment value, none could compete with the late Rebecca West. I met her when she was eighty-seven. She'd begun her career as a columnist on the suffragette weekly *The Freewoman* in 1910, and had once remarked acidly, 'I myself have never been able to find out what feminism is; I only know that people call me a feminist whenever I express sentiments that differentiate me from a doormat or a prostitute.'

The by now half-blind and deaf Dame Rebecca told me that when she was five she watched her mother reading by gaslight about the assassination of Empress Elizabeth of Austria; she was nine when Queen Victoria died and had lived through two World Wars and five reigns. 'Oh yes, I'm *very* old!' she chortled.

She insisted she didn't mind getting old, unlike the French Communist Simone de Beauvoir (long-time companion of Jean-Paul Sartre) whose *The Second Sex* in 1949 was such a seminal influence on the second wave of modern feminism. (A less than devoted fan of Sartre and de Beauvoir described the couple as 'the Fred and Ginger of French existentialism'.)

'De Beauvoir detests me because I've always been anti-Communist and she dismisses me as a frightful reactionary,' said Dame Rebecca. 'Handicapped woman in many ways: can't do her sums, never gets her figures right. I don't really consider her to be a feminist. And you know, there's something so humiliating in the way in which she minds getting old: she quotes a friend of hers saying that the awful thing about getting old is that men no longer pick you up. Ha ha! Silly cow!'

Dame Rebecca was then living in a modern block of flats of an almost nightmarish, mortician-like luxury: discreet commissionaires, concealed lighting, formal flower arrangements, a lobby hushed with reverential carpeting. It looked like the laying-out room in an Evelyn Waugh funeral home for Very Distinguished Remains.

In fact I'd long assumed that this historian, poet, feminist, political polemicist and novelist was already dead. She'd walked with all the literary giants of her age – George Bernard Shaw, Arnold Bennett, Ford Madox Ford, Wyndham Lewis, D. H. Lawrence, Virginia Woolf, and H. G. Wells, with whom she had a stormy and secretive affair for ten years and by whom she'd had a son. They – and several of her other lovers (who included Charlie Chaplin and Lord Beaverbrook) – were now all dead.

And the only reason I realized she was still alive was because *The Birds Fall Down*, the novel she wrote in her seventies, had just been dramatized for television, and Penguin had published a selection of her best writings, which had become classics of journalism. They included her coverage of the trial of the Nazi radio propagandist, William 'Lord Haw Haw' Joyce, whose voice had 'suggested a large and fleshy handsomeness, but he was a tiny little creature and not handsome at all', and her account of the Nuremberg Trials, where she described Goering as being 'like a madam in a brothel' and Julius Streicher as 'a dirty old man of the sort that gives trouble in parks'.

She also wrote vividly about the trial of the society osteopath Stephen Ward (who committed suicide in his cell) and his role in the Profumo sex-and-spies scandal, centred on Lord Astor's Cliveden, which had rocked the British establishment in the Sixties. Shaw had said of West: 'She could handle a pen as brilliantly as ever I could, and much more savagely.'

No wonder I idolized her and no wonder I felt nervous awaiting her arrival in a drawing room stuffed with a lifetime's treasures, including Picassos, Vuillards and Lowrys which clustered thickly on the rough cream-silk walls. In her youth she'd been an extraordinary beauty with a dark and gypsy splendour, sumptuous black hair, glittering brown eyes and a magnificently carved brow.

She hobbled in, small and plump and leaning on a stick. Her beauty might have gone but none of the brilliance of her mind or the cheerful cruelty of her wit. It was January 1979, when the unions were crippling Britain's economic life and a rising new star of right-wing polemicists, Arianna Stassinopoulos (once described as 'the most upwardly mobile Greek since Icarus'), was fulminating against trade union abuse of power. The showy young Cambridge-educated Arianna (who later in America became 'a progressive liberal', i.e. left-wing) had made her name as the author of *The Female Woman: An Argument against Women's Liberation*.

I did not expect Dame Rebecca to admire her, and I was right. 'Don't you think it's *awfully* funny,' she remarked in her measured

Edwardian drawl, 'that this Miss Arianna Stassi, oh, Stassi-whopoulos can write a book about how the world is finally going to the dogs because of women, the End is Nigh and all that, without apparently the *slightest* sense that it has all been written *countless* times before, including by St Cyprian!'

Oh well, that's disposed of Arianna and all the other anti-feminist doomsayers. What next? What indeed . . . ? West gobbled up gossip like a small girl guzzling sweets, sat in her chair sipping neat gin and cutting joyous swathes through forests of carefully nurtured reputations. In no time at all, we'd not only got through a series of delightfully scurrilous stories about the mighty, but had touched on Tolstoy, Mexican painters, Greek ruins, Chinese attitudes towards science, hallucinogenic drugs, the childhood of Goering's wife, modern French literature, the NHS, and Anglo-Saxon poetry which we both loved.

When at nineteen she began writing about feminism she rejected her real name, Cicely Fairfield, as too 'genteel' and chose as her nom de plume the name of Ibsen's brilliant, independent-minded heroine, Rebecca West. Sixty-eight years later she was still not happy with it. 'Chose it in a hurry. It's a hard, harsh-sounding name. Makes people frightened of me and want to hide down rabbit-holes.'

Hiding down rabbit-holes would have been understandable for some of the victims of her gleeful scorn. The then feminist writer Fay Weldon was airily dismissed as someone who 'writes the novels of a very fat woman'. Margaret Drabble: 'Very *Peg's Paper*, don't you think?'

Actually, she was 'rather *crawss*' with Drabble. 'She wrote a book about Arnold Bennett which I thought betrayed a remarkable lack of discernment: if there was anybody who would have detested her it would have been Bennett – who never liked women unless they were marchionesses and very expensively dressed. And she is neither. Not that I'd hold *that* against her.

'In her book she mentions a remark I made and says, "There speaks a writer who has never known poverty." I wrote to her and said, "You must be misinformed. My people lost all their money and we couldn't even afford to light the gas-jet in the hall." And she wrote back saying she knew differently – which I found awfully offensive. Silly, silly gel.'

Later, leaning on her stick, she showed me to her door. 'I don't know how you're going to make an article out of this recondite conversation. Perhaps you could just sell the naughty bits off to *Private Eye*!' To which, Dame Rebecca, I presume you subscribe? Her voice broke into another rich, mischievous chuckle. 'But of course!'

I wondered what she'd have had to say if I'd told her that one of my loopier feminist friends had once invited me to a Speculum Party. What's that, I'd asked. 'We all sit in an earth circle with speculums and look up into our vaginas.' I told her that I never liked looking at my body clothed, let alone naked, and certainly didn't intend to sit on the floor peering up into my privates in public. 'Ann, the nuns have destroyed your pride in your body! You must reclaim it!' I was told I must never shave my armpits or, if I had one, my moustache. 'But fair-skinned women like me don't get moustaches!' I protested.

'Well, if you ever do, you should never get rid of it! Men, thank goodness, are repulsed by women who have moustaches and hairy armpits!'

Not according to my one-time friend, Lady Jeanne Campbell. Jeanne was a sporadic journalist who was the daughter of the raffish Duke of Argyll and the favourite grandchild of Lord Beaverbrook, and she'd been the third of Norman Mailer's six wives. According to one of her friends, James Humes, a former speech-writer for five American presidents, Lady Jeanne was the only woman he was aware of who'd biblically 'known' Khrushchev, Kennedy and Castro – all in the same twelve months.

Jeanne and I, on a journalistic job in Majorca, had to share a hotel room one night and I was curious to know how this striking but not especially beautiful woman had managed to bed so many powerful men – most of them married – at such high speed. (Her lovers also included Henry Luce, founder of Time-Life Inc., Ian Fleming and Oswald Mosley.) When asked by Gore Vidal what had attracted her to Mailer she replied, 'I had never been to bed with a Jew before.'

Clearly not a woman ashamed of her body, she stripped off completely in front of me and I noticed that, for a *grande horizontale*, she didn't have a particularly gorgeous one. On the contrary. And when she raised her arms, huge black tangles of what looked like

Spanish moss tumbled from her armpits. I looked startled. '*Never* shave your armpits, Ann. Hairy armpits are a tremendous turn-on for powerful men!' she informed me authoritatively. 'You see, these men have their lives totally sanitized for them, so they adore women with hairy armpits because it reminds them of the *earthiness* of good sex!' Which may possibly explain why, when Julia Roberts appeared at a premiere with hairy armpits, other women, especially columnists, expressed shock/horror – but not, I noticed, many men.

20

Dancing on the Fault-line

It started with a late-night pizza delivery which I had not ordered – and which the LA District Attorney's office then had tested for what it suspected might be massive, psychosis-inducing amounts of LSD in the pepperoni.

It ended with me outside a Los Angeles courthouse getting death threats from a dangerously batty young woman called Lynette 'Squeaky' Fromme, who was a member of the murderous Charles Manson 'Family' and who was subsequently given a life sentence for the attempted assassination – while dressed as a nun – of President Gerald Ford.

'Squeaky' had form as far as lacing foodstuffs was concerned: she was strongly suspected of loading LSD into a hamburger which had been ordered for a fellow 'Family' member with whom she'd fallen out. So I and the District Attorney's office – which subsequently found no evidence of drugs in my pizza – did have good reason to be wary . . .

Actually, no, the story didn't end there. It ended one year later with me talking at length to the Polish-born director Roman Polanski, whose wife Sharon Tate had been slaughtered, along with a coffee heiress and three others, in the Polanski family home in Beverly Hills by the LSD-crazed 'Family'. Sharon had been eight months pregnant at the time. Her widower Polanski was filming *Macbeth* at Shepperton Studios when I met him; 'the Scottish Play' is, of course, about 'murder most foul'. Standing on the sidelines of the gothic set with me was a tough female writer working for a top American magazine. 'Er, are you writing about Polanski or *Macbeth*?' I asked her tentatively. 'So who the f***', she replied levelly, 'gives a shit about *Macbeth*?'

Everyone on set was nervously aware that the hyperactively

loquacious Polanski wanted no mention of the Manson murders. At one point he almost shouted at me, 'Before tragedy came into my life, I had a reasonably good reputation as a director. Now my main claim to fame seems to be as the husband of the murdered Sharon Tate!'

His *Macbeth* was being financed by Hugh Hefner of *Playboy*, who flew into London on his black-painted 'Big Bunny' DC9 private jet (and for whom I later began to work as the magazine's 'European Photo Correspondent'; during Britain's 'winter of discontent' its Chicago head office once sent me a huge food parcel containing Oreo biscuits, peanut brittle and a Boston ham, to save me from what they assumed might be my impending starvation).

The whole loony – and occasionally rather scary – scenario began with the unlikely figure of Her Majesty The Queen. I was covering the Royal Tour of the West Indies in 1966. Every morning we hacks, pencils aloft, waited on the quayside for the royal party to descend from *Britannia*, the royal yacht, and one of our number included an American freelance photographer called Curt Gunther.

He had thick bottle-glass spectacles, a deeply lugubrious expression and a slightly Jewish/German accent with very pronounced 'Noo Yawk' inflections. That first morning on a Caribbean quayside, Gunther turned his huge nose and specs towards me and pronounced gloomily, 'Who needs dis?'

After about the fourth identical morning greeting from Curt on assorted islands I began to find his sepulchral gloom rather funny. 'Look, Curt, *Express* readers love descriptions of Her Majesty radiating "dignity" among her far-flung Commonwealth subjects. But yes, I do sort of agree with you.' Being told by that fat-head, her Press Secretary Sir Richard Colville (who only got the job because his mother was close to the Queen Mum and couldn't think of what else to do with her son), what the Queen was wearing that day – as if we didn't have eyes – was a mite irritating to us. 'But do shut up, Curt!'

'Okay, but who needs dis?' was Curt's inevitable reply.

Gunther, who was based in Hollywood, had a massive list of showbiz contacts, and my old friend from Manchester days, Derek Taylor, became (as I did) very fond of gloomy Curt. In fact, it was Derek, as the Beatles' press officer, who had insisted that Curt be the only freelance photographer with full access to cover the Beatles' first, record-breaking tour of America in 1964.

Whenever I was working in LA I'd pop into Curt's studio on La Cienaga Boulevard for a bracing bout of 'who-needs-dis' gloomfests. The Manson trials were in progress and virtually dominating the world's news. Those of us who'd been in San Francisco during the 'peace, love and flowers in your hair' period wrote endless po-faced – but accurate – pieces about how the Manson murders proved that those earlier idealistic hippy dreams had curdled into squalor, psychosis and murder.

I'd been interviewing drug addicts in the by now deeply depressing Haight Ashbury district who'd come to San Francisco as wide-eyed, fresh-faced innocents escaping dully conventional homes on the vast plains of the Midwest, and who now found themselves dossing in the streets and injecting themselves between their toes because all other accessible veins were now hopelessly shot.

I'd also been exploring the 'Jesus Freak' cults, born-again hippy Christians who were trying to persuade these poor lost souls on the Haight to get clean and embrace the Lord. Some of the 'stoned on Jesus' groups, run by starey-eyed, ecstatic control freaks, turned thoroughly rancid themselves, and one group, 'The Children of God', ended up using their pretty disciples to go 'flirty-fishing for God' by becoming prostitutes, in order to rope in new believers and new money – and to provide new bed partners for their leader, David 'Moses' Berg.

Initially I'd been rather impressed by the Children of God members I'd interviewed because, although I'm allergic to hippy-dippy evangelists, they did strike me as doing some good among the Haight's lost children. Curt told me I was being naive (which proved to be shamefully true) about 'dese wackos – who needs 'em?'

Of course California, a land of dream-addled migrants, once described as a place where the sunshine 'turns your brain into orange juice', has always sprouted odd, millennial cults of 'wackos', of which the Manson 'Family' was undoubtedly the most extreme.

One day in 1970 I dropped into Curt's studio. With him there was an amiable-looking young man called Bob. 'This is Mr Linda Kasabian,' said Curt, as usual cloaked in gloom. 'I'm tryin' to cut a deal wid you and Linda, aren't I, Bob?'

Linda Kasabian had been one of the Manson 'Family' and she was charged with the murder of Sharon Tate and her friends and of a grocery businessman called Leno LaBianca and his wife. She was granted immunity for turning state's evidence, which resulted in Manson and other members of the 'Family' being sentenced to death (later commuted by a change in Californian law to life imprisonment).

As the trials ground on Linda was in custody but Bob Kasabian could visit her and, as he was extremely short of money, was open to 'deals' of the kind Curt was offering. The plan was that I would write out questions to Linda, Bob would get her to answer them, I'd write up the results, and we'd all make a lot of money. 'If Linda hadn't dropped so much acid, none of this would've happened,' said Bob sadly. I contacted the *Sunday Mirror* in London. Would they like me to cover the trial? Yes, they would; I didn't tell the editor about my contacts with Kasabian's husband as I wasn't sure of Bob's reliability.

And so for the next few days I sat in on the trial of Susan Atkins, Leslie Van Houten and Patricia Krenwinkel, the three women who'd taken an active part in the slaughter. The trio would come into court dressed in black with black crosses marked on their foreheads, looking like a bizarre parody of the Forties singing threesome, the Andrews Sisters.

They shouted insults, mocked witnesses, giggled, pointed fingers. Susan, known as 'Sadie', remarked without any remorse that she'd stabbed Sharon and her unborn baby to death because she was just 'sick of listening to her, pleading and begging, begging and pleading'. She'd then smeared the door with the word 'Pig' in her victims' blood.

At one point Sadie caught sight of me and began winking at me, licking her lips lasciviously, mouthing kisses and obscenities at me, and did so for the next few days. Noting that I was embarrassed and put my chin down on my chest, she would laugh and mime my gestures. A merry old time was being had by this murderous trio, but for those of us in court who had to listen to the utterly grim evidence it was deeply disturbing.

Which is where 'Squeaky' Fromme comes in. Outside the courthouse Squeaky – who, she said, had been made head of the 'Family' by Manson while he was in custody – would shout at us reporters that we were libelling her God (Manson), and we would pay for it.

What really enraged me was that this pale, stringy creature would sit every day on the pavement with other members of the 'Family' knitting pale, stringy garments while casting her anathemas. 'You, Squeaky, are a grotesque little monster – and put away that knitting!' I snapped at her one morning. 'You're disgusting: you remind me of the tricoteuses who sat beside the guillotine knitting, while heads tumbled into the basket!' One of the cops hearing this, grinned at me: 'Careful, lady, this one might mean business!'

I drove back to my hotel, the Chateau Marmont, a weird towering presence perched above Sunset Boulevard. I loved the place because it was pure Americana, a mixture of decadence, fabulous fantasy and glamorous decay, and I'd always stay there if covering one of those 'Only in America' stories. Of which the Manson 'Family's' crime was undoubtedly one.

In 1947 Christopher Isherwood wrote: 'California is a tragic country – like Palestine, like every Promised Land. Its short history is a fever-chart of migrations – the land rush, the gold rush, the oil rush, the movie rush, the Okie fruit-picking rush . . .' The Marmont itself was a fever-chart of the movie rush, and always felt to me to be a mixture of Rick's Place in *Casablanca*, full of 'the usual suspects' escaping their pasts and finagling their futures, with a touch of the creepy atmosphere of *Psycho* and the dead mother in the basement of the Bates Motel. And all contained within an architectural Old Europe pastiche of a Loire chateau.

When it was built in 1929 on the edge of the city amid the sagebrush and tumbleweed that then filled rural Marmont Lane, it was high in luxury and, above all, in discretion. The stars came here to misbehave. As the legendary studio boss Harry Cohn put it, 'If you must get in trouble, do it at the Chateau Marmont.'

Shelley Winters tried to kill her new husband Tony Francioso with a knife during their honeymoon in Room 55. The maids had noticed him constantly creeping off to Room 68 which housed the fiery Italian actress Anna Magnani – and so had the equally fiery Shelley.

From his penthouse suite Howard Hughes used to watch through binoculars the lissom Hollywood bodies lying around the pool. Stars like Jean Harlow, Clark Gable, James Dean, Bette Davis, Katharine Hepburn, Marlene Dietrich, Natalie Wood, Orson Welles, Barbra

Streisand, Janis Joplin, all strolled through the hotel's fake gothic portals, knowing it would guard their secrets.

However, the then manager of the Marmont made private notes about all his famous guests. 'John Wayne showed up today. Just landed first big-budget Western, *Stagecoach*. Asked for "the best room in the house". Explained just wanted "to see how it feels to live like a star". Checked in with unidentified brunette on arm. Length of stay: 2 weeks.'

John Belushi died after injecting himself with a combination of heroin and cocaine in one of the Marmont's garden cottages. Greta Garbo, 'vanting to be alone', would check in and stay for weeks under the pseudonym of Miss Harriet Brown.

By the time I was using the Marmont regularly it had fallen on shabby times, glamour had swept west into Beverly Hills and Bel Air, and it was therefore now quite cheap. I had a large self-catering apartment with musty food cupboards, greasy cutlery and acrid curtains which smelled of ancient cigar smoke. Only one of the two vintage lifts ever seemed to be working at the same time. And unfortunately during the Manson 'Family' trial I had to make lots of phone calls, which annoyed the elderly and crotchety woman switchboard operator who, like Squeaky Fromme, preferred to do her knitting. She'd inform me by the fourth call of the day that 'Ah'm pullin' out your plug *now*!'

One evening I went down to remonstrate with her, and then waited for the only functioning lift to take me back upstairs. A tall woman in a belted mac got in, a fedora pulled half-way down her face; she was like a figure from a Forties *film noir*, one of those mysterious women who, plotting seduction, betrayal and death, drifted like wraiths in and out of the poisoned half-life of Hollywood.

'I mean, this hotel, that old bat on the switchboard, I mean, it's *too much*, isn't it?' I spluttered to the fedora-ed one. She said nothing. But then she lifted up her face to watch the floor numbers going by on the lift wall – and I saw it: the most beautiful face ever seen in Hollywood, and even now, with only the light in the lift slanting across it, utterly heart-catching. It was Garbo. The next day I gabbled to Curt, 'I shared an elevator with Garbo last night!'

'Yeah, don't know why she always calls herself Miss Brown when she's in the Marmont. No one's fooled. Stoopid Swede.'

And then, late one night at the end of the day's hearings, came the unasked for – but happily unpoisoned – pizza delivery . . .

But there was bad news for Curt's planned deal with the Kasabians. One day at court I suddenly saw Joan Didion. She was at the time probably the most famous journalist in America and working for *Life*, its most prestigious news magazine. A native Californian (and few Californians are that), she specialized in writing about the nervy, surreal undercurrents which always lurk beneath the eternal 'have-a-good-day' geniality of her home state.

Raymond Chandler had chronicled the effects on California's inhabitants of the hot, dry, nerve-shredding Santa Ana wind which would sweep in from its eastern deserts. It was a wind that 'makes your nerves jump and your skin itch . . . Every booze party ends in a fight. Meek little wives feel the edge of the carving knife, and study their husbands' necks. Anything can happen.' Joan Didion belonged to the Chandler school of Californian writing.

This trial would therefore be perfect Didion territory. And yes, of course, Didion's magazine had the Kasabians sewn up. I never saw her resulting reports, if they appeared, but she wrote about 'Linda and Bob' in her book *The White Album*. 'Who needs dis?' commented Curt on hearing the news.

The Manson trial had been dubbed the 'Trial of the Century' and I thought of Curt when, in 1995, twenty-five years later, I went to cover the second 'Trial of the Century', this time featuring O. J. Simpson. Alas, dear Curt was now dead. But naturally (not least in his memory) I tried to check in to the Marmont, now under new management and re-creating its past glories. It was full. Not only because of its refurbishment but because it was now crammed with journalists covering this extraordinary story.

Instead I had to check in to the Four Seasons, a very luxurious Hollywood hotel with a swimming pool and garden on its roof, and one day heard Sarah Jessica Parker being paged in the lobby. The Marmont, I thought sniffily, would *never* be so indiscreet with a star name!

Every day I would join the queue for Court 103, surrounded by 'lookie-looks', as the American media had dubbed the ghouls and exhibitionists who helped create the circus atmosphere of the trial. At the end of one day in court I talked to one of the 'lookie-looks' called Samantha who, with other ghouls, was standing outside the courthouse.

It was one of those warm, soft, police-siren-haunted twilights in the 'City of Angels'; just another summer night in Prozac-city, crack-city, an earthquake-prone city of wildfires, riots and mud-slides, a fame-obsessed and febrile city which has always danced on a perpetual moral fault-line – and which has always fed with lubricious glee on its own victims. Victims like Nicole Brown, the bleached blonde, silicone-stuffed former 'beach bunny' and part-time waitress who married O. J. Simpson, the adored and apparently amiable black millionaire sports star and actor who, after seventeen obsessive and abusive years, eventually slit her sun-bronzed throat.

Samantha didn't believe O. J. was guilty: 'Honey, we *know* he was set up by the racist cops of this city, cos he's an African-American like me! We *know* these guys! Listen, honey, you know what? Nicole Brown Simpson won't *never* decompose!'

'Samantha', a six-foot black transvestite clad in mini-skirt, stilettos and hoop earrings, gave a basso profundo laugh, his false eyelashes batting like giant moths. He thumped me flirtatiously with a braceleted arm: 'As we all know, silicone ain't biodegradable – and that rich white-trash bitch was just *made* of the stuff!' Samantha's friends standing with me on the pavement outside the courthouse chortled at his witticism, and I – but no one else – winced.

Earlier that day inside the courthouse, in a small drably panelled neon-lit room on the ninth floor, I'd been listening to a particularly harrowing piece of evidence, a tape-recording of the murdered woman screaming for help. And I'd listened to Juditha, the dead woman's mother, three rows in front of me, quietly weeping with grief and horror at what had become of her beautiful daughter. And, nearby, sobbing and shaking with anger, Fred Goldman, the father of Ron, the young waiter who'd dropped by Nicole's home with a pair of spectacles left behind at the Mezzaluna Restaurant, and who was brutally murdered for being 'in the wrong place at the wrong time'.

Remembering those screams, I angrily protested to 'Samantha' and the other 'lookie-looks', 'But Nicole wasn't just a plastic doll –

she was a real human being, the mother of two young children! Everyone seems to have forgotten about her – and about poor harm- less Ron Goldman! People keep talking about bent cops and racism and celebrities and sex – but *real people* died, and real lives were destroyed!'

But Samantha didn't like me getting 'heavy'; I mean, hey, *enjoy*! 'Honey,' he drawled, 'this is La-la-Land, Nicole wasn't *real*, ain't nobody *real* in Hollywood! This is *showbiz*!' Suddenly I understood why LA's transvestites seemed so attracted to the grotesqueries of the O. J. trial. One man, wearing pearls and a frock, had been thrown out of Court 103 by the Japanese-American Judge Ito for creating a disturbance: 'Oh, Judge *Ego* was just *jealous*!' The same fate nearly befell a rather beefy white transvestite in a tartan mini sitting two seats away from me in row D, who kept hissing petulantly at an old black lady beside him, 'You're sitting on my *skirt*!'

It was clear to all of us in court from the very beginning that O. J. was guilty. There was a mountain of evidence including the 'ugly ass' shoes. A pair of Bruno Magli shoes which handsome, affable, narcis- sistic O. J., that one-time hero of the American Dream, maintained he'd never owned – and which he wouldn't *dream* of wearing be- cause they were so 'ugly'. Their prints had been found at the scene of the double murder. Thirty-one photos of O. J. wearing those 'ugly shoes' turned up. His defence team tried to prove the photos were faked, despite evidence that one had actually been printed seven months before the murders took place. O. J.'s case was not helped by the fact that the 'photo expert' who pronounced them to be fakes turned out to be a high school drop-out, with no degree, and no professional training as a photo analyst, who earned a living writing obsessive books about the Kennedy assassination and acting as a tour guide in Dallas.

But then this trial never hinged on mere evidence.

The original murder trial purported to be about who killed Nicole Brown Simpson and the waiter Ron Goldman. But it soon became something else. A tawdry little tale about love, hate, jealousy and violence among B-list Hollywood celebrities quickly became a tacky, tasteless soap opera which ran live on radio and television for nine months.

The bizarre cast of characters – including the ludicrous Judge Ito, who inspired a popular spoof variety act called 'The Five Dancing Itos' – helped make the soap opera so addictive that, as the original murder trial drew to an end, self-confessed addicts talked about suffering PTS, Post-Trial Syndrome.

O. J. addicts on the internet, calling themselves 'O. J. Anonymous', organized for themselves a 'Trial of the Century Cruise' on which they discussed such crucial trial features as 'The Bloody Glove', 'The Blood in the Bronco', 'The Cut on the Hand', 'The Contaminated DNA', 'The Missing Knife', 'The Great Dress-Sock Mystery', and the 'Dog that *Did* Bark in the Night'.

The syndicated columnist Art Buchwald fantasized that the White House was even now planning a national Task Force, composed of counsellors, therapists, legal experts – and the Joint Chiefs of Staff – to deal with 'the most pressing question Americans face today', which is, 'What will they do with themselves once the O. J. Simpson show is over? It is predicted that millions of people are expected to go berserk when they have nothing to watch in the afternoons and will resort to all kinds of mayhem.'

If the O. J. Trial were just another *Murder, She Wrote* episode, no screenwriter would have dared to come up with a script like this. Okay, perhaps in these politically correct days, a writer would have cast a sexy, dark-eyed single mother as the Chief Prosecuting Lawyer. But would he script in such an extraordinary background for her? Would he name her Marcia Kleks, born into such a strict Jewish Orthodox home that as a teenager she had to go out wearing a veil with a chaperone by her side? And would he then have her train to be a ballet dancer, only to have her run off with a flamboyant professional gambler – and collector of jewellery and guns – called Gaby, with whom the once prim and proper Marcia (complete with pert new nose-job) would patronize the glitzier casinos of the world?

And would he *then* have the audacity to script in the fact that Marcia's glamorous gambling husband was shot and paralysed by his best friend, a dentist-cum-Scientology minister who, *quite coincidentally*, was the minister who officiated at Marcia's *second* marriage to a toy-boy in Tijuana, Mexico?

The dentist/Scientology minister was cleared of attempting to murder Marcia's first husband. And, by the way, Marcia married her second husband before her first divorce had actually been finalized: a not entirely orthodox legal move for a top lawyer to make.

And would a scriptwriter then have Marcia – who earned far more than the now divorced toy-boy second husband – demand more alimony from him on the grounds that she was having to spend so much on new outfits for her appearances on television in the O. J. case?

And would a scriptwriter who possessed any sense of restraint throw in yet another oddity, by casting the slick, gangster-suited Robert Shapiro, one of Simpson's multi-million-dollar dream team of lawyers (Marcia hated Shapiro), as the *very same lawyer* who defended the man who shot Marcia's first husband?

And would a scriptwriter then dare to have the trial take place under the auspices of Judge Ito, who just happened to be married to the 'racist' LAPD's top policewoman, who just happened to have been the model for *Cagney and Lacey* – and who also just happened to have been the boss of a key policeman in the case?

Of course not. The whole thing would be too bizarrely unbelievable.

But it was not simply as an often grotesquely hilarious soap opera that this trial gripped America. The original murder trial became a lurid glimpse into the American psyche. America pored over this X-ray of its own soul, seeing its own decadence, its ethnic balkanization, the souring of its American Dream, and wondered in dismay whether its twin obsessions – with race and celebrity – might prove fatal to its body politic. Through the O. J. trial America put itself on trial – and it didn't like what it saw.

It saw the end of the Great Society illusion, the belief that blacks and whites would come together, if only enough legislation was passed, money spent, quotas enforced, speech codes invented, hypocrisies maintained. O. J. Simpson, before he committed that brutal double murder, had seemed to be proof that the Great Colour-blind Society was possible. He had been so poor that he'd had rickets as a child, but he'd struggled out of a rough black neighbourhood to become a leading football star, minor actor and all-round lovable Good Guy. He married a beautiful white wife, had two beautiful children, played the rich white man's favourite game, golf, joined the right country clubs.

As I pointed out at his trial, the reason why white America loved O. J. so much was because his beauty, his charm and his affability made him (in his own words) 'transcend' race. Here was a black man who did not frighten white America. Here was a black man who did not seem to be consumed with insecurity, fear or rage. Here was a black man who made white Americans feel that they, too, could 'transcend' race. Like Colin Powell and Condoleezza Rice (who both eventually became Secretaries of State) and now like Barack Obama, Simpson made white America feel that blacks and whites need not be enemies after all. He made white America feel good about itself. Hey, this really is the Land of Opportunity, the Rainbow Nation where everyone can make it if they try! I mean, just look at good old O. J.!

Before the trial opened many white Americans longed for him to be not guilty. In the flower-shop of the Four Seasons hotel, a young girl behind the counter was crying, 'I just *know* O. J. didn't do it – he couldn't! Not O. J.!' The unspoken words were: 'He's not just another angry black man who makes me scared. He *likes* me, even if I am white!'

And then the trial began. And while the prosecution team of the tense, frizzy-haired Marcia Clark (née Kleks) and the lugubrious, black and bumbling Chris Darden tried to put O. J. on trial based on the evidence, his own Dream Team, headed by superstar black lawyer Johnnie Cochran, decided to put white America on trial instead. Commentators who, at the beginning, had decided that the 'themes' of this trial were going to be sex, wife-beating, celebrity and money suddenly discovered it was about one thing, and one thing only: the colour of O. J.'s skin.

And blacks, who'd hitherto never seen O. J. as a 'brother' (the white friends, white women, and white money had cut him off from the ghettos), suddenly decided he was a 'brother' after all. And the 'brothers' would use his trial as pay-back time: a chance to punish white America for its hypocrisy, its 'racist' police, its 'racist' justice, its fear and hatred of blacks.

The jury was largely black and female. They took a mere three-

and-a-half hours to deliver a 'not guilty' verdict after an almost nine-month-long trial, featuring 126 witnesses, 1,105 pieces of evidence and 45,000 pages of transcript.

While the jury retired to consider their verdict I thought they would, even if only out of courtesy, take at least a week to do it. So rather than lounging beside the Four Seasons pool or hanging around with Samantha and his 'gals', I'd made an arrangement to visit a man who ran an agency recruiting 'ordinary people' to take part in 'reality' chat shows like the Jerry Springer programme.

Of course every society has its oddballs, but America has turned them (as it had the O. J. trial) into a lucrative branch of showbusiness. Every time I zapped through daytime channels I'd find myself riveted by the multi-channel chat shows. Once there was only Oprah and Donahue. Now there were twenty-seven of them . . . Ricki, Geraldo, Sally Jessy, Montel, Danny, Gabrielle, Charles, Leeza, Rolonda, Jerry, Mark, Richard, Maury, Carnie, Paget, Tempesst . . . One host, Geraldo Rivera (who later turned up in Afghanistan as a hair-raisingly jingo-istic Fox News war reporter), had had his nose broken twice on air which, while being detrimental to his proboscis, was obviously terrific for the *Geraldo* show's ratings.

Where, I wondered, did these programmes find this endless stream of what Curt had rightly called 'wackos'? Actual sample chat-show captions from one day: 'Dad wants to know why he should be discriminated against just because his ex-wife doesn't eat live snakes!' Zap. 'Cruise ship passenger has horror story after run-in with iguana on the island of Cozumel!' Zap. 'Author shows how to see and communicate with your own guardian angels!' Zap. 'Sexy funeral director who bared all in *Playboy* now tells all in *Grave Undertakings!*'

And now the chat-show world had produced its first murder. On a programme about secret crushes, the coquettish blonde host, Jenny Joseph, told a twenty-four-year-old guest, Jonathan Schmitz, that he was about to meet someone who adored him from afar. Preening, Schmitz assumed that his secret admirer was a woman. When Scott Amedure, a young man he knew slightly, emerged from backstage to confess his crush, Schmitz was mortified. Three days later, 'eaten up' by the public humiliation, he went to Amedure's home and killed him with two blasts from a shotgun. As with Geraldo's broken nose, this murder caused Jenny Joseph's ratings to soar.

So, while the O. J. Simpson jury deliberated, I drove out to the San Fernando Valley to see Christopher Darryn, creator of the Talk Show Register, which catered for twenty of these programmes and their insatiable demand for 'ordinary people' with 'wacky tales' to tell on air. I'd already partially interviewed him on the phone.

Forty-year-old Darryn had an invaluable search program which identified who, among his 2,500 'ordinary people' database, could for example fill the bill for a storyline I saw which went: 'Glen – or Glenda? For this hermaphrodite, the choice was easy!' On the phone I put him to the test. 'Okay, Chris, say I'm a producer and I want a lesbian whose husband tried to kill her because she was having an affair with another woman.' Click-click-click. 'Yup, here's one. Name's Cassandra. Says she wants to go on TV to talk about her husband who tried to slit her throat because of her lesbian affair.'

Why does she want to tell all on TV? 'Says she's trying to come to terms with her ordeal with the help of her two children and her lesbian lover. Sees TV chat shows as a kind of therapy.' Oh, so that's all right then.

I bowled him another. 'What about finding me a transsexual who's in a lesbian relationship?' Click-click-click. 'Yup, here's one. Male-to-female transsexual who had gender surgery in December. Her transsexual lover was in a B52 bomber and was shot down over Vietnam. They're also into sado-masochism and body-piercing. Got them both on to *Geraldo*. They were really great on that segment. Audience loved 'em.'

To Chris Darryn, all of the above came under the category of 'normal'. But he had a special affection for those listed in his database under the heading 'Off-beat'. Like, for example, Neil the Messiah. 'He rang me to say he was the first Messiah who was going to run for President. I said, "Great!" Then he happened to mention that he was also the Man from Venus but that he preferred not to make an issue of that. Later I got a call from *The Joan Rivers Show* asking me, "Do you have anyone who says he comes from Venus? We're doing a show about people from other planets and we're short of a Venusian."'

Of course Darryn had a Venusian to hand. 'But the Joan Rivers people complained to me later, saying my Venusian wasn't very focused!' Darryn thought that *The Joan Rivers Show* was being a bit picky: just how much focus have you got the right to expect from a Venusian who's running for President? 'I mean, come on!'

I clearly needed to meet him and explore his database further. But when I arrived at his office in the Valley the entire building was silent, with no one going in or out. I banged on his door. No reply. But I could hear from behind the door the noise of an excited television reporter shouting at viewers. Darryn hastily opened it and gasped, 'They've reached a verdict!' That day most of America was glued to the television and, according to analysts, the economic productivity of the nation took a sudden downturn as no one was concentrating on work.

No chance of getting back to the LA courthouse now, so I had to watch the delivery of the verdict on television. Prisoner No. BK4O13970 sat in the ninth-floor courtroom, his handsome brow furrowed, nervously licking his drying lips, trying to make pleading eye-contact – and failing – with the stony-faced jury as they shuffled into their seats. His lawyer, Johnnie 'the Best that Money Can Buy' Cochran, sat beside him, tense, grim-faced, steepling his expensively manicured fingers in apparent prayer.

I watched the jury, poker-faced, profoundly serious, and it occurred to me that it was significant that these were black *women*. Such women had seen their neighbourhoods destroyed by the rage of their menfolk. They knew that rage, they understood it – but usually they did not, in the end, excuse it. In predominantly black cities like Washington and Atlanta, black juries, often female, routinely convicted their black 'brothers' – because it is black people who suffer most from black violence. And black women, who see their sons, their husbands, their brothers, their lovers dying in drug wars and gang wars, are always those who suffer most.

Such women are, in other contexts, perfectly capable of judging and condemning a black 'brother'. But when it came to O. J. they decided there was enough question over allegedly 'tainted' evidence for them to take sides. They chose to proclaim their ethnic loyalty to one of their own, however flawed, who might well have murdered

some 'rich white trash' but who was assailed by a white legal establishment which they so distrusted. It was, no matter how much they
pretended otherwise, a political decision.

The black jury's decision, of course, enriched that white legal
establishment by millions but also, I hoped, bankrupted their black
'brother'. Even the losing attorneys, Marcia Clark and Chris Darden,
have now made fortunes writing about the case, appearing on television, going on lecture tours. America has around 5 per cent of the
world's population – and 70 per cent of its lawyers. Simpson stated
that his $7 million fortune had disappeared into their greedy paws:
'Now I know a lot of rich lawyers.'

And to many white Americans, this shocking, precipitate not-
guilty verdict (which I, almost alone at the time, predicted) 'proved'
one thing and one thing only: that black Americans were creatures
of emotion, instinct, irrationality, sunk in bitterness and hate,
incapable of judging one of their own on the evidence. O. J. had
therefore, in one sense, 'got away with it'. But he lost the one thing
that he'd fought for all his life: his 'hero' status, the ability to inspire
love in all who worshipped him from afar. The crowds, both black
and white, who'd shouted their support, 'Go, O. J., go!', while he was
fleeing the police in a white Ford Bronco during a long, slow freeway
chase (watched live on TV by 93 million people), now no longer
loved him.

A black reporter who knew him well (and who was certain he was
guilty) had told me, 'O. J. was used to always getting what he wanted,
and hated being rejected – that's why when Nicole finally rejected
him, he couldn't take it. You know, he hated going to Europe, even
though Nicole wanted to, because no one knew who he was over
there. He was a guy who'd made it out of the ghetto and he couldn't
bear the thought of not being adored and the centre of everybody's
attention – especially Nicole's.'

Hollywood, despite its alleged glamour, is a surprisingly small,
incestuous and profoundly dysfunctional 'village', whose spoiled and
neurotic 'villagers' drink at the same bars, eat in the same restaurants, share the same lawyers, pay the same plastic surgeons,
shell out fortunes on the same shrinks. That's why they, like disparate
tribesmen, tend to huddle round the same watering holes and luxury

encampments like the Chateau Marmont, trying somehow to create a fantasy of like-mindedness, a parody of tribal togetherness, while at the same time acting out their own individual obsessions.

Just as 'Samantha' and his friends had dressed themselves in a grotesque Hollywood parody of femininity, this trial had become a grotesque Hollywood parody of justice. It was, as Samantha said, 'showbiz'. There was even a song: 'I've grown addicted to the case/ A case of blood and gloves and race!' Fans of O. J. could buy 'Free O. J.' T-shirts, fans of Judge Ito (and there were some, apart from himself) could buy T-shirts adorned with the words 'Lance Ito – Fair, Just, A Gentleman!' Non-fans of Ito (and there were many) could buy a 'Judge Ito Jello-Mould' in the shape of his smug, bearded face, which they could then pour custard over and slash at with a spoon.

The man who called himself Pilot Bob and who regularly flew his little plane over the courthouse trailing a message streamer would now have to think of something else to do. The day after the prosecution finished its doomed case, Pilot Bob's airborne message had congratulated the team with the words 'Chris and Marcia – Great Closing Arguments!' Maybe – but unfortunately they were on the losing side.

Even the denizens of 'Camp O. J.', the vast, higgledy-piggledy media encampment, full of satellite trucks and trailers parked outside the courthouse, were appalled by the verdict. Most of those I'd spent time with knew perfectly well that O. J. was guilty. One told me how 'amazed' he was at how little was made in the trial of the habitual drug-taking of Nicole and O. J.'s raffish Hollywood set: 'O. J. was particularly into crystal meth.' One woman reporter, wearing a souvenir O. J. watch (its hands featuring the Ford Bronco), reminisced about her own Hollywood-insider days: 'Yeah, I remember snorting coke with O. J. in a friend's bathroom once!'

Camp O. J. regulars admitted they would miss the trial and the camaraderie. And, as one of them said as we bade each other farewell, 'You know, some guys here have read so many books hangin' around this courthouse they could qualify for a PhD. And that includes guys like cameramen who, before the trial, could hardly read!'

21

'What's your operating system?'

How was I to dress for this meeting with the bullying print-union barons at my newspaper – which, if it went badly, could destroy my career?

Sounds trivial, I know, but for women journalists how you dress matters, far more than it ever does for men. The versatility of women's garb does though give you an advantage over men because it makes it easier for you to assume different identities. But it does require a bit of forward planning.

Do I dress like a bird-brain when, say, I'm working with Mexican drug-runners? Bird-brain equals harmless, so I'd settled on that look and it worked. To get into Mugabe's Zimbabwe, where the Western media are banned (with an automatic two-year prison sentence if caught), I chose to plump for bird-brain mode again. Thus in Johannesburg in neighbouring South Africa I bought a baggy T-shirt decorated with garish giraffes, a dotty sun-hat and an old Zimbabwe guide book and filled my huge handbag with its usual detritus.

The role of the handbag has been a major component in my career as a female foreign correspondent. When some axe-faced bureaucrat, immigration official or security apparatchik points out (correctly) that I do not have the required papers, I heave my handbag on to the desk and insist, 'Oh, but I do! It's just that I can't find them!' Then, like some truffle-hunting pig, I begin searching through the bag, fishing out bits of old make-up, broken car keys, snaps of husband and daughter, eyebrow pencil, airline socks, false eyelashes, broken Kit-Kats, parking tickets, a Tina Turner CD, spare tights, dead batteries, empty pill-bottles and an ancient recipe for Irish stew. As the pile of handbag detritus builds up on the apparatchik's desk, it begins to resemble a miniature version of the grotesque Smoky Mountain, the huge refuse dump outside Manila in the Philippines.

After a while, the blocking official begins to get exasperated: he does not want to see all this rubbish piling up on his desk, and he does not want to listen any more to the twitterings of this silly woman. Besides, he is by now convinced that failure to produce the right papers is not sinister, but merely proof that I'm terminally disorganized and batty – in short, 'a typical woman'. Rather than endure any more of this Smoky Mountain stuff, he'll often, with patronizing weariness, wave me through.

And so it was in Zimbabwe. I edited the handbag contents in advance – no spare tights, false eyelashes or Tina Turner CD, because they didn't fit the image I was aiming for, that of a loopy old granny. But I did leave in the recipe for Irish stew (which, incidentally, I've never got round to cooking).

I then flew to Victoria Falls, posing as an eccentric English matron, and feigned utter astonishment on hearing that I needed a visa. Male journalists I knew would sometimes get in by pretending they were obsessional bird-watchers but I wasn't sure I could pull that one off. Anyway, Zimbabwean officials were getting a bit beady about the sudden rush of foreign bird-watchers into their devastated country.

While doing dotty-old-woman things like dropping my specs, guide book, South African postcards and what I call my Housewife Superstar passport (I've got two legal passports, only one of which identifies me by my professional name), I told the official that I wanted to visit the Hwange National Park, and was then going on to Botswana to look at the wildlife there. 'Are you going to Harare?' he asked.

'No. Why would I want to go to Harare? There's no wildlife there, is there?'

He was hot, he was tired, he was bored. Besides, Vic Falls is in Matabeleland and it was likely that he belonged to the Matabele minority tribal group. In 1984 the Matabele had suffered hideously when the Mashona tribesman Mugabe massacred around 20,000 of them for the crime of not voting for him. Mugabe's Shona-speaking murderers were trained and aided by those charmers, the North Koreans.

Ndebele-speakers like that official probably had little sympathy for Mugabe and I didn't feel he was all that determined to stop me coming in. He stamped my passport with a tourist visa and then added with a grin, 'Don't go to Harare! Forbidden!' I then took the next flight to Harare to witness the ruination of that ravishing and once prosperous country by Robert Mugabe – whom, to my lasting embarrassment, I described in 1980 when he first came to power as 'a man of immense moral stature'.

My only excuse for that grave error was that I knew and liked his first wife Sally, a Ghanaian, and believed she would be some kind of guarantor of his probity. I'd got to know her through a most unlikely source, the convivial and boozy Tory MP for Chelsea, Sir Nicholas Scott, and his then wife Elizabeth. Sally was working in London and had no money, and the Scotts – who adopted a mixed-race child and hadn't an ounce of racism in them (indeed, Nicholas had had an affair with the black pop star Mynah Bird) – took Sally in as a lodger. When she and Mugabe got married they were so grateful to the Scotts for their kindness that they asked Nicholas and his wife to be their Best Man and Matron of Honour.

I have a great admiration for Ghanaian women, a feisty, practical lot, and, even though I often disagreed with Sally politically, she seemed grounded, in touch with ordinary Zimbabweans and, to begin with, able to keep her austere, oddly remote and intellectual husband (he gained seven academic degrees, including some acquired when he was incarcerated by the white regime for ten years) more or less grounded too.

Many people, including me, believe that Mugabe went off the rails after Sally died of kidney failure; he then married his stupid, ditzy and spendthrift secretary Grace, by whom this 'devout Roman Catholic' already had two illegitimate children. (Grace, incidentally, became the owner of *Playboy* proprietor Hugh Hefner's 'Big Bunny' private jet.)

Sally and Robert's only child, their son Nhamodzenyika, died aged four from cerebral malaria and (big mistake) the white Ian Smith government would not let his grieving father out of prison, however briefly, to attend his son's funeral. Sally never talked to me about her son's death. But because she had a sense of humour, and could be very funny about some of the couple's political travails, I suspect she'd have enjoyed sharing with me some of the tricks that women, whether dissidents like her or journalists like myself, deploy to circumvent male obstruction.

For example, a woman in a danger zone has the advantage of being able to employ her bra for several different purposes, secret or otherwise. If, as in my case, your bra is quite capacious, you can stow in it – apart from your breasts – items like press passes, passports, mobile phones, currency, airline tickets, iPods, contact-lens cases, mini recorders, spare batteries, and so on. Of course, unless you've remembered to remove all ironmongery from this bosomy storage area, it will excite metal detectors at airports (or, in one scary example at the Erez pedestrian crossing-point from Israel into lawless Gaza, set off klaxon-like alarms and summon posses of armed security police).

But most importantly I use my bra when on the road to store the myriad pills I am obliged to take since I became seriously ill seven years ago. I now have a somewhat fragile immune system and have to take, among other things, antibiotics twice a day for the rest of my life.

But it was in Zimbabwe that, for once, my bra-versatility let me down. Working undercover there, my bra was full of these pills. A Zimbabwean woman friend of mine, who'd previously been jailed for anti-Mugabe activities, was horrified. 'Ann, you can't keep them in your bra! They strip-search you on arrest!' So what do I do? 'Do what drug smugglers do: get some condoms, fill them with pills and stick them up your private parts.' But where to get condoms? Despite the horrendous rate of HIV/Aids in Zimbabwe, African men are averse to using condoms, and besides, because of sanctions and the general collapse of the economy, you couldn't get them anywhere. So I would just have to avoid getting arrested.

I realized one day that I was being followed by the CIO, Mugabe's much feared secret police, not least thanks to the extraordinary courage of ordinary, powerless Zims. One of them, a street hawker, muttered to me, 'That's a CIO man behind you . . . We'll try and distract him – if you go to that shop over there, you can escape because it has a back entrance. The shopkeeper will tell you where it is.' My CIO 'stalker' was clearly not sure whether I was anything other than a middle-aged English matron and, thanks to the hawker and the shopkeeper, I was able to elude him.

But at times dingbat fashion mode has to be rejected in favour of Daughter of the Raj imperiousness. I was faced with this choice in Israel when I was working on a feature about the brutish 'Separation Fence', invariably referred to by Palestinians as the apartheid Wall. While being greatly sympathetic to Israel's desire not to have its civilians, including women and children, blown to smithereens by Palestinian suicide bombers (over the years I'd narrowly escaped death from three such 'martyrdom missions' myself), I also felt uneasy about the allegedly 'temporary' Separation Fence, designed to keep the suicide bombers out, and was now investigating what it was doing to the lives of ordinary non-radical Palestinians.

Like Dr Rasmiyah Hanoun. She was a clinical psychologist at An Naja National University in the ancient Palestinian city of Nablus and a member of the American Psychology Association; she'd been, before the second *intifada*, a popular speaker at international academic conferences and had close professional relations with her Israeli counterparts at Haifa University. But, thanks to the Separation Fence, its razor-wire, its settler-only roads and its checkpoints, she could no longer do the twenty-minute commute to and from her home in the village of Nabi Elias. At one point she was having to do the journey over the stony hills by donkey.

In the village I interviewed her husband who had had a stroke when the Israelis commandeered his 20-acre ancestral farm and grubbed up his orange grove in order to build settler-only roads and the Separation Fence, thus cutting the family off from its land on both sides of their house. And I talked to her son, a medical student, and her daughter, studying pharmacology. They were understandably bitter, and moreover had not seen their mother for a week because every day she would join a long queue of Palestinians at the Israeli checkpoint outside Nablus and every day be forbidden to go back home. 'No reason given.' Her daughter was distraught: 'We're in prison – I can't even return to Cairo University to sit my exams! If this goes on, I think I'll become a suicide bomber myself!'

I rashly promised the family that the next day I would, somehow, get their mother and deliver her to their home. This is where a change of persona was necessary – full imperial rig-out this time. I got dressed up in a long pink Thai silk tunic, black Thai silk palazzo pants, a glamorous sun hat, garden-party shoes and carried an antique embroidered fan. (I always take one 'posh' outfit with me just in case it might come in useful.)

Khalid, my resourceful Arab-Israeli fixer, drove me to the checkpoint. One of the Israeli soldiers spoke excellent English and I informed him imperiously that Dr Hanoun was waiting in the checkpoint queue and I had an appointment with her, so she should be let through *now*: 'This delay is disgraceful!' The soldier said, 'Oh, you must be from the British embassy!' I neither confirmed nor denied this assertion, but as of course I didn't have a diplomatic passport I was relieved that, contrary to the rules, he didn't ask to inspect it.

Instead he apologized sheepishly for the inconvenience and told me that of course I would be allowed to walk, with an armed escort, through the no-man's-land territory between the checkpoints, collect Dr Hanoun and bring her back. The trouble was, I had no idea what she looked like – but I knew that Khalid did. So I announced that I had a bad leg and had no intention, my dear young man, of getting out of the car and limping through the dust in this terrible heat, but that 'my driver' Khalid would fetch Dr Hanoun for me. Which he did. We drove her back to her home and her family were ecstatic. Later Khalid, laughing, said, 'I don't know how you got away with that – it was brilliant!' But of course it was simply the judicious choice of clothes and the grand Lady Bracknell manner which made it work.

Being a female foreign correspondent is not unlike being a spy. Both professions are dedicated to getting information, despite all obstacles. One of Britain's most distinguished former spies, Daphne Park (now Baroness Park of Monmouth), declares (as I do) that women can infiltrate complex situations more easily than men, and thus have an advantage over their male counterparts. And it's because women automatically arouse less suspicion than men that jihadists have now taken to using female suicide bombers.

When I once mentioned the usefulness for a female foreign correspondent of being able to alternate 'bird-brain behaviour and Daughter of the Raj imperiousness' – and that such mode-switching is not readily available to male journalists – the *Guardian*'s feminist Women's Page editor found this statement 'especially disturbing'.

'Why', she wrote, 'does Leslie insist on tempering her achievements with such little-old-me undercut?' I slapped in a letter: 'I did not "insist on tempering my achievements". I merely pointed out that what she calls "little-old-me" devices can be very useful when working in mad, bad, macho countries. But, alas, I fear that many of those feminists who condemn me for using such methods have never had to work anywhere more exotic than Orpington.' And, yes, it was printed.

Again in Israel I mode-switched back to dingbat when trying to get into Bethlehem during the Israeli siege of the city. Palestinian gunmen had taken refuge in the Church of the Nativity and the Israelis had ringed the heart of the city with troops. No one was being allowed in or out.

The Archbishop of Canterbury's Special Envoy to the Middle East at the time was an almost textbook 'muscular Christian' – big, athletic, blithely fearless. Canon Andrew White's silver crucifix swung like a demented metronome across his capacious black-surpliced chest; add a garlic clove or two, and the whole clerical get-up would have looked impressive enough to repel the most determined of vampires.

But this was the Middle East, where vampiric intentions flourish on all sides and require (particularly where 'martyrdom'-obsessed Palestinian militants are concerned) endless supplies of blood – their own, that of Israelis and perhaps a passing cleric or two – as essential sustenance for their cause. Which is why the Canon and I, over endless cups of coffee, tried to work out how to penetrate the armed human wall the Israelis had erected around Bethlehem. 'But I've *got* to get in and deliver these medicines!' he declared. 'There are lots of sick people in there, diabetics and so on, who *desperately* need them!' But the city was sealed off and its allegedly 'martyrdom-loving' inhabitants were currently under total curfew within their homes. For over a fortnight Bethlehem's sacred centre, Manger Square, had been under siege by the Israeli army. The ancient Church of the Nativity on the Square, built above the cave where Christ is said to have been born, had been taken over by around 200 armed Palestinians, trapping clerics, some innocent civilians and the now putrefying bodies of two dead gunmen within its compound walls.

The previous day Canon White and I had been brusquely repulsed by trigger-happy young Israeli soldiers at the final checkpoint outside the town, and were then ignominiously dispatched back to Jerusalem. These soldiers did not like busybody foreign do-gooders and, especially, they hated self-righteous foreign journalists who accused them in print and on air of being 'war criminals' (which I never did). Disastrously lacking in PR skills, these exasperated young soldiers tended to shoot at the newsmen from time to time. Even the holy Canon was mildly outraged at their unmannerly behaviour: '*They pointed their guns at me!*' The checkpoint soldiers were, unsurprisingly, unimpressed by Canon White's laissez-passer letter from their own Foreign Ministry, let alone the endorsement of his peace mission by their own Chief Rabbi.

Back in the (relative) safety of Jewish West Jerusalem, we jointly plotted our return. The doughty Canon insisted that he was going to go to the nearest checkpoint outside Bethlehem and then, clutching a bag full of medical supplies, would walk, run, climb and crouch his way for a mile or two through the rocky fields, dodging behind olive trees in order to avoid Israeli and/or Palestinian sniper fire. 'But Ann, it may be the *only* way in!'

Alas, in the nifty-footed mountain-goat stakes I am a non-starter, and therefore declined to join him: besides, my Palestinian fixer thought this particular Christian Holy Man was mad. 'Does he *want* to be killed?' Thus the Archbishop's Envoy and I, for tactical reasons, decided to go our separate ways.

I've found that one of the best ways of getting into an area where religion plays a part in the conflict is to find a mosque, synagogue or church which is in, or next door to, a trouble epicentre. You can then, as a dotty woman, insist that you need to go to this place of worship and *of course* you want to steer clear of any danger: 'I'm a mother – what mother would risk leaving her children orphaned?' (I'm afraid that I have on occasion pretended that I'm a widow with a whole slew of fatherless children.)

I was the first journalist to get to the besieged city of Gorazde in Bosnia using this 'dingbat-plus-holy-place' ploy. I was working on the Serb side of the lines and every evening would have to listen to long, self-pitying, slivovitz-soaked threnodies about how the *Musselmani* were desecrating Serb churches and how no one in the allegedly Christian West cared two hoots, whereas the West made a big fuss about Muslim mosques being destroyed in 'self-defence' by the Serbs.

I knew of an ancient Serb church on the frontlines at Gorazde, and told the Serbs I wanted to see it because I knew that the Bosnian Muslims had desecrated it and I wanted the world to know about it. The Serbs told me that the Muslims had 'millions of dollars' from Saudi Arabia for their propaganda whereas the poor, noble, suffering and martyred Serbs could never get their side of the story out. But no, they wouldn't take me to the church. Too dangerous.

I pointed out that they deserved a bad press, and would continue to get it, unless they did something to help journalists. Indeed, I said, they did everything to obstruct us, such as putting some of us under house arrest (one German TV team in the *pension* where I was staying in Pale was currently confined in this way) and even issuing death threats to us. It somehow did the trick, and a Serb army patrol eventually got me to the church, which had been, as the Serbs insisted, thoroughly desecrated. And I got to the frontline.

And so it was with Bethlehem. I discovered that in the heart of the city there was a Syriac Orthodox church not far from Manger Square; I invented the name of a Syriac Orthodox priest for whom I allegedly worked and who was imprisoned in his home by the siege.

I emptied my handbag of all evidence that I was a journalist and abandoned the flak jacket. Actually, I've never been keen on helmets and flak jackets – although nit-picking husbands and insurance companies tend to insist on them – because I feel it's insulting to interview victims who have no such protection in the war zone when you yourself are kitted out with as much armour as an Agincourt warrior. Besides, the nearest I've ever come to a war wound was in Croatia when I managed to drop my hefty, double-ceramic-plated flak-jacket on my foot in a Zagreb hotel room, which resulted in a badly bruised big toe that had me limping for days.

Assuming dingbat-mum mode, I tried my luck with the soldiers who were sealing off the centre of Bethlehem. There were 1,200 or so foreign journalists, TV crews and peace campaigners in Israel that week; those crowded round the barricades at Bethlehem, the majority clad in helmets and flak-jackets, were begging to be allowed to go in. 'Too dangerous! Get back! Get back! No one allowed in!' The odd poke in the chest with the barrel of an M16 was a convincing closing argument.

Bizarrely, as a foolish middle-aged 'non-journalist' mum, and an obvious non-Palestinian, I was the only one of the hordes of supplicants allowed to pass. Perhaps I reminded these frightened young soldiers of their mothers, a bearer perhaps of some nice kosher chicken soup to see them through yet another terrifying day.

I walked, utterly alone, through the deserted stone alleyways, picked my way round dozens of bomb-flattened and burnt-out cars and fly-fizzing mounds of decaying rubbish. And tried not to slip on the streams of sewage that were now turning green on the narrow streets between the silent, bullet-marked and sometimes heavily scorched houses. My own fear made my ears hum. (Actually, I did slip in the sewage and fell, and have had a slight hip problem ever since.)

I saw no bodies in the open, smelled none of that all-too-familiar sickly-sweet aroma of death, but there was a throat-stopping stench nonetheless. For the first ten minutes of my cautious peregrination towards the Church of the Nativity and its defiant Palestinian gunmen, the only human beings I saw on the streets were Israeli patrols. I caught sight of one or two Palestinian faces peering through their shuttered windows: if they actually poked their heads out, they knew they'd get shot.

'Where are you going? And why were you allowed in?' a helmeted, heavily armed Israeli soldier barked angrily.

'I'm a voluntary church worker – I've got permission to visit a sick priest who's trapped near Manger Square!'

'But you are very stupid! You have no protection! Even we, with all this' (he tapped his flak-jacketed chest and his M16) 'can be killed at any moment! There are snipers everywhere! This is the most dangerous place in the world right now!'

The chief danger for me at that moment (as far as I could assess) came from the Israeli conscript soldiers themselves. They were very young and seemed determined, in pimply-faced teenage style, to appear thoroughly macho, but they were clearly very, very scared. I walked extremely slowly towards each patrol, a couple of times with my hands up. I dared not take out my mobile phone to ring my worried fixer on the outer rim of the city: a suspicious movement like that would have been a death sentence.

Every sound or sharp movement in this eerily silent world – usually from a stray dog or cat scavenging in the steamy rubbish – made these barely-out-of-their-teens soldiers whirl round, guns at the ready. At one point, an elderly Palestinian couple – she wearing a hejab – and a small child approached them wordlessly from a hundred yards away with their hands up. 'Get back! No nearer!' the soldiers shouted. The couple, their hands still in the air, turned round and silently trudged back towards their shuttered home. Perhaps they wanted food, perhaps medical care; clearly neither was going to be available any time soon.

It was not easy to persuade these jittery soldiers of my innocence. One of the ways I did succeed in doing so was by adopting the 'dotty-old-woman-who-can't-read-a-map' mode. I told the patrol that I was lost, couldn't find the building housing my priest. I suspected that, as Jews, they wouldn't know where the Syriac Orthodox church would be anyway. 'I don't know Bethlehem, do you know it?' They rolled their eyes: typical woman! But no, they didn't have a map. 'Actually, we don't know where we are either,' one of them muttered. 'This city is very strange to us.' Another patrol was rumoured to have a map: it was then fetched. In 'typical woman' fashion, I held it upside down. I then realized that, even holding it the right way up, none of the baffled soldiers could make head or tail of it either.

By now these young, frightened kids in uniform had become enormously protective of me. Each time I left one patrol, its leader would shout out in Hebrew to the patrol round the next corner, warning it to 'hold fire, she's okay!' Gasping with heat, I felt very thirsty: the soldiers happily offered me a water bottle. At one particularly dangerous point, a patrol detached a couple of soldiers to accompany me, their guns pointed upwards towards the shuttered windows of the houses as we passed. 'Snipers . . . snipers . . .'

And then there it was: Manger Square. I was now a few yards from the Church of the Nativity itself. The walls of this street were, as were all walls in Bethlehem, plastered with laudatory posters of dead suicide bombers, the *shahid*, martyrs. Some had posed before their murderous deaths with Kalashnikovs, their heads swathed in the chequered *keffiya*; others were portrayed in front of pictures of Jerusalem's Al Aqsa Mosque, Islam's third most holy site after Mecca and Medina.

Just before descending the steps into the square, in an attempt to allay suspicions I asked the soldiers, 'By the way, what do you think about Beckham's broken foot?' These startling shifts of conversation in the midst of a deeply cruel war occurred here constantly: young Palestinians, even while being shelled by the Israelis, also displayed an intense obsession with the drama of Beckham's foot. As I often do, I feigned a knowledge of football which I do not possess: 'And did you see Michael Owen's goal the other day!' I assumed that, since I'd actually heard of Owen, he must have achieved some 'crucial' goal recently. The jittery, bitter patrol soldiers suddenly became cheerily animated: 'Oh yes, Owen is brilliant – but can he become another Beckham? And what will happen if Beckham can't play in the World Cup?'

I was about to move on to the subject of Posh when suddenly a crackle of nearby gunfire broke out. I had no idea whether it was coming from the Palestinian gunmen within the besieged Church of the Nativity, or from the Israeli snipers surrounding it. Beckham's foot was suddenly forgotten. 'You must get out *now*!' my previously affable Israeli footballing chums shouted. I did not hesitate to obey. But I got nearer to the Church of the Nativity than any journalist would do for at least ten days, and was able to report at first hand on conditions in the besieged city.

*

So yes, given the importance of clothes, I had to pick an appropriate outfit to wear to go to the office of the Father of the Chapel (i.e. print-union local boss; the strange clerical title dated back to the medieval guilds). I was in trouble. The print unions then had an all-powerful grip on newspaper production and could 'black' – refuse to print – your copy if you offended them.

They'd already once 'blacked' one of my pieces – not because of its subject matter but because of something I'd said on the BBC's *Question Time*. I'd supported Rupert Murdoch in his daring, ruthless – and ultimately successful – attempt to crush the bullying and larcenous print unions. I'd described the unions as 'muggers – and along comes Murdoch, who's a super-mugger, and now he's bopping them on the head and stealing their ill-gotten power'.

But this situation was potentially worse for me. The unions forbade the use of computers, which enraged me as I would go to newspaper offices in Third World countries which were full of computers, whereas the unions still locked Britain's newspapers into almost Victorian 'hot metal' methods. When at twenty-two I was given a column on the *Daily Express*, I would be furious to read it the next morning and see lines missing and whole paragraphs transposed. I demanded to be allowed to check my column on 'the stone'. This meant going into the hot, inky, deafening area where the compositors hammered out the lines of type and locked them into a steel 'chase'. I was warned not to insist on going down to work on 'the stone'. 'Well, they don't like women down there. You'll have a hard time.'

They were right. The minute I came in there was a pandemonium of jeers and catcalls and cries of 'Show us a leg, love!' I promptly did a brief parody of a stripper dancing to 'Hey, Big Spender' and then said, 'Okay, boys, fun's over. Let's get on with it!' After that I never had any trouble on 'the stone', except for the time when, in a hurry, I foolishly tried to pick up a line of type which was in the wrong place. Hell broke loose. I, who was not a member of the relevant print union, had committed the demarcation crime of trying to pick up a chunk of type with my own, non-print-union hands. It could have been enough to bring about a total shut-down, but it didn't because of my profuse, girly apologies and my promise never to commit such a grievous offence again.

I could excuse my 'crime' then on the grounds of my youthful inexperience. But not now. In early 1982 I'd bought myself a computer – a slow, clunky machine with a minuscule 32-kilobyte memory – and was totally in love with the new technology; I remember how excited I was when eventually, after some hours, I got my machine to play 'Baa, baa, black sheep'. I even taught myself how to write some extremely primitive programs. I had put myself in touch with my 'nerd' side. I was an ecstatic born-again geek.

So few people in those days had personal computers that when I needed some urgent help I would ring my friend Dr David Barlow, a fellow geek. I'd got to know him because he was part of a semi-professional singing group called Instant Sunshine which performed the musical interlude in Radio 4's *Stop the Week*. He was also a famous sexually-transmitted-disease specialist (indeed, he'd tried to save the life of Terrence Higgins, one of the first British victims of Aids, after whom the gay help group was named). I'd ring David at work at St Thomas's Hospital: 'Please, please, tell Dr Barlow I'm desperate! I have to talk to him *now*! Tell him it's Ann Leslie calling.' After a few calls, I began to sense a few suppressed sniggers at the other end. 'No, no, it's not what you think!' I'd gabble. 'It's my computer!' Pull the other one, was, I suspected, the unspoken response.

I would write my copy on my computer abroad or at home (oh, the joys of automatic word-wrap!) and then dictate it on the phone to copy-takers in the office. The majority of copy-takers were magnificent. Others were dispiritingly miserable old gits who'd sigh heavily, 'Is this supposed to be funny?' Or, 'Is there much more of this?'

Others had great difficulty with names, no matter how often you slowly spelled them out. (Which is why the critic Milton Shulman, who reviewed the opera *Boris Godunov*, was horrified next day when he opened his *Evening Standard* to discover that, according to the copy-taker, he'd been watching an opera entitled *Doris Goodenough*).

Others would start quarrelling with my views, especially one of them, a Marxist, who'd interrupt with comments like, 'I think you'll find, Miss Leslie, that according to Hegelian dialectics . . .' I couldn't be too rude to him and tell him to get a move on (it had already taken me three days to get a phone line out of the Soviet Union), because I'd heard that he was disabled and I'd doubtless be accused of being 'disablist', as well as being thoroughly unreliable on the dialectics front.

But my 'crime' of using a computer did not become apparent to the print unions until the time I sent copy from the Falklands. The 1982 war was now over and the freezing landscape was littered with mines, unexploded shells and the crumpled remains of Argentinian vehicles. I hadn't covered the war itself because the Ministry of Defence wouldn't allow women to join the naval Task Force, and there was no other way then of getting to those windswept islands in the South Atlantic. 'There are no female toilet facilities on the ships,' was one excuse. Funny how a lack of 'female toilet facilities' (how about building them?) has been an oft-cited reason for denying women access to male institutions.

To get to the Falklands then you had to hitch a ride in one of the giant Hercules military transporters flying out of Ascension Island in the mid-Atlantic. The vast belly of the machine was lined with webbed-rope seating for the squaddies and in the middle of it were huge mounds of military equipment. There were, indeed, no 'female toilet facilities', nor much in the way of male ones either. The loo consisted of something that looked like a bucket behind a plastic curtain; when the weather got bumpy it would spill and the contents would spread over the floor and promptly freeze, thus creating a defecatory ice rink.

Before flying to the Falklands you had to sign the Official Secrets Act and state your Next of Kin. Sometimes in an emergency – particularly if the mid-air refuelling failed – the Hercs would have to land in 'an unnamed country' which was, of course, apartheid South Africa. It would be a thirteen-hour flight from Ascension to the Falklands capital, Stanley, where a new airport had just been built. Alcohol, smoking and sleeping pills were forbidden. Especially sleeping pills. In one such emergency landing in the 'unnamed country' the squaddies had been so full of sleeping pills and booze that they had fallen down the aircraft steps in a dopey and embarrassing heap. On our flight the squaddies had stocked up with bottles of Night Nurse, which their superiors clearly had not yet realized has a thoroughly narcotic effect if glugged down in sufficient quantities.

Once again, as so often, being a woman proved to be a huge advantage. I and my friend Diana Goodman of the BBC were the only women on board and after take-off we 'ladies' were kindly invited into the cockpit. We spent the entire journey there, even taking turns to have a doze in the pilots' bunk bed.

I'd wondered how I'd survive thirteen hours without a fag. No problem. Despite the No Smoking signs, the entire flight crew smoked like chimneys throughout. 'Oh, I only forbid smoking during the mid-air refuelling, which could be dangerous. Here, have one of my Marlboros!' said the pilot.

I was reminded of that pilot when interviewing a Serb surgeon at a MASH-type unit on a Bosnian frontline. The unit was in a partially destroyed ski hotel and on the doors there were signs stating 'No AK47s', 'No Rocket-propelled Grenades' – and 'No Smoking'. As wounded men were being stretchered in, some with bloody stumps where their arms or legs had been, the first 'treatment' they received from the nurses was to have a fag shoved into their mouths, if they still had one.

In the wards, the wounded men were bandaged from top to toe so that they looked like Michelin men – and they were all cheerfully puffing away with the aid of kindly, ash-strewn nurses. Even an inveterate smoker like me was shocked. The surgeon said, 'Oh, I only forbid smoking in theatre because it can be dangerous. No, I'm not bothered about ash falling into the wound: ash is sterile. It's just that it's hard for me as a surgeon to see what I'm doing through a thick fog of cigarette smoke. But I don't forbid smoking at other times. If I say to these men, "Smoking kills," they respond, "No, doctor, f***ing war kills." And they've got a point.'

On setting off for the Falklands I had a cunning, union-fooling plan up my huge fur-coated sleeve. I had by now acquired a laptop, powered by torch batteries. I took it with me, along with a sackful of batteries, the requisite bulky modem box, screwdriver, penknife, crocodile clips, and 'acoustic couplers' which you fitted over the earpiece and mouthpiece of a phone, thus transmitting the computer's signal. (You can see why I'm still so dazzled by software modems, Bluetooth, satellite mobiles and WiFi.)

Obviously I couldn't transmit to the office because there were no computers there to receive my copy. But BT had introduced a new service called Telecom Gold whereby you transmitted data to a central computer and it would then automatically re-transmit it as a telex. The print unions allowed telex, so I was feeling triumphant.

On my return the Managing Editor summoned me. 'I'm afraid you're in trouble, Ann. Your Falklands telexes had an automatic Telecom Gold message printed on top saying that your stuff had been generated by computer. The Father of the Chapel wants to see you.'

Thus it was that I dressed with particular care on the morning I was due to answer the summons. Was I going to be 'blacked' for ever? I was in one of my slim periods, so I thought a Miss Scunthorpe 1952 look might be appropriate for these old-fashioned lads: skin-tight white jeans, a Lana Turner sweater-girl red top with matching red stilettos. Perhaps sex appeal and buckets of charm would get me off the hook. I arrived at the office door: it was opened and the union man looked up and down the corridor nervously and then quickly shut the door behind me. There were three or four huge and threatening-looking print men with him. Oh, God. Perhaps the Lana Turner/ Miss Scunthorpe '52 look was a mistake.

'We want to show you something.' They led me towards a cubbyhole at the back of their main office. Of course I didn't expect to be beaten up but I was a trifle alarmed. But to my utter astonishment the cubbyhole contained, hidden under a tablecloth, a computer.

The printers then told me gloomily that they knew the way the wind was blowing, thanks to the hated Murdoch, and they realized that eventually they'd have to give in on the computers issue. I was the only person they knew of who had ever used one and they'd learned that fact from my Telecom Gold telexes from the Falklands. They had no idea how computers worked, so could I help them? I had, of course, to keep this completely secret from their union colleagues, management, and everyone else.

I kicked off the beauty queen stilettos, rolled up the Lana Turner sweater-girl sleeves and settled down in front of this alien machine, which the printers had bought with their own money and smuggled into their office. This was in pre-Windows days, so 'What's the operating system?' I asked. No idea. 'Okay, what are the transmission protocols?' No idea. Gradually, I sorted those questions out and from then on for a while I would, at their request, transmit copy to their secret computer, not for printing but for training purposes.

When the print unions finally lost their hegemonic power and there was a mass culling of print workers, I put in a discreet word for the men I'd been secretly 'training'. They deservedly kept their jobs.

22

Amandla! Awethu!

It's always been a puzzle to me how often pictures of the aftermath of a riot or a natural disaster feature, centre stage, a single lace-up shoe with its laces *still knotted tight*.

I'd long ago got used to that staple of heart-rending disaster shots, the teddy bear in the ruins. Some photographers routinely used to carry a teddy bear with them – though nowadays they're usually canny enough to realize that teddy bears are not appropriate for every culture (as in the case of Islamist Sudan where a British schoolteacher was charged with blasphemy for producing a teddy bear in class and allowing the children to call it Mohammed).

But on the February morning in 1990 when Nelson Mandela was released from the Victor Verster prison in South Africa, both of my tightly laced running shoes left my feet in a minor riot, never to be seen again. I didn't even feel them go.

A month earlier South Africa, and the world, was already rife with rumours that Mandela was going to be released after nearly three decades in prison and that the apartheid regime had finally accepted that its 'separate development' ideology had been a cruel failure which could no longer be sustained.

I had driven to the pretty Cape Dutch town of Paarl, 35 miles northeast of Cape Town, and did an outside recce of the Victor Verster where he was being held. This can't be it, I thought. This flower-fringed estate, with its immaculate playing field and pretty villas nestling amid the vineyards beneath the bright, bony hills of South Africa's ravishing winelands couldn't possibly be a prison.

Where were the watch-towers, the high walls topped with razor-wire, the yelping guard dogs? If it hadn't been for the absence of BMWs in the drive and huge-thighed, freckled Hooray Henries hollering boisterously on their way to a spot of tennis, I'd have thought that the Victor Verster prison was an exclusive, whites-only country club. And yet this was the jail where Nelson Mandela, the world's most famous political prisoner, was waiting out the final days – or weeks (we still didn't know the date) – of his twenty-seventh year of imprisonment.

The then seventy-one-year-old revolutionary, of royal Thembu blood, lived in a 'cell' which many poor whites – in whose cause he was first imprisoned – would have bitterly envied. It was, I learned, a three-bedroomed, air-conditioned cottage, complete with swimming pool, telephone, fax machine and warder servants.

His 'closest friend' (in his own words) was not some fire-eating black revolutionary but an affable white guard called James Gregory. Visitors to this luxurious 'cell' (and there were many, including members of the now supplicant apartheid Cabinet) said that the tall, grey-haired Mandela behaved like an immensely dignified royal personage, and Gregory, his jailer, like a particularly favoured courtier.

Early on the morning of 11 February rumours swept Cape Town that Mandela was going to be released that day. I jumped into my hire car and drove at high speed to Paarl. As I got nearer, the police were already blocking off roads, so I abandoned the car and struggled through the vineyards until I reached the Victor Verster entrance.

At the end of that tumultuous and historic day I filed my copy with these paragraphs:

> As I write this, I am shaking with delayed shock. I have been fleeing gunshots, running shoeless through streets full of smashed glass from looted shops. For the last four hours my head has been spinning with a confused mixture of excitement, fear, joy and foreboding at what has happened, and is still happening today.
>
> In this I am no different from anyone else in this vast and beautiful land, which quivers on the edge of a political landslip because one elderly, dignified, grey-haired man, walking with a slight limp, four hours ago crossed a Stop sign painted on the drive of the Victor Verster prison – and walked slowly out into the turbulent freedom of a new South Africa.
>
> For me and several hundred people – black and white, young and old – who'd gathered outside the bougainvillea-splashed buildings

on a small rural road in the usually sleepy wine country of the Cape, it had been a long, hot wait. In the searing wind, under the wrinkled shadow of the Simonsberg Mountain, the crowd had been singing freedom songs. 'We are going to PREE-TORR-IA! We are going to PREE-TORR-IA!', and 'Soldiers of Communism!'

As the crowd, in exquisite harmony, sang, 'Listen, we are calling you, Mandela!', a Zulu 'praise-singer', an old man in jackal skins, performed a war dance, aiming a ferocious stick at the 150 or so sweating and impassive white policemen massed round the front of the gates. Newsmen whiled away the hours cracking mordant jokes: 'What's he doing now? Getting back the watch they took away from him twenty-seven years ago?'

A tiny black Baptist preacher, Vuyami Mtini, from a nearby township, his shining face beaming with the fatuous but touching innocence of so many men of the cloth, chirruped, 'This is so nice! So nice! I hope it will stop all this fighting and all these moaners!'

A marshal, the slim, black thirty-three-year-old Cheryl Carolus of the Mass Democratic Movement, her hair streaming in the wind and shouting to be heard over the TV helicopters above, told impatient pressmen that there would be a delay because the reception committee 'wanted Comrade Mandela to be with his family and in a sense adjust, because it's going to be a perplexing time on a personal level'.

Then the crowd suddenly stiffened, like a huge, dusty animal sniffing something in the air. It began ululating and whistling with a kind of moaning sound. 'He is coming! Mandela! Mandela! Viva! Viva!' And now Mandela, with the clenched-fist African National Congress salute, came through the gate, accompanied by his wife Winnie, who had, in a rare outbreak of tact, eschewed her favoured paramilitary 'struggle wear'. She did not punch the air, and did not emit her favourite cries of 'Kill the Boer, kill the white farmer!' or 'With our matches and our necklaces' (of burning tyres placed round the necks of her black enemies) 'we shall liberate this land!' Her round, pretty face was serene, gleaming with quiet, proud pleasure.

That's when I lost my tightly knotted lace-up shoes. At their first sight of Mandela the crowd had boiled over with a mad, unfettered joy. As my copy that day described it,

Suddenly I was swept forward in a maelstrom of flailing limbs and sweat, dust and screams. A huge ANC banner pole tore through my hair, my shoes had been ripped from my feet, and I felt my blood warm and sticky on the hot tarmac. For a terrible moment I thought that this was what it must feel like if you're about to die. Of course I would have been just another innocent bystander victim in a war which has claimed so many since the man before me first lost his freedom.

Through the mass of sweating heads and Mandela T-shirts, arms and elbows shoving into my face, I could see the blue uniforms of grim-faced white policemen linking arms with ANC marshals. Tall, khaki-clad youths in tennis shoes and with home-made epaulettes in the once-banned ANC colours safety-pinned to their shoulders were screaming, together with the white police-men, 'Get back! Get back!'

Only later did I have time to remind myself that a mere fort-night ago these marshals would have been beaten and arrested for wearing these gold, green and black strips of cotton on their shirts and these slogans on their baseball caps. Here, for a mo-ment, however reluctantly, the old forces of apartheid and the new ascending order of black power had linked arms against the increasing chaos on this tiny rural road.

Mandela and Winnie were whisked away from the chaos in a motorcade heading for Grand Parade in Cape Town, where we were told he would address the nation. But I had to retrieve my abandoned car, get back to Cape Town, watch Mandela's address and, of course, write and file my copy. But the queue shuffling its way to the nearest road block stretched, I reckoned, for at least two miles. I was having to trudge along with them, shoeless and bleeding: I was desperate because I knew that, at this rate, I'd never make my deadline.

Luckily for me, because I'm a white woman, an Afrikaner soldier took pity on me and gave me a lift. I noted that a pregnant woman who'd collapsed in the road had been ignored, but she was a sari-clad Indian. When I confessed to him that I was a member of the much hated international press, he swore.

At one point three young 'Comrades' waving ANC banners and wearing 'Welcome Mandela' T-shirts jumped exuberantly on to the car and the Afrikaner almost exploded. 'Get off my f****** car, man, you f****** animals! If you f****** touch my car again I won't answer for what I'll do! You're f****** rats out of hell,' he screamed, his tiny blond moustache almost vaporizing with rage. 'And these are the people we're handing this country over to!' When I remarked that they all seemed, given the circumstances, remarkably good-natured and cheery, he continued muttering and grumbling furiously.

When I reached my own car, I gave three women from a Cape Town squatter camp a lift to the nearest bus stop. 'Did you see Madiba?' (his Xhosa clan name). 'We couldn't because the crowd was too big!'

'Yes, I did,' I told them. They gasped, and one of them gripped and stroked my shoulder as though I were a sample of the True Cross. 'Did Madiba look well?'

'Yes,' I replied.

'Oh, thanks be to God,' said a grandmother, a vast sofa-shaped woman in blue sateen which, she told me, was her best church dress. 'We wondered whether he would be killed by the police when he walked out. He said when he was imprisoned that he was prepared to die for his beliefs.'

By now I was in considerable pain and bleeding all over my hire-car pedals. When I reached the environs of Grand Parade, Mandela was understandably running late. The vast crowd was filling in time; some of the Comrades had taken to a spot of looting.

At one point the police started spraying bird-shot at us. I was urged to fling myself face-down on the street but, as my feet were already bleeding profusely, I didn't want my face to suffer a similar fate by burying it in shattered glass. Bizarrely, in the midst of this minor riot, a Comrade who'd been 'liberating' fancy Italian footwear from a boutique, whose windows he and his mates had just smashed, politely offered me a pair of fashionable shoes for a small consideration. 'What size, what colour you like, madam?' He was festooned from top to toe in Italy's finest stilettos. Equally politely I demurred on the grounds that I, albeit in obvious need of footwear, was, right now, rather busy. (Later, when Cheryl Carolus, whom I'd first met outside the Victor Verster, became South Africa's first black High Commissioner in London, she'd take pleasure in introducing me to fellow guests as 'Ann Leslie of the *Daily Mail*. Ann, tell them about the looted shoes and Grand Parade!')

The day after Mandela's release I went to the vast rally held in the football stadium of Soweto township. To the consternation of my white cab driver, I jumped out of the car and clambered into the earth scoop of a giant JCB to join the Comrades and the 'Young Lions' crammed on to every inch of its surface as it headed for the stadium for 'our great leader's' homecoming.

As the JCB lumbered and jerked its way slowly through the crowds, it looked like some huge, hapless insect being devoured by a swarm of hungry ants. I asked them where they got the machine. 'We hijacked it!' the 'Young Lions' shouted back merrily. Hijacking, and often burning, vehicles was an established Soweto sport and one greatly deplored in Mandela's speech in the stadium later that day. The JCB was, presumably, one of the fifty other vehicles hijacked for the great occasion: according to police, none of the owners had yet complained.

My question had however somewhat offended one skinny Comrade with broken teeth who looked about fourteen, and whose tight, dusty curls were crammed into a black beret, a popular 'struggle-wear' fashion item in those parts.

'Hey, man, you with the struggle?' he demanded. '*Amandla!*' (power) I shouted firmly, anxious that there should be no potentially lethal misunderstanding, and for a moment wishing that I'd invested in a few 'struggle-wear' items myself. '*Awethu!*' (is ours) the Comrades around me on the JCB shouted back joyously. Since eight in the morning the entire township of around 2 million seemed to be on the move: from my perch in the earth scoop, it looked as though every red-dust side street between the rows of breeze-block and tin-roofed 'matchbox' houses was crawling with ever more ant-swarms of humanity converging on the stadium. (When I got back to England, the JCB company sent me a miniature version of the earth-moving vehicle which had been my transport that day.)

The 'Black Messiah's' speech was, frankly, rather dull but that didn't matter to the hysterically happy crowds: after all Mandela had been a symbol of black liberation for the twenty-seven years of his imprisonment.

When he became a one-term President, most people now agree he was not an especially wise or skilled ruler. Being cut off from the outside world for almost three decades obviously does not equip you for instantly mastering the mundane political skills needed in a world which has moved on since you were first imprisoned. His main value was, and always will be, as a symbol – and symbolism is what Madiba is good at.

When I'm asked whether I've interviewed him I usually say no. This is partly because I've never been particularly keen on interviewing Great Personages, even if I could get an interview in the first place. The *Daily Mail* is of course an immensely powerful newspaper in Britain, and can usually get any interview it wants, but this doesn't apply overseas.

More to the point, a Great Personage does not rise in a vacuum: he or she is the product, or sometimes the shaper, of particular ideological, economic and social circumstances – and they are what interest me more. Besides, Great Personages are usually very practised at interviews and, unless you can spend an extended period of time with them, and observe them behaving unselfconsciously in their daily context, they will rarely reveal anything surprising.

But actually I did very briefly interview Mandela once, though I still feel faintly ashamed about it. One morning I turned up at a hastily arranged press briefing in Cape Town about student unrest. Already the universities were in uproar as black students went on the rampage, taking hostages, fighting with whites, wrecking buildings in their demands for less 'Eurocentric' teaching and for the abolition of student fees and the cancellation of debts. The hapless President Mandela had appealed to them to demonstrate peacefully, and had been ignored. After all, the argument went, if a man couldn't (as had been evident) control his own errant wife, how could he control other people's kids – particularly kids who adored her?

The press briefing, held at the ANC headquarters, was so unexpected that only four journalists were present – and fifteen people to brief us, including the seventy-six-year-old President himself. He looked exhausted, hiding haggard eyes behind dark glasses, occasionally choking gently into a handkerchief. 'Mr President, you seem to have a bad cough,' I remarked. 'Yes,' he replied sadly, 'I'm afraid I've just come back from a country where the temperature was below 15 degrees Centigrade and it has affected me.' (He'd just flown back from the Copenhagen UN Summit on Poverty: the ANC had been trotting the exhausted old man around the world to assorted conferences to symbolize their own 'virtue'.) I asked him to comment on the story that the Queen, who was about to visit South Africa, would not be awarding him an honorary knighthood, 'because your wife—'

The ANC henchmen, horrified that I was about to bring up the 'Winnie problem', tried to silence me. 'Could I *please* finish my question?' I asked them crossly. Mandela, with a resigned wave of a hand, said, 'Yes, please let the lady continue.'

'*As I was saying*, the Palace apparently fears that your wife might embarrass you, the Queen and South Africa, by swanning around calling herself Lady Mandela!'

With quiet dignity, he replied, 'That is a matter for the British government, not for us.' Such was his grave, sad courtesy, that I suddenly felt like a heel – a typically crass journalist – for intruding on his private grief. Later, he shook my hand and said, 'It has been a pleasure to meet you,' although of course it couldn't have been.

I'd been investigating the background of his by then estranged wife Winnie. Few would go on the record because Winnie still had an important power base in the townships. The wife of a former Robben Island inmate, a hero of the liberation movement, told me, 'We were at school together. I think she was mentally unstable then, even before her ordeals at the hands of the apartheid government. One moment she could be the most charming, warm person – the next, the most cruel and arbitrarily violent creature imaginable. You never knew what she would be from one moment to the next.'

In one township a Comrade called Mandla Mishali and his cold-eyed, well-muscled young mates regarded me and my questioning about their heroine with some suspicion – as well they might. To them I was a representative of the white-colonialist-imperialist-capitalistic media who'd print any old lies to sell newspapers. Like, for example, telling the world that Winnie Mandela was a proven kidnapper, alleged fraudster, ripper-off of charity funds, suspected murderer, and a promiscuous, foul-mouthed, extravagant, hard-drinking slut to boot. 'But to all of us in this squatters' camp, she is our mother, the mother of the nation! When we were oppressed, she fought left and right for us! We love our Mamma Winnie, she's a soldier for the people, she never forgets us. We feel multiple pain for the bad fingers they are pointing at her now! Where is their evidence?'

Well, actually there was rather a lot of it. Her involvement in the murder of fourteen-year-old Stompie Moeketsi, her proven affairs, the kangaroo courts she ran in Soweto, her involvement in dubious diamond deals with a convicted diamond smuggler, the reign of terror she unleashed on the township with a bunch of black thugs who called themselves the 'Mandela United Football Club' – and above all, the huge sums of money this 'mother of the nation' had allegedly siphoned off from charities set up to help the poor. The missing funds had, according to her enemies in the ANC, gone towards maintaining her fifteen-room Soweto mansion, her six cars (she favoured Mercedes), her lovers, and an increasingly lavish life-style. Some graffiti near her home denounced her as 'The Mugger of the Nation'.

'We know some of the bad things Mamma Winnie has done – but no one ever talks of the many, many good things she has done for us! As for the money – well, that is a capitalistic temptation that could happen to any of us, we who have never had money or gone riding in beautiful cars. I, for example, have never held a 500-rand note [then less than £100] in my hand in my life. But if I found that note in my hand, who knows if I wouldn't be tempted like Mamma Winnie?'

Despite his initial suspicions, Comrade Mandla Mishali had agreed to talk to me, taking time out from a meeting of the 'ANC Kliptown Squatters Toilet Committee' – 'we only have 100 toilets for 3,000 people and we're trying to arrange for another 100.' Every time it rained heavily, as it often did, shacks, chickens, cooking pots, a precious portaloo or two – and the odd human being – were swept away into deep gullies by a brown flood. 'Liberation' from white rule had made not a jot of difference so far.

Those Comrades had high hopes for Mandela's Reconstruction and Development Plan, the RDP. According to cynical whites, the RDP actually stood for 'Revenge of the Dark People' or 'Real Darkie Policies' – but whatever it stood for, it hadn't helped the Kliptown

Above. Radio 4's *Stop the Week* team: with Professor Laurie Taylor, chairman Robert Robinson and theatre critic and purveyor of Goldberg jokes, Milton Shulman, 1980s.

Right. With Robert Robinson and *Stop the Week* producer Michael Ember.

Below. BBC TV's *Question Time*, with Michael Heseltine, Robin Day, Michael Foot and David Steel, 1983.

Left. Karla Faye Tucker on Death Row, Mountainview, Texas, 1986. She was executed twelve years after I took this picture.

Below, left. Joe Giarratano on Death Row, Mecklenburg, West Virginia, 1986. His sentence was commuted to life without parole.

Bottom, left. With poet James Fenton, Shek Ho, Hong Kong, 1986.

Below. With photographer Monty Fresco on a train in Guangdong, China, 1986.

A 'Little Emperor', a spoiled only son, the inevitable result of China's one-child policy, Beijing, 1986.

My fixer in Communist East Berlin, Wiebke Reed, ex-wife of the 'Red Elvis', 1989.

Snatching some sleep on the flight to the Gulf in a military Hercules, 1991.

With a Bosnian Serb
soldier near the besieged
UN 'safe haven' of Gorazde
in 1994.

Sitting on a Serb tank in
Bosnia, 1994.

Sir David English, my editor for twenty years at the *Mail*, at an award ceremony in 1997. His sudden death a year later grieves me still.

Granada TV's *University Challenge Special*, 1998: Tabloids v. Broadsheets. Jane Moore (*Sun*), Peter Hitchens (*Express*), Jeremy Paxman, team captain Leslie (*Mail*), Tony Parsons (*Mirror*). The tabloids won.

North Korean orphans, including eight-year-old Hyong-chol, in a secret refuge in north east China near the North Korean border, 1998.

Trying to interview Imelda Marcos in New York at the start of the journey to Hawaii to retrieve her late husband's body, 2002.

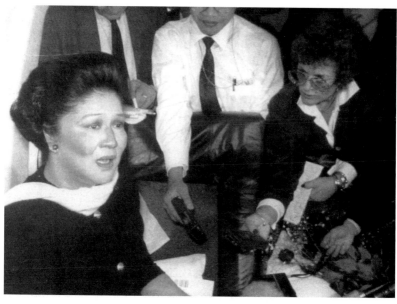

Katharine with proud parents at her graduation from Balliol, Oxford.

With Michael and Katharine.

Investiture as a Dame by the Queen at Buckingham Palace, 2007.

'darkies' yet. But it had certainly 'reconstructed and developed' the lifestyles of the new black elite.

In Jo'burg, Cape Town and Pretoria, former guerrillas had swapped. their fatigues for Hugo Boss suits, AK47s for Mont Blanc pens, and shebeen moonshine beer for Laphroaig single malt; they no longer lived in matchbox township houses, but in fortified, green-lawned mansions in former all-white suburbs and were fawned on by white socialites who'd once regarded them as '*kaffir* Commies'. As Wynne MacOlive, the owner of Club 29, a fashionable 'white shebeen' in Jo'burg's wealthy Houghton, put it to me, 'I was born and brought up under apartheid and I must admit I never thought I'd live to see the day when I would actually *embrace* a black man. And the first time I had to serve one in the bar I felt *very* uncomfortable. But my black guests have turned out to be very nice, very gentlemanly people – frankly, I'd rather have them as customers than some of the white men who come in here!'

But MacOlive's admired gentlemanly blacks were not quite to Kliptown's taste. 'They sit up there, far, far away from us, and we still sit down here,' said a gap-toothed old man in a ragged hand-me-down three-piece suit. 'Frankly, we are very disappointed in them. We do not understand what is happening. Only Winnie listens to us.'

*

Every British Royal Tour has a potential Nightmare Scenario. In Russia, the NS was the fear that Boris Yeltsin might be so drunk that he'd fall face first into the royal soup. This South African Royal Tour in 1995 had several NSs. Would beer-bellied, gun-toting Boers from the *platteland* seek to revenge themselves on the *kaffirboetie*, 'nigger-loving', British for their past persecution of the sacred *Volk*? Other possible NSs included the bitter feud between the Zulu King Good-will and his autocratic uncle Chief Mangosuthu Buthelezi, both of whom were invited to the same banquet on the royal yacht *Britannia*, and both of whom would be mortally offended if the seating plan appeared to downgrade either of them. ('And a mortally offended Zulu tends to be a rather dangerous fellow. Perhaps the pair of 'em could take it in turns to sit on each other's knees,' murmured one exasperated diplomat.)

But the chief Nightmare Scenario involved Winnie, the Queen of the townships, South Africa's Imelda Marcos, its Black Evita. This was the woman who should have been South Africa's first black First Lady, the woman who should have played hostess to the Queen on this tour; instead, 'Queen' Winnie had been cast into protocol's outer darkness. But 'Mamma Africa' doesn't care to be upstaged by anyone, and nervous diplomats wondered whether, surrounded by her bodyguards and fans from places like Kliptown doing a defiant *toyitoyi* shuffle-dance, Winnie would try and gatecrash some solemn royal occasion and emerge, as she usually did, triumphant.

After all, she was still a member of her husband's Cabinet, and an MP who had an automatic right to enter the Cape Town Parliament when the Queen addressed it. But *why* was she still a member of the Cabinet? Why, after the endless embarrassment she'd caused her husband, did he still refuse to sack her?

The answer lay in those squatter camps. As Alan Reynolds, her adoring white personal secretary, put it to me, 'The conservatives in the ANC fear her because she's so popular. Many of her enemies came back from exile; they didn't fight the system within the country, as she did for all those years. Her constituency is among the young, the squatters, the illiterate, the zero-income people – and they are the majority in this country!'

The thirty-year-old Alan Reynolds studied at Moscow's Patrice Lumumba Peoples' Friendship University, and was a former ANC 'Spear of the Nation' guerilla. Reynolds first fell for Mrs Mandela when, as a seventeen-year-old self-described beach bum, he visited her in internal exile in a shack in Brandfort. 'I was immediately struck by her extraordinary beauty, her incredible courage. From that day to this, I have never, ever had any doubts about her.'

Sadly, the unreasonably high hopes held for Mandela's 'Rainbow Nation' have, inevitably, been disappointed; murder (South Africa now has the second-highest murder rate in the world) and especially rape are on the increase, and HIV/Aids has ravaged the population. The Kliptown squatters are no wealthier, but the black elite certainly are.

Mandela's successor, Thabo Mbeki, an austere, academic, apparently cold man, dedicated to long nights with a bottle of Chivas Regal and the internet, has held back South Africa's attempt to deal with

Aids by denying that the HIV virus has anything to do with the disease. As with everything, he sees HIV/Aids through the prism of race. Western campaigns against the disease are, he stated in one speech, mere racism: the white West is 'convinced that we are but natural-born, promiscuous carriers of germs, unique in the world. They proclaim that our continent is doomed to an inevitable end because of our unconquerable devotion to the sin of lust.'

He has refused to take a hard line with Zimbabwe's Robert Mugabe and thus has had no effect on the latter's catastrophic policies (and South Africa could get rid of him overnight simply by cutting off the water, electricity and secret bank accounts it supplies). Mbeki's so-called 'quiet diplomacy' has merely resulted in a major refugee crisis involving desperate Zims escaping across the border.

One seasoned Mbeki observer told me, 'Thabo's tragedy is that he spent twenty-eight years of his life in "the struggle" in relative comfort overseas, whereas his revered father Govan fought and suffered, and was imprisoned for twenty-four years on South African soil. Mugabe did much the same in Zimbabwe. Thabo simply can't reject his father's counterpart.'

Unfortunately, Mbeki's successor as President may well be the corrupt, charismatic Zulu thug Jacob Zuma. Zuma, barely literate, appeals to the same disappointed township dwellers who used to worship Winnie. I only met him once, briefly, when he was master-minding the burning of shacks belonging to supporters of Inkatha, the anti-ANC party spearheaded by Chief Mangosuthu Buthelezi in KwaZulu/Natal. He did not then – and does not now – strike me as the answer to the Rainbow Nation's prayers.

As for Winnie, she didn't serve a day in jail for her crimes. The last time I met her was (as so often with Winnie) a faintly farcical affair. It was in Beijing at the UN Fourth World Conference on Women in 1995 and its opening ceremony was being held in the huge Maoist–Stalinist hulk of the Great Hall of the People on Tiananmen Square.

I alighted from one of the yellow 'bread-box' communal taxis just as Winnie, swathed in one of her magnificent turban-topped Queen of Africa outfits, was alighting from her vast limo and being set upon by a pushing and shoving horde of Chinese police, nicknamed 'bottle-tops' because of the design of their hat badges. Like a swarm of angry wasps, they were hell-bent on stopping the self-styled 'Mamma Africa' from gatecrashing the opening ceremony.

'I'm an accredited delegate and I was invited by the Chinese Government!' squawked Winnie, hotly denying that she was 'too late'. (However, her time-keeping was known as 'African time, doubled' and bore absolutely no relationship to anyone else's schedule.) And Mamma Africa certainly hadn't been invited to be an 'accredited delegate' to her estranged husband Nelson's delegation of twenty-five South Africans. After all, she was currently dodging the serving of the South African President's divorce papers. Women surrounded her shouting, 'Let her in!' and singing, 'We Shall Overcome!' (Not here you won't, sisters, not in Beijing.) Tiananmen Square was, frankly, not a place in which even the ludicrous likes of mad Winnie, clattering her bracelets and waving her clenched fists, should attempt to overstay her already definitely absent welcome.

Suddenly, in the fracas with the 'bottle-tops', she caught sight of me. 'Oh, Ann – how wonderful to see a familiar face!' (This from a woman whom I scarcely knew and whose 'Mandela United Football Club' thugs had once threatened to break my legs.) 'I just don't understand these people – they're not like you and me!' Miraculously, at least from Winnie's side, sisterly solidarity can spring up between the most unlikely individuals, and in the most unlikely places.

23

The Canary, the Champ,
the Snapper and the Crim

I first met Tom Jones in 1970 during his American tour, then the biggest in showbiz history. At the time, Tom (the former bricklayer son of a Welsh miner) was one of the highest-paid singers in the world, earning almost as much per concert as his hero and friend Elvis. I joined the final leg of the tour – Los Angeles, Denver, San Francisco – and most of it was, for me, an exhausting blur. And I didn't even have to sing.

Rarely have I met a sunnier, less complicated showbiz soul than Tom, who turned out to be a nice, down-to-earth, rather old-fashioned Welsh boyo from the valleys. The man whose stage act – thrashing thighs, pelvic thrusts, buttocks like shiny water melons gyrating in his sprayed-on trousers, sudden jack-knifes as if in mortal sexual agony – was virtually pornographic would not, I thought, have a puritan bone in his strutting body. I was wrong. He prissily turned down the part of 'The Stud', opposite Joan Collins, on the grounds that 'I wouldn't like my Mum and Dad to see that sort of thing. It's just short of being pornographic!'

He didn't 'believe in divorce, it's not right', so remained married to lonely, dumpy housewife Linda, his childhood sweetheart; but a boyo's got to do what a boyo's got to do, which, on tour, involved barnacling his crucifix-adorned chest with crotch-grabbing groupies.

The chartered Boeing 727 held around sixty to seventy passengers and an exotic lot they were too – weird birds of paradise in floppy hats, fringed waistcoats, Indian beads, velvet hipster pants, huge dandelion-shaped Afro hairdos, Polaroid sunspecs, every chest, wrist and neck clanking with loops, chains and lumps of solid gold. When one of our number, having partaken too freely of 'substances', slipped over on the plane steps, he clattered noisily onto the tarmac like a freight train crashing into the sidings.

Tom's entourage, who called him 'The Champ', 'Tommo' or 'The Canary', included his personal bodyguard, an amiable former Liverpool boxer called Rocky Seddon, who had a face like a battered owl, tattoos all over his arms and a dog-like devotion to Tom. 'Every day is Christmas Day with Tommo! Had to break the arm of a Mafia feller who was trying to get in to see the Canary in his dressing room at that Copacabana in New York. Came at me with a knife, he did! Yeah, I have a great time I do.'

Damon Runyon would have loved Rocky. He had one leg shorter than the other, which had somewhat hampered his boxing career: a fellow bodyguard declared that 'Rocky rented advertising space on the soles of his feet because he spent more time on his back than he did on his feet.' When Rocky wasn't defending the Canary, he spent his time immersed in a turgid, well-thumbed piece of Victorian pornography called *My Secret Life* which became the tour's unofficial bible, nicknamed 'The Book of the Banger'.

From time to time during American tours Tom would have to escape across the border to avoid the 180-day tax limit: if he spent over 180 consecutive days on American soil he'd become liable to American as well as British tax. On one occasion, the Book of the Banger proved useful.

Over a sweet-and-sour Chinese supper in San Francisco Tom told me, 'Oh, this tax thing has given us some funny moments!' He turned to a member of his entourage. 'Remember that time we was all holed up in some crummy motel on the Canadian border and the manager was convinced we were a gathering of the Mafia and was going to call the police? There was eight of us squashed into this room late at night, so Rocky said, "Now, my children, let us begin at . . .", opened the Book of the Banger, and began reading selected passages from it – as if, you know, like it was the Bible. And then we were told there was a man dying next door. It felt kind of weird, you know, us eight grown men all solemnly listening to readings from a dirty book, and someone gasping out his life the other side of the partition. We wanted to invite him in – a dose of the Book of the Banger might have brought him back.'

On the plane there was strict demarcation. At the front, mainlining on champagne and cigars, sat Tom, his coterie, his groupies and Rocky with the Book of the Banger. I sat in the middle, with some backing musicians and less important staff, several of whom seemed to be nicknamed 'Bubba', and what remained of the black soul group Gladys Knight and the Pips. Through illness we were now deprived of Gladys and two of the Pips. In our Pips section of the fuselage, marijuana and Southern Comfort were the substances of choice. What with the weed and the cigar smoke, the plane smelt like a rancid haystack.

Tom disapproved of marijuana, largely it seemed on social rather than moral grounds. 'It makes people dead boring, they just giggle about nothing. There was this New Year's Eve do where everyone was smoking joints, no one drinking – I had eight bottles of champagne to myself – and I've never been to a deader party in my life.'

Seated silently at the back of the plane were Count Basie and his Orchestra; they were Bourbon-on-the-rocks kinda guys. Basie was not popular with the Canary's people: in the four months he was on the tour the grand old man did not deign to utter a word to them: 'Never even said hello or goodbye.' On one flight, when I'd tired of listening to the stoned ramblings of one of the Bubbas, I strolled down to where Basie was sitting playing cards, as he always was. This time it was poker. 'Oh, I've never understood poker!' I said brightly. No response. 'It must be terribly difficult.'

'Yup.'

'I mean, could you teach me?'

'Nope.' Oh well, back to the Bubbas . . . then 'Siddown'. So I did. And Basie tried to teach me. He failed – but the fact that he'd even tried, however briefly, greatly impressed one of the Bubbas. 'He actually *talked* to you!'

One night backstage an excited tour minion ran in and told us, 'Aretha Franklin is going to drop in!' Which she did. But 'drop in' does not adequately describe the effect that the arrival of the great soul diva had on us all. She billowed in, broad and sassy and bosomy and blindingly charismatic. Our jaws collectively dropped. She declared throatily that she was a great fan of Tom's and Tom, suddenly shy, declared the admiration to be mutual. When she billowed out again (I thought a massive gospel choir should have accompanied her triumphant entrance and her equally triumphant egress) all a gob-smacked Tom could say was, 'What a pair of Cardiffs!'

'But,' I said, 'I thought bosoms were called Bristols!'

'Not in Wales they're not.'

Tom seemed, on the whole, to be free of personal spite. Except when it came to Engelbert Humperdinck with whom he shared a manager, his wary, ulcer-ridden Welsh Svengali Gordon Mills. Mills had created a different persona for each of his clients: Tom was 'Mr Sex' and Engelbert 'Mr Romance'. The latter (real name Gerry Dorsey) had been born in India, as had Mills, and, like Mills, had an Anglo-Indian mother.

There was fierce rivalry between Mr Sex and Mr Romance and Mr Sex would invariably refer, in those politically incorrect days, to Mr Romance as the 'Singing Paki'. Understandably, Mr Romance was furious at this racist – and geographically inaccurate – insult. And, apparently furious that Mr Sex was being interviewed at length by me, he told Gordon Mills that I had to interview him as well. 'Look, Ann, please interview Engelbert,' begged Mills. 'It's a difficult situation.' I agreed. Mr Sex commented witheringly, 'So you're going to interview the Singing Paki, are you? *That'll* be very boring.' (He was right about that.)

But my work at that time didn't just involve pop singers and film stars. I had zilch interest in or knowledge of sport but I'd be sent to interview the likes of Graham Hill, the champion racing driver, and the legendary footballer, Pele. The first, a mustachioed Lothario, was wonderfully racy, in all senses of the word, and the latter was small, courteous and, for a footballer who was a worldwide star, endearingly modest.

One day it was suggested that, despite having the muscle-power of a gnat, I should borrow a tracksuit and do a brisk bit of soccer training with young Kevin. 'Kevin who?' I inquired pleasantly. There was a moment's incredulous silence. 'Kevin Keegan of the Kop, of course!'

'What's the Kop?'

I was told it was part of a football stadium in Anfield and I was to get up there straight away. What had struck my employers down in London as an amusing little jape, looked dangerously like sacrilege up in Liverpool where the People of the Kop had sprayed blackened slum walls with the holy names of their faith: 'Keegan', 'Shankly', 'Keegan'.

In the Players' Lounge at Anfield I learned that the twenty-two-year-old Keegan had a bad cold and, moreover, had injured his knee in Saturday's game. The tea ladies showed motherly concern. 'Couldn't sleep a wink Saturday night worrying about little Kev!' said one. Still, training with a one-legged Kev might, in itself, produce good copy.

But first I'd have to deal with Bill Shankly, the team's autocratic Scottish manager, who once famously remarked, 'Some people think football is a matter of life and death . . . I can assure them it's much more important than that.' When I nervously detailed my little plan to him, an air of dour astonishment slowly suffused his nuggety features. 'You must be joking,' he said flatly. If I'd asked the Pope if one of his younger cardinals could do a fan-dance with me in his Y-fronts, I could hardly have fared worse. But in Liverpool then Shankly was the uncrowned Pope and his word was law. 'My boy's no circus clown! Besides, he's sick. So,' he added with an air of finality, 'I'm not letting him out.'

The nearest I got to my 'training session' was managing to lure 'little Kev' outside on to the sacred turf when Shankly was out of sight. The young superstar striker limped along beside me, muffled from top to toe in a voluminous tweed overcoat, his pink and streaming nose poking nervously through his upturned collar. 'Shanks had better not catch us out here!' he muttered. By the time Shanks found out, I was mercifully back on the train to London, leaving Kev to catch any fallout.

*

Keegan and I got on fine, but the sports star who really surprised me was Muhammad Ali. Again, I hadn't wanted to interview the former Cassius Clay (which he denounced as his 'slave name') because I concurred with the view that boxing was a 'sport' which largely consisted of two black men beating each other up for the entertainment of white men. Besides, I never found all that 'float like a butterfly, sting like a bee' bombast quite to my taste.

But the man I met in a Piccadilly hotel was quite unlike what I expected. He walked very tall, very solid, very aloof, unheeding of the swarms of people buzzing slavishly about in his massive wake. He had a languorous grace and an almost chilling dignity; no emotion ever seemed to rearrange that magnificently smooth, teak-coloured face. But the more we talked, the more he began to sound lonely, restless, embittered, no longer the loud and lovable rogue of yester-year.

'Ah'm just an athlete, nothing more. Everyone asks me questions about religion, about race, about politics, like Ah wanted to be a leader. Ah don't want to be no leader. Ah'm tryin' too hard to lead *myself*. And, all the time, the world is watchin'.'

'But isn't that what you always wanted?'

'Ah want the world to watch me *box*. But the world is watching my private life' (his year-long marriage to a black model was said to be foundering over his newly embraced Muslim faith). 'It's always watchin' my thoughts, my religion. Ah never wanted that. But it don't stop watchin'.'

Why had he suddenly stopped shouting? ''Cos Ah don't need to. Ah don't say, "Ah'm the Greatest" any more. Everyone says, "You're the Greatest, you're the Greatest." Ah'm sick of it.'

And no, his conversion to a strange separatist Muslim sect called the Nation of Islam was no stunt. He turned his eyes on me. 'None of you people come to help us, to understand us. You want to believe lies. You say we are a violent people. Well, there's violence happenin' everywhere and we're not in it. We just want to clean up our own neighbourhoods, marry our own women, mind our own business, like all intelligent folks.'

What about the race riots in Los Angeles? Aren't 'his people' involved in them? 'Ah ain't been reading about that. Ah've been travellin'. Don't want to talk about that. Ah hate violence.' If he hated violence, why was he in a violent profession? He began munching a massive steak, leaving the answering of that and other questions to his extremely voluble entourage. 'De Champ don't like to hurt anyone, do you?' 'De Champ's *sad* when he hurts someone in the ring, ain't you?' 'De Champ knows it's just business, ain't that right?'

A year later I was asked to go to Heathrow Airport to meet an overnight flight from the States. Muhammad Ali was flying in to defend his championship title against the British 'nice guy' Henry Cooper. 'Why me? I'm not the Boxing Correspondent!' But the paper's Boxing Correspondent had apparently declared that it was beneath his dignity to join a press scrum in the Arrivals hall.

I'd already been aware that some of Ali's entourage were not quite as puritanical as he now was over the matter of what they called 'little foxes'. Okay, so I'd dress up as a 'little fox' in a fun fur, high boots and short skirt, and would keep myself separate from the press throng when Ali arrived. One of those waiting for him was a showbiz agent I knew and he spotted me. He sidled up and whispered, 'Want an exclusive with him?' Yup, I sure would. 'Well, nip into that Rolls over there.' Which I did. Shortly afterwards Ali joined me.

There followed scenes of utter pandemonium as the press scrum swirled round the car, photographers fired flash guns in at us, baffled journalists shouted questions. Who's that girl in the Rolls? Has Ali suddenly found himself a white 'little fox'? What on earth's going on? I merely smiled enigmatically back at them all. When the Rolls finally managed to drive off, I rolled down the window, stuck my head out and shouted, 'I'm Ann Leslie of the *Daily Express* and I've scooped the lot of you!' (A fact generously conceded in his column by J. L. Manning, the star sports writer on the rival *Daily Mail*.)

I said to Ali that he seemed to be a happier man than when I'd met him a year previously. 'Yes, ma'am, Ah guess Ah am. Ah feel more relaxed, more free in myself. Maybe it's because my divorce is over.' He even seemed slightly pleased to see me again, but in no way was he an easy interview. Besides, he was exhausted after the long flight. He had, as I wrote at the time, a way of entering a conversation and departing from it quite arbitrarily, provoking all his hangers-on into bouts of loud, nervous geniality, as though humouring a fractious god. But however rackety the circus around him, the former clown now wore a dark shroud of stillness, rendering him inscrutable, impassive, impenetrable.

Nevertheless, by the end of the drive into London he'd talked, or rather mumbled, much more openly to me about his thoughts, feelings and future dreams than I thought he ever would. The result was a triumphant 'Photonews' spread in the paper the next day. Which is why I eventually had to punch him in the jaw.

The editor had been so thrilled with my mini scoop that he asked me if I could go back and get more. Perhaps a two-parter, 'My Life in My Own Words, by the World Champion'? Oddly enough, I thought that might just be possible. I'd guessed that the ever-increasing size and extravagance of his entourage – all of whom had to be housed in top-class rooms in top hotels – might now be affecting his cash flow.

And so it proved. A fairly modest fee of £500 in readies was agreed upon. I would write the Champ's 'own words', but the paper's lawyers insisted that I had to get him to sign approval of each page *in my presence* before we could print the stuff. Ali was not, I suspected, a great reader. I went to his suite with the articles: 'Why don't I read it all out to you and anything you disagree with, just tell me, okay?'

'Okay,' he mumbled abstractedly, gazing into the middle distance.

We both sat down on the floor, surrounded by his hangers-on who were all cracking jokes, tumbling around and playfully punching each other. Ali was at his most impassive and took no notice of either them or me. I began to panic. He wasn't listening, let alone signing anything, and my deadline for getting his signature at the bottom of every page was drawing dangerously close. He started to get up and it looked as if he was going to just amble away. I shot to my feet and punched him on the jaw. '*Now* are you going to pay attention?' The room fell into an astonished and terrified silence. Then a slow, sweet smile spread across his great face. 'Ah *apologize*, ma'am!' From then on, all was plain sailing and we parted on the best of terms.

A year later, I bumped into one of his management team who asked me what I'd thought of the Champ. 'A complete *pussycat*!' I replied.

'Ain't that the truth? But when we say that, nobody believes us!'

*

I may not have been scared of the World Heavyweight Champion, but I was certainly rendered extremely nervous one day when faced with an American photographer called Diane. The *Sunday Times* magazine asked me to go to the States in late 1970 to investigate the new fashion for residential segregation – not by race, but by age. In southern California I went to one gated community (a new concept as far as Britain was concerned) which would not allow anyone over the age of thirty to live there and where residents should preferably be singles. And then on to a very plush community called Sun City where no one under fifty could obtain residence. I disapproved on principle of the separation of generations, as I did of separation by race, but I found all the (inevitably moneyed) pensioners in Sun City to be a harmless, golf-playing, merry lot. I was told that Diane Arbus would take the pictures.

She was already a famous 'visionary' photographer, thanks to her weird, disturbing pictures of dwarfs, giants and freaks and the marginalized in society. But my merry pensioners weren't marginalized by society; they'd chosen to marginalize themselves, and to have innocent, untroubled fun with what was left of their money and their lives. Arbus told me she didn't want to come with me at the same time, but once I'd done the interviews we should meet up at New York's Museum of Modern Art (which had a permanent exhibition of her work) so I could brief her about my interviewees.

In the MOMA café I found a small, thin, nervy woman wearing her famous Rolleiflex twin-lens reflex camera round her neck, attached by a piece of string. Why, I thought, was Diane wearing her Rollei? She never took pictures spontaneously: they were always meticulously planned. As I prattled on, giving her names and addresses, she just stared at me. I began to feel myself morphing into one of her freaks and began to stutter uncomfortably.

When my article – with her pictures – appeared in January '71 under the title 'The Affluent Ghetto' I was appalled. My cheery pensioners had been turned into surreal grotesques; they now feature frequently in Arbus hagiographies. A fictionalized biopic of Diane, *Fur*, was recently made starring Nicole Kidman.

Arbus's pictures were never, despite what she alleged, portraits of real human beings: they were always imaginative projections of her own tortured self. I realized, not for the first time, that I could never be a visionary artist: I would always be just a straightforward, hard-working journalist who tried to reflect, not my own angst, but the reality of other people's. And if that angst was absent – as it was with my sunny Sun City pensioners – I wouldn't be so cruel-hearted as to dream of imposing it. An American wit once said that, to journalists, human beings are just 'copy covered in skin', but there can be few photographers as ruthless as Arbus, who treated human beings as little more than the hapless and unwitting victims of her own self-therapy.

Not long afterwards the *Sunday Times* commissioning editor rang me: 'I'm rather upset. We must meet for a drink.' We did, and he told me why he was upset: 'Diane has just committed suicide.' Frankly I wasn't the least bit surprised; her self-therapy at the expense of her victims clearly didn't work. But hey, she was an artist and evidently, for artists, all is forgivable.

*

While an 'artist' can get away with fictionalizing their real-life subjects, it's rather less easy for a journalist, because he or she can't cite 'creative licence' as a justification. Of course, the more unscrupulous journalists do try to get away with 'fictionalizing' the lives of their subjects. A case in point was when a freelance sold a series to the *Sunday Mirror* purporting to tell the story of life on the run for Angela Reynolds, the wife of Bruce Reynolds who was the leader of the 1963 Great Train Robbery.

The material that the editor Michael Christiansen had paid for was dire stuff, illustrated with ludicrous pictures of a brassy Angela (she'd changed her name from Frances) sprawled on the bonnet of a Rolls, sipping champagne and wearing a blonde nylon wig. As the couple had spent four years on the run with their child – in Mexico, the South of France and Canada – Mrs Reynolds would've been as daft as a brush if she'd sashayed around looking like a B-movie gangster's moll.

And Angela Reynolds was not daft. Like her husband she was barely educated, but both had an acute natural intelligence. Unlike her husband, however, the red-haired Irish Liverpudlian was a deeply troubled, unstable woman, who lived in constant terror of the police and, perhaps more importantly, of her own inner demons.

'Can you do anything with this?' asked Christiansen, who was trying to move his paper upmarket and needed credibility. 'Not unless I spend time with her,' I told him. 'I'm not doing a rewrite job because I just don't believe a word of these quotes – I'll have to check whether any of them are even remotely authentic.' And so I did spend time with Angela, and it was clear that, far from living the life of Riley on the run as they fled from pillar to post with their young son, they constantly dreaded betrayal and the early-morning knock on the door. In reality it had been a miserable, terrified existence (well-deserved, many said, for Reynolds's role in the most sensational robbery of the twentieth century).

No one reading Angela's story as (truthfully) told by me would believe that life with a professional 'crim', as Reynolds has always described himself, was remotely glamorous. He is frank about the adrenaline hit he'd get when successfully pulling off a job, but Angela never even had that. She'd merely plunge deeper into depression and anxiety. True, she was paid £30,000 by the *Sunday Mirror* when Bruce was serving his sentence, which in those days enabled her to buy a nice house in Weybridge for around £8,000. But she was not – and is still not – happy, dogged as she is by a bipolar condition which requires lithium to stabilize her.

Not long ago I spoke to her on the phone but she didn't feel up to meeting me again: 'I'm not very well.' But I did meet up with Bruce in a trendy bar in Clerkenwell where he is something of a fixture. There was evident affection for the seventy-five-year-old 'crim' from the bar owner and the other regulars, but also, I suspected, a certain prestige for Clerkenwell's trendies in having a 'trophy' world-famous criminal like Bruce on the premises.

Reynolds, who drank only coffee, was very thin and his hands shook like an aspen. A ramrod back, goodish suit, bad teeth, slightly deaf, his skinny tortoise-like neck didn't fit his shirt. Age, poverty and prison had removed all traces of the dashing figure of yesteryear who'd inspired several books, films and documentaries.

I suddenly felt rather sorry for the old 'crim', however undeserving he might be. (And to his credit he made no attempt, as other 'crims' have, to solicit my sympathy.) I warmed to him much more than I did to 'Mad Frankie' Fraser, the violent gangland enforcer and murderer who, when I met him, boasted that two Home Secretaries had named him 'the most violent man in Britain' and who revels in his notoriety as one of Britain's most 'legendary gangsters'. Today 'Mad Frankie' markets 'Mad Frank' T-shirts and advertises guided tours round former gangland 'venues', like the Blind Beggar pub in London's East End. The repulsive 'Mad Frankie' is clearly a psychopath, which, for all his failings, the sad, defeated, unboastful Reynolds is not.

Companionably, Reynolds and I swapped tales of our childhood. I told him that someone like me, who'd been sealed up in boarding schools for most of my young life, did have some faint inkling of what it must be like to be in prison. I was obsessed with books and would read under the bedclothes after lights out with an illegal torch and, on hearing this, Bruce's gaunt face lit up. 'Exactly like me! I didn't have no torch, but once – I think after I'd absconded from Borstal – they used to keep a red light on in my cell all night. That didn't bother me, in fact I was pleased, 'cos I could read!'

His son Nick went to a state boarding school, but regularly used to visit his father in prison. On one of his visits he told Bruce that one of his schoolmates was 'an African' who told Nick that he was 'lucky': his own father had been imprisoned, tortured and had then been 'disappeared'. 'At least I can see you,' Nick told his father. The warders were 'very nice' when his son visited. Nick joined the Navy, served in the Falklands War, is now in a band and also works as an artist. His father is clearly proud of him, even though he acknowledges he was scarcely an ideal role model as a father.

Reynolds despises modern criminals – ' 'cos of the drugs'. Indeed, he insists that he was never involved in drugs himself, but when in prison, 'Well, there was grass everywhere. Cheered people up.' Bruce was served divorce papers while he was in jail for his second major conviction, being associated with a former 'crim' friend who manufactured amphetamines. 'I wasn't involved. I'd tell you if I was.' He paused. 'Wrong place, wrong time.' But despite the divorce and much unhappiness Bruce and Angela are now back together. 'Well, you go home with the one you came with, don't you?' explained Bruce stoically.

With a wry smile he suddenly remarked, 'You know, you couldn't stage a Great Train Robbery today, 'cos in them days the trains ran on time! They don't now, and accurate train times were essential for that job.'

Afterwards, we tried to get a taxi for me. He hailed one across the road but the traffic was so heavy we couldn't get to it. He put his arm round my shoulder, and we managed to get to the middle of the road when a passing empty cab nearly ran us down. I said, 'Well, that'd be a good headline: Taxi kills Great Train Robber.'

I got into the cab, Bruce kissed me, and waved at the driver.

Somehow I thought that the cabbie had recognized him: 'You know who he is then, do you?' I said. No, he didn't – but almost crashed when I told him it was Bruce Reynolds. The cab driver was an Algerian who'd been in this country for thirty years and who turned out to be an obsessive Great Train Robbery fan. 'I've watched the documentary made about it on the Discovery Channel thirty times! I can't believe it – this is wonderful! When I get home I'll tell the family that Bruce Reynolds actually waved at me!'

He was so ecstatic that when I got out, he jumped out too, rushed round to my side, refused to accept the £16 fare and kissed me several times on both cheeks. 'Thank you! Thank you! This has been one of the most wonderful moments of my life! Bruce Reynolds *waved at me*!'

Perhaps that's all that remains now for Bruce Reynolds after the robbery which netted nearly £40 million in today's money: a sick wife, and the obsessive adoration of an Algerian cabbie.

24

Po-boys and Chitterlings

The assassination of President Kennedy in 1963 was one of the 'Do you remember what you were doing when . . . ?' moments for my generation.

My boyfriend Michael (later my husband) was and is profoundly irritated by my obstinately tin ear for classical music; he'd decided that massive doses of grand opera or classical ballet would finally cure my affliction. Despite my grumbling reluctance, he'd dragged me off to Covent Garden to see Nureyev and Fonteyn dance in *Marguerite and Armand*. The experience was overwhelming and the whole audience, myself included, was in a state of high emotion.

But instead of the cast taking their bows, the huge red-and-gold curtains abruptly swung shut and a small figure in evening dress came to the front of the stage and announced the extraordinary news from Dallas: President Kennedy had been severely injured in a gun attack. A collective gasp of disbelieving horror swept the auditorium.

I was twenty-two, and had only just begun my career in Fleet Street; Michael was working at the BBC. We pushed our way out of the auditorium and rushed off to our respective newsrooms. In mine there was pandemonium. Conflicting reports were flooding in, everyone seemed to be running around and shouting at one another, 'The President's dead!' 'No, he's hanging on!' 'Jackie's dead!' 'No, she's alive!' 'The President's pulling through!' And then the final, appalling, confirmation.

I have to admit that my initial emotion was sheer, selfish excitement at being present, for the first time, in a great newspaper office when a major news story was breaking. True, four months earlier there'd been another high-profile death, that of the elderly Pope John XXIII. He'd been slowly dying of stomach cancer for some time and the *Express* had prepared a multi-page pullout about his life.

And every night when edition time loomed – and the paper still didn't know whether it could run its fulsome tributes – I'd hear the Production Editor thump the desk in frustration and yell, 'Die, you old bugger, die! Stop hangin' around!'

Obviously the reaction to the youthful Kennedy's murder was very different; later that night when the news of his death was confirmed many of us began to feel an almost personal grief. Although I'd never met Kennedy his assassination hit me much harder than did John Lennon's seventeen years later, despite the fact that, if only slightly, I'd known Lennon.

These days we're all aware of the darker side of the Kennedy electoral success – the vote-fixing, the nepotism, the compulsive adulteries, the Mafia assistance – but to the innocent young at the time Kennedy represented everything my generation wanted to be; to us he was inspiring, powerful, articulate, glamorous, striding the world like a colossus. When he was murdered it was as though a cosmic switch had been thrown; brightness fell from the air and we felt, like Browning in 'The Lost Leader', that there would never be 'glad, confident morning again'.

Perhaps it was that assassination which first drew me into American politics. I've covered virtually every Presidential campaign, including primaries and mid-terms, since 1980 when I went to cover the last gasps of Ted Kennedy's doomed attempt to win the Democrats' nomination from President Jimmy Carter. He was the only surviving Kennedy brother, the other two, Jack and Bobby, having been assassinated.

I didn't get the feeling he actually wanted to be President but, as always with the Kennedy clan, he was being driven by a sense of dynastic obligation. One evening I slipped into a seat on the campaign bus next to the dozing Senator. 'Are you enjoying this?' I asked him.

'No, of course not – I have back problems. The plane crash, you know.' (His back had never been pain-free since a crash in which the pilot and a Kennedy aide were killed.) 'Anyway, it is something that I have to do,' he said with a slow, sad, exhausted sigh. Because you're a Kennedy? 'Yeah.'

It struck me then how odd it was that America, so proudly egalitarian in theory, is actually as dynastic-minded as any ancient aristocratic European family listed in the *Almanach de Gotha*. The heir to an industrial or commercial empire will be named, say, 'Floyd Hackenberger III'; over here we never attach Roman numerals to a person's name unless they're a monarch or a Pope.

The first President elected from the already established Bush political dynasty was George Herbert Walker Bush. In 1988 Bush senior (father of George W.) was Vice-President and I joined him on his campaign. I knew I'd never get a 'one-on-one' with him because the most obscure of American local papers had far more chance of a coveted seat on a candidate's plane than a mere hack from Britain, where there are no votes to be garnered in a Presidential election.

Bush was flying in majestic style on Air Force Two, which was thick with carpeting, aides and armed security men, while I and the rest of the press pack were travelling in a chartered 727. Selected American political correspondents, celebrities in their own right, would join the Vice-President on his plane for airborne 'swings' through assorted states on the campaign trail.

One day, when we arrived in Fort Lauderdale, Florida (where the blue-rinse vote is essential for any Republican Presidential candidate), I nipped behind a hibiscus bush for a quick fag. The Vice-President's Press Secretary was British-born Pete Deeley, who had refused my repeated requests for a 'one-on-one'. 'Oh, Ann, forget it!' he'd reply exasperatedly.

To my dismay Pete suddenly turned up next to me behind the hibiscus bush. 'Eff off, Pete, I'm in the open air, I can have a cigarette if I want to!' (I'd learned of course by then that saying to Americans 'I want a fag' could lead to misunderstandings.)

'No, no, you've got the wrong idea!' he replied. 'I saw the smoke rising and knew someone hiding behind the bush must have a cigarette. Can I borrow one of yours?' It turned out that Deeley had initially refused the post of Press Secretary because he was a smoker and didn't feel he could do that gruelling job if he wasn't allowed to smoke on Air Force Two. 'So George, using his executive powers, allocated two "smoking" seats on the plane! But no one smokes these days, so if I want a cigarette I have to sit by myself feeling very self-conscious. Tell you what, why don't you join me on Air Force Two for the next couple of swings?'

So I did – to the fury and bafflement of those members of the American press corps who'd been denied the privilege. 'How did that *British* reporter get a seat on the next swing?'

'Don't tell 'em!' hissed Pete.

In just one fifteen-hour day we'd had breakfast in Florida, lunch in Alabama, supper in Louisiana; eaten (to me) strange Suth'n foods like chitterlings in Baton Rouge and catfish 'n' turnip greens on the Gulf coast; and glimpsed through the windows of our twelve-vehicle motorcade (plus police outriders) even stranger ones, with names like 'hush puppies' and 'po-boys', flashing past us on the neon signs of roadside diners as night fell.

Up in the brown-tweeded luxury of Bush Snr's 'flying country club' – 'How would you like your *filet mignon*, ma'am?' asked the deferential black waiter – it was all too easy to see why the trappings of power are so seductive and so hard to relinquish.

One of the advantages of being a journalist, a licensed intruder, is that you can dip into and out of these powerful and privileged lives and, because you don't belong there and won't be staying for long, you don't become addicted. Besides, as a foreign correspondent, your next job will usually prove to be a corrective to any corruption-by-luxury tendencies; in my case the next job was just as likely to be in a Lagos slum or a monsoon-swamped Indian village, or in Atlanta's ghettos writing a story about the serial murders of young black boys.

At that time white Anglo-Saxon Protestants, invariably extremely wealthy ones, seemed to have a lock on the Presidency. The one exception was Kennedy, a multi-millionaire 'white ethnic' Irish Catholic (though with thoroughly New England WASP tastes) who only narrowly won the Presidency. Twenty years ago it would have been inconceivable that a black man and a white woman could be competing to win their party's Presidential nomination; America's ability to adapt to a changing world is part of its enduring genius.

Vice-President George Herbert Walker Bush, a courteous and gentlemanly über-WASP – given to uttering weird preppy words like 'Gosh!' (when things were going well) and 'the deep do-dos' (when they weren't) – seemed to belong to another era. And of course conventional wisdom sniggered at Bush and opined that Joe Six-Pack (the ordinary voter slumped in front of the TV with a six-pack of Budweiser near his brawny arm) would *never* vote for what looked and sounded like an upper-class twit with a goofy Donald Duck grin.

Even his aides groaned when their man foolishly explained away his defeat in the Iowa Caucus by saying that he thought his supporters were too busy organizing their daughters' debutante dances to go and vote. 'Poor George,' everyone said; the hardscrabble farm folk of Iowa sure ain't into *debutante dances*!

And how silly 'poor George' looked when he tried to pretend he was a 'reg'lar guy' by eating in greasy-spoon cafés and driving forklift trucks for photo-ops. ('Where's your chauffeur?' yelled a bystander.) Whenever Bush made the effort to come down to the level of Joe Six-Pack by declaring that his favourite food was not *filet mignon* but the pork rinds and Tabasco sauce so beloved of the good ole boys, it was always toe-curlingly unconvincing.

Americans like to deny that social class matters that much to them: gender and, especially, race are the hot-button issues for them. But Bush won – perhaps because Joe Six-Pack didn't despise the WASP upper classes as much as Conventional Wisdom assumed: often he wanted to emulate them, once he had the money.

During the supposedly egalitarian and taboo-breaking Seventies I worked briefly for *Playboy* magazine. I was astonished to find that, after the nudes, the most popular section of the magazine was 'The Playboy Advisor', to which men living in Wisconsin called Kowalski wrote asking whether it was 'good form' to kiss a girl while wearing a hat (I kid you not), and how to pronounce 'Châteauneuf du Pape'. These 'carefree young swingers' were, in fact, desperately insecure social climbers, who feared being snubbed by snobbish maître d's in linen-napkined restaurants almost as much as they feared being laughed at for sexual ineptitude.

The fact is that most American voters don't live in New York, Boston, San Francisco or Los Angeles: they live in 'fly-over' territory – the vast lands which most of the American chatterati only see from 35,000 feet up if they choose to peer down from a plane window. Which is why Conventional Wisdom, usually determined by the chatterati, so often gets it wrong. When the despised Richard Nixon won a landslide, Pauline Kael, the famous film critic for the chatterati bible, the *New York Times*, declared disbelievingly, 'The figures must be wrong! I've never met *anyone* who voted for Nixon!'

On one occasion when Air Force Two had just taken off from yet another state, Bush Snr came back to the Deeley–Leslie ash-strewn sin-bin. 'Please go away, Mr Vice-President! I'm trying to save the sanity of your Press Secretary!' I told him. And, after lecturing us in his reedy patrician Yankee voice on our undeniably filthy habit, he did indeed give me a one-on-one interview. It was of no great import because this sixty-three-year-old grandfather was understandably exhausted, his blue eyes now pink and watery, his lopsided, ever-apologetic smile ragged with over-use. 'You've really got to have stamina for this. You know, Ann, I've had only one twenty-four-hour period off in the last six weeks.' And the election itself was still several months away.

Is this trial-by-exhaustion really the best way to elect the most powerful man in the world? 'Maybe, maybe not.' The ragged smile slipped from his face and he suddenly looked very old. 'But you gotta play by the rules of the game and this is the only game in town. You gotta keep going until you or the other feller drops.' And of course he did keep going and became the 41st President of the United States.

In 2000 I was covering the Presidential campaign of his son, George W., then the Governor of Texas. How could I get a one-on-one with 'Dubya' (which is how the letter W is pronounced in the 'Don't Mess with Texas' Lone Star state)? Clearly there could be no hibiscus-bush-and-illicit-fags scenario with him. He only liked clean-living folks around him and I didn't think I would qualify.

His Amazonian Texan Press Secretary Karen Hughes was, as Pete Deeley had been, routinely badgered by me for a one-on-one. 'Oh, Ann, forget it!' she'd equally routinely reply.

But I'd already learned that George W. adored gossip. When he became President one of his 'spiritual advisers' was profoundly disappointed by the fact that Bush's faith was not in the least bit introspective or ideologically based and, indeed, that in private he could hardly be bothered to talk about God at all. His public 'God talk' was largely an attempt to keep his core constituency of funda-mentalist Christians on side. (Just as Tony Blair's coyness in office about his Christianity was, in secular 'we-don't-do-God' Britain, electorally expedient.)

So every time Bush strolled down to the back section of the plane to josh with the full-time campaign journalists on the flight, I'd try to be in the middle of a gossipy anecdote whenever he passed my seat. The American correspondent sitting beside me was often half asleep from exhaustion, but I'd tell, and sometimes retell, my experiences with the rich 'n' famous and, preferably, the randy, undeterred by the occasional snores of my neighbour. 'So, there was Salvador Dali in front of me with his trousers round his ankles . . . And then Jane Fonda made this *amazing* remark. . . . But then . . .'

I noticed that 'Dubya' was beginning to slow down his peregrinations when he passed my seat. One day he stopped and asked, 'So what happened next?' I replied, 'Governor, I won't give you the punch line unless you give me a one-on-one!' Karen Hughes rolled her eyes wearily and ushered him away. My neighbour, who'd by now woken up, said, 'Nice try! Won't work of course.' Ten minutes later an aide came to the back of the plane and said to me, 'The Governor says he will see you now.'

Almost the first question he asked me was: 'Have you met Camilla Parker Bowles? What's she really like?' I admit I did somewhat exaggerate my 'friendship' with her (though she has sent me Christmas cards over the years and invited me to the occasional party), but he was delighted by my apparent 'insider' status. And was duly astonished when I said that if only Prince Charles had married her when he first fell in love with this warm, unpretentious and earthy country-woman, a lot of misery would have been averted, and when I further explained, in some detail, why I'd never been a fan of 'that neurotic dingbat' Princess Diana.

The jokey, charming, squinty-eyed fellow sprawled on the seat beside me seemed very happy to carry on with this kind of over-the-fence gossiping. But there's a danger in getting on too well with an interviewee and thereby losing control of your agenda. You have to make it clear at some point that you're not his or her new Best Friend: you're a journalist, a quintessential outsider.

To break the affability spell I decided to try to rile him by referring to a disastrous interview he'd given which proved that he hadn't a clue about foreign policy issues – and that we foreigners thought that such blithe ignorance was unforgivable in a man who intended to become the undisputed leader of the free world. 'Governor, we in Europe think you're at least two sandwiches short of a picnic: you confused Slovakia with Slovenia, called the Greeks "Grecians", and didn't even know the name of the leader of Pakistan, the world's latest nuclear power.'

His response: 'What does being "two sandwiches short of a picnic" mean?' I explained: 'Well, it means you're too stupid and uninformed for the job.' Far from taking offence, as I'd hoped, he responded with a mischievous 'heh-heh!' chuckle, 'Of course, you'd have to adapt that saying for different states: "two clams short of a chowder" in New England, "two ribs short of a barbecue" in Texas, "two . . ." He began 'adapting' the jibe according to the differing culinary tastes of assorted states; my God, I thought, we've still got about another forty-seven states to go. My cunning plan – to make him angry – was a total flop; he was running away with the interview, and he knew it. It was the first indication I personally had of how politically sly he was, how skilfully he could use one-on-one charm to de-fang sceptics.

Quite reasonably, he agreed that having been Governor of Texas did not in itself give one much foreign policy experience but added that the team he'd assembled had experience in spades. They included Colin Powell, Dick Cheney, Condoleezza Rice and a host of highly informed intellectual heavyweights. (This conversation was of course before 9/11 and the Iraq War.)

I'd got on the plane assuming (as British newspapers had reported) that this failed Texan oilman was nothing but an amiable nincompoop (the Bombastic Bushkin) with a fruit-fly attention span, who was so stupid he couldn't read a book. Not true – he voraciously read political biographies – and the British media usually neglected to mention that he had been to Yale and Harvard Business School and that in fact his grades had been marginally better than his Democrat rival Al Gore's (although neither's academic scores were outstanding).

In short, I'd assumed he was an archetypal spoiled rich kid born with 'a silver foot in his mouth' (a jibe directed at his father for his clumsy rhetoric, a trait his son inherited) and perhaps with 'a silver spoon up his nose' – rumours of youthful cocaine-taking abounded, which he refused to confirm or deny. And now this wealthy born-again Texan with low-wattage brainpower intended to become the leader of the only superpower on Earth.

But who says you have to be a pointy-headed intellectual to be an effective leader? In fact Roosevelt, one of the most successful leaders in American history, was once described as having 'a second-class mind, but a first-class temperament' (a description applied to Tony Blair by Roy Jenkins). And George W.'s temperament seemed so sunny that it struck me as almost abnormal.

I told him I'd never met an ambitious politician who seemed so comfortable in his skin: 'Sure, I'm comfortable in my skin. I don't worry too much, I just get on with things.' He didn't seem driven by a longing for adulation from the crowd (and from silly women with big hair), as Clinton was, nor was he driven by an almost feral obsession with power, as Nixon was.

Above all, watching him on the road, I detected in him an unerring instinct for what the ordinary (and therefore despised by the chatterati) 'folks' of 'fly-over' country wanted. So what that he strangled his syntax like a serial killer, and uttered baffling statements like, 'I know how hard it is to put food on your family'? Middle America's 'folks' aren't stupid, they knew what he meant, and they weren't too hung up on grammar and 'sophisticated' articulacy themselves.

Given the dysfunctional nature of most politicians' family life, Little Georgie (his mother's name for him) seemed almost preternaturally happy with his wife Laura, a former librarian, his family and his apparently equally affable God. No detectable dark nights of the soul there. Perhaps this lack of dark nights meant that once he'd embarked on what he believed to be right – like the Iraq War – he seemed utterly unabashed by any of its subsequent disasters.

Unlike previous Republican leaders, he didn't seem to be driven by hate for non-Christians, ethnic minorities or even gays: at times, when listening to Republican rhetoric in the past, I'd been reminded of a mocking ditty by the Texan Lounge Lizards group entitled 'Jesus Loves Me, But He Can't Stand You'.

When one such leading Republican declared that all gays were 'kleptomaniacs' and 'sinners', George W. chided him: 'The truth is we are all sinners and the degree of the sin ought to be left to the

Almighty.' Admittedly the Bible Belt had been trying to force Bush to propose a Constitutional Amendment banning 'gay marriage' if and when he came into office. As one furious slogan put it, 'If God had intended gays to marry, he would have created Adam and Bruce.' At first he gave the Christians little joy, muttering on about how marriage law was traditionally a matter for the individual states, not the federal government, and then his private pollsters found that 4 million Christian fundamentalists hadn't bothered to vote in 2000, believing Bush to be too 'liberal'.

So in order to make them pull up their holy socks and head to the polls for his re-election bid in 2004, he threw them a lump of read meat, promising them this Constitutional Amendment. (He knew, of course, that such an Amendment would need a two-thirds majority in Congress, which it wouldn't get.)

He had another problem with the Bible Belt folks over the issue of HIV/Aids. Once he became President, Little Georgie was determined to spend record amounts of money on trying to alleviate the problem, especially in Africa. (Bob Geldof insists that Bush, unsung, has done more for Africa than the ethnically empathizing Clinton ever did: the latter, he says, certainly talked the talk, but actually did 'diddley-squat'.)

But the Bible Belt firmly believed that the HIV/Aids scourge was divinely ordained. 'Perverted lifestyles' had earned 'God's punishment', according to the Reverend Jerry Falwell, leader of the Moral Majority. 'The scripture is clear. We do reap it in our flesh when we violate the laws of God.' But Dubya, with a political skill he's rarely credited with, put the 'let-'em-suffer-and-die' fundamentalists on the back foot by invoking scripture himself, piously reminding them of the parable of the Good Samaritan; it was their Christian duty to help the afflicted and not to pass by on the other side. The discomfited Christians grumbled mightily but, in effect, gave up.

One day, when Bush overheard me making a mildly disparaging remark about him, he looked knowingly at me ('my favourite Britisher') and remarked with a wry grin, 'You know, I've been "misunderestimated" all my life.' His habitual self-deprecation appealed to me because, for an American politician, it seemed so refreshingly 'British'. And yes, I did believe that he was gravely 'misunderestimated', especially by Europeans.

But Bush's political skill, and his instinctive ability to connect with 'folks', which I'd witnessed on the road, seemed to have totally deserted him after he was ensconced in the White House. Take the Hurricane Katrina disaster: he airily remarked that no one could have foretold that the New Orleans levees would break. This was patently untrue since the Federal Emergency Management Agency (FEMA) had, years before, produced a report predicting that the levees would not withstand more than a Category 3 storm – Katrina was a Category 4. And he'd cut the funding for FEMA.

And then – and this caused my jaw to drop in disbelief – the President held a photo-op with multi-millionaire Republican Senator Trent Lott, one of whose homes had been destroyed by the flood. The President chortled, 'The good news is – and it's hard for some to see it now – that out of this chaos is going to come a fantastic Gulf Coast, like it was before. Out of the rubble of Trent Lott's house – he's lost his entire house – there's going to be a fantastic house! And I'm looking forward to sitting on the porch!' More chortles, more chuckles. He was then photographed playing a guitar and laughing.

Trent Lott, whose new porch the President was looking forward to lounging on, had recently been forced to resign as Senate Majority Leader when he said that he regretted that racial segregation had been abolished in the South. And of course the vast majority of those who were dying as their President chuckled on television with his wealthy, segregation-minded old chum were Louisiana's poverty-stricken, abandoned blacks. It was a moment of such insensitivity that it beggared belief.

But perhaps I should have been forewarned of his crassness by one particular incident. I had always been ambivalent about the death penalty, although the *Mail*'s readers were vehemently in favour, largely because they believed it was a deterrent. In 1986 I went to America to look into the issue in depth for the paper and interviewed six murderers (four of whom have since been executed) on two Death Rows, one of which was in Texas. It became clear to me that the death penalty was not a deterrent (except to people who are unlikely to commit murder anyway), not least because none of the killers I interviewed actually knew in advance whether the state in which they committed their crime had the death penalty or not.

One particularly grisly, drug-fuelled double murder during a robbery had been committed by a young, poster-pretty Texan woman called Karla Faye Tucker. She was twenty-six, had once had dreams of Olympic stardom, and had been on Death Row in the tiny town of Gatesville for two years. To reach the Mountain View Correctional Centre, I drove south for three hours from the glittering skyscrapers of booming Dallas and into another, older America: small rural towns, huge windy horizons, men in cowboy hats riding distant ranges under a fiercely hot Southern sun. The men in the cowboy hats, I assumed, were very much in favour of the death penalty.

As, ironically, Karla Faye herself had once been: 'Like, you know, maybe I'd be watchin' television and I'd hear someone got the death penalty and I'd think, "Well, he sure deserves to die for *that*!" But now here *I'm* sittin' on Death Row,' she told me in her breathy, little-girl drawl. 'I reckon no one can really know whether that person deserves to die or not. You gotta know whether they were out of their minds at the time, and whether they've changed. At the time I didn't know what I was doin', my head was too full of dope.'

Now, full of remorse, she was clean of drugs, was educating herself and studying for exams, and had become a born-again Christian. Although I've always been suspicious of 'jailhouse religion' (whereby criminals 'discover' God while inside, and promptly forget about Him when they're out and free to resume their old ways), something about Karla Faye made me believe she should not be killed by the state.

Over a decade later, George W. ordered her execution by lethal injection. Even the Gatesville prison staff, who are not by nature or by calling soft-on-crime liberals, had given evidence to prove that for the last fourteen years Karla Faye had been 'a model prisoner'.

Among the many who campaigned for clemency on her behalf were Pope John Paul II, the Italian Prime Minister, major figures in the UN and – most unusually – two very prominent ultra-conservatives, the tele-evangelist Pat Roberts and the Republican Newt Gingrich. (I even contributed to Amnesty International's campaign myself by donating the photographs that I'd taken of her behind bars twelve years earlier. The main problem I had with taking her picture was that she and a fellow Death Row inmate, Pam Perillo, insisted not only on putting on make-up first – 'We wanna look purty!' – but also smiling radiantly like prom queens into my lens. 'Sorry, girls, but try not to look so happy: I don't think it's, er, appropriate in the circumstances'.)

It was all to no avail: George W. had his sights set on becoming the Republican Presidential nominee. In 1998, after fourteen years on Death Row, Karla Faye had to die for redneck votes and, at the age of thirty-eight, she was duly killed by Dubya's fiat, the first woman to be executed in Texas since the American Civil War.

But what really shocked me was Bush's reaction to her final appeals. A conservative commentator had interviewed Bush for a magazine and asked him what he thought of Karla Faye's television interview with CNN's Larry King. Bush replied, 'He asked her real difficult questions like, "What would you say to Governor Bush?"' The magazine interviewer then asked Bush what Karla Faye's answer was, and was taken aback when Bush began imitating her trailer-park-trash accent. '"Please," Bush whimpers, his lips pursed in mock desperation, "please don't kill me!"' The interviewer's article continued: 'I must have looked shocked – ridiculing the pleas of a condemned prisoner who has since been executed seems odd and cruel – but he immediately stopped smirking.'

While I'd once been too enamoured of Dubya, I'd never been enamoured of his predecessor, the manipulative and mendacious Bill Clinton, or of his cold, clever and equally mendacious wife Hillary. When he first ran for the Presidency Clinton used to claim that his hero was Kennedy, and I noted, when on the campaign with him in 1992, that whenever we crossed north of the Mason-Dixon line his accent would acquire JFK's Bostonian vowels: it would be his forelock-tugging tribute to that earlier political dynasty. However, south of the line his accent would become noticeably more Southern-fried.

He'd drop his G's, assume a cotton-pickin' drawl and come out with impenetrable rural folk sayings like: 'Bush don't know "come here from sick 'um" as far as agriculture is concerned!' No, I didn't know what that meant – and neither, I noticed, did the crowd at one particular rally in Georgia. Hardly surprising as they were comfortable white suburbanites, not rural shack-dwellers who chew tobacco on the front porch. The 'sick 'um' line, however, scored a palpable hit in tobacco-growing North Carolina.

If no man is a hero to his valet – because the latter's seen too much of him – neither is a politician a hero to the exhausted hack on the road, who's attended far too many 'town hall' meetings, television studios and rallies with him or her in the course of an electoral campaign. There are only so many renditions of rally theme tunes – 'Don't Worry, Be Happy!' (Bush Snr), 'Don't Stop Thinking about Tomorrow!' (Bill Clinton), 'Things Can Only Get Better!' (Tony Blair) – that you can be obliged to listen to every day without reaching for the Nurofen and the earplugs. And only so many 'stump' speeches – 'No Child Left Behind!' 'For the Many Not the Few!' 'Forward Not Back' – that you can endure on a daily basis without longing for an escape into the car park for a soothing fag.

You can become utterly impervious to a politician's alleged charm. Particularly, in my case, where Clinton was concerned. His ability to survive in the face of all odds seemed almost superhuman; the late-night TV satirist Conan O'Brien defined Bill Clinton as 'our first cartoon President. He ran off cliffs, was crushed by anvils, and flattened by turn-of-the-century trains. Yet moments later, we always saw him, just like Daffy Duck, completely reassembled, and eagerly pursuing his next crazy scheme.'

Despite endless scandals, usually suffixed '-gate', the constant 'bimbo eruptions', the questionable financial deals (any one of which would have destroyed a better, less ruthless and more honourable man), he managed to defy all the rules of Greek tragedy which require that in the end you have to pay the penalty for your flaws and your hubris. 'Whenever the smoke cleared,' said O'Brien in amused bewilderment, 'Clinton remained standing, covered in soot, and looking at us slightly chagrined . . .'

And usually uttering some words of generalized 'contrition' or defiance, sometimes asking publicly for God's forgiveness for his (that weasel word) 'mistakes' – which, of course, he would promptly commit again. I was in Washington for his State of the Union address in 1995 at a time when his 'bimbo' activities, not to mention his questionable financial arrangements, were in full swing. His first year in office was disastrous and he was at that point the most unpopular man in American politics.

I wrote then that there was something sad, undignified, demeaning about watching him trying, like Rory Bremner's parody of Britain's then Prime Minister John Major, to remind the irritated and dismissive voters that 'I'm still here!' The pleading subtext of his speech was: 'I'll say anything, do anything, co-operate with anyone, just to hang on to this job. Want me to be a caring, sharing, liberal cheerleader for militant gays, feminists, ethnic politics, just like Hillary? You *don't*? Oh, okay, no problem. I'll be whatever you want, do whatever it takes . . .'

But however dishonest or slippery his tactics, this chronically undisciplined and self-indulgent narcissist always got away with it. As he did when I attended a 'Prayer Breakfast' in the lavish white-and-gold East Room at the White House, shortly after he confessed that he'd lied on oath about his relationship with 'that woman, Miss Lewinsky'.

There I heard, with growing disbelief, Big Bubba Bill, gnawing his lower lip to demonstrate his trademark 'sincerity', a hint of moistness in his puffy and crinkled eyes, declare that he now had a 'broken spirit', and that 'if my repentance is genuine and sustained, and if I can maintain both a broken spirit and a strong heart, then good can come of this for our country, as well as for me and my family'. The God-fearing congregation adored the whole nauseatingly hypocritical shebang, as he knew it would.

We were told that his 'moral adviser', the civil rights leader (and egotistical self-publicist) the Reverend Jesse Jackson, was regularly 'counselling' Clinton and his family in the White House, kneeling beside him in prayer to beg for God's forgiveness. At the time God was being somewhat overworked on the forgiveness front in the American political/sexual arena, not least in Jesse Jackson's own case. It was revealed that week that the Reverend – the 'devoted' husband who declared that his campaigns were not narrowly pol-itical, but 'moral crusades' – was conducting an affair at the time that he was 'counsellin'' and 'prayin'' with Bill in the White House. Jackson now had a twenty-month-old daughter born out of wedlock and living in California. The charismatic Reverend's black followers didn't mind, because he shared another characteristic with his equally charismatic friend Bill: he never made a mistake about which par-ticular emotional G-spot a specific audience might be susceptible to.

The dismaying fact is that, even after impeachment, Clinton never paid for his political or criminal (or indeed sexual) misdeeds with loss of office, the desire for which was the driving force of his life.

Nor did he serve time in jail for perjury. But many who worked loyally for him, who had hole-in-corner affairs with him, who financed him illegally, who allegedly laundered funds for him and who (often against their better instincts) lied and cheated for him, paid very heavily indeed. An actuarially improbable number of them ended up in jail and had their careers and reputations unmercifully smeared – especially if they were women whom the 'feminist' couple in the White House believed were exploitable and expendable. Yet for some bizarre and deluded reason the American (and British) liberal left saw, and still see, Bill as a man of political – if not sexual – principle.

This is a couple of no fixed belief, other than in power; and yes, of course, politics is a dirty business, but the first time I felt real revulsion for the Clintons was during Bill's first Presidential campaign. And, as with George W. Bush, it involved the cynical use of the death penalty as a campaign strategy.

Clinton's campaign strategists had spotted a potentially dangerous problem: Southern white voters, who were greatly in favour of the death penalty, were drifting away because they suspected that Bill and his 'uppity' wife might be 'soft on crime'.

No problem. Bill took time out from a hectic Presidential campaign to fly back to Arkansas to sign the death warrant for the execution of a black inmate on Death Row. As State Governor it was in Clinton's power to commute the sentence. But that of course would have been electorally hazardous. No matter that Ricky Rae Rector was virtually lobotomized (after he accidentally shot himself during a robbery) and was now so mentally incapable and so unaware of what the death warrant meant that, when he was served his final meal, he said he'd like to keep the dessert 'for when I return'. Of course he never did return for his dessert – but the Suth'n 'fry-em' vote was safe.

As Joe Giarratano, a convicted killer I interviewed six years earlier on Death Row in Virginia, put it, 'There's always votes to be had in blood lust.' Shades of George W. and the case of Karla Faye Tucker.

Late one night over a cheeseburger in some bleakly anonymous Michigan motel where we were 'ronning' (campaign-speak for Resting Over Night) I tackled a Clinton aide: 'So your man believes in executing the mentally incapable to win votes. Very noble!' The aide yawned, then said, 'Well, Ricky Rae Rector's life was worthless anyway. You could say we did him a favour.'

When in 1998 the black writer Toni Morrison, who won the Nobel Prize for Literature, described Clinton as 'our first black President', Bill, with characteristic moist-eyed hypocrisy, declared that that 'title' meant more to him than a Nobel Peace Prize would. Did Ms Morrison remember, or know, that the ruthless Clinton had executed a hopelessly addle-brained black man just to ensure his own white redneck vote?

In December 2001 Clinton, now out of office, gave the BBC's prestigious annual Dimbleby Lecture, to which I was invited 'plus guest'. I rang my daughter Katharine: I thought that as a firmly left-leaning recent Oxford graduate she might be interested in coming along to see him in action and anyway, as I told her, 'I want you to actually meet the old tart!' At that time Katharine favoured (possibly on a point of principle) dingy clobber purchased from Oxfam, laddered tights, a certain amount of facial ironmongery, and wore her hair in dreadlocks, with orange-tipped ends. There was no possibility of persuading my spirited daughter to dress more appropriately for what the BBC had promised would be a 'distinguished and stellar' audience. 'But do try to look *clean*!'

'Oh, Mummy, for heaven's sake!'

It was indeed stellar: wall-to-wall celebrities from politics, academia, theatre and films – all (bar my daughter) done up to the nines and all chirruping with excitement at the prospect of seeing Clinton in the flesh. Even the BBC 'nibbles' were, for once, stellar.

As I swept through the pre-speech drinks party, I introduced Katharine to as many celebrities as I could lay my hands on. I launched myself, with her in tow, on Jeremy Irons: 'Katharine, meet Jeremy Irons, who used to work as my gardener when he couldn't get any acting jobs: he did *wonders* for my apple tree! And he looked *gorgeous* doing it!' I trilled. I have dined out on this 'Jeremy-Irons-was-my-gardener' story for years, but the now very distinguished Irons, while agreeing that he did, indeed, on occasion clip my shrubs, never seems entirely thrilled to be reminded of the fact. When we were both on Andrew Marr's BBC Sunday morning programme, I repeated the well-worn 'Oscar-Winner-gardening-for-Ann-Leslie-while-unemployed' tale: Jeremy's smile was, I thought, a trifle strained.

And then came the Main Event: Clinton strolled on stage and the audience went mad with excitement. The fraudulent old Loin-Stirrer-in-Chief had done it again, before he'd uttered a single clichéd word. The speech – on 'The Struggle for the Soul of the Twenty-first Century' – was as stuffed full of banalities as we were with BBC nibbles (though I accept that few politicians' speeches are otherwise). On display, the usual Clinton am-dram tricks which I'd got to know so well over the years: the 'thoughtful' stroking of the nose, the 'almost-overcome-with-emotion' biting of his lower lip, the little 'love-me-because-I-love-you' puppy-dog smiles.

When he'd finished, the audience were utterly ecstatic. Indeed, several of them were actually in tears. They leapt up in a mass standing ovation. Katharine whispered, 'Are you going to stand up? I'm not. That was crap.' I agreed with her – 'And anyway, I don't give standing ovations lightly.' We remained resolutely seated. We were the only 'refuseniks' present: even the historian Professor Peter Hennessy, whose opinion of the speech was as scornfully dismissive as ours, admitted that he eventually succumbed to the mass hysteria: 'In the end I'm afraid I did stand up – I really admired you and your daughter for resisting!'

But the main aim of this event as far as I was concerned was for Katharine to meet Clinton. This proved difficult as he was surrounded by luvvies drooling over what one of them declared had been 'the most inspirational speech ever!' Better than Martin Luther King's 'I have a dream'? Mandela's Rivonia Trial defence? Nehru's 'At the midnight hour . . .'? Oh, grow up.

I tried to rack my brains for something I could say to Clinton which would not be insulting. In 1992 I had been in Little Rock, Arkansas, on the night of the Presidential Election results, standing in the midst of a vast crowd outside the Governor's Mansion, all of us gazing up at the giant TV screens broadcasting the results live. When Ohio's vote came in – 'Ohio has taken Clinton over the top!' – the Little Rock crowd became incandescent with joy.

Now, fighting my way through the celebs after the lecture, I grabbed Clinton's arm, while determinedly hanging on to Katharine's: 'Mr President, I must say one of the most exciting moments of my life was being in Little Rock the night Ohio went over the top!'

He turned to me: 'Oh great, you were *there*! Wasn't that just *wonderful*?'

'And, Mr President, I'd like you to meet my daughter . . .' At this point his Secret Service detail took one look at Katharine, the ironmongery, the general attire, the dreadlocks, and decided that she was clearly one of those anti-capitalist, anti-American anarchists who trash Starbucks at WTO summits.

Naturally, a Secret Service agent needed to 'disable' her – which he tried to do by thrusting an elbow so firmly under her jaw that she was nearly knocked over backwards. Equally naturally, my daughter took offence at this manoeuvre, and thumped the Secret Service man in the kidneys. 'Mr President, she's my *daughter*!' I protested. Laughing, he told the security men, 'She's her *daughter*!' Sadly, thanks to this minor fracas, she never did get the chance to talk to the 'old tart' in person. But I consoled myself with the thought that being roughed up by the American Secret Service might perhaps add to her street cred.

Of course, in a televisual age no politician can do without charisma. The days are long gone when a reticent, unshowy figure like Clement Attlee could survive Churchill's famous jibe: 'An empty taxi drew up outside 10 Downing Street and Mr Attlee got out.' Bill Clinton's allegedly charismatic rhetoric is merely proof to me of 'the potency of cheap music'. But then I have never been much into music, cheap or otherwise.

25

'Have you come far?'

The Great Wall of China is a must-do sight for tourists – and for world leaders.

In 1977 Margaret Thatcher was not yet a world leader, and we second-rank hacks accompanying her as Leader of the Opposition on her first trip to China, three months after the death of Chairman Mao, couldn't be sure that she ever would be. Significantly, those chosen to cover her visit were mostly either gossip columnists or women reporters like me, who were expected to be able to chat knowledgeably about Carmen rollers with this blonde, provincial grocer's daughter who wore pussy-cat bows and the kind of outfits favoured by Rotary Club wives.

If our editors didn't yet rate Thatcher, neither did the Chinese. Powerful women weren't much admired by the mandarins: they had long, unadmiring historical memories of their own Dragon Ladies – like Empress Wu, the Dowager Empress Cixi, and Jiang Qing, Mao's widow, the 'White-boned Demon' who had whipped up the murderous excesses of the Red Guards in the Cultural Revolution and was now languishing in prison. But although gambling was forbidden, the Chinese, being inveterate gamblers at heart, usually took a punt on foreign opposition figures if there were the slightest chance that they might come into power.

Protocol demanded that a 'distinguished foreign friend', albeit a woman, must endure baffling multi-course banquets ('What on earth is Five Auspicious Carp Lucky Dish?' whispered a colleague) and also, of course, the compulsory trip to the Great Wall. Mrs Thatcher's visit provided the first glimpse the Chinese would have of the iron will of the future Iron Lady.

The Chinese would routinely take 'foreign friends' like Mrs T. to Badaling where in places the Wall is very steep and slippery; they would then mischievously challenge them by saying, 'Ah, President Nixon, he reach that point!' There would then be a recitation of the distances covered by other foreign friends: '. . . And *he* reach even further, to *that* point.' They repeated to her Chairman Mao's saying: 'He who does not reach top of Great Wall is no great man!' To which her crisp response was, 'It should be changed to no great *leader*!' Oh, how they laughed. (A sure sign that they were embarrassed: the dead Mao was still officially worshipped, and to criticize his sacred sayings in public was the equivalent of being disrespectful about the *a-hadith* of the Prophet Mohammed.) Mrs Thatcher, wearing court shoes, didn't initially look as if she were keen on entering the Great Wall Stakes. 'I do not intend to be athletic, my dear,' she informed me beforehand. But then came the challenge: 'But Mr Edward Heath, he reach *that* point!'

When they uttered the word 'Heath', a glint came into her eye and she shot off up the Wall like a Blue Streak rocket. Awestruck, my government minder Comrade Ma murmured, 'She cannot reach her goal, not in those shoes!' I replied, 'You don't know Mrs Thatcher – she could be on stilts and she'd still get further than her enemy Ted Heath.' And so it proved. Unsuitable shoes? Pah! Some of us tried to catch up with her. When one puffing and gasping photographer in sturdy desert boots arrived at her side, the court-shoed one informed him crisply, 'You are very unfit!' As he was a sinewy Vietnam War veteran, he felt a bit miffed. When I finally caught up with her, I remarked dourly on her fearsome stamina. 'You either have it or you don't,' she carolled. 'But you have to keep in training, you know,' she added firmly.

The Great Wall Stakes could be remarkably revealing, not of the Great Wall itself, but of the 'distinguished foreign friends' obliged to visit it. Which brings me to the Queen . . .

I went to China with her on the first-ever Royal Tour of the country in 1986, and not because I enjoyed Royal Tours: they're both exhausting and boring, so I agreed to cover them only when they were taking place in countries which interested me, like Russia, South Africa, Thailand, Saudi Arabia and indeed China. And this China tour promised to be fascinating, because it was a somewhat contentious visit geopolitically (and, in the case of Prince Charles, personally: he once told me 'other members of my family can go there, but I won't, because I'm disgusted by Chinese behaviour in Tibet').

At Badaling the Queen, also in court shoes, did not deign to venture up the ski-slope section of the Wall. Instead she took out her little Leica camera and innocently turned to someone in her entourage: 'Oh, *do* take a photograph of me, because otherwise no one will believe I've been here!' *What?* Her Majesty was surrounded by hundreds of the world's media, all of whom would splash these historic photos of her on the Great Wall around the globe. Did she really think that 'no one will believe I've been here'?

Perhaps the only way you can survive in her tedious and taxing job is to do what the Royal Family habitually does: 'ostrich' yourself. Whenever the Queen and Prince Philip are faced with a horrendous situation (and of course there've been many, not least the one caused by Charles and Diana), they retreat, as one Palace insider put it, 'into ostrich mode: stick your head under the sand and hope you don't see anything and that the whole ghastly thing passes you by'. If you can 'ostrich out' the world's media (journalists, according to Mao, belonged to the 'stinking Ninth Category' of class enemies), then perhaps you can deceive yourself into thinking that, even though you're standing in full view of the world on the Great Wall, no one will believe you've been there.

As a member of the 'stinking Ninth Category', I've met the Queen several times over the years and have each time reminded myself of the protocol for 'chatting' to Her Majesty: don't speak until you're spoken to, and when the 'conversation' is deemed to be over, the Queen will hold out a gloved hand, her eyes will glaze over, and she will move on to the next recipient of her standard opening line, 'Have you come far?'

But I wasn't prepared for the protocol I should adopt when being introduced, while wearing flip-flops on a Bahamian beach, to her snobbish, spoiled and (to me) spiteful sister, Princess Margaret.

I'd never expected to meet her and certainly didn't warm to the idea, especially after one of her former lovers, a blue-blooded night-club pianist and lounge lizard called Robin Douglas-Home, kept telling me – usually when drunk (as he often was) – that his royal lover was '*so* witty, *so* amusing! When I'd go round to Kensington Palace for you-know-what, she had a little hand-bell which she'd use to signal to the butler, using a code she and the butler had agreed. One ring meant, "Don't come in." And then, when we'd finished, she'd ring it again three times which meant, "You can come in now, we're finished! And we'd like some tea." Oh, she was so amusing!' H'mm.

I was never quite sure whether to believe him: Robin was one of those tiresome men who never stop boasting about their affairs. This pale, thin, professionally 'charming' but, to me, rather unattractive man alleged that his many conquests included Jackie Kennedy while she was America's First Lady. He'd been married to the top Sixties model Sandra Paul, but was always on the hunt for yet another A-list trophy lay. He told me, with pride, that his friend Frank Sinatra fancied Sandra and had made suggestions to him about her . . . 'Oh, God, Robin, don't tell me you thought you might pimp Sandra for your sleazy chum!' (After he left her, Sandra, who's now a successful novelist, went on to marry four times in all. Her final spouse, to whom she's now been happily married for over thirty years, is the Tory politician Michael Howard, an infinitely nicer and more amusing man than Robin ever was.)

One evening at Annabel's, the then fashionable nightclub in Berkeley Square, I suddenly decided I'd had enough: I snappily told Robin that not only did his sex life bore me, but I felt that he shouldn't discuss Jackie Kennedy's or Princess Margaret's underwear with anyone, let alone a journalist on a national newspaper. Eventually, largely friendless and by then short of money, he committed suicide. However, judging by passionate love letters from Princess Margaret which have since been published, that affair, at least, was real.

My first encounter with Robin's 'amusing' lover Princess Margaret came in 1967 when I was working for *Queen* magazine, researching a long feature called 'A Month in the Life of the Bahamas'. Being faintly left-wing, as was fashionable in the late Sixties, I wanted to spend much of my reportorial time with 'real' Bahamians, poor blacks who lived in small wooden houses in a slum area of the capital Nassau called Over the Hill. And there I interviewed poverty-stricken pastors, shopkeepers, servants, strippers.

However, the moneyed readership of the magazine was not tremendously concerned with the travails of poor Bahamian blacks. What they wanted was Bahamian glamour: forget about the 'negroes' (as they were called in those days), they wanted to see glamorous white wealth at play in its Caribbean sandpits. But however purse-mouthed I was about capitalist excess, I found it was impossible not to be seduced by it, however temporarily. As Elinor Robson, an American woman of comparatively modest means, remarked after marrying a multimillionaire, 'A private railroad-car is not an *acquired* taste. One takes to it immediately.'

As indeed one does to a converted Catalina flying-boat, the gun-turrets of which have been removed and replaced with two huge glass 'viewing-bubbles' protruding out of the leviathan's belly like some mutant frog's eyes. The Catalina was owned by a rather mysteri-ous multimillionaire property developer called Sir Harold Christie, who'd offered it to Princess Alexandra and Angus Ogilvy to use on their honeymoon. There had been some controversy about this offer since Sir Harold was widely suspected of having been implicated in the still unsolved 1943 murder of another raffish Bahamian figure, his friend and business partner Sir Harry Oakes, a Canadian former gold prospector.

Among the many thousands of (largely fanciful) words written about this notorious and bloody 'Murder in Paradise', there were allegations that the former Edward VIII, Duke of Windsor, the then Governor of the islands, had been involved in a cover-up after he'd been pressured by the American gangland boss Meyer Lansky not to inquire too deeply into the crime. The exiled Duke, Princess Alexan-dra's uncle, was a lasting source of embarrassment to the Royal Family and the feeling was (according to one courtier at the time) 'that this offer is not wise for her to accept, in view of . . . well, you know . . . all that nasty business'.

Somerset Maugham had famously described Monaco as 'a sunny place for shady people'. But the Bahamas, a scattering of around 700 islands and rocky outcrops in the Caribbean, was of course even sunnier and, when I went there at the height of its property and gambling boom, even more full of exotically shady people. Its history was one of piracy, blockade-running and rum-smuggling during Prohibition. Bootleg liquor had paved its roads, rebuilt its churches, paid for its electricity and its sewerage systems. But now large-scale gambling had replaced bootleg liquor as a source of wealth. The gambling boom had begun only three years before my arrival, and

Mafia figures (many of whom had been expelled from Cuba by Castro) were revelling in its murky proceeds.

As a thirty-six-year-old croupier, a 'resting' British actor (and former bodyguard to Christine Keeler) called Tom Gerrard, told me, 'I trained at Dino Cellini's croupiers' school in London and came over here in a chartered plane with sixty-nine croupiers three years ago when the first casino opened. I liked Uncle Dino a lot.' Unfortunately the British government did not share Tom's fondness for 'Uncle Dino', who was a notorious Mafia don, and had him deported. 'I was really sorry he got expelled. By the way, if you ever bump into any of my old muckers in London, like Albie Finney, Stanley Baker, Mike Caine, tell 'em to come over here and see old Tom!'

Gambling, and the islands' proximity to the United States, had now made every scrap of land valuable: stony little islands with scruffy beaches, which for hundreds of years had slept undisturbed and disregarded except by the odd visiting turtle, now thundered with the roar of dredgers and bulldozers tearing out the palmetto scrub and replacing it with golf courses, club houses, all-American sanitation, nightclubs, and lawns and palm trees imported from Florida. Sir Harold Christie, a small, hunched, deceptively shabby figure in his early seventies, was constantly selling off the bits he owned and which he'd originally snapped up for a song.

I remarked to him that I really couldn't see any potential in some of these islands. He looked at me through his crinkled lizard eyes and said, 'Remember what people said about that boggy piece of swampland in Southern Florida? It's now Miami Beach. And that useless dustbowl in Nevada? That's now Las Vegas.' That, I said to him ruefully, explains why he's a multimillionaire and I'm not. 'Very true, Miss Leslie, very true!'

One day Christie took a fellow property developer and me up in the Catalina: slung under its wings were two steel motorboats, which could be lowered into the water by remote control. I'd heard he'd used it in Alaska. 'No, I never took it to Alaska myself, but that Hickok fellow borrowed it to go there to shoot white whales. Shot a lot of 'em. It's a very good fishing plane. Someone wants to borrow it next week to go fishing off Guatemala, but I told him it has to go to Florida to get fitted with new cushion-covers.'

He and his friend in the glass frog's eyes gazed down at the islands scattered like confetti below us. 'Rose Island. Own a lot of that. Trouble is, its beach is only twelve miles long – think we can do something with it though! Yes, I used to own the land for that development down there on the right. Good development, that. He'll make a lot of money with that. See that beach over there? Own it 50/50 with Lord Cowdray.'

His friend interrupted gleefully: 'Harold, look, isn't that the beach I bought off you? I think I made a 130 per cent profit by selling it almost immediately!' At this news Christie choked slightly and began coughing as if about to explode: 'Do you think I could borrow a cigarette?' As he pointed with veiny, freckled fingers to assorted islands below us, he resembled an aged grandparent identifying his grandchildren in a crowded kindergarten: 'That one's mine. And that's Cowdray's. That one's mine *and* Cowdray's ... Mine ... Cowdray's, I think ... Might be mine ...'

Christie had invented the concept of the Bahamas as a 'smart' destination – which it isn't now, thanks to the mass invasion of cruise ships full of honeymooning hairdressers and Midwest dentists with their portly wives clad in polyester leisure-wear. The smart set, flaring their nostrils, have now largely fled to places like Barbados, St Barts, Mustique and the Virgin Islands.

But Christie and a fellow developer, a Canadian brewer and racehorse owner, were the first to cook up the idea of a secluded, members-only resort where the rich never had to meet anyone (except servants) who wasn't as rich as them. So lots were offered on a 4,000-acre estate in Lyford Cay on New Providence Island to 'the right sort of people' – like Prince Rainier of Monaco, Greek shipowner Stavros Niarchos, Henry Ford II and the Aga Khan.

(Presumably the same tactic is being used today by property developers in Dubai, only their 'right sort of people' are millionaire footballers and their silicone-enhanced WAGS. When I first visited Dubai in 1975 it was a charming, dusty old Arabian port, largely built of mud brick, whose economy still consisted mostly of pearl fishing and gold smuggling; if someone had told me then that it would end up as it is today – loud with the sound of bulldozers and crammed with designer boutiques and super-luxury hotels – I wouldn't have believed them, just as I disbelieved Harold Christie in the Bahamas. That's why I'm *still* not a multimillionaire.)

The photographer working with me was Patrick Lichfield. As a cousin of the Queen, he of course knew all 'the right sort of people', the people who owned sugar-pink, ersatz antebellum villas in Lyford Cay and who never needed to go into Nassau, let alone glimpse the slums of Over the Hill. This super-Butlins for the super-rich had its own security force, its own petrol station, its own golf course, its own church and its own supermarket, which stocked vast quantities of Campbell's Beef Bouillon for making Bullshots, Lyford Cay's favourite cocktail. And of course it had its own bus service, for transporting staff to and from their matchbox homes in places like Over the Hill.

Lyford Cay revealed the fact that, hitherto unsuspected by me, the super-rich – the one species which can really afford to get away from its fellows on holiday – actually prefers to move in 'schools', like porpoises, and is just as anxious to stick with its own kind as any African tribesman or any package tourist eating chicken 'n' chips in Magaluf. There were no bars and the only restaurant, serving lousy food, was at the Lyford Cay Club, by invitation from a member only; but none of that mattered because the super-rich spent their time giving cocktail parties and lavish dinners for one another in their houses. There were no hotels either (just a few rooms in the club-house), because the super-rich rarely stay in hotels.

One of my friends – who once had an affair with the Shah of Persia but who told me 'it became such a bore having to be constantly shadowed by Savak, his secret police' – was astonished when I asked her what were the most sought-after luxury hotels in her starry set. 'Nobody who's anybody stays in *hotels*, Ann! They all stay as house guests with each other, or borrow each other's yachts.' No wonder Tony and Cherie Blair prefer to bum freebies from the super-rich rather than stay in mere hotels; this is the moneyed and internationally nomadic set to which these two former CND members and Labour stalwarts now aspire to belong.

Lyford Cay's definition of 'the right sort of people' was actually quite elastic: its Committee would vet prospective residents and, as one member put it to me, 'We do prefer them not to be too vulgar!' One might therefore have expected the Committee to have rejected the gentleman who was so grateful to the product which had won him his wealth, the humble soya bean, that he christened his two yachts *Soybeana I* and *Soybeana II*; and once he was deemed to be 'the right sort of person' he then, with startling originality, christened his Lyford Cay mansion 'Soybeana'. But apart from inspiring some cut-glass mockery – 'Mr and Mrs Soybean and all the little Soybeans' – the sheer magnitude of his wealth seemed to have automatically absolved him of the crime of 'vulgarity'.

And was it not a teensy bit vulgar for Dolly Goulandris, the Greek shipowner's wife, to decide that not only was her beach 'on the small side', but she thought its talcum-white sand would be much prettier if it was pink? Oh no: if you can afford these aesthetic whims, they're ipso facto not vulgar. When I went to Mrs Goulandris's for lunch (where fellow guests included Prince Peter of Greece and William Randolph Hearst II), we had to endure the sound of bulldozers and earth movers extending the beach and pouring on to it the requisitely pretty pink sand which had been transported from the Out Island of Eleuthera.

A spit of land opposite Nassau called Hog Island (on account of it used to be overrun with wild pigs) had been purchased by the American grocery heir Huntingdon Hertford, who renamed it Paradise Island and, at vast expense, tried to turn it into a luxury resort. But not even his purchase of a genuine fourteenth-century cloister – that he had had brought over from France, packed in foam, and reconstructed as part of the 'Versailles Gardens' in his Ocean Club – succeeded in making it a profitable venture. ('Very naive, young Hunt,' I was told by an old Bahamas hand. 'Didn't understand the way things are done here. Didn't do deals with the right Bay Street Boys.' The Bay Street Boys were not of course 'boys': they were usually old, but extremely wily, white or mixed-blood Bahamian businessmen who controlled the islands' economy and who, like Sir Harold Christie, ran their affairs from deceptively modest premises on Nassau's Bay Street.)

British 'old money' who had built mansions on the spit resolutely refused to call it by its vulgar new name Paradise Island, and doubtless approved of the film producer Kevin McClory who had the 'good taste' to refer to his estate as being on Hog Island. But it was Kevin's extremely boisterous Irishness which made him rather 'below the salt' as far as British 'old money' was concerned. On the McClory jetty a large, showy Irish flag fluttered in the silky Bahamian breeze. 'I mean . . . *really*!' sniffed Lady Baillie, an Anglo-American heiress who owned Leeds Castle in Kent as well as an estate on Hog Island. McClory had produced the Bond movie *Thunderball* (and got involved in a bitter legal dispute with Ian Fleming); his cable address was '007'. He owned an 'amphicar', a red Triumph Herald convertible which could drive off the beach and then motor on across the water. It was, of course, madly glamorous, if rather unreliable. He took me out in it twice and both times it leaked and broke down, and had to be hauled back to dry land by a rescue boat.

Lady Baillie, who so objected to McClory's vast Irish flag, had a 'constant companion', a Tory MP whom my father knew and who'd evidently told her I was on the islands. One day I got a call from her, inviting me to a 'luncheon party'. I innocently asked whether I could bring with me the photographer I was working with. 'A *photographer*?' she expostulated in the tones of Lady Bracknell's 'A *handbag*?' I was about to explain to her Ladyship, tactfully, that Patrick was not some common-or-garden snapper, but the Earl of Lichfield no less. 'Don't tell the snobbish old bat!' hissed Patrick. So I didn't. 'She'll find out soon enough!' he grinned. And she did: from then on I was bombarded with panic-stricken messages from Hog Island telling me that Lady Baillie would be *delighted* if I brought along my photographer. But Patrick refused to go. 'I'm afraid Lord Lichfield is *much* too busy,' I'd regretfully inform her minions.

Whether the likes of Lady Baillie approved or not, the fact was that Lyford Cay provided a wonderful locale for even the 'below the salt' super-rich to acquire a pseudo-aristocratic sheen, if they worked on it. 'Oh, we never have to leave the place! We have a wonderful social life!' trilled Mrs Morgan Reynolds (of the American tobacco fortune). Her favourite headdress of an evening consisted of a huge display of bird-of-paradise feathers, fastened to her head with rubber suction pads. The Reynolds mansion was full of examples of religious art acquired from Europe, a floor-to-ceiling Gobelin, the odd Romney or two, and endless framed photographs of the Reynoldses with their frequent house guests, who seemed to be largely drawn from the ranks of former royal families. 'That picture', gushed Mrs Reynolds, the hibiscus heads on her coiffure quivering adoringly, 'is of dear, dear King Simeon of Bulgaria and his charming family . . . and that's King Peter of Greece, of course, with Queen Alexandra . . . and this, this, and this is dear, dear King Umberto of Italy. Just the easiest of house guests, no trouble or fuss at all! We adore having him. But tell me, do you think the Governor has something against ex-kings? We always invite Sir Ralph to meet them at our parties here and he always refuses to come ... perhaps something to do with British protocol?'

And so of course when Princess Margaret and Lord Snowdon came to the Bahamas for a brief but doomed attempt to save their failing marriage, they did not stay in a mere hotel. They stayed at Lyford Cay in the beachfront house of Jocelyn Stevens, the owner and editor of *Queen* magazine, and his then wife Janie, the Princess's lady-in-waiting.

Patrick was very nervous about his relatively 'plebbie' colleague's forthcoming meeting with his royal cousin. 'Ann, I mean, when you meet her, you will curtsey, won't you? And always call her "Ma'am" when you address her, won't you?' Yes, Patrick, for heaven's sake, yes of course! The trouble was that, when I did first meet Her Royal Highness, she was in the sea, wearing her usual lampshade cozzie (she had an Italian film star's face but a rather dumpy Hanoverian body). A helicopter was clattering overhead. She rose out of the water and started shrieking, 'It's that bloody Bellisario!' Ray Bellisario was the first of the British paparazzi, and had already caused a scandal by photographing her in a similar cozzie three years earlier. But when Patrick informed his cousin, as she emerged at full screech from the waves, that he'd like to introduce her to me, she assumed her royal mode, imperiously stuck out her dripping hand and then looked at my feet. It is, believe me, not easy to do the full curtsey in flip-flops on wet sand.

Ma'am's expression told me that the curtsey was not a success. Besides, I soon discovered to my dismay that both the Snowdons were determined to use me as a foil in their marital battles. The Stevenses had two other house-guest couples staying with them, the industrialist Basil de Ferranti and the banker Evelyn de Rothschild and their then wives. They were all old friends (which I obviously was not) and I was thus fair game. Mind you, even if you're an old friend you're not excused from royal protocol. I was astonished when the three beautiful old-friend wives, turning up in their bikinis on the terrace for breakfast, would always first curtsey before depositing a mwa-mwa kiss on Her Royal Highness's cheeks.

What, I thought crossly, has this vain, trivial and lazy woman done to deserve such obeisance, other than to demand it as of right because of her bloodline? One night I moaned to Patrick, 'I can curtsey to the Queen till the cows come home, because I respect and admire her – but not to this useless, spoiled woman!'

'Oh, Ann, do stop going on!' I got the feeling that he was actually rather scared of her.

One evening Princess Margaret decided to aim her guns at me. Because Patrick was so bothered about my 'not looking right' for his royal cousin I'd grumpily gone in to Nassau and bought myself a gorgeous dress, albeit a cheap Pucci copy: I obviously couldn't afford the real thing and would in any case have regarded it as a waste of money. When I entered the Stevens house for dinner that night, HRH began fingering my dress, like some African tribeswoman confronted with the first Western garb she'd ever seen. 'What's this made of?' she asked, looking round the room expecting – and, of course, getting – sycophantic sniggers. 'Polyester, ma'am, as I think you've already worked out,' I replied evenly.

The Snowdons constantly used me as a hapless ping-pong ball as they viciously thwacked at each other across the conversational net. Snowdon would insist on sitting next to me at dinner and, if his wife interrupted our bouts of Fleet Street gossip, he'd snap, 'In case you haven't *noticed*, I'm talking to Ann – and *for once* I'm enjoying myself!'

While insulting her, he'd make sure she'd be able to hear him. 'Oh, Ann, I made a terrible mistake in New York recently,' he said meaningfully. Oh, God, I thought, *please* don't mention the Lady Jacqueline Rufus Isaacs business. Everyone, including his wife, knew about his rumoured relationship with her, and Ma'am's mood was not improved when they were photographed together in New York. He jumped up, grabbed my hand and took me to what I knew was Princess Margaret's bedroom. He opened some jewellery boxes (by now I was afraid his wife would storm in and thump me; crockery was rumoured to be smashed during the royal rows). He fished out some flamboyant Ken Lane costume jewellery drop-earrings: 'These were my mistakes – when I bought them for my wife I'd forgotten how short her neck is. She looks ridiculous.'

On another occasion we were all supposed to adjourn to the

drawing-room end of the open-plan room for after-dinner coffee. Snowdon refused to get up and refused to let me do so either, slapping his hand on my thigh. 'Don't move! I want to go on talking to you. I've had to give up so much with this marriage. People think it's boosted my career – it's done the opposite. It means I'm not free to do what I want to do.' Princess Margaret sat on a sofa glaring furiously – not at her husband, but at me.

One day Kevin McClory told me he had a problem, and it centred on 'Ma'am'. His boisterous St Patrick's Day all-night parties were legendary. An Irish senator would fly in genuine shamrocks from Ireland (though unfortunately on one occasion the children and nannies in the sprawling McClory household mistook the sacred weeds for watercress, and gobbled them down in sandwiches). The staff had to dress up as leprechauns and everyone got very drunk. One American grocery millionairess forgot to bring her Irishly green emeralds to Hog Island for Kevin's party and had to send her Lear jet back to New York to fetch them from the safe.

'I know I've got to invite the Snowdons,' Kevin told me glumly. 'But I don't want her to come. Unless she's the centre of attention she won't allow anyone to have any fun. She's got eyes like traffic lights and if she's in a mood they always show Stop. Can you persuade her to refuse the invitation?' And I did (well, I wanted to enjoy the party myself). 'Ma'am, I really think it's not something you would enjoy – lots of drunken Irishmen, strippers dressed in Irish flags, that sort of thing. I don't think it would look good if Fleet Street heard about it.'

Whenever Patrick and I went to Lyford Cay we would have to pass through the guarded gates to the estate. Kevin's *Thunderball* movie featured the Lyford Cay entrance, and used a number of its millionaire residents as extras, who found the whole thing '*so* thrilling!'

There were three big stories in the Bahamas that month. There was Aristotle Onassis with his mistress Maria Callas on his yacht *Christina* moored in the bay. There was the Greek shipowner Stavros Niarchos's upcoming divorce from Charlotte Ford, the heiress daughter of Henry, and his fourth out of five wives; the couple were staying with Dolly and Niko Goulandris prior to Charlotte flying to Mexico for an amicable quickie divorce. And of course there was the scandalous story of the Snowdons' failing marriage; Royals in those days simply didn't divorce. The bay was therefore loud with the sound of photographers' speedboats being chased away by waterborne security police. The Lyford Cay entrance area swarmed with photographers and journalists. When several of them realized I too was a journalist – but one who uniquely passed in and out of this enclave without let or hindrance – they began thrusting miniature spy cameras into my hands, telling me how much money I could get in worldwide syndication rights for a picture of the warring royal couple.

Of course I refused. But as the Snowdons' behaviour towards me got worse, I told Jocelyn, their host and my editor, that I wasn't putting up with it any longer, and if things didn't improve, I was going to take up these lucrative offers. 'You, Jocelyn, are rich. I am not. I cannot afford to behave in an honourable way if all I get in return is this rude and childish treatment. I have nothing to do with their rotten marriage and refuse to be dragged into its debris.'

'*How* much are you being offered?' asked Jocelyn disbelievingly. To my astonishment this millionaire 'best friend' of the Snowdons then decided to take advantage of the saleability of his chums. His plan was that Patrick would take some pictures and we'd sell them through Patrick's agent in London, the renowned Hungarian-born Tom Blau of Camera Press. I alerted Blau and he salivated at the size of the fortune we'd all earn.

I wrote to him, 'Alas, alack, we have disappointed you, I fear. Patrick's frightful royal cousin has played cat and mouse with us ever since she arrived. We've been round there drinking, water-skiing and dining with them and when the subject of pix comes up it's always, "Yes . . . no, you must be joking . . . Yes . . . no", etc. Poor Patrick has been almost out of his mind (so's Jocelyn of course!). Thus in the end we decided to do a snatch . . . and Jocelyn and I will work out a good caption. Our plan is to pretend that you have bought some snatch pictures from some unknown source and have cabled me for a good caption, telling me that, whether or not I provide one, the pictures and a caption of some sort will be printed. This will, we hope somewhat faintly, avoid the embarrassing connection between the pictures and Patrick and myself.

'Naturally, no credits and utmost secrecy, as Jocelyn and Patrick will be in dead schtuck for ever more chez Her Royal Highness . . . But if we do sell any of this, no credits for anyone!'

As he lay quivering on his belly in some camouflaging under-brush, the noble Earl's terror of gainsaying Jocelyn – his autocratic paymaster and the mastermind of our sneaky little plot – coupled with his terror of his royal cousin, conspired to render the resulting snatch pictures so wobbly and fuzzy as to be unprintable.

Being very middle-class, I was somewhat shocked that someone related to, or a close confidant of, a Royal would – for a fistful of money which neither of them needed – be prepared to betray them. But that episode did suggest to me that even the Royal Family's beloved 'Uncle Dickie', Lord Mountbatten, might be persuaded to become a willing co-conspirator in another plot which, if it suc-ceeded, would enrage his royal relatives. And so it proved.

26

'The crème de la scum'

Sir Percy Cradock is tall, ascetic, and a mandarin in every sense of the word. He'd been the British ambassador to Beijing, was the leading Sinology adviser to Mrs Thatcher's government, was well versed in the bureaucratic intricacies of both China and Britain, and speaks Mandarin Chinese fluently. And he had a thoroughly mandarin distaste for what he saw as the ignorant low-life of the British tabloid press.

This came to a head during the Queen's tour of China in 1986. One day in the Forbidden City I heard an exchange between him and Harry Arnold, the small, dapper, scoop-winning royal reporter for the *Sun*. Sir Percy looked down, again in every sense of the word, on Arnold and his ilk. His maiden-aunt pursed lips would become as tight as a Victorian spinster's reticule whenever he spotted Harry. Finally, he could no longer tolerate the royal 'fantasies' (which usually turned out not to be 'fantasies' at all) that were routinely published by the *Sun* and the other tabloids. 'You people are *scum*!' he coldly informed Arnold. Harry drew himself up to his full height, which is not a lot, and grandly informed Sir Percy, 'Excuse me, sir, we are the *crème* de la scum.'

'The crème de la scum' were a tribal sub-group of Fleet Street who were greatly treasured by their bosses because their work always put on circulation. Thus at the height of the Princess Diana hysteria many a royal reporter became wealthy through their extravagant expenses, or 'exes', which enabled them to buy race-horses or second homes in France or Florida and ensured that their offspring were able to enjoy a private education. Their bosses' money was never a problem as far as they were concerned. I happened once to be working in the British Virgin Islands for a magazine feature about deep-sea-diving treasure-hunters and was staying in an eccentric hotel called The Bitter End. It was reachable only by sea and catered largely for obsessional divers. Its regular guests were a species which only really felt at home when covered by sea and wearing oxygen tanks and flippers. But it happened to be the landfall nearest to Richard Branson's Necker Island, which was a favourite holiday haunt for Princess Diana. So 'la crème' descended on The Bitter End (which had no room phones in its hillside cottages), lugging their then elaborate and hefty satellite systems which, at vast expense to their employers, they would use to order Room Service from Reception.

This 'crème' had displaced the previous 'crème', the industrial correspondents, who had reigned supreme until Mrs Thatcher broke the unions' stranglehold on the economy. This previous 'crème' were blokes who wore sheepskin jackets, stood beside the braziers of the habitually striking 'brothers', and were always uttering phrases from union lingo like 'composite resolution 194'. Industrial strife was the dominant British news story of that period.

They were all hard-drinking, macho lads who were on 'Arthur', 'Joe', 'Len' and 'Mick' terms with the men they reported on. After the breaking of the unions, this previous 'crème' were at a loss; like Othello, their occupation was gone. Many ended up writing TV reviews, running country pubs, or retiring to ruminate on the vanished glory-days of 'composites' and 'everybody out!' One of them rose to greater heights: my friend and colleague Richard Littlejohn became the most successful of the right-wing polemicists in the press.

At one point my editor David English decided (as he put it) 'to cast against type' and asked me to write a series about the miners' leader, Arthur Scargill. But I didn't belong to the Industrial Correspondent tribe, had never been down a mine, knew nothing about mining culture. No matter. I soon discovered that Arthur, the ginger-haired, balding, tub-thumping working-class hero, was much loathed within 'this great movement of ours' (which is how union leaders saw themselves). He was especially loathed by the higher echelons of the British Communist Party. Arthur always alleged he was a Marxist struggling to create a socialist Utopia in this benighted capitalist land, and he'd been a member of the Young Communists; but the older Communists believed, rightly, that he was such an egotist that he was incapable of adhering to Party discipline.

For Byzantine reasons the Party then decided to shaft him. Which meant that it gave me, a representative of the 'fascist' capitalist press, numerous contacts in the northern coalfields. I'd go to a grimy back-to-back terraced house in some benighted northern town, knock on the door and announce, 'I'm Ann Leslie from the *Daily Mail*' – and, before the door was slammed in my face, I'd quickly add, 'Mick sent me.' Mick was Mick Costello, the Communist Party's industrial organizer, and such was Party discipline that, once I'd produced evidence of my 'Mick' credentials, the door was always opened to me.

(One night in a back-to-back near Middlesbrough I'd been carousing over beer and fish and chips served in newspaper with some Communist miners who were filling me in on scurrilous Arthur gossip. Unfortunately I hadn't realized that the grim little hotel in which I was staying bolted its doors at 11 p.m., and on returning there at 2 a.m. I discovered I was locked out. The hotel had external fire-escape stairways so I climbed up one, found a room which had an unlocked window and clambered in. I was wearing a huge fur coat at the time and the room's occupant woke up to see this fur-coated female easing her way through his window; he stared, transfixed, but remained utterly wordless. 'I'm *so* sorry to disturb you, but there's no night porter and I'm afraid I've been locked out!' I explained in my most gracious manner, before exiting into the corridor. Later I wondered how his 'last-night-this-young-woman-climbed-in-through-my-window-wearing-a-fur-coat' story went down with his mates in the pub.)

A couple of members of the industrial 'crème' jumped ship even before 'this great movement of ours' began to founder, and defected to Harry Arnold's 'crème' on the Royals beat. Instead of blowing on their frozen fingers beside a strikers' brazier they found themselves being whisked to exotic parts of the world on chartered jets with unlimited bar service; they experienced no hassles at airports, no need to bribe officials, no haggling with taxi drivers, and were transported to and fro by limo or press bus to various red-carpet locales. This Royal beat business was evidently an 'exes'-lucrative, free-loading and often drunken doddle – what's not to like? All you had to do in exchange for these goodies was go to the phone and churn out variants of 'The Queen, looking radiant in primrose yellow/apple green/fuchsia pink, yesterday visited the palm-fringed/dusty/oil-rich/poverty-stricken/exotic/typhoon-battered land of . . .'.

For a time during my Fleet Street career I joined, albeit sporadically, the Royal beat and discovered that it was not such a doddle after all. In reality, covering a Royal Tour was like getting involved in one of those claustrophobic house parties in an Agatha Christie novel, in which a large number of disparate characters gather together for what they think is going to be a weekend of laughter and fun, and instead find that, by chapter 2, the drawing room is littered with bodies, daggers quivering in their backs. The fact that the Royal Tour 'house party' spent much of its time scrambling in and out of buses and planes, muttering, 'if this is Tuesday it must be Oman,' didn't alter the claustrophobia; if anything, it slightly increased it. Exhaustion and acrimony would soon set in and the most trivial of irritations – often labelled 'Prince Philip' – would provide an excuse for fits of childish petulance, verging on hysteria.

In 1966 the royal couple were serenely floating through the Caribbean on the royal yacht *Britannia*, which was delivering them effortlessly to various emerald-coloured dots on the ocean, so that they could snip tapes, plant trees and acknowledge the cheers of flag-waving children lined up along the ceremonial route. The royal reporters, who then included me, were there to record the tape-snipping and tree-planting for posterity, but first we had to reach the emerald dots in advance of *Britannia*. This proved to be something of a struggle, usually involving flying in clapped-out planes which seemed incapable of travelling in a direct line to anywhere and which took an extremely elastic view of timetables. (The chronically unreliable BWIA, British West Indian Airways, became the acronym for 'But Will It Arrive?')

Every time we turned up at one of the emerald dots on the itinerary we'd run into a wall of panicking policemen who appeared to be under the impression that the words 'Royal Press Party' on our passes were code for 'These are dangerous anarchists who must not be allowed within sight or sound of the Royal Personages'. One small, prim lady reporter, for whom saying boo to a goose constituted Bad Language, revealed hidden fires when one day she leapt out of our marooned press bus and began screaming hysterically at something resembling a uniformed meatsafe in a policeman's hat: 'If you don't let this bus through *right now*, I'll have your great big black b***s for breakfast!' (The meatsafe staggered back, the press bus was let through, and that night a grateful press corps deputed one of their number to make a pass at her.)

By the time we reached the island where Prince Philip was doing a solo turn opening a hospital, our nerves were raw. The matron said to the Duke, 'We have a lot of trouble with mosquitoes.' The Duke, ever the wag, replied, 'I know what you mean. You have mosquitoes – we have the press.' Right, that's it! Everybody out! Shut notebooks, down cameras. Total boycott! If (as our unofficial union shop steward put it) Philip thinks he can do without us, we'll oblige: he can plant trees and snip tapes all day long, but not a word about him, not a single snap, would record the event. From that moment on, our shop steward decided, Prince Philip – as far as the outside world was concerned – would cease to exist.

The Duke soon realized there was trouble at t'mill: every time he hove ceremonially into view, the press corps took to examining their fingernails, admiring cloud formations and taking 800-mm close-ups of hibiscus blooms. He dispatched an emissary to find out what was going on. The hapless go-between began pinging to and fro like a tennis ball between the two sides. Over the net he came from the Duke's side: er, well, the Duke didn't mean it, just a bit of fun, couldn't we, er, ha ha!, take a joke? No, we said firmly, thwacking him back over the net, we couldn't. Back he came again: ah, er, all a misunderstanding, no harm meant, Duke very upset you're upset. Not good enough: a personal apology was required, the more grovelling the better. The appalled emissary initially refused to go back over the net: can't have His Royal Highness apologizing to the press! Not done, you know. It'd better be, we muttered. Them's our terms, and unless they were met, this little industrial dispute would result in the indefinite 'blacking' of the Duke. And thus it was that we were asked (on the next island, Dominica) to gather beneath a specified mango tree where the Duke would come and eat humble pie.

Constipated with irritation, dragging a rictus of a smile across his face, he approached the assembled hacks and once again tried out the 'couldn't-you-chaps-take-a-joke?' line. No, 'we chaps' churlishly repeated, we couldn't. Did the Duke have *any idea* how difficult it was trying to cover this tour, let alone having to endure endless insults (the mosquito remark being just one in a long list)? Prince Philip, contemplating the prospect of becoming a 'non-person' on the lines of those disgraced Bolshevik leaders who got air-brushed out of Soviet official photographs, finally capitulated. Along with the apology came a promise not to be rude about us again (which, at least on that tour, he wasn't). End of thoroughly childish incident for all concerned.

In fact, the Duke's presence on a Royal Tour has always been thoroughly enlivening to copy-starved reporters: until you've tried it, you've no idea how difficult it is to find different ways of describing little girls presenting posies to the Queen. Women reporters can amuse themselves by giving male colleagues wildly inaccurate descriptions of the Queen's clothes. It was realized long ago by the Palace Press Office that male reporters are quite incapable of describing either the style or even the colour of any frock the Queen was being 'radiant' in, and so it provides typewritten descriptions (which usually arrive too late) of the garments in question. So whenever the Queen stepped off a gangplank in the sort of electric blue which bruises your eyeballs, your male colleagues would ask, 'What's that colour, Ann?' And you'd reply firmly, 'Fuchsia, of course!' Whereupon they would dutifully begin scribbling: 'The Queen, looking radiant in . . . how do you spell that?'

If such minor amusements fail to satisfy, a royal hack longs for things to go wrong. It was usually a waste of time to look to the Queen to provide entertaining cock-ups. In any case, I've noticed that even the most republican of reporters tend to turn into subservient jelly when faced with Her Majesty in person. She can also, incidentally, show herself to be a master of the put-down: at one eve-of-tour cocktail party, a television reporter of legendary arrogance (much disliked by his fellows) was introduced to her as being 'very famous, Ma'am – he's always on the television news!' The Queen sized him up, saw him preening himself in the confident expectation of a stream of royal compliments and, with a dazzling smile, drawled, 'Oh, I'm so sorry – I rarely watch the news, so I'm afraid I've never seen you.' Collapse of arrogant tellyman, who hissed at me as the Queen moved away, 'If you give that story to *Private Eye* I'll kill you!'

Luckily we could usually rely on her husband to provide some comic relief and we'd react to his outbursts of bad temper and tactlessness with the joy of prospectors falling upon gold nuggets (which, in the retelling, would often be carved and polished into such Fabergé gems of royal anecdotage that eventually they little resembled the original raw material). 'Did you hear what he just said to that general?' (this was, I seem to remember, in Brazil). 'He said, "Where did you get those medals?" and the chap said, "In the war." "Oh," says the Duke, "I didn't know Brazil was in the war that long!" and the general replies, "At least, sir, I didn't get them for marrying my wife!"' Or 'Did you hear what he just said to that race-goer?' (this was in Bahrain). 'He said, "Are you all winning a lot of money here this afternoon?" Doesn't he know that gambling is forbidden in this country?' Or 'Did you hear what he just shouted to that policeman with the siren?' ' "Switch that bloody thing off, you silly b****r!"'

If Prince Philip unaccountably failed to come up with the goods, help usually lay at hand in the form of incompetent local officials. One example combined both the Prince Philip and the 'local incompetent' elements in one: in Kuwait, a motorcade bearing the Duke to a dhow-building yard screamed off at high speed in the wrong direction and ended up in the desert, where it got lost. Someone had forgotten to tell the lead driver the way. The Duke was emphatically not amused, but we in the press certainly were. We were somewhat less amused when one morning, also in Kuwait, we missed half the events on the royal schedule due to the fact that our press bus ran out of petrol. Since Kuwait is basically a sandpit on top of a vast petrol tank, this took some doing: 'How the hell can you run out of petrol in Kuwait?' screamed a maddened scribe.

In one Gulf state we were treated to the farce, so familiar to royal reporters, known as 'the red carpet panic'. The Queen was due to fly in on Concorde. (We'd come in on the last Comet on active duty which happily made up in bar service what it lost on speed.) The Ruler was ready, so was the guard of honour, so were the military men, bristling like hedgehogs with machine guns, rifles, daggers and bayonets, so were eighty royal in-laws, so were the press. But not those in charge of laying the red carpet, who'd gone AWOL. The officials were clearly asking themselves, 'Where in Allah's name are we supposed to put it?' Twice the carpet was hauled up, twice it was repositioned. One panic-stricken carpet-laying major-domo finally arrived on post and was seen trying to hammer it into the tarmac with nails. By now the carpet was no longer red: it was indistinguishable from the surrounding dust. Further panic. So busy were we watching the frantic officials and the carpet men hurtling to and fro, like characters in a Buster Keaton film, as they tried to vacuum the carpet and the tarmac, that none of us noticed Concorde landing silently into the wind behind us. I half expected the Queen to emerge from Concorde calling out, 'Coo-ee, everybody! I'm he-e-e-re! Anybody there?'

My admiration for the stolidly dutiful Queen has grown over the years (as, incidentally, has my admiration for her husband). Her uncomplaining self-discipline means that, so long as 'local incompetents' don't let her down, her schedule runs like clockwork. When meeting local dignitaries, for example, she will speak to only about one in ten of the people in the line-up. Prince Charles very often tries to talk to everyone in the line, which drives his entourage mad: 'He's so undisciplined! He must know that we're going to run late!'

At times conversations with the Queen can go on a mite longer than her anxious Press Secretary thinks is wise. I noted that when, at an exuberant service in Cape Town's Anglican cathedral, the ebullient Archbishop Tutu jumped up and down, clapping and ululating – and even Prince Philip smiled and tapped his feet – the Queen just sat there with what one of her Press Secretaries once described as her 'Miss Piggy' face. 'Ma'am, you sat through all that happy-clappy stuff with a face like an axe!' I said to her later.

'Oh dear, did I? I'm afraid that sort of thing is not really to my taste, but I'm sorry that it was so obvious. The trouble is that, unlike my mother, I don't have a naturally smiley face.' The Press Secretary nervously hurried me away.

Her son, of course, has a naturally rather gloomy, basset-hound face. I first interviewed him in 1971. He happened to be fond of the now defunct humorous magazine *Punch*, and its editor Bill Davis had asked me to write a profile of the Prince on the eve of his joining the RAF. *Punch*, founded in 1841, used to host a formal lunch every week to which the occasional distinguished guest would be invited, and this time Prince Charles was one of them. It was a *Punch* Lunch tradition to invite such distinguished guests, or the sometimes even more distinguished contributors, to carve their initials on its revered dining table: among those who'd done so were Dickens, Mark Twain and Thackeray – and Prince Philip, who'd gouged out the Greek letter 'Phi'.

A couple of days before Charles was due to come to lunch, his Royal Protection detective came to do a security recce and was shown round by Sheridan Morley, the magazine's theatre critic. On examining the pockmarked table, the detective remarked, 'I see, sir. Have much trouble with vandalism here, do you?' (Charles's subsequent signature was a capital C enclosing a delicate carving of Prince of Wales feathers.)

I told Bill Davis that I wasn't going to do a cuttings-job profile: I had to have a one-to-one interview with the lad himself. This, the Palace informed Bill, would not be possible. Charles never gave interviews to the press (and had done only one radio interview, to Jack de Manio of the BBC's *Today* programme). It had then been decided by the anally retentive Palace that His Royal Highness wasn't going to do any more – and certainly not for the print media.

But in the end Bill proved persuasive. (His irreverent staff called him 'Kaiser Bill' on account of his German birth, a nickname which understandably he didn't much like.) As an editor he never seemed to hear the word 'No'. 'No, Bill, I can't do the piece, I'm too busy . . .' 'Wonderful! So glad you can, but I will need it next week!' 'I said "No", Bill!' 'Terrific! Really looking forward to reading it!' Keith Waterhouse and I agreed that we usually found it easier to write the damn thing rather than go on trying to make Bill hear our refusals. This clearly had happened to the Palace who gave up saying 'No'. But my 'audience' with the twenty-two-year-old Heir to the Throne was hedged round with conditions: I was not to say that I'd even met him, let alone interviewed him; was forbidden to bring a note-book, forbidden to quote him, and so on.

On a freezing March morning I was ushered by a footman along the red-carpeted corridors of Buckingham Palace into a shiny, old-fashioned mahogany lift: 'Had to get the doors changed,' confided the footman. 'The corgis, you see. Kept getting their paws trapped.' Another longer, wider corridor; green wallpaper, red curtains, huge cabinets full of ancestral china as far as the eye could see. The whole place had, and still has, the rather cheerless air of an extremely grand provincial railway hotel; no wonder the future Princess Diana found the atmosphere so suffocating and hated it so much.

I was then ushered into Charles's surprisingly small sitting room which overlooked a drab, gravelled courtyard. The temperature inside the room was, if anything, even lower than outside; the window was open and little gusts of wind and sleet came whistling in. For the first twenty minutes I perched shivering on a sofa while a rosy-cheeked Prince Charles relaxed in a leather armchair looking comfortably warm, as though basking on a Caribbean beach. The fireplace did contain a two-bar electric fire, but it was switched off. Eventually, through chattering teeth, I asked him if he could close the window: 'I'm so frozen I can scarcely speak!' He leapt up, genuinely stricken by his 'thoughtlessness': he never felt the cold himself. (As his former nanny told me, 'The Royal Family have always been fresh air fiends, Prince Charles especially.' His bullet-proofed Daimler had to be customized so that the back window could be opened – a very expensive stipulation, with security implications, but Charles won't sit in a car with sealed windows. 'I think I've inherited a gene for draughts,' he told me ruefully. 'Queen Victoria used to sit in the corridor at Balmoral because she liked draughts, and I'm the same.')

Three years later in 1974 I had another appointment with him – in the same sitting room on another equally wintry morning. As I trudged down the miles of gloomily grand corridors, I was confident that I was suitably dressed this time: I'd bandaged myself, like an Egyptian mummy, with layers of specially purchased thermal under-wear from a Himalayan climbers' equipment shop. If this stuff was good for the summit of Kanchenjunga, it should be adequate for Prince Charles's sitting room. As I went into the room a slab of stifling heat fell upon me. Waiting to greet me, a faintly sweating Prince. 'I remembered how cold you were last time,' he said. 'So I had the room specially warmed up before you came. I hope it'll be all right this time.' Eventually I could stand the heat no more and asked the Prince, 'Could you *possibly* open the window, sir? I'm so hot I can scarcely speak.' I was touched that he'd remembered how cold I'd been three years earlier. But then he has always been a curious mixture of the disarmingly thoughtful and the extremely self-

centred, and those who work for him are never sure which characteristic will be to the fore at any one time. 'What's the Boss's mood
today?' they'll ask one another before entering his sometimes crotchety presence.

I'd been commissioned by the *Mail* to write a major series on his
life, past and present. Unfortunately, whenever I asked him about
his childhood memories, he'd airily reply, 'Oh, I don't really remember the details. You'll have to talk to Mabel.' Mabel Anderson was his
childhood nanny (and is still a much loved retainer), but the Royal
Family had been so outraged by the publication of the anodyne
memoirs of 'Crawfie', the Queen's governess, that all subsequent
nannies and governesses were shackled hand and foot by confidentiality contracts. 'But as you know, sir, she's not allowed to speak to
me. But if I contact her and say you've given permission, would that
then be okay?'

'Oh yes, of course.'

Being thoroughly aware of the complexities of royal bureaucracy,
I knew that this 'contacting' of Mabel wouldn't be easy. (The Palace
had already concluded that the Prince was something of a loose
cannon who couldn't be trusted to behave according to agreed
protocol.) But luckily I already had the enthusiastic support of the
Prince's adored great-uncle and mentor Lord Mountbatten, 'Uncle
Dickie', with whom I'd done a deal: I would interview him about
Charles 'off the record', and then submit to him any comments of
his that I'd like to use 'on the record'. In such deals you always
submit more quotes than you think your interviewees will accept, so
that when they strike out the more obviously contentious remarks,
they'll often overlook other quotes that, on reflection, they might've
preferred not to have had attributed to them.

Mountbatten was not only immensely vain (he passed most of
his quotes, as they put him in a good light) but also an inveterate schemer. One scheme of his – to get Charles married off to his
granddaughter Amanda Knatchbull – had foundered, but his match-
making activities continued undeterred. After all, he liked to boast
that he'd managed to get his impoverished nephew Prince Philip of
Greece married off to the young Princess Elizabeth, who then
became Queen. 'And that's been a *great* success.'

We discussed the royal requirement of the time for the Heir to the Throne's bride to be a virgin. At least one of Charles's girlfriends had been frozen out of the race because, as one courtier remarked sniffily to me, 'She has "form", if you see what I mean.' The virgin requirement did not, of course, apply to royal bridegrooms. Indeed, 'Uncle Dickie' had strongly advised his great-nephew to 'sow some wild oats' before settling down.

'But thanks to the Sixties,' I pointed out to him, 'I doubt you could now find a well-born virgin the length or breadth of the land!'

'Ah, but you see, you don't know the *Almanach de Gotha* like I do: there are dozens of foreign princesses – probably virgin, because they're mostly Roman Catholics. Though they'd have to change their religion of course!' (It turned out, unfortunately for all concerned, that there was at least one aristocratic virgin left in the land who would not have to change her religion, and her name was Lady Diana Spencer.)

I explained my dilemma about Mabel: 'Can you let me know when Charles and Mabel are going to be together without the Palace bureaucracy, especially any Press Office people, around?'

One morning I got an excited call from Mountbatten: 'This weekend they're going to be together, without any officials, at Sandringham – so you'd better get a letter delivered there to Mabel as fast as you can!' Which I did, by motorcycle courier.

I got a handwritten letter back from Mabel in Sandringham: 'I should be delighted to be of some help.' Which she was, chatting happily in her soft Scottish brogue about how the Prince had been such a sweet-natured, rather biddable little boy. 'He was never as boisterous or as noisy as Princess Anne. She had a much stronger, more extrovert personality: she didn't exactly push him aside, but she was certainly a more forceful child. He was basically a rather shy little boy.' Charles was upstaged by his younger sister even when it came to putting together model toys. 'Princess Anne was very good at model-making but not Prince Charles – all fingers and thumbs, I'm afraid.'

Mabel was the Prince's surrogate mother (and some unkind souls say that that comforting role has now been taken by Camilla). 'You see, the children's parents were away so much on official duties, but

I'm always here. Even now that Prince Charles is grown up he pops in and has his meals in the nursery at Buckingham Palace if he's at home and his parents happen to be away.'

I had, of course, made it quite clear that this interview was to be 'on the record'. But when the articles (which were generally very favourable to Prince Charles) appeared, the Palace bureaucracy became incandescent. They were cross enough that I'd interviewed Lord Butler, the former Tory Cabinet Minister R. A. (Rab) Butler; he was Master of Trinity College, Cambridge, when Prince Charles was an undergraduate there.

A huge, Buddha-like figure swathed in woolly scarves, Butler sat heaped up in his dimly lit, book-lined study and nibbled thoughtfully on a piece of ginger cake. 'When Prince Charles first arrived here he was very boyish, somewhat immature – and perhaps rather too susceptible to family influence. Always does what he's told to do, which has not always been to his advantage.' Butler continued with what the Palace considered to be somewhat 'disobliging' remarks about the Prince's mother. 'Quite frankly, you know, the Queen and the Duke are not university people – they're horsey people, common-sense people. But the boy, you know, has great gifts, great gifts, and is really very clever – much more so than his parents.' He fished into his woolly scarf to retrieve a stray piece of ginger cake and continued ruminatively: 'The Queen is one of the most intelligent women in England, and brilliant at summing up people, but I don't think she's awfully interested in books. You never see any books lying about in her room when you go there – just newspapers, *Horse and Hound*, things like that. But Prince Charles has a tremendous affinity with books, they really mean something to him.'

But what really enraged the Palace was my interview with Nanny Mabel. Charles's private secretary, Squadron Leader David Checketts, even accused me of having 'invented' the whole thing. I informed him that if he repeated this utterly false allegation to anyone I would sue him for slander. He then alleged that I'd 'promised' to clear the material with Prince Charles and his private office. I had done no such thing and, once again, told Checketts that if he repeated this allegation I would, of course, sue him. Checketts (a rather nice bloke actually) then wrote a faintly conciliatory letter. But by then I had become embroiled in reporting the Cold War, and frankly didn't give a fig whether I was shunned by the Palace or not. Supernumerary squadron leaders and royal nannies – who cares about such flummeries when the world might be on the verge of nuclear Armageddon?

At the height of the nanny storm, I had rung Mountbatten: 'I'm in trouble with the Palace!' He laughed boisterously: 'Take no notice! But of course you won't mention my name in connection with Mabel, will you?' And while he was alive I never did. Writing about him after his murder by the IRA, I still didn't mention Mountbatten's role in our nanny plot; I felt that an already grief-stricken Charles might have found it too dismaying. (To my surprise, over the years I'd be rung by royal biographers telling me, 'We've been told by the Palace to contact you because you know more than anyone else about Charles's childhood.')

I last interviewed Prince Charles at Highgrove in 1998 as I'd been commissioned, again by the *Mail*, to write a series about him on the occasion of his fiftieth birthday. Princess Diana had died in the Paris car crash with her coke-snorting Egyptian playboy the previous year and her ex-husband was acutely aware of how unpopular he, and the Royal Family, now were.

I'd only met Princess Diana a couple of times and never warmed to her (or she to me). I used to get barely literate green-ink letters from her worshippers whenever I cast aspersions on their 'saint' on the airwaves, particularly when I said I was allergic to the 'Diana the Holy Martyr' act, and her attempt to promote herself as 'a cross between Mother Teresa and Jackie Onassis: "suffering 'n' shopping" of course being her forte'. (The odd death threat would occasionally be issued.) Even my own newspaper, never given to censoring my work, said, 'But you can't call her *promiscuous*, Ann!'

'But she *was*!' I replied, citing chapter and verse. 'Promiscuous women are usually extremely needy and often aren't interested in sex per se, just in the power they feel it gives them.' But, mindful of the sensitivities of those among our readers who were Di-worshippers, the word 'promiscuous', perhaps understandably, disappeared from my piece.

'The Boss', after months of dithering – including during a trip of his to southern Africa which I'd joined – finally agreed to meet me again for another long private chat, this time over tea at Highgrove.

He'd always hated the press, even before it began mocking him
as the 'Potty Prince' because of his alleged 'looniness' in confessing
that he talked to his plants. (What gardener doesn't? I've often given
my pathetic peonies an earful.) His passion for organic agriculture,
his almost mystical belief in alternative medicine and his 'Disney-
world' taste in architecture all contributed to the press's portrait of
him as a seriously deranged individual clearly ill-equipped to inherit
the throne.

When I'd interviewed him a quarter of a century earlier he
couldn't stop picking at the scars of earlier press cruelty (including
the notorious Cherry Brandy Incident when he was a schoolboy: no,
don't ask – probably only Prince Charles remembers it now). He'd
been portrayed as a rather chubby, faintly stupid boy, trudging hopelessly in the wake of his then dashing *Boy's Own* hero of a dad. And
it hurt. As he said to me, 'I knew I wasn't as stupid as I was made
out to be.'

He can be extraordinarily funny and sharp, especially about some
of the (a favourite word) 'characters' he meets in his work. Like the
colourfully insane Central Asian dictator who engulfed him in
extravagant hospitality and, at the end of a State Dinner, invited the
Prince of Wales to take his pick from a troupe of dancing girls for his
private post-prandial delectation. Unfortunately his Russian interpreter, a very prissy academic, was so disgusted by the specifics of
this offer that she refused to interpret it. The Prince therefore had no
idea what the dictator was offering: 'So I just kept thanking him
profusely for his generosity. It was only later that I was told what this
character had actually been promising me as "a gift"!' Were the
dancing girls slightly mustachioed and on the hefty side – that being,
I seemed to remember, the local taste in pulchritude? 'No, actually
they were very slim and pretty!'

But amid all the anecdotes and the self-deprecating humour you
sense that, even now, self-pity threatens to drown him from time to
time. He was, and is, deeply bitter about 'all the years of vilification'
he's endured, and pretended that he never read the newspapers:
'What's the point?' (He claimed he only read the magazine *The Week*,
a digest of the week's newspapers.) But he seemed fully aware of
what the papers were saying about him: 'Well, one hears things.'

The first anniversary of Diana's death was looming. I asked him, carefully, about 'the events of last year'. Again, he hated the way he had been portrayed 'as cold and unfeeling', and the way the press had apparently convinced the public that he and his family were the undisputed villains in that marital tragedy: 'I wonder how history will judge us.' In an attempt to cheer him up I pointed out that the polls were moving slightly in his favour – and public opinion had by now already embraced many of his allegedly 'loony' ideas. Even my Di-supporting newspaper was now running an alternative medicine page and railing, as he did, against genetically modified crops. He seemed greatly chuffed by a supportive article in *Farmer's Weekly* which, he said, 'routinely used to pour scorn on me'.

He clearly resented Tony Blair who was then at the height of his popularity, not least because the Blair government kept showing off about its latest eye-catching initiatives to tackle the problems of disadvantaged youth. 'As if everything that's being done has only happened since they came to power! What about the Prince's Trust?' He'd founded the organization twenty-two years earlier and there's no question that it's been extremely successful, and (as I know from my own interviews and research) many of those disadvantaged, ill-educated inner-city youths who've benefited from its help hero-worship the Prince. 'Dis man's *cool*!' as one adoring former Rasta put it. One of his close supporters told me, 'He's always banging on about disadvantaged youth, but she [meaning Diana] never talked about these issues privately. And I'm not sure she really cared that much about them, except in so far as they burnished her public image and made her feel good about herself.'

Unlike other members of his family, Prince Charles always knew there'd be a huge outpouring of grief on Diana's death, but even he was taken aback by the scale of it. I covered her funeral and had felt, during the days before it, that there was something disturbing, almost unbalanced, about the mass hysteria which erupted among the once buttoned-up British, as though suddenly they'd transformed themselves into Latin American *descamisados*, ferociously mourning their lost Evita. He sighed: 'I felt it was quite foreign; I felt an alien in my own country.'

'Do you feel guilty about her?' (I'd been assured by his friends that he did.)

'No,' he replied, almost mulishly. 'I've got nothing to feel guilty about.'

After I'd left Highgrove I wrote up my immediate impressions: 'PC strikes me as v. well-meaning, idealistic, romantic, dutiful, conservative (in best sense, not vindictive & exclusionary). Said he'd always been criticized for being too middle-aged when young, but now that middle-aged, thought it probably suited him. Also something rather childlike about him: his enthusiasms, butterfly attention span, longing to believe good of people, occasional petulancy and little-boy tantrums with staff over trivial things like aftershave. Feel he isn't a world-weary man on the verge of his half-century. Still a slightly adolescent chap – feelings too tender, sense of constant betrayal too upfront for his own good.'

Now that the public obsession with Diana is withering away and he has married his lifelong love, Camilla, I'm told he's more relaxed. He clearly adores his 'boys', the two princes, and they him. As for those republicans who'd convinced themselves that Diana's untimely death would bring about the death of the monarchy, their glee has proved premature. Charles is clearly irritated by republicanism, which he believes is partly inspired by envy. Besides, he points out, getting rid of monarchies doesn't automatically improve the lot of the people: his Russian relative Tsar Nicholas II was dethroned and murdered – 'and all that happened was that the Communists took over all the privileges for themselves, and the people suffered even more'.

'The crème de la scum' of industrial reporting will never regain their previous eminence in the papers. But the royal 'crème', despite having lost Diana, and finding middle-aged Camilla too mumsy for their taste, still have their occupation: they've now got the love life, military careers and nightclub antics of the two young princes to feed on. And I dare say their 'exes' are still pretty good too.

27

A Desert Princess

My battered taxi had turned off the tarmac road a while back but had now ground to a halt, drowning like a beetle in a vast sea of blazing white sand.

Ahead in the distance I could see a group of tents shimmering against the sky. Leaving the driver to struggle with his vehicle, I began gloomily trudging towards the camp to get help. It was bad enough being stranded in the desert in a 40-degree C heat but I'd already wasted a great deal of time trying to hunt down a particularly scandalous Dubai princess and now I would probably have to give up the search.

Then suddenly I saw her – a distant, surreal figure among the black tents ahead, surrounded by goats. Like a portly dragonfly, black-and-gold stripes blazing hectically in the desert sun, the figure began whisking its way towards me over the dunes.

Gold lamé gown, a star-spangled black veil, a dark, coppery mask with a rather sinister beak, a mass of gold jewellery, a bizarre pair of white gloves – and below it all, churning briskly though the sand and the goats, an improbable pair of sturdy little desert boots. 'Sheikha Sana, I presume,' I murmured as the apparition drew closer. I nervously half wondered whether somewhere on that small dazzling figure there was concealed her famous bazooka rocket-launcher. Or the .38 that she'd shot her husband's latest wife with. Or the silver-plated Sten gun that she'd allegedly turned on the soldiers who'd tried to stop her from gun-running to the rebel, self-styled 'Lord of the Green Mountains' in the neighbouring Sultanate of Oman . . .

'Huh!' snorted the Sheikha as she stood, golden arms akimbo, looking witheringly through her mask at me and the taxi. 'Your silly car is stuck! I will get it out for you later. But first, come this way. My house is over there'. And off she strode, trailing me, the goats and the mesmerized driver behind her.

This was in early 1975. In late 1973 OPEC, the Middle East oil-exporting cartel, imposed a supply embargo on the Western powers as punishment for providing Israel with oil during the Yom Kippur War; it was this emergency supply to Israel, OPEC believed, that had enabled 'the Zionist entity' to withstand the onslaught of the Arab armies.

Suddenly, ordinary people in the West, enraged by the soaring price of petrol and the resultant galloping inflation, wanted to know more about the people who were causing this chaos to their economies. Who exactly were these Arabs? Until the 'oil shock' of '73 few people (including most of my newspaper's readers) took any interest in the Gulf region. True, there were the Arabists in the Foreign Office (dubbed the 'Camel Corps'), and people like my dashing Uncle Kingsley who, after graduating from Cambridge, at twenty-two was put in charge of a large chunk of the lawless Yemen. But otherwise most people's knowledge of the region was derived from David Lean's 1962 film, *Lawrence of Arabia*.

One day David English rang me: 'I want you to go to the Gulf and write a series on Arab harems. We never hear anything about the wives and daughters of the oil sheikhs, we only hear about the sheikhs and London call-girls.'

'Harems', to a British audience, suggested an erotic, Turkish Delight fantasy world of luscious half-naked, sloe-eyed lovelies in yashmaks feeding their beloved lord and master with sweetmeats, waiting to be chosen for their master's bed. I already knew harems were probably not like that, not least because as a schoolchild in India I had a Muslim best friend called Dureshawar whose mother, along with two of her husband's other wives, was secluded in a *zenana*, the Urdu word for a harem (which merely means 'sanctuary', an all-women enclosure in which wives and children live). Whenever I went into the family *zenana*, from which unrelated adult males were excluded, all I saw were various middle-aged women, together with their children and their maidservants, gossiping companionably together and eating cake. It struck me as all very dull. Dureshawar agreed: 'When I marry I will *never* allow my husband to take other wives – and I won't be shut up indoors all the time like my mother!'

Polygamy is now a dying fashion in the Gulf: the poor cannot afford to support more than one wife (if they can afford to get married at all) and even the wealthy middle class are beginning to feel that the possession of multiple wives is a trifle vulgar. Besides, as one rich Qatari merchant confessed to me, 'Western men think it would be wonderful to have four wives at a time but, believe me, it only causes trouble. If your wives aren't quarrelling all the time, they're ganging up on you. And you have to deal not with one mother-in-law and her extended family, but *four* sets of them. So I divorced three of my wives some time ago and I'm much happier with just the one.'

Are the discarded wives happy? 'I think so. I still support them. Of course, because I'm the husband they cannot refuse the divorce.' (Under Sharia law a Muslim man can divorce his wife by declaring three times, 'I divorce thee' over a period of three months – although one Sharia court has recently ruled that doing so by email or text message is not valid.)

The power of the Arab husband is such that to get into the Gulf harems I had to go through the husbands, and that took time. At one point David English sent me a cable: 'HAVE YOU EMIGRATED QUERY'. No wife could meet me without her husband's permission, and many never left their homes and never went to restaurants or cinemas (where they existed) or even out for a walk. 'Why should I leave this place?' asked Sheikha Fatma, the favourite wife (out of an estimated nine) of the then ruler of Abu Dhabi. 'Everything I want is brought to me here.' Traditional Arab societies even now hardly rate women highly: in its family tree the Saudi Royal Family does not even list the womenfolk.

But I'd heard of an evidently utterly unsubmissive and stroppy royal wife called Sheikha Sana, the sister-in-law of Sheikh Rashed, the crafty merchant prince who ruled Dubai, the former gold-smuggling centre of the Middle East. Dubai had become part of the United Arab Emirates, the then shaky federation of tiny, oil-rich sheikhdoms strung along the shores of the Persian Gulf.

Ever since I'd arrived in the UAE I'd been hearing strange rumours about this princess. Of how, as a child-warrior at nine years old, she'd manned the guns in a savage tribal war against the very family to which she now belonged. And of how she'd watched Rashed's men slaughter her own family, putting their eyes out with swords, and driving her beloved father Sheikh Mana into exile. (Mana had been a reformist who believed in education, even for women.) And of how at thirteen Sana had been forcibly married to Sheikh Rashed's brother, one of her terrible conquerors; and of how, ever since, she'd refused to accept the cloistered, stultifying life of an Arab princess.

Sana, it seemed, couldn't be bothered to wait for oil wealth or formal education to liberate her. She'd simply used her indomitable will as a battering ram to smash her way through the system. After bearing two children, she'd launched herself on a business career, gleefully wheeling and dealing in property and ship-building: many of the wooden-hulled taxi boats on Dubai's then picturesque Creek were hers. Years earlier she had demanded, and got, the first ever driving licence granted to a Dubai woman: 'Why? Because I *like*!'

Clerics in neighbouring Saudi Arabia still declare it is 'un-Islamic' to allow women to drive (or to be driven by anyone other than a close male relative). In Saudi on the eve of the first Gulf War in 1990, I was yanked out of a car by the thuggish *muttawa'in*, the Morality police, because they suspected, correctly, that the driver I was with, a male colleague, was not related to me. They then bundled me into a taxi, despite my pointing out that the cab driver wasn't related to me either. When I later protested at my rough treatment to the American-educated Prince Fahd, a billionaire race-horse owner and Anglophile, he sighed exasperatedly: 'Yes, I agree this is ridiculous. My generation is educated and well-travelled, but I'm afraid we still have to go carefully when it comes to tradition. Too rapid change would be very destabilizing.'

Sana of course had little respect for such religious idiocies. As she later briskly informed me, 'The Prophet, Peace Be Upon Him, allow his favourite wife Aisha to ride camel into battle. If she alive today, she would be driving car!'

As for business interests, the Prophet's first wife Khadija, a divorcee fifteen years older than him whom he deeply mourned after her death, was herself a successful businesswoman and had actually employed the young Mohammed as a negotiator; she was so impressed by his hard work and probity that it was she who proposed to him. It was therefore, Sheikha Sana implied, in itself 'un-Islamic' to forbid women to drive, to run businesses or to behave assertively: 'Aisha very strong lady, speak as she wished!'

So far, so good. Unfortunately, the Prophet himself might have jibbed at what Sana had done six months before I met her. She'd apparently taken umbrage when her husband married his fourth wife, a former slave girl, and had expressed her disapproval by shooting and wounding the unfortunate bride. (It was, it seemed, the fact that the latest wife was black and not of royal blood, rather than marital jealousy, which enraged her. Understandably she was not over-fond of her husband in any case.) After shooting the new wife, Sana had taken off into the desert with her retainers, having first informed the deeply embarrassed Dubai police by telephone that any attempt at arrest would be met with gunfire.

The shock waves rippled across 130 miles of desert to the palace of Sheikh Zayed of Abu Dhabi, the President of the United Arab Emirates. Extra protection was provided for Zayed's wife, Sheikha Fatma – presumably on the grounds that Sana, having gunned down one Sheikha, might fancy taking pot-shots at a few more. But in fact she was never arrested; perhaps the scandal of a shoot-out with a royal princess was too shocking to contemplate. Small wonder though that the ever-charming government officials would shift uneasily whenever I mentioned her name – and that their earnest promises of help in making contact with her somehow never materialized. When I persisted, they'd mumble sheepishly, 'Ah . . . well, she is camping somewhere in desert. No, is impossible to find her.' 'We cannot explain, but she is . . . very naughty lady. Is not good you see her.' 'No, no, you cannot go alone. She is dangerous. Is not safe.'

But now I'd tracked her down at last. And here she was, striding ahead of me into her dusty concrete home in the inland oasis of Aweir. Inside the house, a huge, cool, circular drawing room, hung with gold damask curtains and lined with overstuffed sofas from Maples in London's Tottenham Court Road.

'You sit down. My English not so good. I have no practice, I am too busy with my businesses, my children, my gardens. I have much to say, I will get friend help translate.' The friend arrived, a young unveiled woman called Alia, but the voluble Sana scarcely needed her assistance. Three small children, two with the negroid features of the despised slave stock, came tumbling in and clambered lovingly on to the Sheikha's laméd lap. 'These my children,' she said, kissing their tight little black curls. 'I adopt them from hospital.'

A maidservant brought in tiny, handleless cups and filled them with cardamom coffee. 'Drink!' Sana ordered firmly. Though I dislike the bitter, perfumed taste, I of course did what I was told. The Sheikha briskly tipped up her mask to sip from her cup – and for a moment I glimpsed her face. Although she was then forty-five, the face was exquisite and totally unlined and the rumours of her once great beauty were evidently true. But the dye in the mask, which she'd worn all of her adult life, had over the years penetrated the skin, turning it indigo, adding a slightly farouche air to her features.

But what of the other rumours? Did she really man the guns at the age of nine? 'Ha! No, of course not: they were much too heavy for me. But yes, I help my father load them. But if I had been older, I would have done it . . . Blam! Blam!' She liked shooting, especially rabbits: 'But Sheikh Zayed, he say no more shooting rabbits. He say not enough rabbits left in desert. Ha!' She opened a tin of bright pink, scented biscuits. 'Eat!' Pieces of pink biscuit started disappearing rapidly under the mask. I liked the biscuits even less than the cardamom coffee but knew I had to eat them: 'traditional Arab hospitality', especially from the likes of Sana, can be somewhat overbearingly bossy (and usually does no favours to the waistline).

She scuttled off into another room and returned with a package for me. I unwrapped it and discovered an elaborate pair of gold and turquoise earrings and a bottle of Joy, then the most expensive perfume in the world. 'Is my favourite! I am ashamed this present not worthy of lovely lady like you. But I live in desert. No shops. Next time you come, I have something better!' We beamed delightedly at each other.

If Sana's present life was outrageous by the standards of conservative Gulf society, her savagely medieval past was almost unbelievable by ours. Her father Sheikh Mana was once the ruler of Deira, which until the early 1940s was an independent Sheikhdom but is now part of Dubai. The endless rivalry between Deira and Dubai finally exploded into a bloody tribal war and Dubai emerged the victor. During the hideous days of slaughter most of little Sana's family were wiped out and her father fled into exile. When she recalled those murderous times, she did so in a tone of flat simplicity; only rarely did bitterness creep through. 'I was nine when I saw them kill my family,' she said, sipping matter-of-factly at her coffee. 'And four years later' – she glanced up at the photograph of her husband on the wall – 'I was made to marry the man who killed them.' She paused. 'If I am strong woman now, is because of such experiences. I have lived in hell and I have fought my way to paradise.'

Sana's paradise was now this shabbily magnificent desert palace, filled with the chatter of children, friends and retainers. Here in her beloved gardens she wrote poetry, ran a little vegetable farm and planted trees with manic intensity. 'It is hobby. I love my trees. I plant myself – I like to dig.' It was from here and her palace in Dubai city (when allowed to return, as she did eventually) that she conducted her business deals. 'I have much land. I buy one piece for a million dinars, then I sell for three, four million, I like very much this business. Also I deal in ships. I do not want to just sit in palace and get big salary like other Sheikhas. I want earn my own money. I will not live enclosed like them and just . . . how you say, "goof about".' She leaned mischievously towards me. 'You have met Sheikha Fatma, Sheikh Zayed's wife? Yes? What is your opinion?' I replied cautiously that she seemed very charming. 'Huh!' snorted Sana in cheerful scorn. 'She just Bedou girl who marry big Sheikh, and now she live shut up like little bird in golden cage. If I am her, I commit *suicide*!'

I remarked that Sheikha Fatma seemed perfectly content to me. 'Pah! She know nothing better, poor thing!' Fatma had told me that she'd never been shopping in her life. Not so Sana. Her periodic descents on London stores were like a one-woman swarm of locusts. Alia described with much hilarity the sight of this little masked princess sashaying through Harrods. 'The assistants were absolutely open-mouthed. They kept gasping, "But madam, do you really want *fourteen* of these dresses?" Sana never bothers about sizes because they're all presents for friends and everything will fit *someone*. Last time we came back from London we had to send thirty-two cabin trunks full of presents by sea!'

As we talked, a helicopter flew noisily overhead in the bleached-denim sky. It was Sana's nephew, the dashing, twenty-eight-year-old Sheikh Mohammed, then the UAE Minister of Defence, visiting the flamboyant new palace he was building nearby, and dropping in for some cardamom coffee at a Bedou encampment. Sana sniffed crossly. 'This flying, I not like. I very afraid in aeroplanes. When I fly to London I say my prayers and read Koran all the time.' Sana *afraid*? Surely impossible. 'No point being brave in aeroplane. Courage only of use if you can do something about situation. And if plane goes wrong, what can Sana do?' I asked her if she envied young women like her friend Alia who'd been educated and had the chance of working abroad. 'No, I not envy them. What is the use? I cannot change my past. But I am pleased that things different for them, and misfortunes of women of my generation will not happen to them. When they look at women like us and see how tragic were our lives – how sad it was for us to be forced when children into marriage with men we did not know, and did not love – then they will not accept such a fate for themselves.'

Since Sana in her desert boots had kicked over most of the conventions, I was surprised that she bothered to adhere to any of them, such as wearing the mask. 'Is habit for me now. Anyway, as businesswoman I am meeting often with men, and is expected that a woman of my age and position must wear mask. Also, my brother-in-law Sheikh Rashed, he is in love with the mask,' she added witheringly. 'If his own wife take off mask and he not object, then all we women take it off. Boof! Just like that!' I produced my camera. 'No! No! Not allowed photograph me, my family will be angry. But you must come take picture of my tent. I like to live in tent. Is nice.'

She rose and swept out. On the concrete drive, a maroon Chevrolet Impala, upholstered in red-and-gold flowered velvet. She climbed in, commanded me to sit beside her, hitched up her golden skirt, straightened her mask, and jammed her boot on to the accelerator. The huge limousine shot off into the dunes like a missile, sending sand-devils whirling into the sky, its tyres shrieking. We arrived at the cluster of black tents. Servant girls squatted by fires, others attended to the cattle. 'This my tent. You take picture.' Sana's tent contained an iron bed, a camping stove, an old Bedou woman covered in flies, and a huge colour television. The aerial was rigged up on a nearby camel-thorn tree. 'Soon I get telephone here . . . These my goats. You take picture. These my cows. You take picture . . . Good. Now I take you back over desert to road. Taxi driver will follow.'

Back we shot across the dunes, past the tents, past the concrete palace, and past the astonished driver who by now had freed his taxi. He leapt into it and drove after us in hot pursuit. The Chevy, skidding and fizzing through the sand, eventually reached the road. The Sheikha climbed out of her car and bade me an affectionate farewell.

Evening was falling as I was driven away in the taxi. 'This Sheikha. She is mad, sick, yes?' asked the driver after a few moments of baffled reflection. I turned to look back at the lonely masked figure, a tiny black-and-gold insect, still waving her white-gloved hand at me from that desolate ribbon of road in the dying sunset.

'No,' I eventually replied. 'She's not mad, or sick. She was just the first, and her world was not yet ready for her.' But of course he didn't understand. In silence we drove on through the desert night towards the coast and the distant glow of the city.

Sana had been confident that women in these traditional societies would not have to endure what she had endured. And that is, indeed, to a certain extent true. She was born in 1930 into a desert society which had scarcely changed for over 1,000 years. The fathers of today's Gulf Sheikhs, now among the richest men in the world, were once just illiterate tribal chieftains, whose families had for centuries roamed these sandy wastes, most of the time squabbling with each other, often murderously. They lived off a meagre income from goats, piracy, pearling (until the Japanese invented cultured pearls) and slave-trading, and they fought one another with ancient muskets in endless tribal feuds over precious water wells and scrubby date groves.

And until the discovery of oil no one in the West, bar a few romantic explorers, cared too much about what they got up to among themselves. And so brother plotted against brother, cousin murdered cousin; of the sixteen previous rulers of Abu Dhabi five had been deposed and eight slaughtered by their relations.

Sheikh Zayed, the first President and in effect founder of the UAE, a shrewd and idealistic man who yanked his medieval kingdom into the modern world, first deemed it necessary in 1966 to depose his eccentric and paranoid brother, Shakhbut, who kept his money in tin trunks under the bed (until the trunks burst). Shakhbut only transferred the loot into the safe confines of a dungeon after he discovered that the rats and insects in his mud-walled palace on an offshore island had been eating it. He never reconciled himself to the advent of the automobile: 'I did all my travelling by camel in the old days,' he sighed. 'But now I have to go by car because if the Ruler went by camel, people would think it was peculiar.' Of course Shakhbut had reason to be paranoid, as did most tribal chiefs in the Gulf. He took over in Abu Dhabi in 1928 when his brother was assassinated, having earlier killed their father who, in turn, had come to power by killing his older brother. When Sana was obliged to marry a man who'd murdered her family, this was then considered quite normal in the Arab world. And after all, English history is full of such dynastic alliances in which victorious kings and nobles married the daughters (who had no say in the matter) of their defeated enemies; but that, of course, was centuries ago.

When I was working in Beirut in the early Seventies I had lunch on the Corniche in the achingly chic St Georges Hotel (now still a ruin after both the civil war and recent car bombs) with a Lebanese businessman in the oil trade. 'Dealing with Shakhbut was a nightmare – this new chap Zayed will be better, we hope. But these Gulf Arabs,' he added with a note of contempt, 'they've only just left the medieval camel period – you can't expect them to leap from the fifteenth century to the twentieth and become "modern" overnight just because they can now afford Cadillacs! You know, there's this anecdote about Mohammed: a man comes to him and says, "Oh Prophet! How do you describe this Heaven of yours? Can we Arabs fight one another over there?" And the Prophet says, "There is peace in Paradise, not war." The Arab retorts, "Then that is not our Heaven, because we have been brought up to be warriors." That's what Gulf Arabs are used to.' (To which Gulf Arabs might respond that it's a bit cheeky for a Lebanese to denounce them on this count, given Lebanon's own bloody history of intra-Arab strife.)

But the contempt with which the Lebanese, and especially the Egyptians (whose upper class prided itself on being the intellectual hub of the Arab world), regarded their 'brothers' in the Gulf was, and is, blatant. And it caused a major problem for a French TV team who in 1975 had arrived in the UAE to make a documentary entitled 'A Day in the Life of an Oil Sheikh'.

One night in the bar of the Abu Dhabi Hilton I met the prize-winning Canadian director of the putative documentary; he was sunk in gloom, fury and whisky. 'We're buggered. We've spent *months* fixing this and when we arrive the f****** sheikh isn't there! His dozy staff – when we could get hold of them – told us, "He's gone bustard-shooting in Pakistan"! They don't know when he'll be back, and we can't find another sheikh at such short notice!' I suspected I knew why the TV team had this problem: their fixer was a sleek French-woman with impeccable Arabic, but she'd been born in Alexandria in Egypt and spoke 'Egyptian' Arabic – which instantly marked her out as someone who, ipso facto, would be snobbish about mere sheikhs from the despised, if now wealthy, Gulf. Pleasurable bustard-shooting, as far as the selected sheikh was concerned, would obviously take precedence.

It was two days after I'd interviewed Sana out in the desert and I remembered the sight of Sheikh Mohammed flying his own chopper; and from what I'd heard about him young Sheikh 'Mo' seemed to be thoroughly modern-minded and pro-Western and thus an ideal subject. So I 'fixed' it for the TV team: my lack of Arabic actually worked in my favour, since it carried no internecine class under-tones. Sheikh 'Mo' is now the Ruler of Dubai and the man whose relentlessly modernizing will – and wealth – has created that boom city.

Sheikha Sana may have despised the cloistered Sheikha Fatma, but both women had been illiterate and both had been married, at the age of thirteen, to men they'd never met. But they had another thing in common: an obsession with female education, and both women used their wealth and status to empower younger Gulf women (and both earned international plaudits for doing so).

Indeed, when I interviewed Fatma over thirty years ago she seemed remarkably well informed about the world outside her palace walls. Every morning her briskly efficient Egyptian secretary Hayat translated for her extracts from Western newspapers and magazines, including *Time*, *Newsweek*, *Le Monde*, *Figaro*, *The Times*, the *Telegraph*, the *Guardian* and the *Observer*. And, unfortunately for me, rather less high-minded newspapers as well.

Some of what Fatma had read enraged her and she suddenly burst into a diatribe in guttural Arabic, waving her arms so that the diamonds on her wrists flashed furiously under the vast chandelier which hung above her head. Hayat nervously translated: 'Er . . . Her

Highness wants to know why you Western journalists write such terrible lies about us. When the family last visited Buxted Park [the stately home in Sussex then owned by Sheikh Zayed] your newspapers wrote rubbish about slaves and concubines and everyone sitting eating rice off the floor like savages. Why do you want to make us look backward?'

I tried to placate the masked and cloistered Sheikha by apologizing for some of my Fleet Street colleagues' ignorance: 'You seem to know and understand more about our world than we have ever bothered to learn about yours.' The diatribe ended, the diamonds calmed down, and she became almost amused by my discomfiture. I asked her why she always wore the veil and the beaked mask even among other women: her sister-in-law who was in the room with us wore neither. 'It is a habit for me. And she is of the younger generation. My daughters, for example, unlike me, will go to school, they will not wear the mask or the veil, and they will finish their education and not marry as young as I did. Change will only come by Allah's will, and because Allah is good, and knows all, and decides all, it is not for me to question it.'

Sheikha Sana died, much honoured, in 2006. Sheikha Fatma is still alive and is routinely dubbed 'Mother of the Nation', but you'll never find a photograph of her in the Arab or Western press. So I wonder what they would think of Sheikha Mozah, the powerful second wife (of three) of the Emir of Qatar, who is constantly photographed, never wears the mask and, in the West, doesn't even wear the veil. The concept of power-behind-the-throne, particularly if the power is female, tends to arouse resentment on every continent. (When Bill Clinton first became President, Hillary was constantly criticized for her bossy behaviour: 'You know what I don't like about this new President? She's too pushy.')

There are, I'm told, older, conservative Qatari men who, fingering their worry beads, feel uncomfortable with the glamorous Sheikha Mozah's high profile in the Emirate: the young hussy appears on television, and has even headed an overseas delegation *without her husband*! Worse still, her husband the Emir seems quite happy to sit in the audience when his wife is giving a speech.

But of course the elegant Mozah is no hussy, and not even particularly young: she's the highly educated mother of seven and a grandmother, and is a role model to many young Qatari girls I've met. It's largely thanks to her that Qatar, using some of its vast oil and natural gas wealth, is trying to turn itself into the epicentre of education, both male and female, in the Gulf. Her husband Sheikh Hamad, in time-honoured Gulf fashion, impatiently ousted his father in a bloodless coup in 1995 because the previous Emir was dragging his feet on modernization and, he suspected, in equally time-honoured Gulf fashion had been siphoning off too much of the gross national product for himself.

Sheikha Mozah even had the nerve to declare that using child jockeys (usually destitute young boys imported from Pakistan) in the traditional camel races was 'not humane', and her husband then criminalized the practice. Camels, it seems, don't need goading as horses do: they run like the clappers anyway, and all they need is light guidance on the reins to keep them galloping in a straight line. So Qatari technologists, bowing to the First Lady's will, devised robotic jockeys to replace the small boys and, apparently, the camels race just as well.

When I first went to Qatar in 1975 it was little more than a flat, bleak, burningly hot and windswept sandpit, jutting out into the glassy waters of the Gulf. In the dusty little capital Doha there were only two rather modest hotels and, as Qatar officially belongs to the puritanical Wahhabi sect of Islam, no bars or alcohol. When I checked in to my hotel, the receptionist (male of course) took my details and then, expressionessly, informed me, 'You will need a medical certificate.' What for? 'You will need a certificate,' he said firmly, and handed me a slip of paper. 'Go to the first floor and present it at this room number.'

I knocked on the door of Room 101 (yes, really), which was indistinguishable from others along the corridor. It opened half an inch and I thrust my 'medical certificate' through it. The door chain was then lifted – to reveal a virtual speakeasy heaving with muscled British oil riggers with 'Love' and 'Hate' and 'Mum' tattoos on their brawny arms, raucously swigging cans of lager. Apart from me there were no women, Qatari or foreign, present; we were all, apparently, now registered as 'alcoholics' who needed booze as 'medication'.

These days, whenever I go to Qatar I find it unrecognizable as the country I first visited: skyscrapers, marinas, luxury hotels (with well-stocked, sophisticated cocktail bars from which Qataris, including the women, are not excluded). Offices are full of women workers, Qatari and foreign, veiled and unveiled. Islamic veiling here, unlike in Iran and Saudi Arabia, is optional even for Qatari women. Hard to believe that as late as the 1950s this was still a slave-owning country (and I'm not referring to the then slavish status of its women). In 1953 the Emir was a guest at the Queen's coronation and brought his favourite black slaves with him, and did so again on a visit to London five years later.

The status of Arab women might be seen by some as a 'girly' subject, thus suitable for a female journalist. But the issue is a serious one and has, in this era of Islamist terror, far-reaching consequences for the West. The Arab world, steeped in the culture of self-destructive victimhood, has never tried to examine itself or to analyse the reasons why, despite oil wealth, it is now in catastrophic economic decline compared to the rest of the developing world. Between the eighth and the fourteenth centuries the Muslim world was in the ascendancy – in learning, in intellectual debate, in science. Now there is virtually no technological advance originating in the region. And, in the UN phrase, 'information poverty' is acute in the Arab world: according to the latest available figures, it translates only about 330 books a year, which is one fifth of the number that, for example, Greece alone translates. The Greek population is just under 11 million, the Arab world's is over 300 million.

The Arab world is, of course, bitterly aware of the humiliating fact that it is also slipping rapidly behind the developed world. But it tends to attribute every reverse, every failure, solely to colonialism, imperialism, treachery or Zionism. And then in 2002 came the devastating report by the United Nations Development Programme which laid the blame for this decline almost entirely on political, religious and cultural factors within the Arab world itself.

The report caused a predictable uproar – but no one could accuse it of being the product of yet another Zionist or imperialist conspiracy. It was entirely researched and written by Arabs themselves. One of three main reasons for Arab economic decline, the report stated, was female illiteracy, with its concomitant gender discrimination and lack of female empowerment. And, shockingly, female adult illiteracy in the Arab world is actually increasing.

But even if a girl is educated, her menfolk very often won't allow her to work. I once talked to an Abu Dhabi girl who, when an undergraduate, was discussing her future career with a university adviser when her father burst in, shouting, 'Okay, I've paid for her to be educated – but not so that she can work! Women must get married, have children and stay in the home!' At least that girl had received an education, but more than half the women in the Arab world are illiterate, one of the highest rates in the world (Yemen, for example, has a 75 per cent female illiteracy rate). Illiterate women cannot effectively contribute to a modern economy, cannot help relieve the poverty of their families, cannot even understand basic instructions about nutrition and health. For over half the population to be unable to contribute to the economy obviously has a catastrophic effect on the productivity and development of the countries in which they were born.

One day in Doha I listened to a startling speech by Qatar's Emir in which he told his audience that the time had come when the Arab world should stop blaming everyone but itself for its failures. He pointed out that largely Muslim Malaysia had also suffered under colonialism: but instead of forever looking back at past injustices, it had looked forward and transformed itself into one of the Asian 'tigers'. Today in Qatar the literacy rates for men and women are now virtually equal – an achievement unique in the Arab world.

28

'Song is the devil's pipe'

'You've got exactly nine seconds to put on your respirator, because in ten seconds you're dead!' I was informed by the brisk Scottish staff sergeant at RAF Brize Norton who was instructing me on how to survive a nuclear, biological or chemical attack.

I was heading for Saudi Arabia on the eve of the first Gulf War against Saddam Hussein in 1991, and it was assumed that Saddam, who'd invaded and occupied Kuwait and declared it to be 'the nineteenth province of Iraq', possessed biological and chemical weapons – a reasonable assumption, because he had already used them on his own people as well as on the Iranians during the eight-year war that he'd launched on them.

After his defeat in that first Gulf War international atomic inspectors scoured Iraq and discovered that he did indeed have huge stockpiles; those that they discovered, they destroyed. (Unfortunately Saddam's insistence before the second Gulf War in 2003 that he didn't have any weapons of mass destruction was not believed by Western intelligence agencies, since that psychopath had consistently lied about possessing them in the past.)

But Saddam's psychopathy was not at the forefront of my mind that morning at Brize Norton. My clothes – and Saudi 'sensitivities' – were. Having worked in the country before, I'd arrived for my training session wearing what I knew I'd be obliged to wear in that grimly imam-ridden Kingdom: it was my 'Widow Twankey' outfit, a long, flowing, figure-concealing, utterly impractical but thoroughly Islamically approved get-up. Otherwise, I reckoned, if Saddam's Scuds didn't get me, Saudi's *muttawa'in*, the religious bullies employed by the Commission for the Promotion of Virtue and the Prevention of Vice, just might.

Waiting in the Departures area before flying out to Dhahran, I gazed ruefully out of the window at the soft morning light. I felt acutely aware that just beyond the RAF base there lay a plump, peaceful landscape of Oxfordshire manor houses, golden stone villages, meandering rivers – Kelmscott, Minster Lovell, the Evenlode. And it seemed faintly unreal to me that here I was preparing to go to yet another war in the broken, violent, humiliated and desperately dysfunctional Middle East.

Unfortunately, thanks to Saudi sensitivities about female garb, my training session had been an embarrassing failure. As he watched me struggling to get myself and my Widow Twankey outfit into the NBC protection suit, the RAF staff sergeant had barked, 'If this was for real, Miss Leslie, you would have been dead four minutes ago!'

He then held up a white pad stained with a range of colours as though from a child's water paints: 'This stain tells you you're dealing with a nerve agent . . . this tells you it's a choking agent . . . this one tells you it's a blister agent.' What if I got that stuff in my eyes? 'Wash your eyeballs immediately, otherwise within five minutes your eyes will blister and you've had it!' Depending on the colour, I would then have to jab a hypodermic into my thigh through the NBC suit (if, that is, I'd been able to get the thing on in the first place).

Training session abandoned, I flew out to Saudi to report on the build-up to the war about to be waged by a thirty-four-nation coalition in order to wrest Kuwait from Saddam's bloody fingers. But I chose not to cover the war itself.

I'm *not* a war reporter, I told myself. My speciality is foreign politics; but, more relevantly, I'm a wife and mother: I'm not going to risk irretrievably damaging the lives of my husband and our twelve-year-old daughter by getting myself killed – by 'nerve agents', 'choking agents', 'blister agents' or anything else – out here in the desert sands, just because one bunch of Arabs is bent on slaughtering another bunch of Arabs. After all, I thought, they're always doing that, aren't they? The vast majority of the world's refugees are Muslims fleeing other Muslims. And nothing we do – or report – seems to be able to stop the carnage. Indeed, if we non-Muslim outsiders try to, we're accused of imperialistic interference in their sovereign affairs.

Nevertheless, I felt guilty: it was my job to go wherever the stories were and 'Operation Desert Storm' was the biggest story in the world at the time. In past conflicts I had usually felt the excitement that soldiers feel when they first go into action. Mortars crump into the earth not far away, snipers' bullets ping into nearby walls, the adrenaline pumps through your veins, your eyes, skin and the roots of your hair prickle; and when the attack's over and you're still unscathed, you become infected by a slightly deranged exhilaration: 'Ha ha! You b******s didn't get me this time!'

But somehow this time I knew that that excitement wouldn't buoy me up as it had done in the past. 'Why aren't you coming with us into Iraq?' an astonished colleague in Saudi asked me one evening. 'You're not using your family as an excuse, are you? It's never stopped you in the past: I've always thought of you as being utterly fearless!'

And, indeed, I'd always given that impression. Maybe fear of being seen as fearful had sometimes driven me to take (what others considered) insane risks in pursuit of a story which would merit, at most, 2,300 words on two inside pages. One evening in Addis Ababa in Ethiopia, the late Jon Akass, an old Fleet Street friend, embarked on his favourite theme (which would usually be gloomily delivered over a triple gin): 'One day, Leslie, they'll find us out.' Find out, that is, that we were not nearly as competent or as brave as 'they', the outsiders, deemed us to be. 'You and I know it's all a con.'

Oddly enough, I've never been particularly afraid physically. But in the past the gut-wrenching fear which would grip me just before doing a story was that this time I wouldn't be able to pull it off – especially if I was going to a country to which I'd never been before and where I'd established no contacts. But long before the first Gulf War that kind of fear had subsided. I knew by now that it wasn't, as Akass had put it, 'all a con'. Having expunged one fear, though, another replaced it: the fear that by constantly 'proving' myself I risked inflicting a grave cost on those who loved me. It may not sound convincing, but the fact was that now I was frightened, not for myself, but for them.

At the end of the war, when the Iraqis had been driven out of Kuwait, I returned to the city. When I'd first worked there, it was a fantastically wealthy, carelessly comfortable, perhaps a rather smug and lazy little emirate. Saddam's brief and bloody 'annexation' and the subsequent war had changed all that. On the coastal road, the beaches still lined with Iraqi bunkers, flattened cafés and tangled webs of 'porcupine' wire, the British army jeep I was riding in passed the remains of 'Entertainment City', Kuwait's one-time answer to Disneyland. Farewell the 'Sindbad the Sailor' ride, now a heap of twisted metal. Farewell the thrills of the 'Atom Smasher'.

Kuwaitis needed no such ersatz excitement now that they had to contend with 'Dodge City' (as the army driver described it to me), where unexplained gunshots would regularly shatter the acrid night air. 'Bang goes another Palestinian!' a British journalist joked uneasily. Kuwait's 400,000 stateless Palestinians, who did much of the administrative work in Kuwait, had been expelled in revenge for Yasser Arafat's support for Saddam; some had not yet left and were having to dodge vengeful Kuwaitis. (The Palestinians seem ordained to be on the losing side of history, and they, their catastrophically bad leaders, and their fellow Arabs – let alone the Israelis – seem determined that they should stay that way.)

I doubt that any Kuwaitis missed the scary fun of the 'Oasis Express' ride, not when their city was full of unexploded bombs, live grenades (I found one in the hotel's underground car park) and of course innumerable Iraqi mines. 'This is not a particularly friendly little beast,' Lieutenant Pete Williams informed me, pointing at a deceptively endearing Dalek-like object with spikes on its head; its particular party trick was to leap out of the sand and blow your face off. And what *son et lumière* tourist spectacle could compete with the sight of the burning oil wells? 'A terrible beauty' had indeed been born: fiery orange flowers performed a wild dance of death beneath ostrich-feather smoke plumes, in constantly swirling shades of livid white, dove grey and inky black.

And 'dance of death' is not mere purple prose – it was, on at least one occasion, literally true. The military wouldn't allow me to get close to the burning oilfields, but I wanted to interview the specialist American firefighters trying to deal with the oilfield blazes. I found an abandoned but working car and a willing Egyptian driver, and we drove out into the area. A couple of days later two other journalists and their driver did the same: the wind suddenly changed direction, the 'fiery orange flowers' swung down across the road, and all three were instantly incinerated.

To my surprise the city was not, despite the Allied bombing, a smoking ruin; this was no Dresden. In fact, remarkable numbers of sumptuous villas, Mercedes and even valuable artworks in wealthy homes remained intact. In one still occupied and unvandalized house I visited I saw a Picasso sketch and two Dalis; perhaps understandably Saddam's hapless conscripts, who had been looting mundane things like buckets, packs of disposable nappies, bathroom fittings and children's toys for their families back home, would've been unable to assess the monetary worth of what might have seemed to them to be merely weird Western daubs and scribbles.

The Kuwaiti Royal Family and most of the elite had already fled to safety before the war, leaving behind the poor, the migrant workers, the Palestinians and the myriad Filipina maids whose passports they'd impounded. The stranded Filipinas proved extremely resourceful on behalf of some of the incoming Western media. Food and water, let alone electricity, were scarce, but large media organizations like the American networks and the BBC had driven into Kuwait across the Saudi border in vehicles crammed with water bottles and tins of food. Working alone and, as a woman, forbidden by the Saudis to drive, let alone hire a vehicle in the Kingdom, I couldn't bring in my own supplies, so was obliged to cadge the odd tin from the BBC.

One evening in our Iraqi-vandalized hotel (they'd shot off all the locks on the doors) I sniffed the aroma of scorching meat drifting down the corridor. The female producer for Sky News had rounded up some stranded Filipinas and sent them off on food-foraging expeditions; miraculously, they'd returned with plentiful supplies of steak which were now being cooked over a camp stove.

Had these steaks been 'liberated' from abandoned deep-freezes? Or was their provenance more sinister? Kuwait City was littered with now homeless pedigree dogs and I'd seen these once doted-upon chihuahas and spaniels with matted hair rootling hopefully in piles of rubbish, a few of which gave off the sweet stench of rotting human flesh. 'Are you sure we're not eating barbecued chihuahua?' I asked the Sky producer. 'I don't ask, and I don't care,' she replied as we tucked in.

The Kuwaitis don't seem to have suffered *that* much, I thought at first. But I soon felt ashamed of my self-justifying flippancy about 'one bunch of Arabs slaughtering another bunch': as you would, when you first hear about thirty-two-year-old Asra al-Qabandi, who had been secretly sending out intelligence reports using a satellite phone before the Iraqis arrested her; after which they tortured and killed her, scooped out her brain, wrapped her mutilated body in a cloth and dumped it on her parents' front lawn ...

And as you would, when you're faced with Kuwaiti women, faces haggard with grief, who tell you through stuttering tears about how their sons, husbands, brothers, fathers had suffered torture at the hands of the occupying Iraqis – 'they blinded him', 'they crushed his arms', 'they castrated him under interrogation' – and who, almost more poignantly, begged you for help in tracking down those who had been 'disappeared' by Saddam during Iraq's seven-month occupation ...

And as you would, when you stand on the ceasefire line in southern Iraq, under a jaunty banner declaring it to be 'Checkpoint Charlie – Freedom's Frontier', and listen to the distant thumps of Saddam's gunships now pulverizing his southern Shias, to punish them for their attempted uprising ...

It all makes it very difficult for even the most cynical observer to stick to the view that *il faut cultiver son jardin*, and that the appalling things that people do to one another beyond our own borders is none of our business and they should simply be left to get on with it.

I was up at Checkpoint Charlie on the first day when the peace treaty signed between Saddam and the Allies came into operation; we had, as mandated by the UN, driven him out of Kuwait. But the UN did not mandate us to carry on to Baghdad and effect 'regime change'. So we'd stopped here, at this ceasefire line in the desert.

Standing beside me, looking towards Basra and the desperate Shia refugees and their families who were fleeing in our direction across the blisteringly hot, mine-infested sands to 'Freedom's Frontier', was a burly American sergeant from North Carolina. He was wearing Polaroid sunglasses and at first sight resembled a caricature of the 'kick-ass' Bruce Willis-style military killer. But below the mirrored lenses, tears were forming rivulets in his sand-covered cheeks: 'Sorry, ma'am, but Ah'm really choked – Ah cannot believe that the United Nations and our President don't allow us to save these folks. Look at these children, look at that little girl, look at that baby – got one that age back home – how can we leave innocent folks like this to be gassed and murdered by Saddam?'

But we could, and we did. Which is why many of us felt then that there was unfinished business here. After all, the first President Bush had encouraged the Shia to rise up against Saddam, and when they did, he abandoned them. 'Why America leave us now?' an agonized young refugee, a male nurse from the holy city of Najaf, had asked me at 'Freedom's Frontier'. 'If America and Britain leave, he kill us all. We human beings, just like you! Why you do this to us?'

And over the years, when trying to answer similar questions from ordinary exiled Iraqis and on hearing, detail after grisly detail, about Saddam's persecution of trade unionists and the torture and murder of human rights activists and their families, I'd become infuriated by those anti-war protesters on the left who seemed content to let this cruelty continue indefinitely, and who preferred to vent their self-righteous 'humanitarian' ire on Bush and Blair instead.

When the novelist Alice Walker declared soulfully, 'I firmly believe the only punishment that works is love,' and Shirley MacLaine, in equally daffy terms, insisted that the best way to deal with dictators and terrorists was to 'melt their weapons, melt their hearts, melt their anger with love', I found myself asking, 'What planet do you soppy women live on?'

And that's why, unfashionably (and unlike my own newspaper), I supported the second President Bush's decision, twelve years after the first Gulf War, that America should go to war against Saddam again. Because of Saddam's unequivocally stated intention to obliterate all his enemies and to exert Iraqi hegemony over the Middle East, I concluded that eventually another war with him was going to be inevitable – and that it was therefore better to strike while his defences were still relatively weak.

I was not so naive as to suppose that once Saddam had been deposed a golden age of enlightened Western-style democracy would flower like primroses across that blighted land; thirty-five years of a cruel, incompetent and corrupt Ba'athist dictatorship had brutalized Iraq, and of course war itself is brutalizing. But I had been naive enough to believe that George W.'s government would not be as astonishingly inept as it proved to be in the management of the aftermath; nor how ignorant about tribal, Arab and Muslim culture so many of its administrators and contractors on the ground would turn out to be.

Even mere journalists like myself know that before going to work in an alien land you must, even if only for survival's sake, hoover up as much information about its culture as possible. To understand all is not to forgive all, but before you can decide which aspects of the culture are wholly unforgivable, it helps if you have some understanding of it in the first place. So-called 'honour' killings, for example, simply cannot be excused on the grounds of 'traditional culture'. And that isn't just a 'Western perspective': in Egypt, Turkey and Britain, I've met brave Muslim women who campaign against 'honour' killings, and who correctly point out that this practice is not prescribed by Islam, but derives from patriarchal tribal traditions, most of which pre-date Islam. Alas, this doesn't save such campaigning women from threats and abuse in their own communities.

Fundamentalism is growing stronger throughout the Muslim world, which is why I keep some Islamist-approved female gear to wear, where necessary, when working in the Middle East. And every time I pack it into my suitcase, I reflect on the purported reason for all these hejabs, jilbabs, chadors, burqas, niqabs, abayas. This 'religiously mandated' clobber is not stipulated in the Koran, which merely says that 'it is better' for Muslim women to dress and behave modestly when they're in public.

Moreover, elements of this attire only became the norm in the Muslim world in medieval times when the Arab warriors had established their empire (and had picked up styles of dress from Jewish tribes and from upper-class Byzantine Christians who used to veil their women to distinguish them from the vulgar hoi polloi). Of course it's always been the habit of conquerors to try to impose their sartorial norms on the conquered, usually on the grounds of religious rectitude.

When I first went to Polynesia in the Sixties I asked why the women were all trussed up in those long, shapeless sacks called muu-muus; 'It is our cultural tradition,' I was informed. No it isn't. Polynesian cultural tradition used to involve a 'shockingly' easygoing attitude to nudity – until the Christian missionaries took over in the nineteenth century and told the women that they had to cover up lest sight of their unfettered breasts inflame masculine (and perhaps missionary) lust. As far as I know, the muu-muu is not ordained by the Bible, any more than the burqa is ordained by the Koran.

In Arabic the word *fitna* means 'schism' or 'strife'; significantly, it is also used as a synonym for 'beautiful woman', a glimpse of whom by unrelated adult males will supposedly give rise to uncontrollable lust and thereby lead to appalling amounts of 'strife'. The puritanical Wahhabi-sect Saudis do not of course put the onus on men to control their nether regions – but on women (beautiful or not) to refrain from 'provoking' these virtuous but hapless males into hell-deserving vice by letting them glimpse a single, apparently maddeningly erotic, strand of hair.

Sometimes even the glimpse of a bare female wrist is deemed to be enough to engorge a Saudi male's propensities and thus cause *fitna* – which is why, however bakingly hot the weather (as it was during one of my visits to Riyadh), I saw several heavily black-swathed and veiled Saudi wives wearing black gloves. Fundamentalist Islam, far more even than fundamentalist Christianity, seems to me to be unhealthily obsessed with sex.

We godless souls in the consumerist West may trivialize the activity by draping half-naked bimbos over car bonnets and publishing lip-smacking kiss 'n' tell confessions, but in the Middle East the obsession with sexuality, and especially the denial of it, has rather more dangerous consequences for us, let alone for the Arab world itself.

It means that millions of young Arab men, unable to afford to get married (marriage is particularly expensive in the Middle East) and forbidden, under the threat of hellfire, to express their hormonal urges with anyone to whom they are not married, take other, sometimes deadly, routes to fulfilment. (As in gender-segregated boarding schools in England, testosterone-fuelled Arab youths may indulge in a little light homosexuality, but this route is frankly not advisable since in radical Islamist eyes homosexual acts must be punished by death.)

Unfortunately, one of these routes out of endemic sexual frustration is driven by the delusional belief that if these young men become martyrs and die fighting us, the *kuffar* unbelievers, they will be provided in Paradise with seventy-two virgins and all the carnal pleasures which their society and their version of Islam has denied them on earth.

Not all suicide bombers are frustrated virgins, of course (several have been married men with children); some, including the 9/11 bombers, had a high old time with *kuffar* prostitutes before their self-induced deaths, believing that all this sexual depravity would be instantly forgiven once they became a *shahid*, martyr, and that Allah – 'the most Compassionate, the most Merciful' – would reward their 'self-sacrifice', and their indiscriminate slaughter of innocents, with unlimited guilt-free sex for eternity.

And of course I know many good, decent, sophisticated and devout Muslim men, both here and in the Middle East, who do not subscribe to 'all this medieval seventy-two-virgins rubbish' (as one of them described it to me). But then, these are not the sort of chaps who'd strap explosives to their chests and kill themselves, along with as many bystanders as possible, in order to get lots of celestial leg-over in the hereafter.

But however well I'm prepared on the Islamist-clobber front, I have occasionally made careless mistakes. Shortly after 9/11, I flew to Cairo to explore the background of al-Qaeda. Egypt gave birth to bin Laden's ideology through the writings of the philosopher of jihad, Sayyid Qutb, who was hanged by the Egyptian secular dictator Gamal Abdel Nasser in 1966. Qutb was the leading intellectual in the Muslim Brotherhood movement, whose slogan is 'Islam is the Answer' (to more or less everything).

Those who blame the West's support for Israel – and Israel itself – for the burgeoning of Islamist terrorism forget, if they ever knew, that the Brotherhood itself was created in 1928, twenty years before Israel even came into existence. The Brothers believe that if the *ummah*, the Muslim world community, returned to the seventh-century virtues and unadulterated beliefs of Mohammed and his successors, 'the Rightly-Guided Caliphs', then Allah would wipe out centuries of humiliation inflicted by the victorious 'Crusaders' of the West and would restore temporal power to Islam.

I'd read my Qutb in translation and I knew he was particularly fierce about women who were not veiled; Muslim women who did not wear Islamic garb were, he insisted, no longer Muslims because they had disobeyed Allah's instructions.

Obviously, I had to talk to someone in the Muslim Brotherhood, preferably its aged Supreme Guide. The movement has inspired not only bin Laden and his Egyptian deputy and theological overseer, Ayman al-Zawahari, to commit atrocities against unbelievers, but also a host of murderous sub-groups. Death is decreed by them not only for unbelievers (especially Jews and Christians whom the Brotherhood's co-founder Hassan al-Banna said 'it is necessary to kill'), but also for those Muslims they denounce as not being Muslim enough.

When I'm accused, as I occasionally am, of 'not understanding Islam', I feel thoroughly exasperated. Which version of Islam am I supposed to 'understand'? Which lot represent 'the true Islam' and which lot are *takfir*, heretic? I've worked in Northern Ireland during the 'Troubles' and, believe me, understanding the doctrinal differences between Unionist Protestant Ulstermen and Catholic nationalist ones is a walk in the park compared to Islam.

Depending on which devout Muslim you are talking to at any one time, Shiites are *takfir*, heretics, or Sunnis are, or Ismaelis are, or Deobandis are, or Sufis are, or Ahmadiyyas are, or Barelvis are, or Wahhabis are, or Salafis are. The one thing all these myriad 'heretics' seem to agree on is that all the rest of us are *kuffar*, infidels.

But while in Cairo, I was also interviewing leading Egyptian secularists, two of whom were on a fundamentalist 'death list', and they were understandably appalled at the growth of the Brotherhood in their cosmopolitan city. (Incidentally, the Brotherhood, though technically illegal, is hugely popular among Egypt's myriad poor because it provides an efficient welfare system for them, which the corrupt and authoritarian secular government has signally failed to do.) Naturally it would not be tactful to wear a hejab with these determinedly anti-Brotherhood secularists.

One afternoon I was talking to a retired doctor, who was both anti-Brotherhood and anti-Government (he'd been imprisoned for fifteen years for denouncing its human rights record); the doctor had been an ally of Farag Foda, a leading intellectual and satirist, who'd been assassinated in 1992. The doctor had himself been put under police guard for a while, 'but my wife and I eventually refused it because we thought it put us in greater danger as it drew attention to us wherever we went'.

Foda had been murdered because he argued that, contrary to Brotherhood mythology, there'd never been a golden age of unity and virtue under the four 'Rightly Guided Caliphs', the Prophet Mohammed's successors; after all, three of them had been assassinated by their fellow Muslims. Moreover, he pointed out, the 'sword of Islam' which fundamentalists so yearn for had, during the 'golden age', beheaded far more Muslims than it ever did infidels. And continues so to do. Worse still, Foda had mocked a popular blind Islamist preacher, Abdel Hamid Kishk, who, among other things, declared that singing was un-Islamic, because 'song is the devil's pipe, the courier of fornication'.

Kishk's obsession with sex, according to Foda, led to him 'telling his audience that Muslims who entered paradise would enjoy eternal erections and the company of young boys draped in earrings and necklaces'. Foda's punishment for this 'attack on Islam' was a lethal shot in the head by two masked gunmen while he was working in his Cairo office. The Brotherhood insists that it is moderate and non-violent, but a suspicious number of its offshoots and disciples – including bin Laden and al-Zawahiri – believe that violence is not only necessary, but Allah-mandated.

The problem for me was Cairo's endemic traffic jams. I'd just received a message saying that Mamoun al-Hodeibi, the Supreme Guide of the Brotherhood himself, had finally agreed to see me but I had to get round to his office in half an hour. Unfortunately I'd left my hejab at the hotel and didn't have time to go back and retrieve it, let alone stop off to buy another.

I arrived at his office in Sharia Malek Salah in what appeared to be a semi-derelict building. But the polished mahogany door, and the sounds of prayer and Koranic recitations thrumming out through it into the corridor, confirmed to me that, despite the building's appearance, this was indeed the headquarters of the most serious threat to the secular regime of President Hosni Mubarak. (Mubarak alternates between pandering to the Islamists and imprisoning them, depending on the political exigencies of the moment.) The Supreme Guide's staff of bearded young men took one look at my unveiled head and panicked. 'No! No! *Haram*, forbidden!' One of them seized a large, yellow nylon tablecloth, sending a vase of plastic flowers crashing to the floor, and ordered me to cover my head with it.

The Supreme Guide, as it happens, was charm itself. The sort of chap you'd be happy to have round to tea, so long as you didn't intend discussing Allah. The problem was that I did intend discussing Allah and whether he had indeed ordained jihad against the likes of godless me. Unfortunately the yellow nylon tablecloth kept slipping off my head in a loud crackle of static, and every time it slithered to the floor, one of his underlings would frantically windmill instructions to me to reinstate it before I proceeded further. It's hard to concentrate on making notes, operate a tape-recorder *and* ask hopefully forensic questions while attempting to anchor a nylon tablecloth on to one's head. But al-Hodeibi clearly had no intention of letting me, an infidel, off the hejab hook.

Nor had he any intention of letting the Mubarak regime off the Islamist hook either. 'Because this government refuses to institute Sharia in full, it is anti-Allah. For example, it is *haram*, forbidden, for a man or a woman who is born a Muslim to convert to another faith, or to no faith at all; he has therefore committed apostasy, for which the penalty is death. But does this government punish the apostate? No, it does not. There is, under Sharia and even under this government, no such thing as "civil marriage". Even if a man and woman have lived together for fifteen years, pretending they are man and wife, they are still guilty of fornication, which is *haram*. But does this government punish them as it should? No, it does not! Alcohol is *haram*, but if an Egyptian drinks alcohol, does this government punish him? No, it does not!'

Clutching at my tablecloth hejab, I asked, 'If the Muslim Brotherhood came to power, would you institute flogging for drinking alcohol? Death for homosexual acts? Death for adultery?'

'Yes, of course. Those punishments are decreed by Allah, so those instructions must be obeyed.'

Throughout all this the Supreme Guide beamed benignly. 'So do you approve of the Taliban regime in Afghanistan?' I inquired.

'No, no, of course not!' he replied, as if I'd asked the stupidest question imaginable. But why on earth not? This advocate of the harshest aspects of Sharia looked surprised at my question. 'Well, because obviously the Taliban are *much* too extreme!'

When I left the Supreme Guide's office, having returned the tablecloth to his staff, I headed back to my hotel and its cocktail bar where I was meeting a young Egyptian friend. Whenever I needed guidance on the minutiae of the four Sunni schools of Sharia jurisprudence, I'd turn to him. He had studied Sharia in great depth from the age of twelve and had graduated in the subject at the oldest Islamic university, Cairo's Al Azhar.

He was nursing a vodka and orange and said bitterly, 'The more you know about Sharia, the more you realize that about 80 per cent of it was created by men for their own purposes, not by Allah. Believe me, if and when the Muslim Brotherhood comes to power in Egypt, I and most of my friends will emigrate.' Of course I'm not naming him: according to the Muslim Brothers he is an apostate, and therefore deserves to die.

29

Tulips in Tehran

So this is the place where they beat her to death, I thought, looking up at the dingy-white hulk of Evin prison in Tehran. They tortured her first: several of her fingers and her nose were broken, her skull was fractured, an eardrum was perforated, some fingernails were missing and there was evidence of lash marks on her body; they may also have raped her. (The doctor who examined her while she was in a coma could not examine her vaginally because he was male, but a female nurse told him that she'd seen 'brutal' genital injuries. The doctor has since defected.)

Before her murder she'd been doing what I was now doing – trying to report on the human rights abuses of the Islamic Republic of Iran, which routinely imprisons, tortures, and murders its own citizens, allegedly in the name of 'Allah, the most Compassionate, the most Merciful'. Zahra Kazemi, a fifty-four-year-old Canadian photo-journalist of Iranian descent, had worked in danger zones in Latin America, Iraq, Afghanistan and Africa, but it was Iran, the land of her birth, which finally did for her.

I kept my camera hidden under my all-enveloping black *chador*, but Kazemi had been openly photographing student protesters and the families of jailed political prisoners, who regularly came to the pavement outside Evin to try to find out what had happened to their loved ones.

She may have thought that her official press pass from the Islamic Ministry of Guidance had given her some sort of immunity, but she was wrong. In June 2003 after her arrest she was imprisoned in cellblock 209, the high-security section in Evin reserved for the enemies, real or supposed, of the theocratic Iranian regime.

At first officials announced that she'd died of a stroke while under interrogation. Or had 'banged her head' when she fell over, due to weakness from a hunger strike. But finally, under pressure from the Canadian government and international protests led by her son Stephan in Montreal, the authorities admitted that she had, indeed, been beaten to death. A low-level Ministry of the Interior interrogator was arrested, put on trial and acquitted; he then disappeared into the Iranian woodwork.

'The trouble with Ziba [her nickname] is that she was very determined, very brave but also probably too confrontational,' I'd been told by a family friend. 'She may well have insulted one of her interrogators, and it all escalated from there.'

Like Kazemi, I too had official Islamic Ministry of Guidance accreditation, but in view of what had happened to her, less than a year earlier, I wasn't going to hang around too long outside the prison; least of all did I intend to be 'confrontational' with this murderous lot. In any case, what I was intending to do might have been considered quite 'confrontational' enough: I was on my way to a nearby hospital to visit a very sick old man who was one of Iran's most famous dissidents.

In order to get to seventy-four-year-old Siamak Pourzand, a former film critic and director of a Tehran cultural centre, I'd had to shake off my obligatory regime minder, pleading a migraine (as I occasionally did when trying to avoid official 'Guidance') which would confine me to my hotel room. And for once, I was grateful for the black-swathed anonymity of my 'good hejab', the term of approval given by the mullahs to the regime's Islamic dress code.

For criticizing the regime Pourzand was sentenced to eleven years; he had been brought from cellblock 209 to the hospital in iron shackles. Did his Evin jailers really believe that this virtually crippled old man, whom they'd repeatedly beaten, could somehow make a gazelle-like sprint to freedom unless he were shackled?

I had no idea where he was in the hospital and realized I'd have to ask the staff. To my astonishment, not only were they happy to give me his ward number, but one of the nurses, wreathed in smiles, insisted on showing me the way to his bed. Were they tricking me? Were they about to alert the authorities to my presence? Not a bit of it. I soon realized that they not only respected the old man but actually wished him well. Frail though he was, Pourzand still bravely criticized the regime to me, and with a croaking voice asked me to tell his daughters in America that he was grateful for their efforts to get him released.

And he was, eventually, released on the grounds of ill health, but today, according to his family in exile, he is living under virtual house arrest. And as his sentence has not been formally cancelled he can at any time, on the whim of the mullahs, be thrown back into cellblock 209; although now almost eighty, he is officially still regarded as a dangerous anti-Islamic criminal. The satellite dish – an illegal window on the outside world – which he shared with others in his apartment block has been confiscated. 'All he can watch now is the fundamentalist crap put out by the mullahs on state television,' says Banafsheh, his daughter in America. Her father is still forbidden to leave the country. Such is life – and sometimes death – under the 'mullahcratic' Mafia.

After decades as a roving foreign correspondent I've always assumed that, if I do enough prior reading and research on a region's history and culture, I'll be able to operate effectively once I'm there. But Iran remains one of the most perplexing countries I've ever worked in.

Since the 1979 Islamic Revolution, inspired and led by Grand Ayatollah Khomeini (he who issued a fatwa demanding the death of Salman Rushdie for *The Satanic Verses*, which the Ayatollah had never read), Iran has become one of the world's most oppressive regimes.

The Islamic Republic stones male and female adulterers to death (though the legal process is heavily weighted against the women). Article 104 in its Penal Code even prescribes the size of the stones to be used: they should 'not be large enough to kill the person by one or two strikes, nor should they be so small that they cannot be defined as stones'. In other words a bloody, slow and agonizing death is required by law. And this despite the fact that stoning to death is not mentioned in the Koran, even though it was a standard punishment in the tribal mores of the seventh century; its religious 'legitimacy' is allegedly derived from the Shia-approved a-Hadith – the reported sayings of, and anecdotes about, the Prophet. 'Most of the a-Hadith are, I'm afraid, just seventh-century gossip,' was the opinion of one young Islamic scholar I talked to in Egypt, who wants to modernize Islam and render it more relevant to the twenty-first century.

A former political prisoner in Evin told me that some adulteresses took too long to die (twenty minutes is considered the average dying time). 'The vast majority, even of religious Iranians, don't want to take part in these stonings,' he told me. 'So the authorities have to bus in common criminals or religious fanatics to do it. The woman was buried in a pit up to her shoulders, as the law commands; but she took a long time dying, and it was very hot and the stoning pit was outside, so this guy said, "I'm fed up with this!", picked up a rock and smashed her head in. He seemed to enjoy it because he actually boasted about it to me. I felt physically sick.'

But bizarrely, a nation which decrees that adulterers be stoned to death also permits religiously approved *sigheh*, 'pleasure marriages'. A married man can 'marry' a woman, so long as a mullah agrees (and the seedier mullahs can earn a tidy sum simply for charging fees for their services): the 'marriage' contract can last from ninety-nine years down to nine minutes, and the man can break the contract any time he wants. But not the woman.

A man is formally allowed only four wives at a time, but there's no limit to the number of temporary 'wives' he can enjoy. So what's the difference between 'pleasure marriages' and prostitution? None, according to Iranian feminists whom I met at a clandestine meeting one afternoon. 'It just means that poor women can be exploited for sex, and mullahs can have as much sex as they want – and also make money!'

Most Sunnis regard this custom as lightly disguised prostitution, but fundamentalist Shias insist that 'temporary marriage' was sanctioned in the seventh century by the Prophet himself. So that's all right then. While I was at the women's meeting it was discovered and broken up by the police, and one of those I spoke to, a devout, heavily veiled management studies student, twenty-one-year-old Hanieh Nemati, was arrested. Feminism, particularly if it 'infects' devout women, is not popular with the authorities.

The influential Ayatollah Ahmad Elmalhoda recently preached in the holy city of Mashad that Iranian feminists are 'whores who, clutching a piece of paper in their hands to gather signatures, are working for foreign powers and want to destabilize the Islamic Republic'. And that unveiled women automatically 'turn men into beasts'.

Religiously permitted prostitution does not stir up international outrage. But stoning adulterers to death does, and under international pressure, the regime in 2002 announced there would now be a 'moratorium'. But, as with most things in the mullahcracy, what it says is not what it does, and this grotesquely medieval punishment continues. In 2007 Jafar Kiana, a man who had already spent eleven years in prison for his 'crime', was judicially stoned to death in Qavzin province; his partner Mokarrameh – who has already served eleven years herself – is still in prison, along with their two children, awaiting her own death under a hail of stones.

Zahra Shojaei was the Presidential Adviser on women's affairs: I went to her office to challenge her and found a smiling figure swathed in 'good hejab'. I'd expected her to insist (as the daughter and the wife of powerful mullahs) that stoning to death was decreed by Islam. She was after all a 'regime woman', the scornful name used by Iranian feminists to describe her type – the kind of devoutly religious woman who is given a high-profile, but unelected, government job so long as she toes the fundamentalist line.

But this 'regime woman' surprised me by saying, 'Well, obviously we must get this stoning clause out of the Penal Code, but this takes time and many arguments with religious leaders. But the fact is that the stoning penalty no longer fits the needs of a modern, educated generation.'

So presumably she'd be in favour of abolishing the death penalty for adultery – by whatever means it is carried out? 'Oh no, of course not! It's essential to have the death penalty for that. Otherwise how can you preserve the integrity of the family?' But, I protested, I don't need the threat of the death penalty to prevent me straying from my husband of the last thirty-nine years! She continued to beam comfortably and, almost teasingly, replied, 'Perhaps you are an exception!'

When the Islamic regime came to power in 1979 it immediately instituted its version of Sharia law, which not only introduced stoning for adultery but also lowered the marriageable age of girls to nine years old. This was because the Prophet, who had around eleven wives and concubines, married his favourite wife Aisha when she was six, and consummated the marriage when she was nine. I told Zahra Shojaie that to us in the West there seems to be a paedophiliac element in Iran's marriage law which, in effect, appears to us to sanctify child rape.

Once again she surprised me: 'Oh, I agree, reducing the marriage age of girls to nine is not appropriate in this day and age. Which is why our reformists in the Majlis [the Parliament] introduced a bill raising the marriage age to eighteen for both boys and girls.' But, I pointed out, the bill was rejected by the hardline clerics, on the grounds that it was 'un-Islamic'! She shrugged: 'Well, you know, politics is a game and if you know the rules of the game, you can usually effect change.'

After two years of passionate intra-mullah argument, the marriage age was raised to thirteen for girls and fifteen for boys – but with the qualification that children could still be married at an earlier age, if that was the wish of their fathers. 'But we still hope to get it raised to eighteen,' she said. 'Actually, the average age of marriage in Iran is twenty-three and it's even higher among educated, urban women, so changing the marriage law is broadly symbolic – but of course symbols always matter.'

But while there's argument about marriage law, there seems to be none about the death penalty for homosexual activity. Not that gays exist in Iran, according to the current President, Mahmoud Ahmadinejad (described to me by a young Tehrani man as 'a complete fruitcake'), who insists that the Holocaust is a 'myth', who has promised that Israel will be 'wiped from the map', and who declares that Allah has decreed that Islam will 'conquer the world'.

To jeers and catcalls from his student audience at Columbia University in America in 2007 the Iranian President had asserted: 'We don't have homosexuals, not like you.' Presumably that's either because his regime has executed these 'non-existent' gays (occasionally by hanging them in public from cranes in city squares), or because they've wisely fled abroad. 'Homosexuals deserve to be tortured or put to death, preferably both,' Mohsen Yahya, a high-ranking Iranian official had told an astonished British Parliamentary delegation in 2007.

Just as *sigheh*, so-called 'temporary marriage', is allowed for married men – while other married men are stoned to death for adultery – so the regime's attitude towards homosexuality seems bizarrely inconsistent. Indeed, it can be remarkably generous towards those gays, or men with gender dysmorphia, who want a sex-change operation to 'cure' them of their 'illness'. The government even contributes half the cost of the operation, and the result is that Iran is now second only to Thailand in the number of sex-change operations performed. When the alternative is being put to death, you can hardly blame gays who opt for genital mutilation and demotion to the inferior status of being a woman, just so that they can 'marry' their male partners without fear of ending up hanging from a crane. In 2006, when the lover of one man who was about to undergo a sex change came to visit him in hospital, he wasn't immediately arrested: 'Instead I was treated with respect as his fiancé.'

Britain recently granted asylum to an Iranian student, studying in England, whose boyfriend was hanged for sodomy and who, just before his execution, named him as his lover. Claiming to be gay (or lesbian, for which the penalty is also death) is one sure-fire way of receiving asylum overseas.

One day I visited an internet café (they keep being closed down by the clerics but somehow seem to spring up again almost immediately: Iran is now said to have the second most active blogging community in the world). In the booth beside me, a twenty-year-old girl was writing in English to an overseas friend: 'I'm really in despair. It's getting harder and harder to be a Christian here, and I don't have any friends here any more because they've all emigrated. Boys who used to be my friends have all gone to Sweden and claimed asylum saying they were homosexual. Perhaps I should say I'm a lesbian. But I hate to tell lies.'

Were your friends gay, I asked. 'No, of course not!' She laughed bitterly. 'The minute they got asylum in Sweden – Sweden is very kind to gays – they start dating lots and lots of Swedish girls and now they're having a wonderful time. You can't have a wonderful time here. And I'll never be able to get married, because no Muslim man here dares to marry a Christian girl. And even if I pretended to convert, no one would believe me, and his family would shun me.

Sometimes I just wish I could die.' So many unnecessary deaths, so much unnecessary despair.

But that's the way the fundamentalists like it: Western hand-wringing about the abuse of human rights in Iran is simply further evidence of the inherent wickedness of 'infidels'. Mohammed Reza Jaafari, the commander of the 'Lovers of Martyrdom Brigade' (which recruits potential suicide bombers), is like many of his ilk utterly uncompromising. 'The leaders of the Islamic world need to be brave and announce: Islam and Western democracy have nothing in common. Islam has nothing in common with the Universal Declaration of Human Rights. Islam has nothing in common with Western liberalism and that kind of freedom. Islam stands in opposition to these ideas.'

But Iran's young don't seem to agree: in the holy city of Qom, one 'moderate' mullah, wearing the black turban which denotes direct descent from the Prophet, told me how distressing it was that mosque congregations these days were dominated by the middle-aged and the old. 'The young must be reminded of their religious duties.'

Well, they're reminded all right, day and night – and take absol-utely no notice. Iran, formerly Persia, has over 2,500 years of history behind it, but its current population is one of the youngest in the world. Seventy per cent are under the age of thirty. And they're fed up – with the corrupt mullahs who rule their lives, with unemploy-ment (around 25 per cent and rising), with inflation (around 20 per cent and rising), with their isolation from the outside world. Even the issue of Palestine, while it does tug at their heartstrings, can fuel anti-mullah exasperation: the Islamic Republic finances and trains anti-Israel and anti-West terrorist groups overseas but, in the words of one furious and unemployed youth: 'They should shut up about Palestine! What about us? Why don't they spend the oil money on us?'

And they're utterly fed up with being told to hate America. While I was in Tehran in 2004, a poll showed that 75 per cent of Iranians wanted rapprochement with the 'Great Satan'; the two pollsters who revealed this inconvenient truth were, of course, promptly jailed.

Virtually every young person I talked to would tell me (so long as they weren't in earshot of some religious vigilante) how they longed to escape into the arms of the 'Great Satan', and far from denouncing President Bush – as did most of Britain, Europe and the Middle East as a result of the Iraq War – some even declared that the so-called 'Toxic Texan' was their hero. According to Kianoosh Sanjari, a young dissident, 'Bush is a symbol of freedom to us.' Although banned in Iran, Madonna, thanks to smuggled videos, is one of young Iranians' favourite pop stars, and most of them know far more about her than I do.

All of which must be somewhat distressing for Iranians like Massoumeh Ebtekar, who was one of the most famous figures in the virulently anti-American Islamic Revolution of 1979. By the time I met her, Ebtekar had become a Vice-President of the regime. Naturally this clever (a qualified immunologist) and relatively powerful woman was wearing the *chador*, which means 'tent' in Persian. I was similarly be-tented in black. Almost the first thing Vice-President Ebtekar said to me when I entered her office was, 'You know, you really don't have to wear black all the time in Iran!'

Evidently not, I replied: young Iranian women I saw in the street seemed to be using their version of the mandatory Islamic Dress Code (flogging is the official penalty for disobedience) almost as a sexual invitation. In relatively wealthy North Tehran young women, many from mullah families, sashayed along the pavements in short, skin-tight, pastel-coloured *ropoosh* coats, their hectically colourful hejabs sat perched on the back of their heads, displaying elaborately blonde-streaked hair and faces lacquered with make-up: the whole get-up seemed designed to incite 'sexy nun' fantasies among passing males.

Some even proudly sported large pieces of sticking plaster across their noses: rhinoplasty to reduce the noble Iranian nose is one of the most popular cosmetic surgery procedures here, and these young women seemed to me to be, almost literally, thumbing their noses at the mullahs. Ebtekar merely laughed indulgently: 'Well, the young are always rebellious!'

Indeed they are, but youthful rebellion so far seems to be largely directed against the Islamic dress codes. The wearing of ties is, according to a Tehrani friend of mine, considered counter-revolutionary: ties were banned after the fall of the Shah as being an 'un-Islamic' Western import.

My friend's fifteen-year-old son was now being so stroppy with his father that 'Would you believe it, he's taken to wearing a tie! And hair gel! If he carries on like this our whole family will be in trouble!' And the father of this tie-wearing, hair-gelling rebellious teenager is, like parents in the West, afraid that his son is going to get into drugs. Iran, with a population of 66 million, now has one of the highest drug-addiction rates in the world and, to its credit, the regime has recognized that fact.

Drinking alcohol is of course forbidden, and although I was told (even in puritanical Qom, the 'Vatican' of Shia Islam) where I could buy it – 'You see that intersection? Just round the back of that building you can buy anything you want' – I decided, for safety's sake, not to be tempted.

I was going to stick to all Islamic codes, especially as regards dress. Unfortunately my black hejab, thanks to the heat and Tehran's chronic filth and pollution, had become rather rancid, so one day I went to the bazaar to buy a replacement. The *bazaaris*, the devout, mosque-going merchant class, had been at the forefront of the revolt against the secularizing, autocratic Shah Mohammad Reza Pahlavi, so surely they'd have black hejabs galore. They didn't. 'I don't stock them any more because you can't sell them these days. Young women won't wear them,' said one grizzled old *bazaari* who told me he'd been heavily involved in the uprising against the Shah.

'Pahlavi was a very bad man but our mullahs are very bad men too, and everyone except them and their families is getting poorer every day. May Allah preserve us.' I was therefore obliged that night to wash my hejab in the hotel room's basin: the next morning it was still damp, still rancid, a fitting symbol, I thought, of this increasingly rancid and dysfunctionally dangerous regime.

In view of the 'sexy nun' outfits I'd seen in North Tehran, I asked Vice-President Ebtekar whether the authorities had given up trying to enforce their religious views on these 'chaos-and-depravity-causing' young women. She laughed: 'Traditionalists have to adapt to the needs of the younger generation; anyway, we reformists are still in power!'

No, you're not, I retorted. You never were: the ruling clerics can always overrule any allegedly 'un-Islamic' laws, even if they've been passed by the popularly elected Parliament. 'Yes, but because there are now so many young people in Iran, including highly educated women, we have to adapt in order to ease the tensions that are building up in our society.'

She certainly knew a lot about 'tensions in our society'. She'd already taken part in one (pro-Islamist) revolution and was anxious to prevent another – this time an anti-Islamist one. At the age of nineteen Massoumeh earned the nickname 'Machine-Gun Mary', because of her leading role twenty-five years earlier in the siege by Islamist students of the American Embassy in Tehran. Having been educated partly in America, her English was flawless and, during the 444-day siege during which fifty-two American diplomatic staff were held hostage, the then fundamentalist Massoumeh became known round the world as the students' implacable spokeswoman.

At the time when 'Machine-Gun Mary' had told me that 'We reformists are still in power' she clearly didn't suspect what would happen next. She'd been given her job by the weakly 'reformist' President Ayatollah Khatami, but he's now out of power and the 'fruitcake' son of a blacksmith, Ahmadinejad, has replaced him.

President Khatami had become known as 'The Smiling Ayatollah' which, to begin with, endeared him greatly to Iran's young. Smiling, something which Iranians do a lot of, is not approved of by Shia fundamentalists. The late Ayatollah Khomeini, who had never been caught with a smile creasing his grim and crafty face, clearly feared that ordinary Iranians had a secret tendency to be far too merry for his religious tastes.

'Smile less, grieve more!' he would command. 'Allah did not create man so he can have fun. The aim of creation was for mankind to be put to the test through hardship and prayer.'

Shiism itself is founded on grief, a sense of injustice and martyrdom, and sprang from an inheritance dispute in the seventh century in which their faction lost out to another faction, the Sunnis. Shiites constitute a 10–15 per cent minority in the Islamic world but in Iran are a majority.

The word 'Shia' is a shortened version of the Arabic phrase for 'the followers of Ali': Ali was deemed by his followers to be the rightful successor to Mohammed because, as the Prophet's cousin and brother-in-law, he belonged to the same bloodline, but was assassinated by the Sunnis. Later the Prophet's grandson Hussein, along with seventy-two of his acolytes, was slaughtered by the dominant Sunnis at the Battle of Karbala in 680. This martyrdom is the defining moment in Shia Islam: his death is remembered every year at the festival of Ashura, where devotees, still grieving at the injustice of his fate over 1,300 years ago, inflict bloody wounds on themselves with chains and knives.

This 'celebration' of violent death is not, of course, unique to Shia Islam: the Cross is central to the Christian faith; but that ugly instrument of death has, in the largely secular West, been 'de-bloodied', and is even used as pop star bling. (But not everywhere: one day in the predominantly Roman Catholic Philippines a guide in my luxury Manila hotel told me that he had arranged for a coach to take his happy-snappy tourist flock to a village about an hour away to view the 'Crucifixion Ceremonies' on Good Friday. 'Why don't you come with us? Terrific video opportunities – lots of blood!' I rather sniffily declined to join the tourist hordes who gleefully film devout young Filipinos flagellating themselves and getting themselves nailed to wooden crosses; in full Health and Safety mode the Philippine government every year warns that 'crucifixion is bad for the health,' and advises flagellants to take tetanus jabs, keep their whips 'well maintained', sterilize the nails before use. As a former Roman Catholic, I find all this ecstatic, almost erotic celebration of bloody death repulsive, a view shared by the Filipino Roman Catholic hierarchy, which is however unable to prevent this Grand Guignol religious street theatre.)

Sunni Muslims also have a feeling of revulsion about the Shiite Ashura rituals, but only on political/religious grounds. So much so that Sunni fundamentalists like Al-Qaeda, who regard Shiism as heretical, are very partial to blowing up Shiite pilgrims, thereby creating their own grotesque Sunni version of Grand Guignol.

The last time I'd been to Iran had been long before the Islamic revolution. But, having immersed myself in Shiite theology and culture, I'd returned there in 2004 half-expecting to find a now fiercely puritanical, enclosed people. After all, in fundamentalist Sunni Saudi Arabia I'd found exactly that: although I had easy access to Western-educated reformists, who were perfectly comfortable in the company of 'infidels' like me (and extremely partial to scotch whisky, for the consumption of which lesser citizens get flogged), I found ordinary Saudis impossible to relate to, not least because they didn't want to relate to me. The school textbooks in their grotesquely intolerant education system have told them that Christians and Jews are respectively 'pigs' and 'monkeys' who must not be befriended, an instruction they dourly carry out to the letter.

In contrast, ordinary Iranians are some of the warmest, most charming – and most irreverent – oppressed people I've ever met in a long career of talking to the oppressed around the world. And they are passionately addicted to Persian poetry – Ferdowsi, Rumi, Omar Kayyam, Sa'adi, Hafez – much of which is extremely sensuous, even homoerotic, extolling the joys of sex, wine and music (the last two of which the mullahs routinely denounce).

'Would you allow me to play some music?' I was asked hesitantly by the cab driver who was taking me back to Tehran from the mullah-filled city of Qom. In the intense heat I felt almost stifled by my hejab. 'Okay,' I replied cautiously, 'but only if you let me take this thing off – and if you don't report me!' As soon as we passed the city limits and were out on the empty desert road, I tore off the hejab and let the wind stream into my hair, and he joyously slammed on a cassette of forbidden Bollywood dance music: he was singing along, and we were both laughing, exhilarated by an almost childish delight at having seized this brief bout of freedom from the holy turbaned ones.

Who, I had assumed, would be disapproving of Persian love poetry. A favourite couplet by the fourteenth-century poet Hafez runs: 'A rose without the glow of a lover bears no joy/ Without wine to drink the spring brings no joy.' Surely they'd have banned lyrical stuff like this? Not at all: they've simply 'reinterpreted' it, to allege that, actually, it's all just the colourful expression of the poets' love for Allah.

Iranians are also addicted to anti-mullah jokes, some so scabrous (concentrating as they do on mullahs' private parts) that even I find them faintly shocking. And many are cast as versions of Mullah Nasruddin anecdotes: Nasruddin (an ancient folk figure in those parts) is a legendarily clownish mullah endowed with sublime stupidity. 'Have you heard the latest Mullah Nasruddin joke? A devout man comes to him and says, "How do I become a mullah?" And he says, "Oh, it's easy: all you have to do is what I did, remove your brain and then put on the turban!"' The young man and his friends in a Tehran café creased up with merriment (well, okay, it probably sounds funnier in Farsi).

But even Iranian fundamentalists can sometimes be warm and generous. One day, after Friday prayers, I encountered a young Basij, an Islamist militiaman, wearing the black shirt and red scarf of his fanatical calling, who suddenly stopped lecturing me about the infidel West and its 'plot' against Islam, disappeared for a few minutes and returned – not with a 'sacred sword' or a 'sacred' AK47, but with a bag of fresh fruit: 'Please take, very hot today! You want ice cream? I get!'

And it is impossible for a godless infidel in an Iranian market to gaze on a huge mound of pistachios (which, along with oil and rugs, are a primary Iranian export) without someone insisting on scooping up a bagful and giving it to you for free. At which point you then have to enter into the Iranian etiquette ritual of *taarof*, an elaborate game of manners – whereby you must first refuse, then the pistachio-giver must insist, then you must again refuse, he must insist – and so, confusingly, and flowerily, on and on.

This can make negotiation tricky: what does the other side *really* mean? In the chatterati tribal sect of media London, there are equivalents like, 'We must do lunch!' Sometimes we mean it, sometimes we don't, but usually we can instinctively divine, because we know our own tribal customs, whether or not the statement is genuinely meant. However, faced with the Iranian smoke-and-mirrors version of *taarof*, you're often at sea. (To my surprise, in Iran I found myself occasionally longing for a spot of Russian bluntness, a trait which used to infuriate me until a Russian friend explained to me that bluntness was not necessarily a sign of aggression: 'What you English call "politeness" we see as hypocrisy.')

One evening I visited a dedicated secularist, a former nationalist politician who'd fallen foul of the mullahs. On the wall of his large but sparsely decorated flat, instead of the usual lurid portrait of the seventh-century Ali or the current Supreme Guide Ayatollah Khamenei, this small, wizened old man with paper-thin skin sat beneath a vast portrait of his own secular saint, Dr Mohammad Mossadegh. That eccentric, pyjama-wearing former Prime Minister had nationalized Britain's Anglo Iranian Oil Company, and in 1953 the CIA, with British help, mounted a coup against him and reinstated the hated pro-Western Shah.

The old Mossadeghist insisted he was willing for me to use his name. But was that merely *taarof* – did he really mean it? After all, he'd been imprisoned first by the Shah and then by the Islamic regime, and I'd seen the secret graves of other Mossadeghists: should I further endanger him in the twilight of his days by naming him, simply to identify him for my readers – who, frankly, couldn't care less about yet another baffling foreign name? Not unreasonably they're more interested in issues than in names.

I'd used the names of young dissidents like Kianoosh Sanjari and Ali Afsari whom I'd met undercover, because they had insisted. And I knew that they meant it: both had been imprisoned by the mullahs, but like political dissidents I've met all over the world, they hoped that international publicity would offer some protection. Both, however, have now had to give up and escape; today they live in exile, but an exiled dissident does not, alas, command much interest in the West. The anti-regime Mossadeghist was now too old and too frail – and probably too obstinate – to flee, so I did not, and will not, use his name.

As every foreign visitor knows, you can't go into an Iranian home without being ambushed with plates of sweetmeats, and this time was no different. Huge platters were spread across a large coffee table but when my nationalist host began describing the regional origins of each pastry, alarm bells began to ring in my head. 'This is *gaz*, a speciality of Qom ... this is *sohan*, a speciality from Isfahan ... this is a speciality from Khuzestan...' I launched in to the obligatory bout of *taarof*, but his steady, unsmiling gaze seemed to me, in my slightly paranoid frame of mind, to be a warning.

When I finally succumbed, as *taarof* required (even though I wasn't hungry), would it matter which regional sweetmeats I nibbled? I feared it would: if I refused some but not others would I be signalling (in a land where 'symbols always matter') that I didn't believe in the inviolable unity of Iran? If I only ate the sweetmeats of Khuzestan, would I be inadvertently symbolizing the fact that I was on the side of the minority Iranian Arabs, who mostly live in Khuzestan, the province in which most of Iran's oil is located?

After all some of these Iranian Arabs want to secede from their Persian overlords who, they say, discriminate against them; from time to time, these Arabs plant the odd bomb to prove their disaffection. The Iranian embassy siege in London in 1980 arose out of this ethnic dispute: the men who took over the embassy were Iranian Arabs demanding the release of ninety-two fellow Arabs being held as terrorists in Iranian jails.

So, to be on the safe side, I ate one sample pastry from each of the Iranian provinces. But I wasn't yet in the clear: I was British. Everyone in the West is used to seeing on the news crowds of demonstrating Iranians chanting, 'Death to America! Death to the Great Satan!' Occasionally, the chant includes 'Death to the Little Satan!' Who the hell is that? Well, actually it's us.

Iranians are acutely aware of their history, and Britain's role in that history still raises hackles; to this day they credit us with far more power and influence than we have in reality. 'Lift a mullah's beard, and you'll find "Made in England" written underneath,' goes an Iranian saying. And it was clearly one with which the old Mossadeghist concurred: 'We can never forget your responsibility for inflicting national humiliation on our country! And you still want to humiliate and destroy us!'

Suspicion of the 'Little Satan', aka the 'Little Fox', is surprisingly widespread. One day after Friday prayers at Tehran University a Revolutionary Guard said affably to me, 'You know that you English are the source of all evil?' Er, why? 'Because you English are controlled by the Jews, and you created Israel!' Well, actually Israel was created by the United Nations, I replied. 'The United Nations is controlled by Jews!' (Many Britons have never even heard of the Balfour Declaration of 1917 promising a homeland for the Jews, but Iranians most certainly have.)

Beside the entrance to the outdoor mosque was a large list urging Iranian women not to buy products from assorted Western companies – including Marks and Spencer's – on the grounds, I was told, that 'they are owned or controlled by Jews'. (No matter that most of these Western products are unavailable, due to sanctions and the shortage of foreign currency; 'symbols are always important'.)

But what is really making the West jittery is Iran's nuclear pro-gramme. Iranians ask why their country shouldn't have nuclear weapons (although they deny that's what they're aiming for). Britain, America, China, France, Russia, India, Pakistan, Israel and probably North Korea already have them. Islamist fanatics insist that the nuclear powers in the West oppose Iran's programme because these countries are anti-Islam. Nonsense: Muslim Pakistan exploded the first 'Islamic bomb' and, apart from a lot of huffing and puffing, the Western powers did nothing and Pakistan remains an allegedly 'reliable ally' of the West.

But Iran is different. President Ahmadinejad's statements about Israel and the Holocaust shouldn't have surprised anyone: the destruction of Israel has been part of the Islamic Republic's Consti-tution for almost thirty years. But this rhetoric has never been taken very seriously outside Iran and Israel; so why is everyone – including the Arab states – so bothered by it now? Because, unlike previous 'pragmatic' Presidents, this President actually means what he says.

His 'source of emulation', or spiritual adviser, is Ayatollah Mesbah-Yazdi, a once obscure cleric, who believes that Iran must cut itself off completely from the 'infidel' West – prior to conquering it. Both men are obsessed with the return of the Mehdi, the Twelfth, or 'Hidden', Imam, who disappeared down a well, aged five, in 941. They believe that, after worldwide chaos and bloodshed, the Hidden Imam will return and establish Islamic world dominion.

Ahmadinejad, the first non-mullah to be elected President, noisily declares at every opportunity that he has made a pact with the Hidden Imam, promising to pave the way for his return, and has obliged his ministers and civil servants to do the same. It's as if Gordon Brown, that son of the manse, obliged his Cabinet, civil servants and advisers to prepare for Armageddon and the Second Coming, or face the sack.

Can we tolerate a regime, armed with nuclear weapons, which dedicates itself to the obliteration of 'liberal democracy' and 'the evil of human rights', and which may, alarmingly, give some of its nuclear material and know-how to the terrorists it finances? (Iran is already supplying specialized weapons and technology to Hamas, Hezbollah and Iraqi insurgents.)

Needless to say, Iran insists that its nuclear programme is purely for peaceful purposes in order to generate electricity, but since it sits on the second-largest oil reserves in the world, that takes some believing. Besides, despite its treaty obligations, Iran concealed its nuclear programme for eighteen years, and until incontrovertible evidence was produced by an opposition group, the West and the UN's atomic inspectors never suspected a thing.

By denying the truth, Iran was exercising *taqqiya*. This is the name given to telling lies that are considered permissible by religious authorities. The Shia, in order to defend their branch of the faith against the dominant and often oppressive Sunnis, have always believed that *taqqiya* is an Allah-approved method of outwitting their enemies.

But what can the worried West do? Diplomacy by the Europeans has failed. And sanctions, the favoured diplomatic course, have never forced rogue regimes to behave: they only further impoverish the poor and strengthen dictators, as the example of sanctions against Saddam proved.

Could America or Israel 'take out' Iran's nuclear facilities with surgical strikes, as the Israelis did with Saddam's Osirak nuclear reactor in 1981? Unfortunately Iran learned from Saddam's mistake: its nuclear facilities are scattered all over this vast nation and many are hidden deep underground.

Should we then try to enforce 'regime change' by invading? Not an option at the moment: the only power capable of enforcing regime change is America, which is still struggling with the consequences of its actions in Afghanistan and Iraq. And the minute it or Israel attacks, any support for Western liberalism will, thanks to Iranian nationalism (common even among anti-regime dissidents), disappear in a puff of smoke with the first bomb.

On a hot summer morning, muffled in my hejab and chador, I walked into a tangled copse in a Tehran park for a meeting with the dissident student, Kianoosh Sanjari. These wooded parks are the places where young Tehranis, fed up with enforced gender segregation, meet up for clandestine romances, flirting, and sometimes a little more. Often they will detail one of their number, armed with a mobile, to act as a look-out.

As indeed did Sanjari and I. But that was because he had already been imprisoned several times, sometimes in solitary confinement, for campaigning for a secular democracy; I didn't want to give the regime an excuse to arrest him again. (Nor, frankly, was I anxious to be arrested myself.) I reckoned that if anyone would want the Western powers to invade and put an end to the theocracy, it would be Sanjari.

He was appalled by the idea: 'Oh no, military overthrow by outsiders would be a very big mistake. No Iranian wants another country to invade us!' He, and every theocracy-hating Iranian I met told me that the solution had to lie within Iran itself. After all, the regime is not a monolith: even within the ruling clerical elite there are numerous quarrelling factions, mullah pitted against mullah. The ultimate power lies in the hands of the Supreme Guide, Ayatollah Khamenei, who still keeps lavishing praise on his protégé Ahmadinejad; but he may, in view of the dire economy, and the increasing industrial unrest, suddenly withdraw his support.

Not least because some of the most conservative mullahs are becoming thoroughly exasperated by their excitable, and economically illiterate, President. He recently declared that the way to rescue the stuttering economy was to 'encourage the cult of martyrdom'. How urging thousands of young men and women to kill both themselves and others is supposed to pay the wages of unpaid and striking factory workers beats me.

And it beats most Iranians too, bar a few Armageddon-minded 'fruitcakes' like the President. He insists that the Twelfth, the Hidden Imam, the one who disappeared down the well in the tenth century, is personally guiding his every move. Ahmadinejad is said to have written the names of his proposed Cabinet members on pieces of paper and then thrown them down the well for his approval. In which case the Hidden One must have given gravely misleading advice because the Oil Minister, whose appointment he had presumably approved, soon had to be replaced when it became clear that he knew absolutely nothing about oil. The oil industry is Iran's chief foreign currency earner but it is already so badly managed and maintained, and has so few refineries, that for domestic use the country actually has to import over 40 per cent of its oil.

All this divinely inspired incompetence is proving too much for some of the governmental mullahs: Gholamreza Mesbah-Moghaddam, an arch-conservative cleric and a member of Parliament, gave a furious interview to an equally conservative Iranian newspaper in May 2008: 'If the President is saying that the Twelfth Imam is supporting the government, we say he is wrong! Surely the Twelfth Imam is not supporting the current 20 per cent inflation rate in Iran!'

*

I used to be very fond of red tulips, planting dozens of bulbs in my little north London garden, but then the marauding squirrels got them. And actually I'm now grateful to them: after my last visit to Iran, I never want to see a red tulip again. The giant propaganda murals on the sides of office blocks feature Shia martyrs and are always decorated with painted red tulips: the entrance to the vast Martyrs' Cemetery at Behesht-e-Zahra ('The Paradise of Zahra', the Prophet's daughter) is adorned with a giant white hand holding a red tulip, and even the Iranian flag features a stylized version of the word Allah in the shape of a red tulip. The flower is not chosen for its intrinsic beauty; it is because it symbolizes the spilling of blood, the blood of martyrdom.

Mind you, the regime won't award you with a celebratory rash of post-mortem tulips unless you've been martyred in the correct cause. One afternoon I surreptitiously visited two mass graves outside Tehran; unlike the elaborate martyrs' graves at Behesht-e-Zahra, all I could see were low, grassy humps: no headstones, no portraits of the dead, no loving tributes from their families. Lying beneath the humps, the dead bodies of intellectuals, Bahais, monarchists, Mossadeghists, Communists, secularists – and very often their families – all murdered by the implacable mullahs.

Two or three times I spotted a tin can or a bottle containing plastic flowers stuck into one of the grassy humps and small coloured stones marking out a grave. Who'd put them there? 'Their families – if they know where their loved ones are buried,' said my contact. 'My uncle, we think, is buried over there. Families will sometimes come at dead of night and leave these tributes, but from time to time the authorities clear them away.' No tulips? 'No, definitely no tulips.'

Last Mother's Day I watched a teenage girl buying a bunch of red tulips in my local market for her Mum and was tempted to say,

'Don't buy them! Don't you know that red tulips symbolize the joys
of violent death?' Which, I agree, would have been a foolish remark
to make, because outside Iran, with its almost pornographic cult of
death, a tulip is, well, just a tulip. If only I could feel that way again
myself.

30

'The glacier in the cupboard'

'No matter how imperfect things are, if you've got a free press everything is correctable, and without it everything is concealable,' says a character in Tom Stoppard's *Night and Day*, his play about foreign correspondents and the morality, or otherwise, of the press. Journalists who may never have seen or read it will happily recite that now clichéd line of dialogue as though it were the sacred mantra of our often grubby (and, despite its claims, not always high-minded) trade. In response another character, Ruth, drawls, 'I'm with you on the free press. It's the newspapers I can't stand.'

And every foreign correspondent winces at these withering lines: 'A foreign correspondent is someone who lives in foreign parts and corresponds, usually in the form of essays containing no new facts. Otherwise he's someone who flies around from hotel to hotel and thinks that the most interesting thing about any story is the fact that he has arrived to cover it.'

As one of those who 'flies around from hotel to hotel' I've never thought of myself that way, but I have known those who do. Journalism has never been an ego trip for me, and (at the risk of sounding pompous) I do, passionately, believe in a free press – because, without it, everything is indeed 'concealable'.

We in the West (because we're spoiled) tend to mock and belittle our media, putting journalists at the bottom of the popularity polls, along with politicians and estate agents, rather too enthusiastically for our societies' own good. But dictators routinely prove the importance of a free press by banning it, and by jailing, torturing and sometimes murdering its practitioners: Putin's Russia, Mugabe's Zimbabwe, Iran's theocrats, Burma's junta, North Korea's 'Great Leader' and most Middle East regimes – the list is depressingly long.

But I'm eternally grateful to the *Mail*, and to other newspapers which Tom Stoppard's Ruth 'can't stand', not least because they've given me the chance to enjoy the most exhilarating, exhausting, absorbing career that life can offer. As the great foreign correspondent the late Lord Deedes told an interviewer at the age of eighty-nine, having just come back from reporting on yet another forgotten war, this time in the Upper Nile: 'Getting into a dangerous place and then escaping – well, it's an adventure, better than sex!'

But for me no emotional hit, not even a sexual one, can compare with 'smelling' a new place, a new situation, for the first time; the joy – or the darkness – which you encounter that first time can conjure up complex emotions inside even the most matter-of-fact of hacks like myself.

That complexity of feeling is for me best expressed by the Georgian poet Edward Thomas, who wrote about an ancient shrub, then common in English gardens, called Lad's Love or Old Man: if you crushed its leaves and sniffed its bitter scent between your fingers as you walked up the garden path, it opened strange pathways in the soul:

> I sniff the spray
> . . .
> No garden appears, no path, no hoar-green bush
> Of Lad's Love or Old Man, no child beside
> Neither father nor mother, nor any playmate
> Only an avenue, dark, nameless, without end.

In this job, which I'd embarked on by accident, I've been paid to venture down those dark, nameless avenues and, as someone who has a safe and loving family behind me, I've always been made acutely aware of the horror which can underlie the most banal of domestic existences. I'm always being ambushed by disturbing reminders of anonymous, broken people who once lived and breathed and sweated and laughed like me; there, I think, but for the grace of God . . .

One day in Bosnia, heading towards a front line (there tended to be several in that bloody civil war), I passed an abandoned caravan beside the road, and I noticed that the family had been in such a hurry to flee its 'ethnic cleansing' that the mother evidently didn't have time to remove the family washing – knickers, blouses, tights, underpants – which dangled from a washing line rigged up between two blossom-covered apple trees. 'The glacier knocks in the cupboard,' wrote Auden,

> The desert sighs in the bed,
> And the crack in the teacup opens
> A lane to the land of the dead.

Was that family still alive, or had they now been sent to 'the land of the dead'? I had no time to find out, but the memory of the quotidian banality, the shattered intimacy of that line of hastily abandoned knickers and tights, the crushed and scattered blossoms beneath it – and of course what these now mud-spattered remnants of family clothing symbolized in that ravaged land – haunts me to this day. 'The crack in the teacup opens . . .'

But sometimes what I see makes me so angry that even favourite lines of elegiac poetry prove inadequate to express what I feel. Which was the case in the late Nineties when a largely government-induced famine in the 'hermit kingdom' of Communist North Korea killed up to 3 million of its own citizens.

Journalists couldn't get visas to North Korea, but a few selected tourist groups were being allowed in. Naturally, to ensure that none of these 'tourists' were journalists in disguise, there were stringent conditions. Not only did you have to submit a detailed CV, but it had to be verified by a solicitor. I was using my 'housewife superstar' passport issued in my married name, and was posing as an expert in Korean textiles.

But it proved surprisingly difficult to find a lawyer who would attest to the veracity of my CV (where's a bent solicitor when you need one?). When one solicitor refused me he said, with an air of righteous dismay, 'But you're *not* a Korean textile expert! I recognize you – you're Ann Leslie of the *Daily Mail*. The North Koreans could report me to the Law Society!' Oh, for heaven's sake.

So I forged a suitably convincing solicitor's letter, giving the home address of a helpful colleague as the 'solicitor's' office, and flew to Beijing to meet up with my group. But on arrival I was given the bad news: the tour had suddenly been cancelled. Doctors who'd been working in North Korea with Médecins Sans Frontières were disgusted by the way other NGOs had been concealing facts about the famine (in order not to be thrown out of the country), and they broke ranks and published evidence that the people were now so hungry that they'd resorted to cannibalism. With the exception of the UN's World Food Programme, all foreign aid workers were expelled and all tours cancelled.

But I had an old friend in Beijing who spoke fluent Chinese and Korean and I turned to him for help. I was damned if I was going to fly back to London immediately (not least because my doggedly acquired knowledge of Korean textiles would now be completely wasted): come what may, I was determined to cover the famine story. My friend knew, from past experience, that he could trust me, and so arranged for me to meet up with some Chinese-Korean contacts of his who lived in Yanji, the capital of the Yanbian Autonomous Korean Region of Jilin province in the far northeast of China, close to the North Korean border.

One of them, a Chinese academic at the university, spoke not only Korean but good English, and told my Beijing friend that she was willing to help me find North Korean refugees who'd crossed the Tumen River border and were hiding out in China. If the Chinese authorities discovered them they would deport them back to their homeland, where they would be executed or, at best, used as slave labour in the North Korean gulags.

My contact in Yanji found me a helpful Chinese-Korean driver who had a relative in the local Politburo and therefore had 'access' to a curtained official car. Luckily for foreign correspondents, the world is full of Arthur Daleys, natural-born duckers and divers, and the jolly and spivvish Mr Li was one of them.

The cost to me, apart from a fistful of *yuan*, was having to endure a five-hour trip on dirt roads to the narrowest part of the Tumen River, listening to Mr Li's Celine Dion cassettes played at full blast. As this is a highly militarized zone (the nearest big city was Vladivostok in Russia's Far East), there were several military checkpoints. And every time our black limousine reached one, soldiers of the People's Liberation Army would scramble to attention and salute us: unable to see the occupant of the Politburo car through its grey curtains, they naturally assumed that I was a powerful local cadre whom it would be unwise to offend.

In a small Chinese hamlet in the blossom-drenched foothills of the Great White Mountains, I found Kwong-yong, a fifteen-year-old North Korean refugee (all names have been changed for obvious reasons). At this point the Tumen River is only about 25 metres wide and is the favoured spot, especially in the harsh Manchurian winter when the river freezes over, for refugees to escape into China. Sometimes the corpses of emaciated men, women and children who had stumbled crossing the river ice, and who'd been frozen to death where they fell, are left on the ice until the spring thaw.

The teenager was small and thin and frightened and, thanks to chronic malnutrition, looked about nine. He'd first taken refuge in a *kimche* pit in a small garden plot belonging to an elderly Chinese-Korean widow, Mrs Han. *Kimche* is an extremely pungent Korean dish of fermented cabbage, garlic and red pepper, and the widow had stored her home-made supplies in the pit; the boy stank of it. Every time local officials came round, Kwong-yong and other North Korean refugees would hurry to the *kimche* pits and hide in them.

Kwong-yong was not strictly speaking a 'political' refugee: he'd simply known that he couldn't survive any longer eating nothing but grasses, roots, nettles and tree bark. His father had died of starvation three years earlier, and his stepmother told him she couldn't feed him any more and had thrown him out to fend for himself. 'She had already sold my little brother to a rich family in exchange for food, but couldn't find a rich family she could sell me to.'

He'd been taught to worship North Korea's self-styled 'Great Leader' Comrade Kim Jong-il, whose other titles include 'Benevolent Father', 'Iron-Willed Brilliant Commander' and 'Most Noble Genius of the World'. He is, in reality, a short, pudgy, middle-aged sybarite with bouffant hair and lifts in his shoes, who's scared of flying, and who watches Rambo movies, cavorts with imported Swedish tarts, and has 'traitors to the Revolution' executed in public.

And while the 'Iron-Willed Brilliant Commander' plays with his tarts and his lethal toys (which include ballistic missiles and matériel – possibly nuclear – which his regime sells to places like Syria and Iran), his once highly industrialized nation slowly disintegrates. In Kwong-yong's district there was a coal mine, 'but it closed because the workers weren't getting food, so they left to try and find some. And only six children in my class, which used to have thirty, still came to school. The rest were too weak, or too busy trying to find food. Our teachers were also weak: they'd ask us to go out and try and find herbs and grasses for them to eat.'

So hermetically sealed is the Great Leader's country that Kwong-yong told me that he didn't know that man had landed on the moon (well, it was the American imperialists who'd pulled off that feat, so naturally the Great Leader would rather it wasn't mentioned). Nor, I learned from my Chinese-Korean contact, did the guides at the two vast, air-conditioned, underground 'International Friendship Exhibitions' at Mount Myohyang – which contain the '61,000 valuable presents' given by 'world leaders' to the Great Leader and his late, and even 'greater' father, Kim Il-sung – know that in a revolution nine years earlier Romania's Ceausescu, who donated a stuffed bear, was, not unlike the bear, ruthlessly shot dead.

Kwong-yong told me that his village had contained around 500 people 'and 100 have already died. Some die in their homes, but sometimes you see their bodies lying in the street. We heard rumours that people in other places were eating dead bodies, but it didn't happen in our village. In my village it is mostly the older people who died, because they would try to feed the children first.'

But not all the dead were adults: two years earlier, his best friend, a thirteen-year-old boy at his village school, also died of hunger. 'I miss him a lot. We used to have fun together after school, playing running games. I wish he did not die.' I suddenly wanted to hug his skinny little bones in motherly comfort, but his innate dignity and his evident fear that he might break down stopped me.

His ambition had been to join the North Korean Army, whose motto is, 'Let Us Defend the Nerve Centre of the Revolution and the Great Leader Comrade Kim Jong-Il with Our Lives'. Why be a soldier? 'For the love of the motherland, because I wanted to defend it against the American imperialists and their South Korean puppet regime.' He suddenly burst out bitterly: 'We were taught in school that socialist countries like ours were the richest in the world, and that capitalist countries were the poorest. We knew we were very poor, so we thought capitalist countries must be even poorer, and we wondered how people could live like that. But now I'm in China I can see that capitalist countries have a much better life.'

Ironic, considering that the most Kwong-yong had ever seen of 'capitalism' was this remote, dirt-poor Communist Chinese village.

But its relative prosperity – and the fact that these villagers could feed themselves (despite having suffered the same floods and droughts which had afflicted North Korea across the 25-metre-wide river border) – had struck him like a thunderbolt.

There are times, in a long journalistic career, when I wonder whether I can bear to hear very much more of human misery and the human venality which so often causes it. I've also wondered whether readers too can bear much more; the lifestyle travails of Britney and Amy Winehouse are perhaps more to their taste. But there are also times like this when I feel extraordinarily privileged to be able to witness, at first hand, so many quiet, unrewarded, unpublicized examples of selfless human goodness.

Like that of Kwong-yong's benefactor, the aged Mrs Han. It's a crime for her to shelter the young boy: if she were caught she'd be fined 5,000 *yuan* (around £385), a lottery jackpot-sized fortune to peasants like her. (And now, as famine once again threatens North Korea, the Chinese authorities have upped the fine.)

'I could never in my lifetime pay such a sum, but I feel so sorry for these people. My life is very hard – please don't ask me about the sufferings I've endured, because I won't be able to stop crying – but their lives are so much harder. These refugees, when they come here, are really amazed: they see our animals eating better than they do. And I say to them, if you are shocked when you see our poor village, if you ever get to the big city you will be even more amazed.'

Mrs Han chattered away while she prepared us a generous meal cooked in little ovens set into the floor next to her brick-platform bed – virtually her only furniture. She and other Chinese-Koreans living along the border try to fatten up the refugees they take in: 'You see this boy?' she said proudly, 'he is getting fatter every day!'

The year before, she'd taken in a young North Korean couple for six months. The husband came first; the wife, dodging North Korean army patrols, then crossed the frozen Tumen River at night. 'She had only thin clothing and she got frostbite in her right foot: I cut off her shoe but the foot went bad.'

The desperate couple eventually went to a local Chinese hospital to try to treat the gangrene; they were arrested, then sent back over the border, shackled, in a truck. The husband (she'd heard through the refugee grapevine) was in a North Korean labour camp, but all she knew about his young wife is that 'they took her to hospital on the other side and amputated her toes, without anaesthetic or medicines. They just don't have any. I was so upset, I wanted to send some medicines to her, but I don't have the money to buy them and I wouldn't be able to find her.'

If the generosity of this elderly Chinese-Korean widow was moving, so too was the case of Mr and Mrs Choi who ran a secret orphanage located down a filthy dirt lane on the outskirts of a drab industrial town ('Don't say where it is, who runs it, who finances it – it's very dangerous,' I was warned by my contacts. 'There would be prison sentences, and the children will be sent back to starve.')

Did these abandoned children ever cry, I'd asked Mr Choi. He smiled sadly: 'No, they never cry. Only two of the thirty I've taken in ever cried for their mothers: in fact, they're always very good, very quiet.' Not surprising, really. Starving children rarely cry; a kind of blank-eyed apathy settles in, their energy levels too low for outward expressions of grief.

In fact, most of these children weren't orphans: they'd been abandoned by their desperate, fleeing mothers. They were too young to recognize that the 'Benevolent Father' of their once passably modern state had, like his father before him, inflicted on its citizens the most grotesque personality cult the world has ever known (and that includes those of Stalin and Mao), even as his country slowly starved to death.

And while this catastrophe unfolded the Great Leader's hagiographic media continued to heap fresh titles on him. Comrade Kim Jong-il is 'The Priceless Master of Witty Remarks', an official example of which included: 'To expect victory in the Revolution without the Leader is as good as to expect a flower to bloom without the sun!' Another of the Great Leader's rib-ticklers: 'Trust produces loyal subjects – but doubt produces traitors!' I don't imagine that eight-year-old Hyong-chol, whom I met in the secret orphanage, will ever find the Great Leader's witticisms amusing.

After all, 'the Priceless Master of Witty Remarks' had in effect killed the little boy's father and condemned Hyong-chol to life as a fugitive. He, with his mother and older sister, had scrambled across the icy Tumen River; his father, thanks to a North Korean border patrol, didn't make it. The last the boy heard of his father, who'd been behind him, was a shot, a scream, and then silence.

Perhaps his parents had already guessed the hollowness of the official propaganda which assured them that the Great Leader 'foresees both the remote future as well as the present. He ensures that miracles and innovations are made in all fields, with outstanding leadership which rallies the masses into one, with grand worldwide operations'. ('Operations' which include, incidentally, terrorism: North Korea had blown a South Korean airliner out of the sky, kidnapped young Japanese citizens, and once killed half the South Korean cabinet in a bomb attack.) Its Great Leader, who has allegedly published 890 'masterpiece' works in thirty years, is apparently possessed of a 'noble mind' and 'a brilliant clairvoyance which ensures that he is a model for the entire world'.

Mr and Mrs Choi are Christians belonging to an illegal 'house church' (in itself a somewhat risky thing to do in China), and they proudly showed off their little classroom with its brightly painted orange desks secretly donated by well-wishers and other 'unofficial' Chinese Christians. Under the Chois' care children like Hyong-chol had begun to blossom.

Like Kwong-yong, he was very small for his age and his little chest was pockmarked with skin disease. Pulling up his sweatshirt, Mrs Choi said, 'Look at that, they all have skin diseases! But we've managed to get private help from some local doctors. We've even got a dentist secretly helping us.'

Mr Choi told me that, after their escape, Hyong-chol's mother had deserted her two children: as far as he knew, 'Their mother married a Chinese man to have a better life.'

Hyong-chol and another eight-year-old, who'd been sold to a Chinese family by his North Korean mother and had then been abandoned by the buyers because he was too sickly, asked if they could sing me a favourite song. It was: 'I am a King! I am always a King, even though I am weak. I can overcome all difficulties. I am a King!' Mr Choi smiled fondly at them as they sang. 'Of course, according to the law, I have to send them back. But how can I? I will only send them back when their country is rich enough.'

Unlike the two once half-starved little boys bravely singing 'I am a King' in this secret hideaway, some North Koreans are already 'rich enough'. Many of the Great Leader's cronies are now so wealthy that their wives are a common sight in Beijing's shopping malls buying expensive designer handbags; one day I went to the luxury Swissotel where the crony wives like to congregate. They all wore Kim Il-sung badges on their cashmere coats; the man died in 1994 and was posthumously awarded the title 'Eternal President'.

Every North Korean over the age of eighteen has to wear his Kim Il-sung badge: it is a crime to deface it, to sell it or to throw it away. The differing badge designs denote your status – a kind of identity card on your lapel. It's even a crime to crumple a banknote bearing the previous Great Leader's face: when I bought a 100-*won* banknote on the North Korean border (they're smuggled across by refugees hoping to sell them as souvenirs), I was warned: 'Keep it completely clean and flat, otherwise you'll be in big trouble if you ever try to use it on the other side.' One foreign visitor to the North Korean capital Pyongyang inadvertently crumpled up a newspaper which happened to bear the late Great Leader's portrait and was promptly arrested.

So where did these pampered wives get the money for their cashmeres and their foreign jaunts? Drugs, for a start. The bankrupt and criminal regime is so desperate for hard currency to maintain its system and ensure the loyalty of its elite that it's become a major international drug dealer. North Korean diplomats overseas have been caught smuggling cocaine, rhino horn, ivory and gold. Another little wheeze which helps North Korea's depleted coffers is currency fraud: so skilled were their state forgers at flooding the Far East with convincing 100-dollar bills that the US was obliged to change the design.

In public Kim Jong-il is treated like a divine being (although there have been several high-level defections from his regime). Every time the Great Leader reaches some milestone, the North Korean media announce that blossom has appeared 'miraculously' out of season, that double rainbows have appeared in the sky, that a rare white sea-cucumber of vast size has just been caught.

When he was born, allegedly in a humble log-cabin on the slopes of the sacred Mount Paektu (in reality his birthplace was Stalin's Russia), a similar slew of miracles came to pass. Indeed, before he even emerged from the womb, a swallow was said to have swooped down from heaven and to have informed a startled traveller that 'A prodigious general, destined to rule the world, will be born on February 16, 1942.'

Looking at these plump, well-fed North Korean wives in the Swissotel, and remembering those children in the orphanage, I had to fight the urge to rip off their Great Leader badges and give them a good thump. But of course I didn't. In any case, perhaps as a result of my nomadic childhood, separated from my family for long periods of time at a very young age, I've always instinctively tried to put a lid on my emotions. I rarely cry and once, when asked why not, I simply shrugged and said in hard-boiled been-there-done-that manner, 'Crying is pointless, it just smudges your mascara.' Besides, what reason have I to weep, a privileged middle-class woman of the affluent and, comparatively, safe West? Self-pity, sometimes paraded as a virtual fashion accessory in the West, is not something in which those I've interviewed across the world can afford to indulge.

But I suppose I could not have stayed in this job for so many years if all I had witnessed had been misery, deprivation and death. There's always comedy, albeit often black, to be found when out on the road.

For example, the absurdity of trying to deal in a war zone with a fixer who's addicted, not to drugs or booze, but to Cadbury's Fruit and Nut. Alexandra, a Serb fixer of mine in Bosnia, kept moaning to me that she couldn't survive much longer without the stuff; it was of course unavailable. One day she came to me, with the staring, half-delirious eyes of an addict who's just learned the whereabouts of a favoured drug: 'Ann, we have to go to the MOs' house – now! There's a British MO in there and there's a rumour that he's got stockpiles of Fruit and Nut!' MOs were UN Military Observers and the Bosnian Serbs had put them under house arrest; later, they tied them to posts as human shields in order to deter the NATO bombers.

I protested: 'But Alex, the MOs will know even less than we do! It's a waste of time!' Alex informed me that she was going on strike unless we wangled our way into the house where the MOs and the Fruit and Nut were sequestrated. Which, with difficulty, we did. The British MO did indeed have industrial quantities of Alex's drug. I was right that neither he, nor the Norwegian MO imprisoned with him, knew what the hell was going on outside. 'All we can do is listen to the BBC's World Service on our shortwave radio,' the Norwegian told me gloomily, 'and we write our official reports based on that.'

And while Alex stuffed her face with slabs of Fruit and Nut and was thus calmed down, the British MO and I discovered we had something in common. He lived near me in north London and we had a long and passionate discussion about whether the expansion of Lemonia, our favourite Greek-Cypriot restaurant in Primrose Hill, had been an improvement or not.

The American Senator Tip O'Neill had once famously remarked that, in the end, 'All politics is local.' The imprisoned MO and I at that moment waxed more passionately about the future of Lemonia than we did about the bombings and atrocities going on around us, let alone the long-term future of the Balkans.

Sheltering one day with another foreign correspondent in a bunker above Sarajevo, I found my fellow shelterer was far more anxious to find out what was going on at his beleaguered newspaper back home than he was about analysing Serb military strategy. 'Have you heard anything? Do you think the paper's even going to survive?' he asked as yet another mortar thumped into the city down below us.

Neither the imprisoned MO nor my fellow correspondent in the bunker was being crassly self-centred: very often it is dwelling on the apparently trivial 'local politics' of your life back home that, oddly enough, helps keep you sane amid the surrounding madness.

And then of course there's the pleasure of being paid by one's employers to make genuine friends out of total strangers. When the Soviet Union began opening up in 1986, I spent many a long night sitting with newly acquired Russian friends in their cramped kitchens in ugly, high-rise *doms*, talking *dusha* to *dusha*, soul to soul, and watching them weep with intensely Russian romanticism as they recited their favourite bits of Pushkin or Akhmatova or Yevtushenko over pickled cucumber, black bread and strong, sweet Armenian brandy.

But you can sometimes find that your newly acquired friendships can become, at least on your side, a trifle exhausting. One evening in oil-rich Azerbaijan I was invited to have dinner with a group of Azeris, not in some new, lavish and eye-poppingly expensive Western-style restaurant, but at a patriarch's home, along with (it seemed to me) most of his large extended family. After being urged by all these jolly Azeris to partake in many a fraternal toast (and having had thrust on me huge, yellow, blue-veined lumps of their favourite dish, 'Fat-Bottomed Sheep'), my heart sank when the dread word 'Nizami' was uttered.

'Now we will recite for you from our great national poet Nizami!' This twelfth-century court poet is principally renowned for his five long epic poems. An old man with gold teeth began reciting . . . and reciting . . . and reciting. In Azeri. At last, I thought, as his audience clapped joyously, the ordeal is now over. But no such luck. 'Now Fatima, as favour to you our friend, will recite you Nizami in English!' And a charming young geology student stood up and recited . . . and recited . . . and recited.

The *Mail* had asked me to go to Azerbaijan in 1998 to write about the new oil boom in the Caucasus and the multi-billion-dollar pipeline which was being built by an international consortium to pump Caspian oil from Baku 1,100 miles to Ceyhan in Turkey. Because of my family's background in oil I've always been fascinated by the glamour, the energy, the technicoloured wealth and the often murderous squalor of 'pipeline politics'. And Azerbaijan had them all a-plenty – and still has. It lies on one of the greatest political, ethnic, religious and seismic faultlines in the world: Christians, Shias, Sunnis, Zoroastrians, old Communists, new predators, squabbling tribesmen with moustaches and Kalashnikovs – and a trembling earth endlessly leaking oil and columns of flaming gas.

Baku, the muddy, oil-stained capital of war-shattered, eternally windswept Azerbaijan, a once forgotten corner of the old Soviet empire, was suddenly the new Klondyke, the West's new billion-dollar Eldorado, the Last Great Frontier, the new Black-Gold Rush. And in this new Klondyke, a new Great Game – the name given to the nineteenth-century rivalry of the Great Powers for control of this region – was being born.

In fact Baku in the late nineteenth century had been the site of the world's first ever Black-Gold Rush. Illiterate Azeri tribesmen discovered that, by simply sticking a shovel into the bubbling earth, huge oil gushers would pour upwards into the blackening Caucasus skies, showering them with wealth. They hired Armenian architects to fan across Europe to copy its finest mansions in order to replicate them in downtown Baku: which is why in the old city you can still find streets full of glorious fake Loire châteaux and Venetian palazzos, now defaced by oil pollution and the habit of its old Soviet bosses of plastering them with the hammer-and-sickle.

The Nobels, the Samuels and the Rothschilds came here to build 'the Paris of the Caspian' in Baku, which then became the richest oil city in the world. And the incompetent and brutish Soviets almost destroyed it.

I've seen many Soviet crimes against the environment, but the Baku oilfields – like the grotesque Oily Rocks settlement built out over the sea, which (after the odd massacre) the Russians left behind when they pulled out of here in 1991 – left me almost winded with rage.

On the Western consortium's spotless Chirag 1 platform, 60 miles out in the freezing Caspian Sea, a tattooed Scottish oilman, Peter Boyd, said to me in disgust, 'I couldn't believe it when I first saw Oily Rocks! As a professional, I felt really angry. Makes you wonder now why we were so frightened of the Soviet Union in the first place, when they couldn't even maintain their rigs and their oil industry properly!'

He, like me, was appalled by acre upon acre of arthritic 'nodding donkeys' and Baku's stinking black lakes and its rusting derricks, which looked like a forest of petrified trees that had suddenly been shorn of their leaves in some post-nuclear storm.

And now Baku was being transformed, yet again, into a boom city; but it was a city where, despite the new Givenchy boutique, the luxury car showroom, the 'Natashas' (the prostitutes) clad in Versace, and the visiting Asprey salesmen, peasants still casually slit the throats of tethered sheep in the potholed streets. And where packs of stray dogs scampered across the runway of the then utterly dec- repit Soviet-built airport – even while the West's merchant adven- turers were attempting to land on it in their gleaming private jets. As one Russian-American-Israeli 'import-export' businessman (i.e. arms dealer) told me, 'Those f***ing dogs – I nearly lost my Gulfstream that way!'

Neighbouring Iran's theocratic mullah regime was so disgusted by the laid-back Azeris' lack of Islamic fundamentalism that it even aided Christian Armenia in its 'ethnic cleansing' of Muslims in the disputed enclave of Nagorno-Karabakh. Iran's former Ambassador to

Baku shouted furiously at a group of protesting Azeris, 'What distinguishes you from the infidel enemy? Both you and the Armenians drink alcohol, eat pork and – forgive me my words – fornicate all day!'

The name Azerbaijan means 'Land of Eternal Fire', and one late afternoon I went out with a couple of Azeri contacts and a British oilman to visit a small shrine in the Burning Hills, the place which is said to have given birth to the fire-worshipping Zoroastrian faith, the world's oldest surviving religion.

It was a movingly elemental sight: hectic flames, which no wind ever extinguishes, licked up out of the flanks of hills covered in snow; the Burning Hills were an almost primeval landscape of fire, wind and ice. My two Azeri friends were nominally Muslim and the British oilman and I were nominally Christian. But in that deserted, sacred, lonely place at sunset we all, albeit with some embarrassment, instinctively bowed at the shrine, paying a kind of awestruck homage to those eternal flames spurting up through the snow from the bowels of the earth.

During the last World War, Hitler's Luftwaffe used those flames as beacons in their bombing raids; the oil-starved Nazi regime was desperate to capture Azerbaijan's oilfields. 'Without Baku, the war is lost,' declared the Führer. His Nazi empire is now dead, and so too is the Soviet one. Empires come and go, but these ancient flames flicker on.

*

And as these empires come and go, the journalists, and the men and women who work alongside them, soldier on – trying, albeit imperfectly, to tell the truth. Sometimes it needs poets to tap into that often submerged vein of emotional, rather than merely factual, truth which mere journalists find hard to articulate.

I first came across James Fenton, who subsequently became Professor of Poetry at Oxford, in China. He was then working as a foreign correspondent in the Far East and I once popped round to his house in Quezon City in the Philippines. He had invaluable contacts among Marxist guerrillas and that evening, after a delicious dinner of herb-stuffed baked fish, I chatted to one of the Filipinos present about the so-called 'sparrow squads'. After we'd switched off a TV show featuring President Aquino's tone-deaf daughter warbling some excruciating love song, I asked him: 'Why "sparrow squads"?' 'Well, sparrows peck, and when a member of the squad "pecks" you sharply in the neck with a knife, you're dead!' he chortled.

Fenton, who had covered the wars in Vietnam and Cambodia and who had seen much death, recently wrote 'Memorial', a poem about all those who've helped us foreign correspondents over the long, turbulent years:

> Drivers, interpreters, these were our friends.
> These we loved. These we were trusted by.
> The shocked hand wipes the blood across the lens.
> The lens looks to the sky.
> . . .
> Death waved them through the checkpoint.
> They were lost.
> All have their story here.

Amen to that. I too loved them; and no foreign correspondent, basking in by-lined glory, should ever forget those who were imprisoned, or were tortured, or died in the cause of helping us tell an often indifferent world about its many dark, savage corners. One of the duties of journalism is to shine a torch into those dark places, to face the glacier in the cupboard, and to expose its coldness and cruelty to the bright, clear and humanizing light of day.

Index